Irish Elites in the Nineteenth Century

Irish Elites in the Nineteenth Century

WITHDRAWN

Ciaran O'Neill
EDITOR

FOUR COURTS PRESS

Set in 10 on 12.5 point Bembo for
FOUR COURTS PRESS LTD
7 Malpas Street, Dublin 8, Ireland
www.fourcourtspress.ie
and in North America for
FOUR COURTS PRESS
c/o ISBS, 920 N.E. 58th Avenue, Suite 300, Portland, OR 97213.

A catalogue record for this title
is available from the British Library.

ISBN 978–1–84682–351–0

Printed in England
by Antony Rowe Ltd, Chippenham, Wilts.

Contents

PORTRAYING THE POLITICAL ELITES

REVISITING BLOCKED MOBILITY

Illustrations

FIGURES

TABLES

Abbreviations

Add.	Additional
Berg	The Henry W. and Albert A. Berg Collection of English and American literature, New York Public Library
BL	British Library, London
BM	British Museum, London
DFA	Department of Foreign Affairs
DIB	James McGuire and James Quinn (eds), *Dictionary of Irish biography, from the earliest times to the year 2002* (Cambridge, 2009); online edition, http://www.dib.cambridge.org
DUM	*Dublin University Magazine*
EHR	*English Historical Review*
GAA	Gaelic Athletic Association
HC	House of Commons sessional papers
(H)CMS	(Hibernian) Church Missionary Society
HL	House of Lords sessional papers
IHS	*Irish Historical Studies*
IPP	Irish Parliamentary Party
IRC	Irish Research Council
LSE	London School of Economics
NAI	National Archives of Ireland
NHI	*New History of Ireland*
NIAH	National Inventory of Architectural Heritage
NLI	National Library of Ireland
NUI	National University of Ireland
ODNB	Colin Matthew, Brian Harrison and Laurence Goldman (eds), *Oxford dictionary of national biography* (Oxford, 2004); online edition, http://www.oxforddnb.com
PRONI	Public Records Office of Northern Ireland
PRTLI	Programme for Research in Third-Level Institutions
QC	Queen's Counsel
QUB	Queen's University Belfast
RCBL	Representative Church Body Library
RIA	Royal Irish Academy
SEG	Shannon Estuary Group
SPG	Society for the Propagation of the Gospel
SSNCI	Society for the Study of Nineteenth-Century Ireland

TCD	Trinity College Dublin
TYE	Three Years' Enterprise
UCC	University College Cork
UCD	University College Dublin
V&A	Victoria and Albert Museum, London
YWCA	Young Women's Christian Association

Contributors

MERVYN BUSTEED graduated in geography from Queen's University Belfast. He lectured in Manchester University Geography Department and chaired the British Association for Irish Studies. His research interests are in Irish settlement and identities in nineteenth-century Manchester and the historical geography of eighteenth-century Ireland. He is an honorary research fellow of the Institute of Irish Studies at Liverpool University.

FINTAN CULLEN is professor of art history at the University of Nottingham and has published widely on art and representation in Ireland. His most recent book, *Ireland on show: art, union and nationhood*, appeared in 2012. He is presently on secondment as dean of arts and humanities at the University of Nottingham Ningbo China.

PAMELA EMERSON BSc (Hons), MA, MRes. is completing a PhD at the University of Ulster at Coleraine. Her research is based on the origins and users of book clubs and libraries in nineteenth-century Ulster. Pamela previously worked in the education and museum sectors.

SUSAN GALAVAN is an architect with fifteen years postgraduate experience in Ireland and abroad. In 2009 she was awarded an IRC scholarship to engage in doctoral research at Trinity College Dublin. Her work entails a multidisciplinary examination of Victorian domestic architecture in Dublin within the broader contexts of the nineteenth-century city.

BRIAN GRIFFIN is a senior lecturer in history at Bath Spa University. He is the author of *The Bulkies: police and crime in Belfast, 1800–1865* (1997), *Sources for the history of crime in Ireland, 1801–1921* (2005) and *Cycling in Victorian Ireland* (2006).

JOHN HUTCHINSON is a reader in nationalism in the Department of Government at the London School of Economics. He has authored and edited several books in the field of nationalism, including *The dynamics of cultural nationalism*, *Modern nationalism* and *Nations as zones of conflict*. He is currently completing a monograph on warfare and nationalism.

RAPHAËL INGELBIEN is associate professor of literary studies at the University of Leuven. His current research focuses on the European dimensions of nineteenth-century Irish writing. His articles on Irish literary and cultural history have appeared in *Comparative Literature Studies*, *Éire–Ireland*, *New Hibernia Review* and *Irish University*

Review and in volumes including *Affecting Irishness* (2009). He co-edited *Irish women writers: new critical perspectives* (2011).

FELIX M. LARKIN is chairman of the Newspaper and Periodical History Forum of Ireland. A retired public servant, he has written extensively about the press in late nineteenth- and early twentieth-century Ireland. His *Terror and discord: the Shemus cartoons in the* Freeman's Journal, *1920–1924* was published in 2009.

PATRICK MAUME is a full-time researcher with the Royal Irish Academy's *Dictionary of Irish Biography*. He is a graduate of University College Cork and Queen's University Belfast, who has written biographies of Daniel Corkery (1993) and D.P. Moran (1995), *The long gestation: Irish nationalist political culture* (1999) and many other publications on nineteenth- and twentieth-century Ireland, including seven essays in previous SSNCI conference proceedings volumes. One of his long-term projects is a study of William Cooke Taylor in the context of pre-Famine liberal unionism.

JOANNE MCENTEE is finishing doctoral research on order and the nineteenth-century Irish landed estate. The PhD forms part of the Texts, Contexts, Cultures programme in the Moore Institute, NUI Galway and is funded by PRTLI 4. She was awarded a BA in history and English from the University of Limerick in 2008.

KEVIN Mc KENNA was awarded a PhD by the National University of Ireland (NUI) Maynooth in 2011 for a dissertation entitled 'Power, resistance and ritual: paternalism on the Clonbrock estates, 1826–1908'. The research was funded by an IRC Postgraduate Scholarship and the John and Pat Hume Scholarship awarded by NUI Maynooth.

TIMOTHY G. MCMAHON is associate professor of history at Marquette University. He is the author of *Grand opportunity: the Gaelic Revival and Irish society, 1893–1910* (2008) and was the Revd William B. Neenan SJ visiting fellow at Boston College-Ireland in 2011. He is currently engaged in research on the part played by Irish men and women in the British Empire.

NICOLA K. MORRIS lectures on history at the University of Chester. She researches the interaction of religion and politics in Ireland in the late nineteenth and early twentieth century, particularly the politics of the Methodist Church and the Home Rule crises. She has also recently published articles on the attitudes of Protestant clergy to the Ulster Covenant.

CIARAN O'NEILL is Ussher lecturer in nineteenth-century history at Trinity College Dublin.

MAEVE O'RIORDAN is a PhD candidate at University College Cork. She holds an IRC scholarship for her project 'Home, family and society – women of the landed class, *c.*1860–1914: a Munster case study'.

ANNA PILZ is a PhD candidate at the Institute of Irish Studies, University of Liverpool, working on a critical study of Lady Gregory's drama. She has presented papers at conferences including those of the Society for the Study of Nineteenth-Century Ireland, the International Association for the Studies of Irish Literatures and New Voices.

MATTHEW POTTER has lectured at the University of Limerick, Mary Immaculate College Limerick and Limerick School of Art and Design. He is the author of several books and articles including a biography of William Monsell of Tervoe (2009) and a history of municipal government in Ireland (2010). He is currently employed in Limerick City Archives, where he is working on a history of Mount Saint Lawrence Cemetery, Limerick.

NEIL SMITH is pursuing a PhD at the University of Liverpool on 'The Irish middle classes in nineteenth-century Manchester'.

ANDREW TIERNEY currently lectures at the Institute of Irish Studies in the University of Liverpool. He is engaged in researching the architecture of the Irish midlands for the Buildings of Ireland Charitable Trust, and has published several journal articles on Irish architecture and social history. He received his PhD in archaeology from University College Dublin in 2006.

Acknowledgments

This edited collection is the lasting legacy of a conference co-convened by James H. Murphy and me at the University of Liverpool in the summer of 2011. The idea for the conference 'Irish elites in the nineteenth century' came about as a result of a conversation between James and me in Chester back in 2009. With his encouragement, and the consent of the steering committee of the Society for the Study of Nineteenth-Century Ireland, the conference was held at Liverpool at the Institute of Irish Studies. We owe a great debt to Dorothy Lynch, Nick Jackson and Viola Segeroth for doing so much of the organization for the conference. My thanks too, to the academic staff and students who helped out at Liverpool – Marianne Elliott, Frank Shovlin, Diane Urquhart, Niall Carson and Whitney Standlee in particular. Financial assistance was forthcoming and very much appreciated from both the Irish embassy in London and the Gaelic Athletic Association. That support is gratefully acknowledged and the society would like to thank Ciarán Byrne and Dermot Power of the DFA and GAA respectively for their help in securing it. The contributors are thanked for their diligence and hard work in producing such good material and for meeting the various deadlines imposed on them with impressive regularity. Lastly, it is important to acknowledge the continued support of Four Courts Press for our series, and to praise the professionalism of Michael Potterton for his role in guiding this volume to publication.

The collection is dedicated to the memory of a much-missed stalwart of the Institute of Irish Studies at Liverpool, Dr Ian McKeane – a gentleman who had no time for elites or elitism.

Introduction

CIARAN O'NEILL

> A century ago, a rich Irish trader, the manufacturer, even the lawyer or the doctor – unless by chance he could produce a pedigree – held little place in the social scheme; but today his granddaughters flaunt it with the best.
>
> Katherine Cecil Thurston, 1908[1]

We live in an age when 'elite' has become a multi-purpose and no-purpose word, a diluted concept that is often equated with everyday services or video-game culture.[2] It can refer to any powerful group or sectional interest in society, and is often asked to do so. The problem is now so acute that one of the leading British academics in the area, John Scott, has argued that the word 'elite' is one of the 'most misused in the sociological lexicon', leading many scholars to conclude that the concept has become 'completely vacuous and without any significant analytical value'.[3] As if to illustrate the point, Ireland's premier business directory lists companies as diverse as 'Elite Copier Services' (Celbridge, Co. Kildare), 'Elite Dental Practice' (Belfast), and 'Elite Oil Products' (Tuam, Co. Galway).

This is the first volume of collected essays to directly address the topic of elites, elite behaviour, or elite formation in nineteenth-century Ireland. This flourishing of interest in a neglected topic is thanks, in part, to the publication of Fergus Campbell's timely study of the 'Irish establishment' between 1879 and 1914.[4] Campbell's book stands alone as the only full-length attempt to classify an Irish elite. The present collection of essays seeks, therefore, to build on Campbell's work. This will be done chronologically, by extending the parameters further back into the nineteenth century, and thematically, by offering examples of Irish elites which fall outside of Campbell's categorization. Before allowing the contributors to go about this task in their own voice, this introductory essay surveys the literature in this area, defines what is meant by concepts such as 'power' and 'elite' in this volume, and points to areas that might benefit from further analysis.

---

1 Katherine Cecil Thurston, *The fly on the wheel* (New York, 1908), p. 3.   2 In this volume, I have chosen to use 'elite' rather than the more correct 'élite', respecting the conventions of much of the English-language scholarship on the subject.   3 John Scott, 'The transformation of the British economic elite' in Mattei Dogan (ed.), *Elite configurations at the apex of power* (Leiden, 2003), p. 155.   4 Fergus Campbell, *The Irish establishment, 1879–1914* (Oxford, 2009).

ELITES AND IRISH HISTORIOGRAPHY

How is it possible that so little has been written on the subject of Irish elites? The temptation here is to bemoan or at least acknowledge the usual factors whenever a yawning gap is pointed out in Irish historiography. These factors include an infatuation with political history, the conservatism and caution that has been characteristic of the historical profession in Ireland, the relatively late development of the discipline of sociology in Irish universities, the continuing sorry state of disciplines such as social history and historical sociology, and even the simple dearth of Irish historians gainfully employed. All those factors are, of course, relevant, though the twentieth-century reticence to explore issues such as social stratification and social mobility in Ireland ought not to be dismissed as easily as that, reflecting as it does a general unwillingness to admit to an enduringly unequal society in the postcolonial context.[5]

Nonetheless, it is important to note that much of the history written in or about Ireland is skewed towards a fascination with the rich and most powerful in society. Students of Irish history can hardly complain of a shortage of biographies of charismatic leaders, chronicles of leading political parties or source material on landed families. There is, however, a distinct lack of theoretically sophisticated surveys of elite groups, reflective of a wider unwillingness to engage with perspectives or frameworks inspired by or drawn from other disciplines. Outside of Ireland, the topic has experienced three discernible peaks in twentieth-century scholarship. The first was inspired by the scholarship of Gaetano Mosca and Vilfredo Pareto, two Italian theorists whose work has subsequently become linked with the national socialist or fascistic regimes, which, to some extent at least, appeared to take on board their ideas and then to apply them in a largely negative manner.[6] Mosca and Pareto espoused a vertical, linear conception of power that sought to explain how, in their society, it came to be concentrated in the hands of so few. Theirs was not an overt critique of the process, however, rather accepting that all societies had been characterized by the dominance of a small cadre of leaders over the masses who were 'led' by them. The next upsurge was a more 'scientific', community-based approach pioneered by scholars such as C. Wright Mills and Floyd Hunter in 1950s America. Mills, in particular, stimulated American academics with his study of power relations among top US

---

5 The classic text for pre-Celtic-Tiger era social mobility in Ireland is still Richard Breen and Christopher T. Whelan, *Social class and social mobility in Ireland* (Dublin, 1996). For more on social mobility in twenty-first-century Ireland, see Richard Layte and Christopher T. Whelan, 'Class transformation and trends in social fluidity in the Republic of Ireland, 1973 to 1994' in Richard Breen (ed.), *Social mobility in Europe* (Oxford, 2004), ch. 7. **6** We could easily include Robert Michels, a former student of Max Weber, in this list of 'traditional' elite theories. The classic texts for these theorists are Robert Michels, *Political parties: a sociological study of the oligarchical tendencies of modern democracy*, trans. Eden & Cedar Paul (London, 1915, from 1911 original); Vilfredo Pareto, *The mind and society*, trans. Andrew Bongiorno et al. (London, 1935, from 1916 original); Gaetano Mosca, *The ruling class*, trans. Hannah D. Kahn and rev. by Arthur Livingstone (London, 1939, from 1896 original).

officials, politicians, and business tycoons in *The power elite* (1950). This book is now the ironic and unwitting inspiration behind the Forbes lists and other celebratory chronicles of accumulated wealth, but it was originally a strong critique of capitalism as well as a pioneering study of how power can be conceived of as something that can come to be wielded by a very select few with no prior conspiracy or cosy agreement. Mills, and those who followed him, were increasingly characterized as leftists, their community-focused work inspiring later 'democratic' theories of power by Robert A. Dahl and others. The last discernible peak in elite studies came in a more diffuse manner with the onset of neo-Marxian critiques of capitalist society in the 1970s, the theories of nationalism (most usually connected with the London School of Economics) and the re-imagination of Durkheim's 'French School of Sociology' by scholars such as Pierre Bourdieu and Victor Karady. Elite studies have fallen from the forefront of the social sciences in the past two decades, undermined by what Mike Savage and Karel Williams have termed the 'pincer movement' of, on the one hand, structuralist and post-structuralist critiques of the ability of established elites to remain dynamic actors in modern societies. The other 'pincer' was a methodological one, the rise of 'orthodox, positivist and neo-positivist social science'. The widespread use of quantitative source data, such as national statistical surveys, meant that the traditional conception of an identifiable or visible elite simply faded from academic discourse.[7]

To a great extent, all of these later scholars were preoccupied with institutional or infrastructural power, and committed to the study of those who peopled such hierarchies or were controlled by them. However, the work of scholars such as Pierre Bourdieu, Jürgen Habermas and Anthony Giddens all aimed to remodel earlier perceptions of the 'circulation of elites' as seen by Mosca and Pareto. This remodelling led to a greater interest in defining elites as plural rather than singular entities, with imprecise rather than precise boundaries and codes. Recent work on elites, therefore, has tended to emphasize their distinct institutional character, seeing them instead as 'politically diverse groups of national leaders'. This muddying of waters has arguably contributed to the word itself being so confused and inexact in its contemporary usage. It is also, however, the point at which this volume may be differentiated from the work of Campbell, whose characterization of the Irish elite is much closer to that of a 'closed' singular elite than any definition we will endorse. Following scholars such as John Higley and Robert D. Putnam, Irish elites may be defined much more loosely, as Trygve Gulbrandsen posits in relation to Norwegian society, as 'the holders of top positions in central institutions and organizations within significant sectors' of society.[8] This definition, more elastic than others, allows us to

---

7 See Mike Savage and Karel Williams, 'Elites: remembered by capitalism and forgotten by social science' in Mike Savage and Karel Williams (eds), *Remembering elites* (Oxford, 2008), p. 3. 8 Trygve Gulbrandsen, 'Elite integration and institutional trust in Norway', *Comparative Sociology*, 6 (2007), 190–214 at 191. For the classic studies which prefer this more fragmented approach, see Robert D. Putnam, *The comparative study of political elites* (Englewood Cliffs, NJ, 1976); Michael G. Burton and John Higley, 'The elite variable in

conceive of power as something that is not doggedly maintained or monopolized by state forces, monarchies or hereditary stake-holders, but something altogether more fluid and difficult to characterize. The question of whether power and authority was coercive, legitimate or an inconvenient blend of both in nineteenth-century Ireland is one that goes right to the heart of the great debates of Irish history.

Yet Irish historiography has remained somewhat aloof from the international debate on the subject. Those scholars who *have* contributed to this debate in an Irish context have been greatly influenced by theories of nationalism and exercised more by the idea of theorizing the rival 'Catholic elite' than the dominant Protestant elite – which is often taken for granted as an elite *in situ* but also in irreversible decline. The potential problem with this interpretation is that it is an inherently present-centred approach, not incompatible with a nationalist viewpoint, and one which analyses nineteenth-century Irish society as if it ought to be taken for granted that an established elite of (mostly) Protestant composition was morally suspect and, in any case, doomed to failure and marking time before an inevitable Catholic takeover.

The issue of Irish elites barely arose until the 1980s, when both Tom Garvin and John Hutchinson produced full-length studies of aspirant nationalism (the radical sort by Garvin; the cultural sort by Hutchinson) in the second half of the nineteenth century.[9] To a great extent, both of these studies honed in on the 'blocked mobility' theory of mass mobilization, popularized and modified by figures such as Miroslav Hroch, Ernest Gellner and Hutchinson's own mentor, Anthony D. Smith. Broadly speaking, the 'blocked mobility' thesis seeks to explain the radicalization and politicization of formerly excluded groups (usually intellectuals) who have found themselves suddenly eligible but nevertheless excluded from positions of power in an unequal and anti-meritocratic elite. It is, in other words, a way of seeing political or social revolution as a product of frustrated ambition and rising expectations. This thesis, when applied to a specifically Irish context, would, without some qualification, lead a believer to the conclusion that Catholic dominance was inevitable from the second half of the nineteenth century as greater access to elite positions became possible as a result of more widespread access to education. It would lead too, potentially, to the conclusion that the downward pressure exerted by a largely Protestant and 'alien' ascendancy was morally suspect, moribund and structurally doomed to failure. It rather neatly explains the 'surprise' of 1916 and the subsequent revolution to 1923, as well as the apparent collapse and dispersal of the ascendancy class after independence. Garvin, in particular, is seduced by this possibility, and by focusing his attention on the background of the revolutionary generation (by which he means a narrow stratum of advanced nationalists), he makes them exemplars of an entire generation of lower middle-class Catholics. The inference here is clear enough. Had there been a greater degree of upward social mobility available to the rising Catholic

democratic transitions and breakdowns', *American Sociological Review*, 54 (1989), 17–32.
9 Tom Garvin, *Nationalist revolutionaries in Ireland, 1858–1928* (Oxford, 1987); John Hutchinson, *The dynamics of cultural nationalism: the Gaelic revival and the creation of the Irish nation state* (London, 1987).

lower middle class, then the social revolution of 1916–23 would not have occurred. The wide acceptance of this thesis within Irish historiography has important implications for our analysis of Irish elites.

These studies were later modified by Senia Pašeta, who indirectly critiqued their depiction of a homogeneous rival Catholic elite in her influential monograph *Before the revolution* (1999), building on an earlier revision of Catholic 'penetration' into various elite groups in Lawrence McBride's *The greening of Dublin Castle* (1991). Pašeta and McBride, in pointing out what they saw as a greater diffusion of Catholic wealth and influence prior to Independence, posed a threat to the 'blocked mobility' reading of elite competition. These works, representing the bulk of sociologically informed historiography on the subject, have been widely cited and highly influential, and have remained largely unchallenged until the appearance of Campbell's *The Irish establishment* (2009).

Campbell's monograph represents a shift away from Pašeta and McBride, and a conscious return to the 'blocked mobility' thesis of Garvin and Hutchinson. Looking back from a distance of twenty-five years, Hutchinson replies to some of the subsequent criticism of his work in an essay included in this volume. While Hutchinson pointed to the importance of three 'cultural' revivals, Campbell's analysis rests on his identification of the six elite groups he considers the most influential in society – namely large landholders, top civil servants, police officers, leading religious figures, wealthy businessmen and politicians – and is based on an impressive control group of *c.*1,200 biographies. This 'positional analysis' leads Campbell to conclude (supported by statistical analysis) that Catholic penetration into the upper echelons of power and influence was, *pace* McBride and Pašeta, very limited between 1879 and 1914 and that power in nineteenth-century Ireland was something that was concentrated in the hands of a closed cartel, access into which was controlled according to a religious affiliation. His subsequent characterization of the Irish elite as illegitimate, unrepresentative and a 'head without a body' is therefore grounded in solid empirical research and constitutes a significant challenge to scholars interested in the area. This challenge is issued in admirably clear terms:

> The Irish Revolution may have been partially directed against those Catholic Unionists and Home Rulers who had been assimilated into the Irish establishment. But the main target of the Irish Revolution was the British state in Ireland, which had presided over a society that continued to regard Irish Catholics as second-class citizens and denied them access to the positions in society to which – by virtue of their qualifications and talents – they were entitled.[10]

Arguing that Mosca's definition of an actively excluding 'closed elite' appears to have some application in the Irish case, Campbell states that 'the revolution in Ireland was

---

10 Campbell, *The Irish establishment*, p. 318.

a consequence of structural inequalities in Irish society at the beginning of the twentieth century, and of the discontent that some sections of Irish society felt at the time.
If we are to take Campbell at his word, any meaningful exploration of an Irish elite
prior to Independence would require its creator to acknowledge that the 'establishment' was a 'closed elite' of (mostly) Protestant composition, which actively excluded
Catholics from its membership. If we are to reject this as a simplification of Irish
history pre-1914, leaving aside the problematic use of imprecise terms such as
'Catholic Unionist' and the insistence that a 'revolution' took place, on what basis
might we do so?

A MORE OPEN ELITE?

There are several points of contestation open to us as we search for a wider definition of Irish elites. The first, and most compelling, is the complete absence of women
from the debate thus far. Of the work done on Irish elites, Campbell is the only one
to really acknowledge this absence, before compounding it by excluding them from
his analysis because 'in most cases women were formally excluded from positions of
power'.[11] This constitutes a now unforgivable blind-spot in Irish historiography, as
several important and relatively recent studies have demonstrated just how integral
women were within elite culture.[12] Diane Urquhart's work on three generations of
Ladies Londonderry and their role in pushing the political and social claims of their
husbands, sons, and confidantes, is perhaps the most striking proof of salonnière-style
influence in an Irish context, but the exclusion of women from studies of power-
relations is an absurdity that blights almost all scholarship on the subject, leading to a
situation where the original (but contestable) oppression and subjugation is reinforced and in some cases worsened by the myopia of later scholarship.[13] In the case
of Irish history, if we continue to concentrate on the political system, the state
bureaucracy, the military, the clergy, and the 'public sphere' in search of power, then
we will, of course, continue to find it in male hands. If we conceive of power as
'influence', or indeed as an enabling or 'empowering' force rather than uniformly
coercive or repressive, then more exciting and holistic work awaits us.

We must also address the question of a homogenous elite structure, the so-called
'closed elite'. In a nineteenth-century context, we can say that the state developed
rapidly as a bureaucratic organization from the 1820s onwards at a gradually accelerating pace. State control over Irish lives was probably at its greatest in metropolitan

11 Ibid., p. 6. **12** See Oonagh Walsh, *Anglican women in Dublin: philanthropy, politics and
education in the early twentieth century* (Dublin, 2005); Diane Urquhart, *The ladies of
Londonderry: women and political patronage* (London, 2007); *Women in Ulster politics, 1890–1940*
(Dublin, 2000); Catherine Morris, *Alice Milligan and the Irish cultural revival* (Dublin, 2012).
13 For an excellent discussion on precisely this problem, see Amy Allen, 'Feminist
perspectives on power' in Edward N. Zalta (ed.), *The Stanford Encyclopedia of Philosophy*
(spring 2011), http://plato.stanford.edu/archives/spr2011/entries/feminist-power.

and policed areas and at its weakest in rural and remote districts. The classic example of this is the infamous Maamtrasna murders, which took place very far from the gaze of the state, even at a point when the bureaucracy had reached relative sophistication in the early 1880s.[14] We cannot, therefore, speak of a coherent or centralized state structure for much of the first half of the century. Critics of C. Wright Mills, such as Robert A. Dahl and Arnold C. Rose, saw this as a problem even in the twentieth century. Rose, challenging Mills' argument that a small closed elite controlled mid-twentieth-century America, argued that there were 'large-scale historical forces – often of an economic character – which constrain, limit, push and direct any society in ways beyond the control of any segment in it'. Rose pushed instead for a pluralistic understanding of the dispersal of power, maintaining that the substructure of an advanced society was only 'to a very limited extent manipulable by any one group'.[15]

This need for greater elasticity in relation to any definition of an 'Irish elite' paves the way for a discussion of relevant literature affecting the essays that follow. Perhaps the leading chronicler of Irish elites and elite institutions was the late R.B. McDowell, whose work on Trinity College Dublin and two socially exclusive Dublin clubs complements his earlier classic surveys of nineteenth-century state bureaucracy in *Public opinion and government policy, 1801–1846* (1952) and his indispensable *The Irish administration, 1801–1914* (1964).[16] McDowell was a practitioner of a statist history at a time when the welfare state was at its peak, and his work remains the starting-point for those interested in how nineteenth-century administration developed in Ireland. In terms of history-from-below, the work of US scholars James S. Donnelly and Samuel Clark stands out for its critique of Irish social relations. Their 1979 collection of essays, *Irish peasants*, was a significant contribution to Irish social history and, for a moment, it seemed that the QUB historian K.H. Connell was finally to be aided in his pioneering work on the history of the excluded and forgotten Irish labouring classes.[17] That never materialized, however, with much of the scholarship in this area remaining focused on rioting, social banditry and social protest.[18] Influential and accomplished young historians such as Joe Lee and Paul Bew gradually relinquished their earlier social history tendencies in favour of pursuing political history, albeit with no diminution in the quality of their output.

---

14 See Jarlath Waldron, *Maamtrasna: the murders and the mystery* (Dublin, 1992).   **15** Arnold M. Rose, *The power structure: political process in American society* (Oxford, 1967), p. 18. **16** R.B. McDowell, *Public opinion and government policy, 1801–1846* (London, 1952); *The Irish administration, 1801–1914* (London, 1964); *Land and learning: two Dublin clubs* (Dublin, 1993); R.B. McDowell and D.A. Webb, *Trinity College, Dublin, 1592–1952: an academic history* (Cambridge, 1982).   **17** K.H Connell, *Irish peasant society: four historical essays* (Oxford, 1968); Peter Berresford Ellis, *A history of the Irish working class* (London, 1972).   **18** Michael Beames, *Peasants and power: the Whiteboy movements and their control in pre-Famine Ireland* (Brighton, 1983); Tom Garvin, 'Defenders, ribbonmen and others: underground political networks in pre-Famine Ireland', *Past and Present*, 96 (1981), 133–55. See also Todd B. Quinlan, 'Big Whigs in the mobilization of Irish peasants: an historical sociology of hegemony in pre-Famine Ireland (1750s–1840s)', *Sociological Forum*, 13:2 (1998), 247–64.

The trend of Irish history had not been substantially altered and the 1980s brought with them a gradual return to more familiar territory, with the bulk of the so-called 'revisionist' canon concentrating on dismantling the myths and legends of Irish history through the medium of deconstructivist political biography or large-scale surveys. The landmark work on the Irish land system, the cause of so much social strife in the nineteenth century, was W.E. Vaughan's *Landlords and tenants in Ireland, 1848–1904* (1984). This work steered clear of theory, offering a valuable appraisal of the social structure without over-elaboration.[19] Vaughan has had no obvious successor, though the appearance of Terence Dooley's *The decline of the Big House in Ireland: a study of Irish landed families* (2001) brought rural hierarchies once again to the fore and has recently been complemented by a much-needed study of the Big House in Ulster by Olwen Purdue.[20] Historians of eighteenth-century Ireland have been lucky to have had scholars of the calibre of S.J. Connolly, David Dickson and Toby Barnard to help bridge this gap with a more holistic approach, but nineteenth-century specialists have had nothing like the accumulation of small-scale studies with which to produce a synthesis comparable to the work done on the English land system by Lawrence A. Stone and David Cannadine in the 1980s and early 1990s.[21] Leaving these major conceptual questions aside, then, what might we object to in how elites have thus far been presented in Irish historiography, and most recently by Campbell?

Of the elites identified by Campbell, the 'landed' elite is ostensibly one of the most obvious and acceptable of the six categories identified. If we were to accept the landlord–tenant system in Ireland as a fundamental axis of power, then we might still seek to qualify Campbell's identification of those with the most land as being the most influential of the landed gentry. Kevin Mc Kenna, in an excellent essay contained in this collection, shows us the extent to which landlords were themselves 'locked' into the system of primogeniture and entail with little opportunity to facilitate any fluidity of ownership within the landed class even if they had desired it.[22] The land system, until it was reformed by a series of parliamentary acts, arguably forced those who had inherited land to remain tied to it, therefore limiting their agency and controlling their behaviour. Campbell demonstrates that although

---

19 Other important and contemporary contributions to the work on land and social structure include Liam Kennedy, 'Social change in middle Ireland', *Studies: an Irish Quarterly Review*, 74:295 (autumn 1985), 242–51; William J. Smyth, 'Landholding changes, kinship networks and class formation in rural Ireland: a case study from Co. Tipperary', *Irish Geography*, 16 (1983), 17–36. **20** Terence Dooley, *The decline of the Big House in Ireland: a study of Irish landed families* (Dublin, 2001); Olwen Purdue, *The Big House in the north of Ireland: land, power and social elites, 1878–1960* (Dublin, 2009). See also Mark Bence-Jones, *Twilight of the ascendancy* (London, 1987); *Life in an Irish country house* (London, 1987). **21** David Cannadine, *Lords and landlords: the aristocracy and the towns, 1774–1967* (1980); *The decline and fall of the British aristocracy* (New Haven, CT, 1990); Lawrence A. Stone and Jeanne C. Fawtier Stone, *An open elite? England, 1540–1880* (New Haven, CT, 1984). **22** Kevin Mc Kenna, 'Elites, ritual and the legitimation of power on an Irish landed estate, 1855–90', this volume, pp 68–82.

Catholics constituted over 40 per cent of landholders with more than five hundred acres by the 1860s, the bigger estates remained in Protestant hands. We might just as easily characterize that land as being trapped within such families for as long as they continued to procreate, leading in some cases to an apparently anachronistic situation where a landlord such as the earl of Kenmare might own 118,000 acres while heavily indebted and unable to service his £146,000 debt to Standard Life.[23] If we begin to look at the land system in this light then Irish landlords begin to look less and less like the archetypal elite group with leverage and dynamism. Furthermore, while the system of entail, even after the passing of the Encumbered Estates Act in 1849, accounts for Protestant domination of the landed class, the arbitrary measurement of elite-composition-by-acre does not allow for any estimation of their actual influence in either local or national affairs. Theo Hoppen has shown us, many years ago, the extent to which the participation of the landed classes in national politics waned as the nineteenth century progressed and it is possible to suggest that their influence at a local level came to an effective end with the passing of the Local Government Act in 1898.[24] We might even argue that the less land a landlord had the more likely he was to project or exert influence on a national scale. Andrew Tierney's perceptive point about the 'minor gentry' status of the Burke family behind the bible of British and Irish landed elite membership, *Burke's landed gentry of Ireland* and *Burke's peerage*, is itself an indication of the extent to which those with less land might wield significant influence. Tierney's demand that we reappraise the overemphasis on the Big House in both architectural and social terms is complemented by Maeve O'Riordan's insistence that we reappraise the role played by women in the management of the landed estate, while Brian Griffin shows us that neglected pastimes and sports such as archery can reveal much about gender relations among the landed elites.[25]

Campbell's identification of the police as an elite group is questionable at a more fundamental level. One of the most important considerations in historical sociology has been the question of social capital, social status and the informal socialization of elite groups. This is a feature of the work of Bourdieu, of C. Wright Mills, of Dahl, even of the classical elite theorists. Campbell's inclusion of police, and to a lesser extent, the merchant class, points to a potential conceptual weakness in the work. There is no question that, outside of the top three or four figures in the Dublin Metropolitan Police and the Royal Irish Constabulary, those engaged in the business end of policing would have been excluded from the social elite. Indeed, within the penal triangle that exerted corporal power over Irish citizens in the nineteenth century – the law, the armed forces and the prisons – the police were arguably the

23 Michael Moss, *Standard Life, 1825–2000: the building of Europe's largest mutual life company* (Edinburgh, 2000), p. 110. **24** K. Theodore Hoppen, 'Landlords, society and electoral politics in mid-nineteenth-century Ireland', *Past & Present*, 75 (May 1977), 62–93. **25** Andrew Tierney, 'Architectures of gentility in nineteenth-century Ireland', this volume, pp 31–50 at p. 49; Maeve O'Riordan, 'Assuming control: elite women as household managers in late nineteenth-century Ireland', this volume, pp 83–98.

least significant actors. Campbell also includes a section on the religious elite but the omission of two of the three 'ancient learned professions', law and medicine, strikes us as anachronistic, especially when we consider the long-standing link between radicalism, law and politics through the pantheon of Irish heroic figures from Theobald Wolfe Tone and Robert Emmet, through Daniel O'Connell and Isaac Butt, to Edward Carson and Patrick Pearse.

This increasing influence of the professional class is something we can also trace in other European societies at the time, albeit with no convenient or neat pattern. In France, for example, scholars have analysed the legal bourgeoisie in the nineteenth century as a self-selecting elite group, a *bourgeoisie de robe*, who retained privilege through their domination of the lycées, even while school reforms ostensibly aimed at equalizing society in the 1880s.[26] This group proved to be much more dynamic than the traditional nobility, who had by then lost a great deal of political influence to the middle classes (as in Ireland) and effectively dominated only the social heights of metropolitan Paris and the localized government of rural Brittany, Franche-Comte and south of the Massif Central. The influence exerted by barristers in the burgeoning associational culture of nineteenth-century Ireland is given short shrift by Campbell in *The Irish establishment*, and this detracts somewhat from our understanding of the nuances of class consciousness in Irish society. A group such as this complicates the issue and points to a gradual infiltration of democratic ideals, and indeed the apparently paradoxical use of those ideals to improve social mobility. It would not, for example, be difficult to see Daniel O'Connell's career in this light. Fintan Cullen's essay mines the figure of O'Connell as found in the work of the celebrated London-based cartoonist 'H.B.', whose caricatures of O'Connell reached thousands and helped to shape the legend of that particular barrister. Joanne McEntee's essay offers us a new perspective on even a relatively lowly social group in the Irish *bourgeoisie de robe* – solicitors – by proving how central they were to the operation of the land system in rural Ireland, far away from the metropolitan base of the bar in Ireland. Her essay, along with that of Susan Galavan on the Meade family's rise and fall in Victorian Dublin, show that civic and social lives were interwoven and complementary, both in town and country, in a way that implies Campbell's vision of a closed elite is too restrictive and may not be the most useful way of thinking about Irish elites.

In literature, the question of elites and elitism has usually been bound up with the fate of the Big House, the crumbling edifices of which provide us all with an all-too seductive metaphor for the declining aristocracy. From the fiction of Maria Edgeworth and Sidney Owenson to the short stories of Somerville and Ross, to the literary memoirs of Elizabeth Bowen, the literature of elitism has been inextricably linked to both the topography of power and prestige and, somewhat more strikingly, to the tradition of women's writing. There are a number of seminal works worth

---

26 Christophe Charle, 'La bourgeoisie de robe en France en XIXe siècle', *Le mouvement social*, 181 (1997), 39–52.

mentioning in relation to these traditions. W.J. Mc Cormack is the doyen of elite literature in nineteenth-century Ireland, and Vera Kreilkamp has contributed much to our understanding of the 'Big House' novel.[27] Literary theorists such as Terry Eagleton have provided sometimes far-fetched but always provocative readings of nineteenth-century literature, which alert the reader to the existence of elites by virtue of a rather gleeful critique of their existence and legitimacy.[28] Claire Connolly has recently added much to our understanding of the cultural construction of the Irish novel in the early nineteenth century, while James H. Murphy and John Wilson Foster have provided exhaustive surveys of Victorian literature in Ireland that rescue from obscurity some long-forgotten novelists who specialized in dissecting middle-class and elite social circles.[29] We could include Ladies Hartley and Blessington, Rosa Mulholland and Hannah Lynch in this list of knowing critics. Indeed it is worth remarking that R.F. Foster's magisterial two-volume consideration of William Butler Yeats stands out as the yardstick of how informed biography can elude its narrow confines to illuminate an age, however transitional that age was. So too has Eve Patten's in-depth reconsideration of Samuel Ferguson renewed our perspective on elite metropolitan culture early in the nineteenth century.[30] Anna Pilz, with her essay in this collection on Lady Gregory, blends these inherited traditions in her appraisal of that most diplomatic of female Irish writers, whose careful negotiation of the political and cultural elites may have had less to do with self-aggrandizement and more to do with the career advancement of her only son than was previously thought. Patrick Maume reminds us, through a detailed analysis of the antiquarian Samuel Hayman, that the dominance of the 'Protestant ascendancy' was defended resolutely not only by the landed rural families usually supposed to be at its core, but also by metropolitan civic elites throughout the nineteenth century.

Hayman's defence of the Protestant interest raises one further issue connected to the history of Irish elites: that of the 'two nations' or two states. It became somewhat fashionable to conceive of Irish history in an essentialist, almost racist, formulation where the populace (and its politics) might easily be split into Catholic-nationalist and Protestant-unionist monoliths. Facilitating this formulation is the idea that the Catholic Church, in particular, acted as a 'state within a state' – a cliché so entrenched in Irish historiography as to make us reluctant to query it. The work of scholars such

---

27 W.J. Mc Cormack, *Ascendancy and tradition in Anglo-Irish literary history from 1789 to 1939* (Oxford, 1985); Vera Kreilkamp, *The Anglo-Irish novel and the Big House* (Syracuse, NY, 1998). J.C. Beckett's classic study, *The Anglo-Irish tradition* (Cornell, NY, 1976), also merits a mention here. **28** This is most true of Terry Eagleton, *Heathcliff and the great hunger: studies in Irish culture* (London, 1995). **29** Claire Connolly, *A cultural history of the Irish novel, 1790–1829* (Cambridge, 2012); James H. Murphy, *Catholic fiction and social reality in Ireland, 1873–1922* (London, 1997); *Irish novelists in the Victorian age* (Oxford, 2011); John Wilson Foster, *Irish novels, 1890–1940: new bearings in culture and fiction* (Oxford, 2008). **30** R.F. Foster, *W.B. Yeats, a life. I: the apprentice mage, 1865–1914* (Oxford, 1997); *W.B. Yeats, a life. II: the arch-poet, 1915–1939* (Oxford, 2003); Eve Patten, *Samuel Ferguson and the culture of nineteenth-century Ireland* (Dublin, 2004).

as Emmet Larkin and J.H. Whyte has helped to embed the idea of the Catholic Church as a viable rival (rather than aspirant) elite structure from the mid-nineteenth century and onwards.[31] This rather downplays the cross-community and inter-class engagement with state bureaucracy which is evident throughout the century, however, and gives the impression that the church was attempting to claim territory that was properly regarded as none of its concern. In fact, this was true of quite specific issues, education being perhaps the most celebrated of these, though health and wellbeing were others. Arguably, secular church interest in these areas was mainly targeted at those most in need of care, the working and non-working sector: thus competing with well-intentioned but often misdirected public and private provision of welfare with the intention of protecting the faith of those in receipt of aid. There seems ample room to argue that, outside of specific concerns such as welfare and education, the churches had little enough interest in areas of national fiscal or military policy, policing and law, except where any or all of them impinged on the rights of their respective flocks.

The 'legitimate' political elite, as one might expect, has been well-mined in Irish historiography. The early work of J.H. Whyte marked a turning point in historical analysis of politics; his *Irish Parliamentary Party, 1850–59* is in continual use. Later studies, mostly emanating from Trinity College Dublin and the influence of T.W. Moody, filled in the subsequent gaps in the 'parliamentary tradition'.[32] The more recent work of Alan O'Day, Eugenio Biagini and Alvin Jackson has provided us with much of merit in the interim.[33] Though the political elite inspired several of the papers given at Liverpool, they are here considered by three essays. Felix M. Larkin interrogates the link between the media and the political class, while Fintan Cullen revisits the portrayal of Daniel O'Connell by the caricaturist John Doyle, and Nicola K. Morris contributes a piece on a political 'outsider' in Jeremiah Jordan, the Methodist Home Ruler whose career path reveals much of the complexity of the Irish Parliamentary Party as well as the tensions within the Methodist elite. The

31 Emmet J. Larkin, 'The devotional revolution in Ireland, 1850–75', *The American Historical Review*, 77:3 (June 1972), 625–52; *The consolidation of the Roman Catholic Church in Ireland, 1860–1870* (Dublin, 1987); *The Roman Catholic Church and the emergence of the modern Irish political system, 1874–1878* (Dublin, 1996); J.H. Whyte, 'The influence of the Catholic clergy on elections in the nineteenth century', *English Historical Review*, 75 (1960), 248.   **32** I refer here to the graduate research done by Moody's students, much of which can be traced on a continuum and was subsequently published, such as that of F.S.L. Lyons, 'Irish parliamentary representation, 1891–1910' (PhD, TCD, 1947); Conor Cruise O'Brien, 'Irish parliamentary party, 1880–90', ii (PhD, TCD, 1954); David Thornley, 'Isaac Butt and the creation of an Irish parliamentary party, 1868–79' (PhD, TCD, 1959); R.F. Foster, 'Charles Stewart Parnell in the context of his family and social background' (PhD, TCD, 1974).   **33** Alan O'Day, *The English face of Irish nationalism: Parnellite involvement in British politics, 1880–86* (Dublin, 1977); Alvin Jackson, *Home Rule: an Irish history, 1800–2000* (Oxford, 2003); *The Ulster Party: Irish unionists in the House of Commons, 1884–1911* (Oxford, 1989); Eugenio Biagini, *British democracy and Irish nationalism* (Cambridge, 2007). A recent and important addition is Gerald R. Hall's *Ulster Liberalism, 1778–1876* (Dublin, 2011).

dominance of 'high politics' in Irish historiography has meant that few have focused on how policy percolated down from that lofty height, or how it was accepted or resisted by special interest groups. The absence of a centralized local government structure in Ireland until the last years of the century has led to near absence of historical debate on local political agitation and advocacy, or indeed the roles of vitally important local vectors of power such as the grand juries, high sheriffs, deputy lieutenants and justices of the peace who effectively ran Ireland day-to-day throughout the nineteenth century.[34] In his essay on the Shannon Estuary Group, Matthew Potter goes to some length to show that localized elites were also well-informed and both national and international in their horizons. Felix M. Larkin reinforces a recurring theme in the collection by pointing out how the political and print media elites overlapped, and how a worrying proportion of Irish print media was controlled by newspapermen from just one county: Cork. The importance of the local features heavily, too, in Pamela Emerson's essay on Belfast book clubs in the first half of the nineteenth century – reinforcing our earlier point that history-from-below and local studies are chronically insufficient in Irish historiography.

Our received image of the Irish emigrant is that of a forlorn and desperate youth forced out of a homeland they would forever lament. An essay in this collection from Mervyn Busteed and Neil Smith challenges this by highlighting the diverse class composition of the Manchester Irish. We have also become familiar with the thoughts of radical or elite tours of Ireland in the nineteenth and early twentieth century, with the musings of travellers as diverse as William Thackeray, Gustave de Beaumont, Friedrich Engels and L. Paul-Dubois all cropping up in mainstream accounts of the century. Raphaël Ingelbien inverts this navel-gazing in his essay about Irish elites on tour, which brings to life the withering observations and heightened insecurities of the leisured Irish elite as they toured other societies. Timothy G. McMahon, for his part, allows us a glimpse at the strategic migration of the Hibernian Church Missionary Society as they toiled assiduously to redefine their role as a Protestant elite within the imperial context.

The collection ends, appropriately, with an essay by John Hutchinson – a scholar who has done more than most to highlight the question of Irish elites in the late nineteenth century with his seminal work on the third Irish revival. The essay returns to themes such as 'blocked mobility' and cultural revival, which are central to our present understanding of how modern Ireland developed and poses new questions about how – on the eve of a centenary decade – the First World War might

---

34 There are several exceptions here; for local government structure, see William L. Feingold, *The revolt of the tenantry: the transformation of local government in Ireland, 1872–1886* (Boston, MA, 1984); Virginia Crossman, *Local government in nineteenth-century Ireland* (Belfast, 1994); Matthew Potter, *The municipal revolution in Ireland: local government in cities and towns since 1800* (Dublin, 2010); Mary E. Daly (ed.), *County and town: one hundred years of local government in Ireland* (Dublin, 2001). For resident magistrates, see Penny Bonsall, *The Irish RMs: the resident magistrates in the British administration of Ireland* (Dublin, 1997).

be the most useful prism through which to understand both the radical and conservative nature of the Irish revolution. It is hoped that the essays that precede it, grouped together thematically and chronologically where possible, will bring a similar blend of forward-thinking and reflection to a topic in need of invigoration.

Architectures of gentility in nineteenth-century Ireland

ANDREW TIERNEY

Ideas of gentility and politeness were central to the elite culture of the eighteenth and nineteenth centuries. However, recent academic debate has queried the usefulness of such terms in demarcating any meaningful boundaries of class.[1] Material cultural – in particular architecture – served to both articulate and enforce social and economic boundaries while at the same time diffusing a taste for such culture to a rising class of middle-income consumers. While the genteel aspirations of the Victorian middle class are visible in the spread of polite suburban housing developments, this essay examines the material equipage of 'gentility' – from architecture to landscape – among the lesser gentry and rising class of rural farmers. The cultural relationship between the 'Big House', small but polite houses of the minor gentry, and the homes of wealthier tenant farmers remains under explored territory. With some notable exceptions, architectural studies – often concerned with issues of attribution and stylistic development – have tended to focus on larger and better-documented houses where a coherent line of architectural and ornamental development can be retrieved.[2]

Maurice Craig, in his *Classic Irish houses of the middle size*, commented that 'the gulf between the "Big House" and the cottage has perhaps been over-emphasized by historians, and too much has been made of the absence of a middle class'.[3] The term 'parish gentry' has been used to describe those families whose supremacy was merely local, and in the nineteenth century this group included the more affluent merchants, professionals and farmers.[4] Indeed, the more ubiquitous homes of the minor gentry constituted the 'Big House' in most localities and were designed in such a way as to articulate their membership of an elite, however localized that might be. Terms such as 'seat' and 'demesne', traditionally associated with the upper ranks of the gentry, have been subject to relatively little scrutiny. As I argue below, their broad usage during the nineteenth century denotes an increasingly democratized context for polite culture in Ireland. For this reason, I have used the term 'architectures' to describe the scope of domestic buildings that expressed 'gentility' in nineteenth-century Ireland.

1 For a general review of the debate, see Lawrence E. Klein, 'Politeness and the interpretation of the British eighteenth century', *Historical Journal*, 45:4 (2002), 869–98. 2 For a recent overview of the historiography, see Terence Dooley, *The Big Houses and landed estates of Ireland: a research guide* (Dublin, 2007), pp 117–18. 3 Maurice Craig, *Classic Irish houses of the middle size* (Dublin, 2006), pp 3–4. 4 Lawrence Stone and Jeanne C. Fawtier Stone, *An open elite? England, 1540–1880* (Oxford, 1984), p. 180.

Not only is the period defined by aesthetic and, indeed, moral antagonism over style – particularly the Classical v. Gothic debate – but also over scale – cottage, farmhouse, villa and mansion – all of which, in their way, might indicate genteel status.

'A MIDDLE CLASS OF GENTRY'

The notion of gentility was all the more fraught and contested in a country where the ruling class was derived largely from a colonial elite politically and religiously alienated from the general populace.[5] 'Englishness' long remained a core element in definitions of good taste. Unsurprisingly, the country house in Ireland never assumed the role of national heritage that it did in Victorian England.[6] More recent attempts to repackage it as such have not gone uncontested.[7] This unease over elitism, gentility and national identity was palpable when a new Catholic middle class first began to assert itself, as Gustave de Beaumont noted in 1839:

> We must not be astonished if aristocratic inclinations display themselves in the middling properties which are gradually being formed in Ireland; there is not a middling proprietor who, at the sight of the privileges attached to the possession of land, is not tempted to enjoy them himself: he is delighted at possessing in his condition some analogy to a noble lord, his country neigh-bour, whom he hates as his political and religious enemy, but from whom, to convert his hate into love, he probably waits only for a kind smile, or a complimentary recognition … Will they persist in their hostile feelings to the privileged, now that their property gives them, besides all political rights, the chance of being named justices of the peace, being summoned on grand juries, sitting on the bench with the aristocracy in petty and quarter sessions?[8]

When did such material aspirations to gentility first emerge among the farming class? Until the 1780s, most farmers had lived in single-storey, vernacular 'cabins' partly due to what Kevin Whelan has described as 'a typically cautious, low-profile mentalité among Catholics'.[9] He gives the example of the Aylwards in Walsh moun-tain, who ran a 'dairy empire' and enjoyed a 'gentry-like income' but occupied houses little distinguishable from the peasant.[10] Despite their material invisibility,

5 For some discussion on this point, see Patrick Duffy, 'Colonial spaces and sites of resistance: landed estates in nineteenth-century Ireland' in Lindsay J. Proudfoot and Michael M. Roche (eds), *(Dis)placing empire: renegotiating British colonial geographies* (Aldershot, 2005), pp 15–40. 6 See Peter Mandler, *The fall and rise of the stately home* (New Haven, CT, 1999). 7 Hugh Maguire, 'Ireland and the house of invented memory' in Mark McCarthy (ed.), *Ireland's heritages: critical perspectives on memory and identity* (Aldershot, 2004), pp 153–68. 8 Gustave de Beaumont, *Ireland: social, political and religious* (Cambridge, MA, 2007), p. 248. 9 Kevin Whelan, 'An underground gentry', *Eighteenth-Century Ireland/Iris an dá chultúr*, 10 (1995), 37. 10 Ibid., 36.

there were many small freeholders among this group. Thomas Power records the estimation in 1807 that of the '6,500 freeholders in the county [Tipperary], 5,500 or 84 per cent were Catholics, showing that beneath the level of gentleman the base of the Catholic landed class was wide'.[11]

In Ireland prior to the nineteenth century, a shared reliance on the vernacular was more likely to bind the lower gentry and wealthier farmers more than any common dabbling in the niceties of architecture. From the seventeenth century, the new Protestant elite had been content to occupy the castles of their dispossessed Catholic predecessors or make do with unpretentious thatched houses,[12] many only begin-ning to 'quit their cottages' towards the end of the eighteenth century.[13] This seems particularly true of the lesser gentry. For example, William Roulston notes that although formal architecture makes an appearance among the northern Irish clergy in the early eighteenth century, simple rural residences remained 'commonplace' until much later.[14] According to Toby Barnard, as late as 1790, Co. Down had a commis-sion of the peace of eighty-seven but only forty-eight of those had 'notable seats'.[15] A similar familiarity with the vernacular existed among the gentry of Cork during this period, according to local memory recorded in the nineteenth century.[16]

Certainly, among eighteenth-century Catholic middlemen, a strong sense of gentility based on dress, education, pedigree, hospitality and local prestige was often retained within a vernacular architectural tradition. Occasionally, this might assume a hybrid form through the employment of symmetry.[17] The process that saw a wide-spread move to a consciously formal architecture among the elite is now often difficult to recover. It has been argued that the 'thatched mansions' that characterized the dwellings of well-off farmers and minor gentry in the eighteenth century were often demolished or remodelled beyond recognition, suggesting that the line between vernacular and polite architecture was more assertively drawn as rising agri-cultural prices (in the second half of the eighteenth century) drove both the construction of towns and the establishment of a more prosperous farming class.[18]

---

11 Thomas Power, *Land, politics and society in eighteenth-century Tipperary* (Oxford, 1993), p. 107. **12** Barry Reilly suggests that a number of the surviving two-storey vernacular dwellings – often five or six bays wide and 'the largest houses in their townlands' – are datable to the late seventeenth and early eighteenth century. See Barry Reilly, 'Hearth and home: the vernacular house in Ireland from *c.*1800', *Proceedings of the Royal Irish Academy*, 111C (2011), 197. **13** Toby Barnard, *Making the grand figure* (London, 2004), p. 22. **14** W.J. Roulston, 'Accommodating clergymen: Church of Ireland ministers and their houses in the north of Ireland, *c.*1600–1870' in T.C. Barnard and W.G. Neely (eds), *The clergy of the Church of Ireland, 1000–2000: messengers, watchmen and stewards* (Dublin, 2006), pp 106–27 at p. 119; Roulston also gives the example of the single-storey thatched 'cabin' known as 'Belville', seat of Edward Bayly, treasurer of Co. Down, see p. 117. **15** Barnard, *Making the grand figure*, p. 35. **16** David Dickson, *Old world colony: Cork and south Munster, 1630–1830* (Cork, 2005), p. 529, n. 185. **17** Whelan, 'An underground gentry', 24. **18** Caoimhín Ó Danachair, 'Traditional forms of the dwelling house in Ireland', *Journal of the Royal Society of Antiquaries of Ireland*, 102:1 (1972), 91; Kevin Danaher, *Ireland's vernacular architecture* (Dublin, 1975), p. 49; Susan Hood, 'The significance of the villages and small towns in rural Ireland during the

These improvements were reflected in furnishings as well as architecture. Arthur Young, writing in 1776, noted 'numerous exceptions' to the generally impoverished cabins of the poor with 'much useful furniture, and some even superfluous; chairs, tables, boxes, chest of drawers, earthen ware, and in short most of the articles found in a middling English cottage'.[19] These acquisitions, he pointed out, had all been made within the last ten years, which he regarded as a sure sign of a rising national prosperity. The same process was occurring across Britain. In 1825, William Cobbett, writing about England, expressed disgust at the transmutation of the farmer and his family into 'a species of mock gentlefolk' through their acquisition of parlours and genteel furniture.[20]

Unsurprisingly, it is at a local level, where the paths of landlord, middleman and tenant farmer frequently crossed, that we find the idea of gentility at its most malleable. Yet here, geography played its part. Thomas Power has noted that the northern baronies of Tipperary had far fewer large leaseholders than south Tipperary, where there was a substantial class of gentrified Catholic head tenants – many of whom built country houses indistinguishable from those of the landlord class. For example, Mr Macarthy of Spring House was leasing nine thousand acres in the late 1770s, while another such farmer, James Scully, a well-off grazier, was leasing some fifteen thousand acres in 1796.[21] In contrast, farms in the northern Tipperary barony of Lower Ormond were far smaller, in the region of five or six hundred acres – and many had no substantial buildings.[22] No farmer in the northern Tipperary barony of Ikerrin held more than a hundred acres.[23] Although landownership was certainly used as one of the criteria to define membership of the gentry as a class, vast lease-holds could render any such distinction redundant.[24]

Testament to these blurred social boundaries, in 1795 the English architect, John Miller, produced in the same volume designs for a 'gentleman's house with a farm-yard' and a 'genteel farmhouse and offices', of similar scale and pretension.[25] Although clearly some social distinction was intended, it is difficult now to differentiate the two architecturally. However, the occupants of such houses – whatever status they might claim – were clearly distancing themselves from the vernacular traditions

eighteenth and nineteenth centuries' in Peter Borsay (ed.), *Provincial towns in early modern England and Ireland: change, convergence and divergence* (Oxford, 2002), pp 241–63 at p. 245; Whelan, 'An underground gentry', 38. **19** Arthur Young, *A tour in Ireland* (2 vols, Dublin, 1780), ii, p. 30. **20** Cited in Michael McMordie, 'Picturesque pattern books and Victorian designers', *Architectural History*, 18 (1975), 43–59, 109–12, n. 19 at 53–4. **21** Whelan, 'An underground gentry', p. 39; Young, *A tour in Ireland*, ii, p. 157. **22** Young, *A tour in Ireland*, ii, p. 227. **23** Power, *Land, politics and society*, pp 113–14. **24** Toby Barnard, 'The gentrification of eighteenth-century Ireland', *Eighteenth-Century Ireland/Iris an dá chultúr*, 12 (1997), 154. While Kevin Whelan has argued for the survival of an 'underground gentry' of Catholic former proprietors who maintained archaic gentility within their own tradition, Toby Barnard has pointed to the 'imported' nature of both the language used to articulate gentility and the materiality through which it was expressed. **25** John Miller, *The country gentleman's architect, in a great variety of new designs, for cottages, farm houses, country-houses, villas, lodges for park etc.* (London, 1791), pp 10–13.

of the peasantry. Already in 1801 Charles Coote, writing of Queen's County, observed a 'middle class of gentry', who were engaged in improvement and whose residences were 'handsome, and generally well calculated for good family farm houses'. These he contrasted with the 'hovels' of the peasantry.[26]

The spread of polite architecture among farmers appears to have been much slower in Ireland than in England, however, and was not apparent to every observer. In 1807, Henry Colt Hoare remarked 'we see no conveniences of sheds, stalling, fenced rick yards &c. as in England; nor is the house of a farmer, renting three of four hundred pounds a year, at all better than many of the labouring poor', a problem he attributed to the insecurity of sub-leasing from avaricious middlemen.[27] Edward Wakefield in 1812 attributed the material impoverishment of wealthy farmers to a desire to avoid hearth and window tax.[28] One visitor remarked in 1836 that 'the whole surface of England is covered with substantial farm-houses; in Ireland they are scarcely to be seen', a dearth he attributed to the low wages of Irish labourers, reckoned at half that of their English counterparts.[29]

Inevitably, the quality of housing erected by well-off farmers varied considerably from region to region. Wakefield, despite his more general comments, noted the very fine farmhouses around Gorey, Co. Wexford, all rebuilt with slated roofs since their destruction during the 1798 rebellion.[30] As late as 1837, Samuel Lewis recorded that the residences of rich farmers in the region of Kilkenny were 'generally inferior to their means',[31] while Arthur Atkinson noted that farmers' houses in the county of Carlow were distinguished by iron gates and stone piers, 'an appendage which until my entrance into this county, I did not see attached to concerns of the same character'.[32] It is possible that such variation depended on the size and quality of farms available in each region, as noted above in relation to Co. Tipperary.[33] However, statistical evidence from Munster suggests that the period from 1790 to 1840 was an extraordinarily transformative one in terms of residential improvement for the farming class.[34] Regional disparities made farmers hard to pin down in terms of class as – in the words of one early twentieth-century commentator – 'an Irish farmer may be anything from a private gentleman on a small scale to a labouring man on a large one'.[35] Throughout the nineteenth century, farmhouses would vary from 'imposing

---

26 Charles Coote, *General view of the agriculture and manufactures of the Queen's County* (Dublin, 1801), p. 22.   **27** Richard Colt Hoare, *Journal of a tour in Ireland* (London, 1807), pp 306–7.   **28** Edward Wakefield, *An account of Ireland, statistical and political* (London, 1812), p. 468. The lack of farmyards and poor state of farm offices contributed to a desire to economize.   **29** Baptist Wriothesley Noel, *Notes of a short tour through the midlands of Ireland in the summer of 1836* (London, 1837), p. 359.   **30** Wakefield, *An account of Ireland*, p. 409. **31** Samuel Lewis, *A topographical dictionary of Ireland* (2 vols, London, 1837), ii, p. 108. **32** Arthur Atkinson, *Irish tourist* (Dublin, 1815), p. 406.   **33** For a broader view of the regional variations in the quality of housing by county in the nineteenth century, see W.E. Vaughan, *Landlords and tenants in mid-Victorian Ireland* (Oxford, 1994), pp 271–2. **34** Dickson, *Old world colony*, p. 317.   **35** Robert Lynd, *Home life in Ireland* (London, 1909), p. 11.

stone-finished dwellings, fitted out with pianos and Victorian furniture, down to small two-roomed and even one-roomed cottages, white-washed, and with thatched roofs …'[36]

INTERROGATING THE 'BIG HOUSE'

A 'democratization of aesthetics' from the late eighteenth century saw the discourse on landscape and architecture open up to those without means to build on an extensive scale.[37] Rousseau's celebration of rural simplicity had elevated the status of the humble cottage and revived the popularity of indigenous place names.[38] Gentility was defined not by building alone but through participation in aesthetic discourse, allowing those on the fringes of the gentry to pass judgment on the taste of their social and economic superiors. Stephen Bending has spoken of the 'battles for control over socio-aesthetic taste' that emerges in the second-half of the eighteenth century in a range of literature produced beyond the confines of the patrician elite.[39] In this guise, Arthur Atkinson, an impoverished King's County Protestant whose *Irish tourist* was published in 1815, was often derogatory about the lack of aesthetic judgment in the design of larger houses and demesnes he visited. Like other educated but impecunious travellers, Atkinson took pleasure in talking down to the upper ranks of the gentry, often giving detailed instructions on how their demesnes might be improved. High walls built to inspire awe could be quickly pulled asunder by a disapproving stroke of the pen – and one wonders how many campaigns of rebuilding in the early 1800s were prompted by some slight in a tourist guidebook. The enlargement of Oak Park, Co. Carlow, in the early 1830s[40] came in the wake of Atkinson's comment that the house was 'neat but not extensive' and his dismissal of its eight-hundred-acre demesne – enclosed by a ten-foot-high wall – as 'completely destitute' of a decent prospect.[41] Another travel writer, later in the century, criticized the Kildare seat of the earl of Mayo for having 'a low situation' and a view 'greatly confined' before recommending 'a splendid site not many perches from the front door'.[42] The seat of the barons Courtown was likewise 'confined … [and] almost smothered in the trees, which prevents the free circulation of air'.[43]

36 Ibid., pp 15–17.   **37** Stephen Bending, 'One among the many: popular aesthetics, polite culture and the country house landscape' in Dana Arnold (ed.), *The Georgian country house: architecture, landscape and society* (Stroud, 2003), pp 61–78 at p. 63.   **38** See Arthur Atkinson's discussion of this revival in the context of a broader Celtic revival in *The Irish tourist*, p. 229. **39** Bending, 'One among the many', p. 63.   **40** See Ann-Martha Rowan, *Dictionary of Irish architects*, http://www.dia.ie, accessed 10 June 2011.   **41** Atkinson, *The Irish tourist*, p. 369. **42** James Godkin and John A. Walker, *The new handbook of Ireland* (Dublin, 1871), p. 223. **43** Ibid., p. 196.

'SMALL BEAUTIES'

Participation in aesthetic discourse by lower-ranking gentry and professionals was part of a broader diffusion of genteel culture in the early nineteenth century, seen also in the 'democratisation of fashions' wherein 'the lady's maid could dress in the style of her mistress'.[44] This cultural interchange was not one-way only, for at the same time that the lower economic ranks sought the traditional trappings of gentility, the elite also took a close interest in the material culture of the peasantry – albeit in an idealized form. The landscape of early nineteenth-century Ireland was something of an architectural dressing up box; indeed, the line between well-intentioned improvement and picturesque fantasy was often a fine one. The contemporary popularity for the *cottage ornée* and *ferme ornée* – sometimes in highly ostentatious forms, such as the Butler's Swiss Cottage at Cahir – created a sylvan refuge for an idle elite rather than a better class of farmhouse.

When foisted on tenant farmers and estate workers, the picturesque style was not always well-received or understood. At the start of the nineteenth century, Charles Coote expressed astonishment that the peasantry seemed to prefer their own vernacular dwellings to those of their improving landlord.[45] Yet small farmers and estate labourers could hardly have wished to celebrate the faux-bucolic lifestyle dreamed of by their masters. In 1825, James Brewer, the travel writer, castigated Mr Jefferyes of Blarney for over-embellishing the dwellings of his tenants when building the town of Blarney, arguing that 'such superfluous circumstances of embellishment were derided by the rich, and viewed with indifference by the tenants and the poor' leading to a state of dilapidation.[46]

Among the lesser gentry, cottage architecture eased the material expectations involved in housing impoverished maiden aunts and displaced dowagers, while disguising the reality that many of them had, in the previous century, been served by houses of a less intentionally vernacular character. Despite the air of aristocratic indulgence, designs for cottage architecture were often propagated by lower middle-class professionals who, 'within a modest compass, made the genteel life possible by their arrangement'.[47] Lewis' *Topographical dictionary* of 1837 includes the thatched, mud-built – yet symmetrical – house (fig. 1.1) of the local Catholic curate among a group of 'seats' in the parish of Jamestown, Queen's County – a group that includes a large neoclassical mansion by William Vitruvius Morrison.[48] Clearly a remodelling of an earlier vernacular dwelling, its name, 'Abbeyview Cottage', cleverly appropriated the genteel language of the picturesque to make a virtue of its humble scale and materials.[49] The name also asserted a visual relationship with the fanciful Gothick

44 Mairead Dunlevy, cited in Claudia Kinmonth, *Rural interiors in art* (London, 2006), p. 50. **45** Coote, *General view of the agriculture and manufactures of the Queen's County*, p. 144. **46** James Brewer, *The beauties of Ireland* (2 vols, London, 1826), ii, p. 379. **47** Michael McMordie, 'Picturesque pattern books and Victorian designers', 50. **48** Lewis, *Topographical dictionary*, p. 248. **49** The owner, Michael Dempsey, has ascertained an early modern date for the building using carbon dating (pers. comm.).

1.1 Abbeyview Cottage, Co. Laois (photograph by the author,
with thanks to Michael Dempsey).

revival mansion of the earl of Drogheda, Moore Abbey, built in the 1760s – reducing
the aristocratic pile to an eye-catcher in the Revd Maher's masterly field of view. In
this way, visual conversations opened up between cottage and castle in a newly shared
cultural landscape.

More so than the strong farming class from which they were drawn, Catholic
priests had the education and leisure time to engage with art and architecture.
Another Queen's County cleric of this period, the Revd James Walsh, was remembered as 'a man of genius, taste and learning, painter, sculptor, designer'.[50] Frequently
classed among the gentry, priests in wealthy parishes often occupied quite substantial
houses[51] with genteel interiors. A painting of 1878 shows the high-ceilinged parlour
and marble fireplace with overmantel mirror that exemplified the plush gentility of
the Irish priest's house. As Claudia Kinmonth has observed, these features provide a

50 Monument on south side of nave of Durrow RC church.   **51** The more common view
of the Catholic priest is perhaps that relayed by a correspondent of the *Daily Telegraph*, 4 Jan.
1880, who described a Fr Conway in Ballina, Co. Mayo, as 'a lodger in one of the larger
farmhouses adjoining the road': see T.M. Healy, *Why is there an Irish land question and Irish
Land League?* (Dublin, 1881), p. 73. Those priests who could raise money to build new
chapels might also raise funds for a new parochial house. Blake's 'Father Peter Morrissey',
resident in a large parish, makes the transition to 'a comfortable glebe-house', which afforded
'more ample accommodation than the modest two rooms in a farmhouse heretofore
occupied by the parish priest' – see his *Pictures from Ireland*, p. 55.

1.2 Moneycleare House, Co. Laois (image reproduced courtesy of the NIAH).

'studied contrast to the simple poverty of [a] barefoot girl and her mother, who bends in deference to the priest'.[52] Such an interior might be found in the home of the Revd James Delaney, resident at Moneycleare House on the outskirts of Ballinakill, Co. Laois, in 1850. Approached down a winding avenue, a genteel flight of stone steps accessed an attractive fanlit, Gibbsian door. A two-storey servants' wing extended to one side (fig. 1.2).[53] Similarly, in the small village of Puckaun, Co. Tipperary, the genteel and picturesquely titled demesne of 'Riverview' was the mid-nineteenth-century residence of a parish priest who leased it from a member of the local gentry.[54] Parochial houses built later in the century, often in towns and close to the church, shed something of this earlier glamour. While they enjoyed the trappings of a genteel lifestyle, priests were answerable to those who paid for it. There were at least two instances in Carlow in the early nineteenth century of outraged parishioners reclaiming parochial houses from the relatives of deceased priests. In Clonegal, they literally dragged the secular 'heirs' of the priest out of the house.[55]

Although every type of building from the castle to the cottage might articulate some notion of polite living, the minor gentry – particularly the Protestant clergy who built extensively in the early nineteenth century – followed a reserved architectural template for gentility: the symmetrical astylar block, two storeys high, three

52 Kinmonth, *Rural interiors in art*, p. 159. 53 http://www.askaboutireland.ie/griffith-valuation, accessed 15 June 2011. 54 Daniel Grace, *Portrait of a parish: Monsea and Killodiernan* (Nenagh, 1996), p. 172. 55 *Nenagh Guardian*, 29 Oct. 1842.

1.3 A typical glebe house near Terryglass, Co. Tipperary
(image reproduced courtesy of the NIAH).

bays wide, with fanlit doorway (fig. 1.3). The influence of neoclassicism and theories of landscape design recommended a three-dimensional articulation of the house
as 'villa' within a landscape. Regular fenestration on at least three sides allowed views
out into the free-style parkland – popularized by Capability Brown – which in turn
framed views back towards the house. This was a departure from their more rigidly
oriented early eighteenth-century precursors, which sat in gardens of geometrically
designed groves and parterres – more expensive and harder to imitate by those in
straitened circumstances. Inside, the simple plan of dining room and drawing room
flanking a narrow hall was nothing new, but presented the rising middle class with a
formula for architectural respectability.

Aspiring farmers extend the life of this villa style well beyond the nineteenth
century, and Atkinson noted with approval the 'growth of taste' among this class. 'It
would be utterly incompatible within the limits of this volume', he remarked, 'to
introduce to public notice, all the rising villas of this kind which mark the improvement of the country'.[56] He repeatedly favoured what he called 'small beauties', which

---

56 Atkinson, *The Irish tourist*, p. 307. Cloth merchants in the north of England had similarly
clung to the old-fashioned style of the 'Tudor manor' well into the seventeenth century due
to its enduring associations with the landed classes – see Nicholas Cooper and Marianne
Majerus, *English manor houses* (London, 1990), p. 88; Patrick and Maureen Shaffrey comment
that this classical type, generally denoting a farm of over a hundred acres, was still being built
by farmers as late as the 1950s – see their *Irish countryside buildings* (Dublin, 1985), pp 41–3.

he equated to his own 'standard of rural excellence'.[57] The 'demesne' was no longer exclusive to the 'Big House' and Atkinson employed the term at every scale, including a series of 'cottages in the English style' on the Cosby estate of Stradbally, to each of which, he remarked, 'a few acres of demesne are attached'.[58] While landlords were often the sponsors of such domestic improvement among their tenantry, these improvements are necessarily described with a vocabulary borrowed from the Big House (around which the discourse of improvement had first arisen). Certainly, an air of cultivation and maturity in the plantations around smaller houses hinted at the gentility of their residents, sometimes making their social status difficult to ascertain. In the 1870s, Godkin and Walker commented that, in addition to the beautiful mansions of the Offaly gentry, there were also 'substantial dwelling houses sheltered by old trees, showing either that the owner is a smaller proprietor or that he or his forefathers had a long lease'.[59] A few decades later, an observer described such a dwelling as having 'little plantations of trees around it, and an orchard and flower-beds, and often a lawn for games', the houses 'stone finished and four-square and roofed with slate'.[60] To what extent landlords were involved in improvements among more prosperous tenants is uncertain, though there is evidence to suggest that their influence was more limited in this sphere.[61]

Although farmers were what Atkinson termed the 'useful class of the community', he encouraged them to cultivate genteel surroundings for themselves. Commenting favourably on the 'villa' of a farmer named Morris near Bray, Co. Wicklow, he suggested that utilitarian farm equipment be kept out of view of the visitor approaching the house and trees used to screen farm activity. The surroundings of a farmhouse could, in classic villa style, be divided into the genteel and the utilitarian.[62] Elsewhere he described the 'demesne' of a farmhouse (fig. 1.4) on the estate of the absentee Lord Stanhope, and lauded the house itself in the following enthusiastic terms:

> ... a neat white-washed edifice of about thirty-six feet by twenty-four – it might have contained two small parlours, a hall, pantry and kitchen, on the ground floor, and as many apartments above them; but certainly not much under or over – its extent was exactly adequate to the accommodation of a family of taste and small fortune, and the garden, offices and demesne exactly corresponded with this – all compact and in good order, bore the aspect of

57 Atkinson, *The Irish tourist*, pp 174–5.   **58** Ibid., p. 319.   **59** Godkin and Walker, *A new handbook of Ireland*, p. 237.   **60** Lynd, *Home life*, p. 38.   **61** Patrick and Maura Shaffrey argue that 'the stronger tenant farmer and minor gentry were responsible for more improvements in agricultural techniques than many a great landlord': see *Irish countryside buildings*, pp 41–3. Was the same true for architectural improvements outside the sphere of the estate town? At a lower social level, Patrick Bowe has shown that some nineteenth-century manuals for cottage improvement were aimed directly at cottagers themselves – see P. Bowe, 'The traditional Irish farmhouse and cottage garden', *Irish Architectural and Decorative Studies*, 3 (2000), 77–101.   **62** Atkinson, *Irish tourist*, p. 606.

1.4 Valleyfield House, Co. Laois (photograph by the author,
with thanks to the Delaney family).

comfort; but save one or two objects in the little domestic landscape, nothing
had the appearance of grandeur.[63]

He asserted that it was 'one of the prettiest little villas which I have yet seen in this
part of Ireland', recommending gentlemen travelling through the area to visit it. It
was, he said, 'the epitome of English neatness and beauty'. Atkinson here uses terms
like 'demesne', 'lodge', 'villa', 'ornament', 'offices', 'garden' and 'lawn', and the occupants he describes as people of 'taste'. Although he was unsure whether the small lake
close to the house was intentionally ornamental or not, given the farm's proximity
to Heywood, one of the country's most important landscape gardens – which it overlooked – it is certainly feasible that it was.

Keen not only to describe the improvements and tastes of the humbler classes,
but also to include them among his readers, Atkinson created four separate ranks of
subscriber, each paying a separate price. One such subscriber he recounts seeking out
in a decent-looking cottage, poor, Protestant and in the linen trade – and a
'respectable' member of society.[64] We can detect in Atkinson's enthusiasm for 'small
beauties' the contemporary picturesque taste for the rural idyll and an evangelical
fervour for honest living. There is also a criticism of a purely materialist notion of
'improvement'. He wrote:

63 Ibid., p. 175.   **64** Ibid., p. 50.

> I connect every idea of comfort … with a neat lodge and demesne, in a neighbourhood highly cultivated and improved, but cultivated and improved in a sense much more important and extensive than is conceived necessary by some of those who have been placed by public suffrage in the first class of taste and correct judgment.[65]

'ESQUIRES' AND 'GENTLEMEN'

Deciding who exactly qualified as a 'gentleman' in an Ireland where political and religious supremacy was increasingly contested was a difficult task. Certainly, by the nineteenth century, many conservatives across Britain viewed the term 'gentleman' as having been thoroughly debased.[66] As a result, the somewhat archaic label of 'esquire' took on a new importance in distinguishing the established gentry from those regarded as their social inferiors. Various forms of nineteenth-century literature carefully pursued this distinction. In describing the provincial Tipperary town of Nenagh, *Slater's Directory* of 1846 included an extensive list of esquires among the 'nobility, gentry and clergy' but also a smaller number labelled merely as 'gent' – mostly distinguished by their Irish names – Mr Consedine, Mr Flinn, Mr Kennedy, Mr Murphy, Mr Talbot. In contrast to the 'esquires', these men had addresses in the town rather than the surrounding country.[67] This is not to suggest that this class was merely urban, but rather that those members of the lower gentry residing outside the town were omitted from the list. Their influence was clearly judged to be more geographically limited than that of the 'esquires'.

The distinction was by no means an Irish one alone. In 1842, *The Spectator* had, in an article entitled 'Dilemmas of gentility', described the attempts of jurors in Chelsea to move from those listed as 'gentlemen' to those listed as 'esquire'.[68] Jury lists also raised eyebrows in Ireland. John O'Brien of Hogan's Pass, Co. Tipperary, occupant of a small but genteel two-storey, five-bay house on the outskirts of Nenagh, had his status downgraded from 'esquire' in 1841 to 'gent' in 1845.[69] Edward Flinn, 'gent', occupied a modest but polite residence – named grandly as 'Fox Hall' – outside Newport, Co. Tipperary, and appeared as both 'esquire' and 'gent' in separate publications.[70] Only those who held the rank of 'esquire' (loosely classed as landowners, bankers and merchants) were eligible for inclusion in special juries and an inquiry into the status of jurors in 1867 showed that many returned themselves as 'gentlemen' rather than 'esquire' to avoid the more onerous duties of the latter class, while describing themselves as 'esquire' in town directories. Only the better sort of

---

65 Ibid., p. 202.   **66** For a broad overview of these changes, see Penelope J. Corfield, 'The rivals: landed and other gentlemen' in N.B. Harte and R. Quinault (eds), *Land and society in Britain, 1700–1914* (Manchester, 1996), pp 1–33.   **67** *Slater's national commercial directory of Ireland* (London, 1846), p. 295.   **68** *Spectator*, 15 (1842), 1236.   **69** *Jurors (Tipperary)* [380], HC 1844, xliv, 18; *Jurors (Tipperary)* [393], HC 1846, xlii, 34.   **70** See *Slater's directory* (1846), p. 301; *Jurors (Tipperary)* [393], HC 1846, xlii, 33–4.

tradesmen, such as wine merchants and builders, were deemed eligible to sit on grand juries – but not shopkeepers. It was decided that the only means of establishing the true class of any individual was by reference to the character and location of his house.[71] On paper, houses could be just as misleading as anything else, as their names were often more grandiose than their appearance would justify. While house names with 'mount', 'park' and 'lodge' proliferate among those listed as 'esquire' in the returns of jurors for Tipperary (North Riding), such genteel names were also adopted by those only granted the status of 'gent': 'William Ryan of Mount Alt', 'John M. Fletcher of Shannon Hall', 'Obediah Holland of Mount Falcon', 'William Vere Cruise of Mount William', 'Edward Flinn of Fox Hall' and 'William Nagle of Fortfield' were all classed among the lower gentry.[72] Although many of these 'seats' were significantly smaller than those occupied by the local 'squires', they also culti-vated a certain gentility in their architecture and surroundings. Mount Alt, for example, was modestly scaled yet occupied a politely laid-out parkland with an orchard to the rear. Very similar in size is the equally grandly titled 'Shannon Hall' (fig. 1.5), where the orchard out-scaled the parkland. However, some houses of this class, such as Garryvenus – the seat of William Fogarty, which neighboured Mount Alt – made do with just an orchard.[73] The maintenance of such social division in the classification of the gentry was inevitably a source of friction. In 1850, a Galway town councillor and poor law guardian 'lost several of his teeth from the blows of a guest, at his hospitable table ..., in a dispute about the gentility of their respective fami-lies'.[74]

Such disparities in material status were more difficult to disguise in towns where there was often a readily apparent distinction in the architectural quality of certain streets. Slater's directories of Irish towns from the 1840s give an indication of the urban localities most favoured by the patrician class, such as Nenagh's Summerhill, where the architecture parallels that of Georgian Dublin, with houses reaching four and five storeys high, embellished with fanlit doorways and stone steps to their entrances (fig. 1.6). Popular with those ranked 'esquire', the clergy (Catholic and Protestant), wealthy professionals and tradesmen, none of the town's lower ranking 'gentlemen' were found among the tenants.[75] Similarly, zones of upmarket architec-ture served to delineate status in many other small Irish towns in the late eighteenth and early nineteenth centuries. The neighbouring village of Borrisokane featured terraced villas in the polite 'modern' style on its south side, totally distinct from the townhouses in the centre. Mountrath, Queen's County, a small town of similar size,

71 *Reports from committees: special and common juries* [425], HC 1867, ix, 32.   **72** *Jurors (Tipperary)* [393], HC 1846, xlii, 33–4.   **73** See first-edition OS map.   **74** *Nenagh Guardian*, 20 Apr. 1850.   **75** Residing at Summer Hill, Nenagh, during the mid-1840s were ten members of the gentry and clergy (of both denominations), six attorneys, one barrister, one doctor, two architects, two building contractors, three carpenters, three stone masons, five schools or academies, two land agents, two corn dealers, one newspaper, two public houses, one saddler, one shopkeeper and one baker, one shoemaker, one straw bonnet-maker, one tailor. See 1846 *Slater's directory* (1846), pp 295–8.

1.5 Shannon Hall, Co. Tipperary, with remodelled windows
(image reproduced courtesy of Peter Clarke).

also had a series of polite villas on its north side; its south side, in contrast, featured small two-storey, two-bay labourers cottages. Unsurprisingly, these polite areas tended to be closer to the Protestant church – except in Nenagh, where the church was at the opposite end of the town until moved to the town's genteel quarter *c.*1850. Urban wealth increasingly spread outwards in suburban demesnes surrounding towns and villages in the same region, a pattern common in other parts of the country. Lindsay Proudfoot, in his study of the 'Big House' in Co. Tyrone during the nineteenth century, described the clusters of notably small demesnes around provincial towns, as part of a 'process of socially driven land purchase by petty urban capitalists'.[76] The superficial trappings of landownership – the Big House, demesne, gate lodge etc. – clearly had a role in articulating claims to genteel identity among this class, despite their dependence on trade and commerce.[77]

76 Lindsay Proudfoot, 'Place and mentalité: the "Big House" and its locality in Co. Tyrone' in Charles Dillon and Henry A. Jefferies (eds), *Tyrone: history and society* (Dublin, 2000), p. 511. **77** David Dickson has commented on this 'glittering allure' of landed gentility around Cork, arguing that 'however important merchants may have been in the great economic transformation, the dominant element in the region's power structure remained the county gentry'. See Dickson, *Old world colony*, pp 170, 421.

1.6 Summerhill, Nenagh, Co. Tipperary (photograph by the author).

LANDLORDS AND TENANTS

Lewis' *Topographical dictionary* of 1837 expanded the parameters of gentility considerably to include prosperous Catholic farming families. We find Clopook House near
Luggacurren, Co. Laois, described as the 'seat' of the Catholic Mahon family (fig.
1.7), who rented a 247-acre farm from a local Protestant clergyman. The family were
also freeholders of almost four hundred acres at a value £176 per annum, partly leased
to fourteen separate tenants.[78] Built in 1821, the house is very clearly distinct from
the vernacular dwellings of their tenants, having a symmetrical two-storey façade and
an emphatically genteel block-and-start doorway of limestone with fanlight.[79]
Similar in size and character was the 'seat' of their neighbour John Dunne of
Raheennahown, a 'gentleman of extensive means', who leased 1,300 acres from the
marquess of Lansdown.[80] The Raheennahown demesne was distinguished from its

78 http://www.askaboutireland.ie/griffith-valuation, accessed 12 June 2011. **79** The
house has been dated by a scrap of newspaper discovered by the present owner behind the
skirting, recounting the coronation of George IV. **80** Virginia Crossman, *Politics, pauperism
and power in late nineteenth-century Ireland* (Manchester, 2006), p. 87.

1.7 Clopook House, Co. Laois (photograph by the author).

neighbour by its gate lodge built in the Tudor Revival style. Tenants with similarly sized holdings but more aristocratic pretensions could build on a much more lavish scale and in more exuberant style. The Lenigan family, who leased 1,600 acres from the earl of Portarlington in Co. Tipperary, in the early 1800s built a large castellated mansion (fig. 1.8) to advertise their descent from the noble Gaelic family of O'Fogarty.[81] Like most castellated houses in Ireland, it subscribed to the 'English style of architecture' in a line with accepted notions of genteel taste.[82] A popular novel of 1823 made fun of such pretensions, referring to 'the Fogartys of Castle Fogarty, as they now choose to designate themselves', while in the 1840s, *Tait's Edinburgh Magazine* attacked them as impoverished 'castellated gentry'. Thackeray, in *Vanity Fair*, made 'Lord Castle-Fogarty' an acquaintance of 'that tattling old harridan, Peggy O'Dowd'. Lady Morgan, on the other hand, compared their gentility favourably against that of upstart English baronets who had made their fortunes in industry.[83]

81 http://www.landedestates.ie/LandedEstates/jsp/estate-show.jsp?id=3359, accessed 10 Jun 2011; *Dublin Penny Journal*, 4:183 (1836), 249. **82** *The Parliamentary Gazetteer of Ireland* (Dublin, 1846), p. 361. **83** Miss Cramp, *Isabel St Albe: or, Vice and virtue* (3 vols, Edinburgh, 1823), i, p. 166; Andrew Tierney, 'Noble Gaelic identity in medieval and modern Ireland', *Virtus: Jaarboek voor Adelsgeschiedenis/Yearbook of the History of the Nobility*, 16 (2009), 168; See G. Saintsbury (ed.), *Miscellaneous contributions to* Punch *by William Makepeace Thackeray, 1843–54* (Oxford, n.d. [1917]), pp 138–53; William Thackeray, *Vanity Fair* (New York, 1848), p. 60;

1.8 Castle Fogarty, Co. Tipperary (*Dublin Penny Journal*, 6 Feb. 1836).

While architectural grandeur might invoke snide remarks from certain quarters, a family's gentility might equally be undermined by their status as tenants rather than landowners. The McCutcheons of Kilmore, Co. Tipperary, occupants of a polite dwelling house on 157 acres, suffered the indignity of having their chattels seized during the Land War. Their absentee English landlord, Colonel Maberley, expressed an extraordinary degree of contempt for assertive tenants of this class, wishing to reduce another local Protestant family of gentleman farmers, the Daggs, to the poor house:

> The building I shall burn down, and let the land run waste to recover the fertility, of which, no doubt, owing to your style of farming, you have pretty well deprived it. I have few wants, no debts, no family and a good English income. The loss would be a mere nothing to me, and I shall have the satisfaction of punishing you, and, I trust, rendering you for life an inmate of the Nenagh Union.[84]

Toby Barnard has observed similar attempts to demote the pretensions of genteel tenants during the previous century – see *Making the grand figure*, p. 38; Lady Morgan, *The princess, or the beguine* (2 vols, Philadelphia, 1835), ii, p. 66.   **84** *Nenagh Guardian*, 31 Aug. 1881.

Much more substantial families, such as the Dunnes of Raheennahown, were evicted during the Plan of Campaign in March of 1887 to set an example to smaller tenants.[85] The trappings of architectural gentility were therefore no barrier to experiences more commonly associated with the thatched cottage.

Tensions between the lower and upper gentry came to the fore in a widely publicized lawsuit taken by Michael Kelly of Mirehill, Co. Galway, in 1843. An occupier of a modest dwelling on a leasehold of 272 acres, Kelly had been disqualified as winner of a race in Athlone when Moore of Moore Hall asserted that he was not a gentleman. Kelly successfully sued for the return of the £55 trophy in a court case that saw both sides grapple with the definition of gentility. Although it was asserted in the evidence that Mr Kelly's wife did not receive visits from the upper ranks of the Galway gentry, the case was ultimately decided in his favour by virtue of his family's inclusion in *Burke's guide*.[86] Sydney Owenson's Celtic Revival romances had glamorized the pedigrees of the impoverished native gentry, who, from the 1830s, were received with notable enthusiasm into this well-known register of genteel families. Concerned with the notion of 'the house' in its genealogical and material form, *Burke's guide* vied with earlier books such as Lodge and Debrett's to define the parameters of gentility not just in Ireland but throughout Britain and the empire. Here, the antiquity of three branches of the Galway O'Kellys was prominently displayed. Its writers – several generations of the Burke family of Elm Hall, Co. Tipperary – were provincial Irish Catholics who earned a living as lawyers and genealogists and were anciently connected to clans such as the Kellys by marriage.[87] They boasted an ancestor in the Austrian service and proclaimed themselves descended from the O'Reillys, 'Princes of Brefny', in the female line, a pedigree decidedly out of kilter with the mainstream Protestant establishment in Ireland.[88] 'Elm Hall', like Mirehill, was of decidedly humble scale.[89] A short avenue from the road led to a modestly scaled house with a walled garden to the rear and a small park to the front. In material terms, the Burkes existed at the very margins of the class they sought to define – a fact obscured by the publication of their books in London.

This Irish Catholic background may explain why they sought to promote pedigree over material wealth as the true measure of gentility and why they could be quite dismissive of new English and Cromwellian blood of more recent vintage. The real aristocracy of Ireland, they explained in one edition, was to be found in very low

85 *Nenagh Guardian*, 24 Aug. 1881 and 31 Aug. 1881; Crossman, *Politics and pauperism*, p. 87; see also Leigh-Ann Coffey, *The planters of Luggacurran* (Dublin, 2006), p. 20. **86** For the Kelly leasehold, see Griffiths Valuation (www.askaboutIreland.ie). For an account of the squabble, see *American Turf Register and Sporting Magazine*, 15 (1844), 264; see also Tierney, 'Noble Gaelic identity', 168. **87** John Burke, *A general and heraldic dictionary of the peerage and baronetage of the British Empire* (2 vols, 1832), ii, p. 248; Joseph Jackson Howard and Frederick Arthur Crisp, *Visitation of Ireland* (London, 1973), pp 23–4. **88** John Burke (ed.), *The Patrician* (London, 1848), v, p. 501. **89** The scale of the house and garden is visible on the first-edition OS map. The house was demolished about twenty years ago according to the present owner (pers. comm.).

places – the Old English and Gaelic Irish. Dispossession and exile might therefore be worn as badges of the old Irish family.[90] The Burkes' close neighbours, the Aylmers, who lived at the very small and remote Derry House, Rathcabbin, Co. Tipperary, were also representative of this class. Although their current 'seat' was very insubstantial, they appeared in *Burke's guide* as 'the Aylmers of Lyons', the large Kildare estate they had sold in the previous century to the woollen manufacturer in Dublin who later became Lord Cloncurry.[91]

CONCLUSION

The spread of polite architecture and landscape in rural Ireland during the nineteenth century reflected the growing social and political confidence of the middle classes. Already by the late eighteenth century, polite consumer goods were making an impact in rural Ireland, a process accelerated by the eradication of smaller holdings in the post-Famine years.[92] Terms such as 'seat', 'demesne' and 'villa' were applied quite far down the economic scale and sweeping avenues, gate houses and fanlit doorways were no longer the preserve of the landlord class. Tenants on even relatively small acreages appropriated a visible gentility in parallel with their newfound political and social power. Catholic priests, in the years following emancipation, similarly acquired – at least in richer parishes – the material trappings of the landlord class. Fine parlours or drawing rooms asserted the new liberty of the Catholic Church in the same way as ambitious programmes of church building by fashionable architects. The contemporary taste for polite architecture on the small scale – cottages and villas – accommodated the aspirations of small landowners on the fringes of the gentry. Those with aristocratic pretensions but who were unable to build grandly could find refuge in *Burke's guide* and it is revealing that this authoritative social register, which was ostensibly a prop of the Protestant ascendancy, emerged from the ranks of the Irish Catholic professional class. Certainly, such claims to gentility were more assertively made as the spread of formal architecture and the democratization of elite culture saw the lines between prosperous farmer, middleman and landlord increasingly blurred.

---

90 Tierney, 'Noble Gaelic identity in medieval and modern Ireland', 167. **91** Sir Bernard Burke, *Genealogical and heraldic history of the landed gentry of Great Britain and Ireland* (London, 1879), p. 55. **92** For these broader improvements, see Alan Gailey, 'Vernacular dwellings of Clogher Diocese', *Clogher Record*, 9:2 (1977), 207; Danachair, 'Traditional forms of the dwelling house in Ireland', 91.

Building Victorian Dublin: Meade & Son and the expansion of the city

SUSAN GALAVAN

At the dawn of the Victorian age, Dublin was a comparatively small city, clustered around a medieval heart, its municipal boundary marked by a series of roads and canals built the century before. Dublin's Georgian city was essentially complete, with its grand squares and streetscapes of red-brick terraces. The influences of the Fitzwilliam and Gardiner estates had ensured that development was focused to the east of the city, both north and south of the river. But on the west side, large tracts of undeveloped land were dotted with market gardens and suburban villages (fig. 2.1).

This was a city on the verge of major expansion. During the nineteenth century, Dublin's population increased by over 43 per cent as the city expanded to form new residential suburbs.[1] Speculative developers entered the frame, carving out new streets in empty fields, both inside and outside the canals. A growing middle class sought refuge in these new areas, away from the disease and overcrowding that characterized Dublin by the mid-nineteenth century. Out of this context emerged a new house form, as a high-density urban building model gave way to one more suitable to a suburban context. Today, Dublin's Victorian architecture extends across a vast area from the city to the surrounding county. The level of architectural sophistication and the quality of materials and craftsmanship are testament to the skills and status of their creators. This essay explores the role of one of these protagonists – the firm of Michael Meade & Son, a prolific family of Dublin builders. The Meades emerged in the post-Famine period to forge new business opportunities in a rapidly advancing city. Part of a rising Catholic elite, they expanded their building empire until it became one of the city's largest employers. How did their entrepreneurial spirit and drive help to shape the ever-shifting nineteenth-century urban landscape?

BEGINNINGS

Born in Dublin to a Catholic family in 1814, Michael Meade first appeared on the scene in the 1840s as a carpenter and builder in Townsend Street, to the north of Trinity College. By 1843, he was insolvent, but he must have recouped his losses fairly quickly, as within two years he was back in business at the same address.[2] From

---

1 Mary Daly, *Dublin, the deposed capital* (Cork, 1984), p. 3.   2 *Freeman's Journal*, 28 Oct.

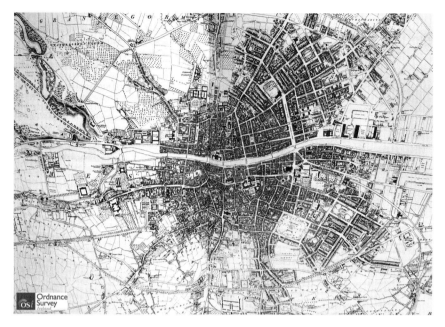

2.1 Dublin, 1837 (© Ordnance Survey Ireland/Government of Ireland, copyright permit no. MP 0004712).

the outset, Meade was active politically, campaigning for Catholic rights and the repeal of the Union. His earliest recorded project was the Turkish Baths at Lincoln Place in 1858, followed by two houses in Rathgar designed by the architect Rawson Carroll. Meade began to benefit from a golden age of church building, as the lifting of anti-Catholic legislation enabled the clergy to commission major works to cater to a burgeoning laity.[3] He built up an ecclesiastical client base, commencing with the Passionist monastery at Mount Argus for the renowned church architect James Joseph McCarthy. He also began work on the first of many public projects: in 1858, he broke ground for a new building to the rear of the Four Courts designed by James Higgins Owen, architect to the Board of Works.

Clearly, a growing enterprise such as this needed to source large quantities of building materials. By the end of the 1850s, Meade was in the process of building a sawing, planing and moulding mill at Great Brunswick Street (present day Pearse Street). A carpenter by trade, it was a natural fit for Meade, but it would also provide him with an important material resource for his burgeoning building empire. The mill was located on a large site adjoining the terminus of the Dublin and Wicklow railway and was built to house 'powerful machinery' to process timber for building. The machine age had arrived and new steam power could manufacture doors, sashes

1843. **3** Brendan Grimes, *Majestic shrines and graceful sanctuaries, the church architecture of Patrick Byrne, 1783–1864* (Dublin, 2009), p. 2.

and mouldings faster and cheaper than ever before. Meade claimed to be the first to introduce the new technology, boasting that his was 'the only manufactory of the kind in Dublin'.[4] At Great Brunswick Street he produced flooring, skirtings and mouldings 'of all sizes and patterns' as well as doors, sash frames and shutters. It must have been a conspicuous sight in the city – its 150-foot-high chimney was reported to be 'the tallest structure of its class in Dublin'.[5]

THE HOUSING BOOM

By 1859, the outskirts of Dublin were in the course of rapid transformation:

> Passing to the south side, we find the same steady march in the path of improvement … where villas, single and semi-detached, terraces &c., are springing up with an almost fairy-like rapidity, and the green sward speedily gives way to macadamized roads and populous thoroughfares, justifying the supposition that there is a universal move in that direction.[6]

Meade's timing could not have been better: a housing boom had just taken off and timber was the main raw material required to fuel it. By 1862, there were eight saw mills operating in the city, many with a wholesale yard on the quays from which shiploads of raw timber were sold. Meade placed advertisements in the *Dublin Builder* alongside those by the 'prince merchants' Martin & Sons, illustrated here operating from North Wall Quay (fig. 2.2).[7] The drawing demonstrates the potential enormity of such an operation, with a labyrinth of yards storing a wide variety of raw and sawn timber. In the bottom right hand corner, a timber wharf was being extended on a continuous basis to cope with the increasing loads of lumber arriving mainly from Canada and the Baltic. By 1862, Great Britain and Ireland were importing annually over half a million loads of Canadian pine timber. Most of it was processed on the Ottawa River, giving employment to over 40,000 men.[8]

Throughout the 1860s, Meade's business continued to prosper. In 1862, the *Dublin Builder* announced that he was in the process of rebuilding two houses in Eustace Street for the solicitor Mr Pickering.[9] The designer was William Caldbeck, who had trained under the eminent architect William Deane Butler and who was also working with Meade on new Italianate premises at 24/25 Grafton Street. Ecclesiastical work continued to thrive, and during this period Meade worked with the architects Pugin & Ashlin on a cathedral and four Catholic churches. Ashlin was the son of a Cork corn merchant and had received a privileged education in Belgium and England. In 1860, he went into partnership with the London architect Edward Welby Pugin and opened a Dublin office to run the Irish side of the practice. With

4 *Dublin Builder*, 1 Nov. 1859. **5** Ibid., 1 June 1862. **6** Ibid., 1 Nov. 1859. **7** Ibid., 1 Feb. 1860. **8** Ibid., 1 Jan. 1862. **9** Ibid., 15 Jan. 1862.

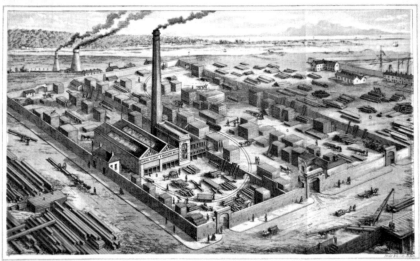

A. *Mahogany Mixed & Red Pine Store Yard*
B. *Sawing and Planing Mill*

SAWING, PLANING & MOULDING MILLS.

C. *Spruce Deal Store Yard.*
D. *White Pine Store Yard.*

2.2 John Martin & Son saw mills, North Wall Quay, Dublin (courtesy of
the Board of Trinity College Dublin, *Dublin Builder*, 1 Feb. 1860).

a predominately Roman Catholic client base, Ashlin soon became the leading ecclesiastical architect in Ireland, and completed more than sixty church and cathedral projects throughout the country. One of these was the church of Saints Augustine and John in Thomas Street in Dublin, which Meade began work on in 1866. It remains one of Dublin's most important churches, and has been described as 'the most original Victorian Gothic church in Dublin'.[10] Two years later, the foundation stone was laid for Pugin & Ashlin's largest commission: St Colman's Cathedral in Queenstown, Co. Cork. Meade was involved in the first phase of the project, but, when the design was significantly altered, he refused to negotiate the contract and left the site. Work on the cathedral was carried out in a piecemeal fashion thereafter and did not reach completion for another fifty years. O'Dwyer declares it as 'one of the grandest and certainly the most costly Irish ecclesiastical building of the Victorian era'.[11] Other collaborations included parish church commissions in the expanding Dublin suburbs, such as the church of St Patrick in Monkstown (1861–6) and the church of the Sacred Heart in Donnybrook (1863–6).

During this time, Meade became involved in one of the largest public works projects in Ireland: Ennis Lunatic Asylum (1863–6), designed by the Limerick architect

10 Christine Casey, *Dublin* (New Haven, CT, 2005), p. 627.   **11** Frederick O'Dwyer, 'A Victorian partnership: the architecture of Pugin & Ashlin' in John Graby (ed.), *150 years of architecture in Ireland: RIAI, 1839–1989* (Dublin, 1989), p. 55.

William Fogerty (fig. 2.3). This enormous complex was built in an Italianate style and was Fogerty's largest commission. The complex cost £35,000 to construct and was so large that it was said 'one would imagine this establishment could accommodate all the indoor and outdoor idiots, madmen, women and children in the whole kingdom of Ireland'.[12] As work began on the asylum, Meade was commissioned to build the Dublin cattle market in Prussia Street by Dublin Corporation. The facility would later become the biggest cattle market in Europe, serving the needs of the ever-growing populations of Ireland and Britain.[13] Operations continued unabated at Meade's saw mills in Great Brunswick Street, providing many of the raw materials for his building contracts.

The 1860s also saw Michael Meade acquiring sites for house building. In 1862, the company was in the process of building eight houses and a villa in Bray for William Dargan, the railway entrepreneur.[14] Dargan was 'the great figure of the Irish Railway Age' and was responsible for the development of practically every such project in the country, including the first one in 1834 from Kingstown to Dublin. Railway companies promoted the attractions of open sea bathing, an activity which had spawned a growth of seaside resort towns across the United Kingdom.[15] An enthusiastic supporter of Bray, Dargan determined to make it the 'Brighton of Ireland',[16] and it seems that by 1862 development there had been 'literally gigantic; houses here, there, everywhere', with 'hotels of monster form' catering for the crowds arriving during the summer season.[17] Meade's Bray houses were designed by the architects Lanyon, Lynn & Lanyon who had recently set up partnership in Belfast and Dublin.[18]

Meade then turned his attention to Ailesbury Road, a new thoroughfare that had just been opened up. It had been created by the Pembroke Estate to connect Donnybrook with Sydney Parade Station, resulting in 'over a mile of potential building frontage'.[19] Meade was the first to build there, acquiring a prime corner site of over two acres on the junction with the Merrion Road (fig. 2.4).[20] A testimony to his growing success, he built a grandiose Italianate villa for himself there in 1865. Its most striking feature is the seven-storey tower said to be modelled on Osborne House, Queen Victoria's country retreat on the Isle of Wight. A spiral staircase rises through the campanile, affording views far and wide from the city to the sea and the

12 Quoted in Brendan O'Donoghue, *The Irish county surveyors, 1834–1944* (Dublin, 2007), p. 89. **13** Liam Clare, 'The Dublin Cattle Market', *Dublin Historical Record*, 55:2 (2002), p. 180. **14** Irish Architectural Archive, *Dictionary of Irish architects, 1720–1940*, Michael Meade (http://www.dia.ie/), accessed 31 May 2012. **15** John K. Walton, *Wonderland by the waves* (Preston, Lancs, 1992), p. 2. **16** Maurice Craig, *Dublin, 1660–1880* (London, 1952), p. 302. **17** *Dublin Builder*, 1 Jan. 1862. **18** Irish Architectural Archive, *Dictionary of Irish architects, 1720–1940*, Michael Meade & Lanyon, Lynn & Lanyon (http://www.dia.ie/), accessed 31 May 2012. **19** E. McAulay, 'The origins and early development of the Pembroke estate beyond the Grand Canal, 1816–1880' (PhD, TCD, 2003), p. 217. **20** Original lease from Lord Pembroke to Michael Meade for piece of ground on the south side of Ailesbury Road in the city of Dublin for 150 years from 29 Sept. 1865.

2.3 Lunatic Asylum, Ennis, Co. Clare (courtesy of the National Library of Ireland).

Wicklow Mountains. As De Breffny & Ffolliott have noted,[21] suburban houses of this scale were a rare sight in Ireland, where there was always a good selection of Georgian houses on the market. But Meade was determined to put his stamp on the new suburbs.

The builder continued with his vision, acquiring plots next to his mansion in Ailesbury Road. The land was acquired by leasehold agreement from Lord Pembroke who gave him two years to build 'two good and substantial dwelling houses'.[22] The estate administered strict building leases, which set overall develop-ment guidelines by fixing plot size, building line and form. Only the best quality materials were to be used: the lower levels were to have punched or chiselled granite with the 'best red bricks' to the upper storeys. Out of the specifics of this lease, a new type of domestic architecture emerged, where wider plots and greater setbacks allowed houses to separate into pairs, resulting in a semi-detached building model (fig. 2.5). Although similar in form to those emerging in other streets of the Pembroke Estate, Meade's houses exhibit a high quality of execution and the stone window surrounds are unusually extravagant features for the time. By 1870, the builder had completed ten semi-detached houses there, providing the catalyst for future development.[23] Catering to an elite class, they were let to high-ranking

21 Brian De Breffny & Rosemary Ffolliott, *The houses of Ireland: domestic architecture from the medieval castle to the Edwardian villa* (London, 1975), p. 216. **22** Registry of Deeds, 1866, vol. 24, memorandum 131. **23** *Thom's Dublin street directory*, 1870.

2.4 St Michael's House, Ailesbury Road, Dublin (photograph by the author).

professionals, or those in the upper levels of the public service.[24] These high-quality structures have ensured that Ailesbury Road remains one of the most valuable pieces of real estate in Dublin today.

24 *Thom's Dublin street directory*, 1875–1885. Most of the occupants were solicitors, but other residents included an army colonel, a land agent and a county court judge.

2.5 Meade's houses, Ailesbury Road, Dublin (photograph by the author).

MEADE & SON

In 1870, Michael Meade's son Joseph married the daughter of William Carvill, a timber merchant from Co. Down. The two families had much in common: Carvill was also part of a rising Catholic merchant class and had developed housing on his estate in Rathgar. Each family brought property to the marriage: the Meades entrusted two of their Ailesbury Road buildings and the Carvills conveyed a pair of houses in Rathgar. The following year, Joseph became partner in the building firm and the company was renamed 'Meade & Son'.[25] Working from the saw mills in Great Brunswick Street, Joseph began to acquire property in the city. In 1872, the Pembroke Estate wrote to him for the third time about rent due on a holding in Denzille Street, and the following year he was party to a mortgage on a number of properties in Dublin and Wexford: two plots on the Portobello Estate, nos 10 and 12 Crosthwaite Park and thirty-five acres of ground in Kellystown.[26] The 1870s was certainly Meade & Son's busiest period in terms of building activity, beginning with the laying of the foundation stone for the new Gaiety Theatre in South King Street.[27] The inspiration for the project came from the Gunn brothers, who had run

25 Irish Architectural Archive, *Dictionary of Irish architects, 1720–1940,* Joseph Michael Meade (http://www.dia.ie/), accessed 31 May 2012. **26** Registry of Deeds, 1873, vol. 13, memorandum 259. **27** *Irish Builder,* 1 July 1871.

a music business nearby on Grafton Street. They appointed C.J. Phipps, the eminent theatre architect, who designed a two-thousand-seater auditorium on the site. The building was completed in a record five months, with 'workmen labouring through the nights by torchlight'.[28] The *Irish Builder* considered the design too utilitarian, but expressed confidence in the calibre of the builders:'the contractors are Messrs Meade and Son, of Great Brunswick-street', it announced; 'there is little doubt but the builder will carry out his contract according to design and specification'.[29]

The Catholic Church continued to be a lucrative source of work for Meade & Son, and by 1870 the firm had completed five ecclesiastical projects for Pugin & Ashlin.[30] Collaboration continued throughout the 1870s, as they worked together on at least three new church projects. Meade also began to break ground for some new buildings in the growing suburb of Kingstown (now Dun Laoghaire), including the new town hall and St Michael's Hospital. As townships all over the United Kingdom expanded to fulfil the desires of a rising middle class, civic building had emerged as a symbol of urban pride and identity. In Kingstown, the chairman of the township put up £20 in prize money for the best design in campaigning for a new town hall.[31] The competition was won by the Dublin architect John Loftus Robinson, who had recently set up practice in Great Brunswick Street. Built in the style of a Venetian Gothic palace, the building is a reflection of the wealth and confidence of the township. Meade and Robinson worked together next on St Michael's Hospital, but the project was more functional in design, built to 'meet the wants of the poor in Kingstown'. The Sisters of Mercy, who commissioned the project, engaged Meade a number of years later to build the new Jervis Street Hospital in Dublin. Towards the end of the decade, Meade and Robinson worked together on two more schemes: a new wing to the male orphanage in Glasnevin and a new laundry and Magdalen asylum at Glasthule.

Although Meade was busy with civic projects in Kingstown, he continued to be involved in domestic building construction. The Dublin Artisans' Dwellings Company was established in 1876 by members of the Dublin Sanitary Association. The company was made up mainly of the city's unionist business elite and became the 'only sizeable semi-philanthropic housing body in Ireland' which aimed to build housing for the working classes.[32] Meade was the first contractor to get involved, and constructed a housing project in Buckingham Street, designed by the Belfast-born architect Sir Thomas Drew as a 'model tenement block'.[33] Meanwhile, on a personal note, tragedy struck for Joseph's growing family, as he and his wife Catherine lost three of their five children between 1876 and 1879. The first was Elizabeth, a 'dearly beloved daughter', who died of bronchitis at fourteen months, followed by two boys:

28 Douglas Bennett, *The encyclopaedia of Dublin* (Dublin, 2005), p. 82. **29** *Irish Builder*, 1 Nov. 1871. **30** Irish Architectural Archive, *Dictionary of Irish architects 1720–1940*, George Coppinger Ashlin (http://www.dia.ie/), accessed 31 May 2012. **31** Peter Pearson, *Kingstown* (Dublin, 1981), p. 107. **32** M. Fraser, *John Bull's other homes, state housing and British policy in Ireland, 1883–1922* (Liverpool, 1996), p. 71. **33** M. Daly, M. Hearn & P. Pearson, *Dublin's Victorian houses* (Dublin, 1998), p. 45.

2.6 Nos 46–52 Northumberland Road, Dublin (photograph by the author).

Michael (infant) and Joseph (aged three and a half). Two of Joseph's brothers and two of Catherine's siblings also died during these years. Premature deaths such as these were not unusual during the period; Sir Charles Cameron, Dublin's chief health and medical officer, lost five of his eight children early in life.[34] Frequent outbreaks of disease transcended class divides and were often related to inadequate sanitary provisions.

By 1880, Michael Meade had laid out approximately £30,000 in building on the prestigious Pembroke Estate.[35] Soon his son began speculating there in a new street south-east of the city, acquiring a plot of ground on Northumberland Road.[36] This streetscape of red-brick houses had been one of the first to be opened up in the new suburbs and was largely complete by the time the builder entered the scene. Finished in 1885, his scheme is in the High Victorian Gothic style and displays a high degree of architectural sophistication (fig. 2.6).[37] The mark of the builder is proudly displayed in the signature Meade monogram, 'MM', which is cast in terracotta on the front gable (fig. 2.7). With this first set of houses, Joseph Meade was instrumental in creating the most successful architectural composition of the whole road. He also continued to acquire property in the growing suburbs: in 1882, he sold his interest in

34 Ibid., p. 10. **35** H.C. Parliamentary Papers, 1880, XXX.327 C.2725, 'Municipal Boundaries Commission (Ireland). Part I. Evidence, with appendices. Dublin, Rathmines, Pembroke, Kilmainham, Drumcondra, Clontarf and also Kingstown, Blackrock and Dalkey', p. 188, para. 5056. **36** Registry of Deeds, 1882, vol. 6, memorandum 76. **37** *Thom's Dublin street directory*, 1885, Northumberland Road.

2.7 Michael Meade monogram (photograph by the author).

a holding at Brennan's Terrace, Bray's earliest and most complete seafront terrace.[38] He was also resident at a property there named 'Bella Vista', which probably served as a seasonal home.

Building work at Meade & Son seemed to slow down during the 1880s but, for the first time, property deeds began to appear under the company name. A deed dated 1884 refers to a number of allotments in Donnybrook, consisting of over two acres with houses, mills and offices.[39] In addition, large parts of their saw mills were sold off to the adjoining railway company, possibly forming part of a compulsory purchase agreement.[40] Meade & Son were also involved in quite a few commercial building projects in and around the city centre. During the rebuilding of no. 110 Grafton Street for the house agent James H. North, the neighbouring property collapsed, resulting in a lawsuit against both Meade and North. The firm were also involved nearby at nos 96–100 Grafton Street (now Weirs) when they built a block of new shops for Dublin Corporation. Three years later, in April 1884, Joseph Meade's wife Catherine died, and this was followed five months later by the death of their two-and-a-half-year-old daughter. The causes of death are not known, but Joseph Meade was left with three children between seven and twelve years of age.

38 *National inventory of architectural heritage*, Bray. See Reg: 16301103 (www.building-sofireland.ie/), accessed 31 May 2012. **39** Registry of Deeds, 1884, vol. 50, memorandum 75 & 1885, vol. 47, memorandum 66. **40** Registry of Deeds, 1885, vol. 51, memorandum 277 & 278.

THE PASSING OF THE FOUNDING FATHER

Two years later, in May 1886, Joseph's father, Michael Meade, died at his mansion in Ailesbury Road after a long illness. The *Irish Times* paid tribute to the 'eminent builder and contractor', who had been engaged in business in Dublin for more than thirty years:

> during that time, he erected many of the churches and other public buildings which ornament the city ... He was highly esteemed and respected, not only for his business qualities, which were eminent to a degree, but also for the way in which he always exerted himself to forward every object of a charitable and deserving nature. His straightforwardness, coupled with his charity, made for him a very wide circle of friends, by whom his death will be deeply regretted.[41]

Michael Meade died with assets worth over £32,442, a considerable fortune for the time (equivalent to 477 times the yearly salary of a building labourer), and quite an achievement considering Meade's humble beginnings as a carpenter. His son, Joseph, inherited the building firm aged 47 and his business and political career continued to soar, as that year he was elected to Dublin Corporation as alderman for the Trinity ward. Building was in a depressed state during this time, and the firm completed few projects, though the saw mills in Great Brunswick Street continued to operate. Joseph continued to speculate in the Pembroke Estate and in 1887 he acquired a second plot on Northumberland Road beside the red-brick terrace he had completed two years previously. He also got married for the second time, to Ada, daughter of the late Thomas Willis of Ormond Quay. Willis had been a well-known apothecary, a purveyor of medicines and a campaigner for better social and sanitary conditions for the working classes.[42] His daughter was 18 years of age when she married Meade, who was thirty years her senior. The second plot at Northumberland Road formed part of the marriage settlement, where the builder was about to complete three dwelling houses.[43]

After his father's death, Joseph and his family moved to the family home, St Michael's in Ailesbury Road. By this stage, he was becoming an important business and political figure in the city and in 1887 he was elected to the board of the Hibernian Bank.[44] Two years later, as high sheriff for Dublin city, he could be found selling a large site on Grand Canal Quay for a considerable £14,000.[45] The position of high sheriff was one favoured by high-ranking nationalists and Meade's election marked his rise through the hierarchy of local government. In January 1889, some

41 *Irish Times*, 26 May 1886.   **42** *The hidden Dublin: facts connected with the social and sanitary condition of the working classes in the city of Dublin*, ed. D. Dickson and members of the Trinity History Workshop (repr. Dublin, 2002).   **43** Registry of Deeds, 1887, vol. 7, memorandum 199.   **44** *Freeman's Journal*, 15 Feb. 1887.   **45** Registry of Deeds, 1889, vol. 50, memorandum 6.

members of the Pembroke Town Commissioners proposed him to the board and, although the motion was not passed, the chairman was anxious to elect the builder, since he had 'such a large stake in the township'.[46]

In the summer of 1890, Dublin Corporation proposed Alderman Joseph Meade to the office of lord mayor. Meade was praised by the chairman for his 'great intelligence and industry' in a report carried by the *Freeman's Journal*:

> Alderman Meade and his family had been connected with the city for a number of years. He was a large employer, a merchant prince, respected by the citizens of all classes, and in his opinion the council could make no better selection for the office of lord mayor.[47]

Joseph Meade appears to have been a successful and popular mayor. During his first year in office, he presided over many important developments in the city, such as the introduction of electric lighting, improvements in drainage and plans for a new fish and vegetable market. The following year, the corporation praised him for his skills as a public speaker and this, combined with his 'sound practical judgment', rendered him most deserving of a second term of office. In January 1892, the Right Honourable Meade began the second year of the mayoralty, 'with the entire approval and good wishes of every section of his fellow-citizens'.[48] Soon afterwards, he was awarded with an honorary degree of Doctor of Laws at Trinity College Dublin. When the university celebrated its tercentenary later that year, Meade commemorated the occasion by holding a grand reception and ball in the Mansion House.[49] The year 1892 must have been a busy one for the mayor, as he went on to contest Stephen's Green in the Parnellite interest, but was narrowly defeated by Mr William Kenny, a Catholic unionist lawyer who went on to serve as solicitor-general for Ireland a few years later.[50]

In 1893, Meade stepped down from the mayoralty and resumed his role as alderman for the Trinity ward. That year, he was honoured with the ultimate distinction when he was appointed to her majesty's most honourable privy council in Ireland.[51] His work as lord mayor was also recognized, when the city's aldermen and councillors gathered at his mansion in Ailesbury Road later that year. The officials made reference to Meade's 'dignity and strict impartiality' in addition to his 'practical knowledge and business capabilities'. Sir Charles Cameron presented Mrs Meade with a tiara of diamonds and a marble bust of her husband.

46 *Freeman's Journal*, 22 Jan. 1889.   **47** Ibid., 8 July 1890.   **48** *Irish Times*, 2 Jan. 1892.
49 Ibid., 6 July 1892.   **50** *Freeman's Journal*, 6 July 1892.

THE DEMISE OF A GEORGIAN STREETSCAPE

In 1894, Joseph Meade invested in the city's most important Georgian streetscape by purchasing eight properties on Henrietta Street (fig. 2.8).[52] Built for the elite in the early eighteenth century, the mansions are of an overwhelming scale and some are double the width of a standard Georgian terraced house. Numbers 3, 4 and 5 are palatial in size and were originally occupied by the earls of Kingston and Thomond and the Rt Hon. John Ponsonby.[53] Meade's purchases equated to the whole of the north side of the street and he proceeded to strip out many of the original features such as grand staircases and valuable chimneypieces, turning the buildings to tenements. In doing so, the builder transformed himself into 'one of the most notorious slum landlords of the late nineteenth century'.[54]

While converting Georgian mansions for the poor, Meade was also busy building villas for the rich. By the close of 1894, Charles Ashworth had completed drawings for him on Shrewsbury Road, just north of his villa in the southern suburbs. Ashworth had been appointed architect to the Dublin Artisans' Dwelling Company in 1890 and although there is no record of previous collaborations, he and Meade were certainly acquainted.[55] By 1900, Shrewsbury House was complete, a fine detached six-bedroom residence on the junction with the Merrion Road (fig. 2.9). This was followed by four semi-detached houses adjacent, also designed by Ashworth (fig. 2.10). It seems that the builder was slow in developing these sites as John Vernon, agent to the Pembroke Estate, wrote to him frequently about lack of progress during this time. Although he was in contravention of his lease, Vernon was willing to turn a blind eye, due to Meade's expenditure of 'large sums in building on his lordship's estate'.[56]

Meanwhile, debate continued to rage in the council chambers on the state of the poor in Dublin city, who inhabited insanitary and overcrowded houses such as those in Henrietta Street. The debate reached the House of Commons, where it was pointed out that Meade 'was the owner of a considerable number of the tenement houses complained of, and which the corporation were desirous of sweeping away'.[57] As Mark Crinson has shown, several leading Dublin councillors were known to be slum landlords, and it appears that the former lord mayor was one of them.[58] By the turn of the century, the eight mansions that he presided over in Henrietta Street produced a substantial annual rent of £1,500. Yet Meade was known for his philanthropy, and was a founder of the association for the housing of the very poor.[59]

---

51 Ibid., 28 Jan. 1893. **52** Registry of Deeds, 1894, vol. 36, memorandum 89. **53** Maurice Craig, *Dublin, 1660–1860* (London, 1992), p. 103. **54** Peter Pearson, *The heart of Dublin* (Dublin, 2000), p. 361. **55** NLI, Visitors' book of Alderman Joseph Meade, lord mayor of Dublin, 27 Jan. 1891–2 Aug. 1892. MS 19,707, acc. 3383. Charles A. Ashworth of 2 Ballsbridge & 42 Dame Street made three visits to Lord Mayor Meade at the Mansion House in 1891. **56** NAI, PEP, Letter books, vol. 24, Vernon to the Rt Hon. J.M. Meade, 7 Mar. 1899, p. 492 (acc. 97/46/3/21). **57** *Irish Times*, 26 June 1900. **58** Mark Crinson, 'Georgianism and the tenements', *Art History*, 29:4 (Sept. 2006), 644. **59** Daly, *Dublin, the*

2.8 Nos 3–10 Henrietta Street, Dublin (photograph by the author).

2.9 Shrewsbury House, Dublin (photograph by the author).

2.10 A Shrewsbury Road house, Dublin (photograph by the author).

How do we equate the philanthropic endeavours of Joseph Meade with his notoriety as a slum landlord? The answer to this apparent hypocrisy perhaps lies in a cynical cartoon appearing some years after Meade's death. During a visit to a Dublin slum, a public inspector queried the identity of the landlord:

> and being told he is the eminent philanthropist who represents the Kill-em-all Ward, he wearily remarks that his eyesight is growing worse each year, then retires to make room for the doctor, coroner and undertaker. And public health goes to sleep again, and the slum-owner takes the chair at a large and influential meeting for 'the better housing of the poor', and makes his audience weep with his heart-rending description of life in the tenements.[60]

CONCLUSION

By the time of Joseph Meade's death in 1900, his building empire employed some nine-hundred men.[61] It is not surprising, therefore, that the winding up of the firm led to a dramatic increase in unemployment among building workers in the city.[62] Success and wealth came to the Meades – not from inheritance of title, but from a strong work ethic and an entrepreneurial spirit. Emerging in the post-Famine period, Michael Meade began in the carpentry trade, placing himself at the centre of opportunity in a rapidly advancing city. His son Joseph built on his father's success and continued to expand the building business, while forging a formidable political career of his own. However, as a builder to the rich and slum landlord to the poor, Joseph Meade was also an opportunistic capitalist who benefitted from both sides of the economic divide. He died as a new century dawned, leaving behind an estate worth over £89,000, including fifty-three properties in the city and surrounding county. The power, wealth and influence amassed by the Meades are manifested in the architecture of Victorian Dublin.

61 *Irish Times*, 16 July 1900.   **62** Daly, *Dublin, the deposed capital*, p. 63.

Elites, ritual and the legitimation of power on an Irish landed estate, 1855–90

KEVIN Mc KENNA

One of the most prominent, and well-studied, relationships in nineteenth-century Ireland is that of landlord and tenant, and for most of the century it was the traditional authority of the rural landed elite that dominated positions of power at local and national level. This essay, drawing on theory from the social sciences, will examine the role of ritual in legitimizing the elite position of the landed class at local level in the 1850s and how, through the forces of historical change, its efficacy became greatly diminished as the century drew to a close. Howard Newby's aim in his 1975 paper 'The deferential dialectic' was to explain 'the relational and normative means by which [rurally based] elites maintain their traditional authority [and] the strategies they employ that attempt to ensure the stability of their power'.[1] Deference, he argues, is neither 'a type of behaviour' nor 'a set of attitudes', but rather a combination of both as 'a form of social interaction which occurs in situations involving the exercise of traditional authority'.[2] He uses the dialectic to explain the interaction between the superordinate and subordinate partners in a paternalistic relationship and argues that this dialectic requires attentive management, on the part of the superordinate partner, in order that the relationship's destabilizing 'tensions' can be addressed. The root of these tensions, he explains, is the inegalitarian nature of paternalistic social relations and that the successful management of these tensions necessitates the superordinate group entering into an inherently contradictory relationship with the subordinate one in order to strike a balance between the conflicting elements of *differentiation* and *identification* that constitute deferential interaction.[3] Because of the hierarchical nature of the relationship, *differentiation* from subordinates is a prerequisite in order to effectively wield power over them, but so too is it necessary to cultivate a level of *identification* to promote the relationship as mutually cooperative so that the subjection of the subordinate partner is less obvious.[4]

Newby's concept of the deferential dialectic was formulated following sociological research among agricultural workers during the twentieth century, but his thinking was informed by the historical development of traditional relationships such as those of landlord and tenant in the nineteenth century. While his research was focused on rural England, his model of the deferential dialectic is applicable to aspects

1 Howard Newby, 'The deferential dialectic', *Comparative Studies in Society and History*, 17 (1975), 139–64 at 149, 161–2. 2 Newby, 'The deferential dialectic', 142. 3 The terms *differentiation* and *identification* and will appear in italics to indicate a specific reference to Newby's concept of the 'deferential dialectic'. 4 Newby, 'The deferential dialectic', 161–2.

of the landlord–tenant relationship in Ireland during the nineteenth century. This essay, using the Clonbrock estate in east Galway as a case study, will examine the coming-of-age of Irish landed heirs in the second half of the nineteenth century as rituals of power in which the conflicting elements of *differentiation* and *identification* were finely balanced. Using the 'thick description' as an analytical tool, it aims to provide a deeper understanding of rural class relations by focusing on the symbolic significance of these elite events and the strategies employed by the tenantry to challenge them.[5] It will argue that, in the mid-Victorian period, the rituals facilitated the maintenance of an ideological hegemony that defined the rate of exchange between landlord and tenant as free and fair, and explore how the expansion of the public sphere and the land acts undermined this hegemony and the effectiveness of a coming-of-age as a legitimizing force.

W.E. Vaughan has argued that in mid-Victorian Ireland various events associated with landed families provided occasions for spectacle.[6] The birth of an heir was often marked with bonfires on estates, his coming-of-age with extensive celebrations, his marriage with the presentation of addresses and gifts, and finally the funeral of the landlord was often marked with an exhibition of deference such as the drawing of the hearse and remains by the tenantry. These life-cycle rituals, or what Larry Geary has described as 'significant family occasions',[7] were a prominent feature of estate life at Clonbrock in the second half of the nineteenth century. Mark Girouard has argued that 'in most [English] country houses of the time, the high point of entertaining was the coming-of-age' celebrating the twenty-first birthday of heirs.[8] This also holds true for the Irish country house, but they had significance beyond mere entertainment as rituals that legitimized the power of the landed elite. Their importance was closely associated with the practice of primogeniture that celebrated the forging of another link in the chain of male descent and increased the likelihood that a family's title and estates would persist in the future. Furthermore, there were implications associated with the complex legal intricacies of 'strict settlement' that made these the seminal events of a landed estate.

5 The technique of 'thick description' was advocated by the anthropologist Clifford Geertz in *The interpretation of cultures* (New York, 1973). Geertz, following Max Weber, argued that human beings were suspended in webs of significance that they have spun. These webs, he continued, were cultural and, rather than attempt to ascribe laws to them, he advocated a search for meaning within the signs and symbols of a given culture at particular moments in time. Through close examination of the signs and symbols he argued that it was possible to uncover the layers of significance that would provide a 'thick description'. See Clifford Geertz, *The interpretation of cultures* (New York, 2000 ed.), pp 3–30. See also Aletta Biersack, 'Local knowledge, local history: Geertz and beyond' in Aletta Biersack and Lynn Hunt, *The new cultural history* (Berkeley and Los Angeles, CA, 1989), pp 72–96.   **6** W.E. Vaughan, *Landlords and tenants in mid-Victorian Ireland* (New York, 1994), p. 4.   **7** Laurence M. Geary, 'Anticipating memory: landlordism, agrarianism and deference in late nineteenth-century Ireland' in Tom Dunne and Laurence M. Geary (eds), *History and the public sphere: essays in honour of John A. Murphy* (Cork, 2005), pp 127–34 at p. 131.   **8** Mark Girouard, *Life in the English country house* (New Haven, CT, 1978), p. 290.

From the 1650s, strict settlement became the preferred legal mechanism for transmitting estates from one generation to the next. It used the earlier medieval device of 'entail' to restrict the inheritance to specific named persons to try and ensure that the estates were inherited through the line of direct patrilineal descent, which favoured contingent male heirs over heiresses. Before the 1650s, entail named specific persons, usually eldest sons, as heirs, but the entails of strict settlement named sons and sometimes grandsons that may not have been born when the settlement was drawn up. The effect was that the sitting landowner became a mere 'life tenant' rather than the outright owner and this restricted his capacity to dispose of land and other fixed assets. 'His interests were subordinate to those of the family, and the family was of more importance than he was. He was the king in check, his freedom of manoeuvre limited' in order to protect the estates for future generations.[9] When an heir came of age, he became the 'tenant in tail' and, in many cases, if he and the 'life tenant' – usually his father – came to an agreement, a new settlement could be drawn up to reflect the financial needs of the estate and the family. Therefore, when an heir came of age he was vested with certain powers to change the settlement and this added to the importance of event because from this point forward he was recognized as a significant actor in the affairs of the estate and its future.[10] This system permitted the landed class to maintain a stranglehold on land for centuries as the entails within the settlements could not be broken except by an act of parliament. Even if an estate was bankrupt, it was protected from sale by the entails and this was the case with numerous estates in the aftermath of the Great Famine, so parliament passed the Encumbered Estates Act in order to free them from these constraints and permit sale. This underscores the inflexibility of the system, which, on well managed estates, facilitated a smooth transfer from one generation to the next, but in cases where a profligate or misfortunate generation borrowed heavily then the future heirs, with limited access to capital, often faced an insurmountable task in returning estates to financial stability.[11]

When Luke Gerald Dillon, the heir of the third Baron Clonbrock,[12] came of age in March 1855, bonfires were observed 'blazing in all directions' to mark the occasion, and a few months after, once he had completed his studies at Oxford, a coming-of-age was staged at Clonbrock in June.[13] Representatives of the *Galway*

9 Laurence Stone and Jeanne C. Fawtier Stone, *An open elite: England, 1540–1880* (Oxford, 1995), p. 48.   10 Barbra English and John Saville, *Strict settlement: a guide for historians* (Hull, 1983), pp 20–2.   11 Among the critics of primogeniture and entail was Adam Smith, who, in *The wealth of nations*, 1 (Hartford, CT, 1811 ed.), argued that they were factors that contributed to the underutilization of land and retarded economic progress, p. 274.   12 Robert Dillon (1807–93), third Baron Clonbrock, inherited the Clonbrock estates as a minor in 1826. With *c.*26,000 acres in east Galway, he was one of the largest landowners in the county, enlarging his estates to 28,246 acres by 1876. He played an active role at local and national level, acting as a Poor Law guardian as well as lord lieutenant and representative peer for Co. Galway. These positions were also held by his son, Luke Gerald (1834–1917), fourth Baron Clonbrock.   13 *Galway Mercury*, 17 Mar. 1855.

Mercury, the *Western Star* and the *Tuam Herald* were present as invited guests and their reports of the celebrations were extensive. The main events of the day were the presentation of an address to Luke Gerald by representatives of the tenantry, a 'sports', a tenants' dinner and an exhibition of fireworks. By midday, when proceedings had been scheduled to commence, several thousand people, including tenants' families and others from outside the estate, had assembled near the Big House. At 1pm, they greeted Luke Gerald with repeated rounds of applause when he appeared at the front of the house and then dancing commenced on the lawn 'to the music of a number of fiddles and other familiar instruments'.[14] At about half past three, a deputation of tenants, comprising those with the most extensive holdings, approached the house with an address to Luke Gerald and they were 'received in the grand hall by Lord and Lady Clonbrock'.[15]

The content of the address was a mix of hyperbole, which eulogized the Dillon family, and what might be described as a paternalistic social contract, which reminded Luke Gerald that, while he had privileges, there were also duties to be fulfilled. It described the attainment of his majority 'as a matter of deep concern' not only to the tenantry but to his country, and expressed expectations that he would become involved in promoting the interests of Ireland as well as those of the tenantry. They (the tenantry) expressed confidence that when he came to manage the estates he would

> follow in the footsteps of his noble father, who has at all times with much zeal and justice, discharged his duties as a landlord, and who, intimately acquainted with the requirements of the tenant farmer, has ever been ready with his purse and advice to advance the true interests of those who are placed under him.

That the ritual promoted the landlord–tenant relationship as contractual is further evidenced by the tenants' assertion that, although Luke Gerald's position in life conferred certain privileges, he would 'never overlook its duties'.[16] It reminded him that he had obligations and allowed the representatives of the tenantry to express a degree, albeit limited, of agency.

From the centre of the hall, Luke Gerald replied to the tenants, thanking them for the kind words expressed in the address. He referred to how he was 'most closely connected' with them and that their 'happiness and welfare … must ever be the object of [his] life to promote'. Acknowledging that they were in a contractual relationship, he expressed hopes that throughout his life his 'conduct [would] meet with [their] approval' and if he ever strayed then he would follow the shining example that had been set by his father.[17] With the conclusion of the address and reply, Lord Clonbrock then introduced Luke Gerald to the deputation, who 'expressed their

sincere and hearty congratulations'.[18] Lord Clonbrock introduced his son to them as
his heir, a man in full enjoyment of his rights, prepared and entitled to take control
of the running of the estates when the time came, and the members of the deputation were recognizing him as such. Clonbrock was paving the path of succession for
his son by introducing him to representatives of the tenantry; in effect, he was stating
'here is my son, someday he will inherit these estates and he will replace me as your
lord'.

After the formalities of the address and reply were dispensed with, a celebratory
tenants' dinner was given in a large pavilion erected in the demesne. It was bedecked
with flags, some of which were inscribed with 'Irish harps', while others were embla-
zoned with slogans such as 'Welcome' and 'Erin go bragh'. The newspapers listed the
invited guests of Clonbrock beginning with the aristocracy then moving on to the
gentry, clergy and others among whom the principal tenants, Michael and John Carr,
were mentioned, indicating that they were the elite of the tenantry. The rest of the
'general company, which numbered upwards of 600' tenants from all sections of the
estates dined on 'everything substantial and delicate with wines of the purest vintage'.
At the after dinner speeches, Clonbrock proposed a toast to his son and pointed out
the many qualities he possessed, he expressed hope for the transmission of the family
name and title to Luke Gerald, who, he expected would 'perform the duties of the
station in which God has placed him'.[19] The various speeches that ensued were of a
similar nature, referring to the benevolence of Clonbrock and the hopes that Luke
Gerald would follow in his footsteps. Charles Filgate, the land agent, spoke of how it
had been his pleasure to have served Clonbrock for thirteen years, as he had been
permitted to 'distribute the favours at all times so liberally bestowed by their noble
landlord'. He referred to the reductions of rent that had been made during the
Famine, but that the calamity had now passed and he expected the rents to be paid
in full. He pointed out the difference between the 'improving and the slothful tenant'
and that a landlord was as entitled to his rent as a merchant was entitled to payment
for goods.[20]

Concluding the speeches, Clonbrock proposed a toast to the press and remarked
that the celebrations at Clonbrock that day were a private affair that was hardly worth
reporting, but there were 'many absent friends that would like to know their doings
on the occasion' and he hoped the press would oblige them. Jasper Kelly, of the *Tuam
Herald*, spoke of Lord Clonbrock's reputation as a benevolent landlord and expressed
hopes that his son would 'sustain his ancestral name as nobly and as well as his
respected and honoured father had done before him'. The banquet was then brought
to a close and dancing resumed on the lawn and later that evening a fireworks display,
the event's grand finale, took place in the village of Ahascragh.[21] It was reported that

> a large number of the respectable inhabitants of Ballinasloe had arrived to
> witness the fireworks … In that part of the country the scene was a novel

18 *Tuam Herald*, 16 June 1855.   **19** Ibid.   **20** Ibid.   **21** Ibid.

one, and excited some deep interest in some thousands who had never before witnessed such a display.[22]

Such was the extent of the pyrotechnic illuminations that 'in Ballinasloe [eight miles away] they were quite observable'. The celebrations continued until 1am and the press was of the opinion that the event was enjoyed so much that it would 'long be remembered by all who were present on the occasion'.[23] That the illuminations and fireworks would 'long be remembered' was, of course, the reason for such a display, and the impact of the spectacle on a nineteenth-century Irish smallholder must have been great. Stories of the display could then be told to children years after the event had taken place and the next coming-of-age would have been looked forward to in expectation of such spectacle.

The coming-of-age of an heir was the central ritual of the landed class that celebrated the forging of another link in the chain of descent and, while the main focus of the celebrations was on the heir, there was also a symbolic celebration of the virility of the landlord who had produced an heir and reared him to maturity. Lord Clonbrock mentioned that the celebration of his son's majority was a private affair, but, with several thousand people crowded into the demesne and reporters from three newspapers present, nothing could be further from the truth. It was a statement of power to tenants that were present but also to the public at large, as the event was extensively reported in the newspapers. Throughout the speeches, the paternalistic message of hierarchy was conveyed, outlining the duties and responsibilities that each class had to each other. It was acknowledged by all that Lord Clonbrock was as good a landlord as any tenant could hope to have and the continuity of the family was repeatedly asserted through the hope that Luke Gerald would follow in his father's footsteps.

Examining the coming-of-age festivities of landed heirs in the nineteenth century provides an opportunity to feel the pulse of landlord–tenant relations at those particular moments. On the surface, these rituals seem somewhat generic as there appears to be little difference between one and the next. If carefully examined, however, they reveal much about the landed family and the tensions that may or may not have existed between them and their tenants. The coming-of-age celebrations at Clonbrock were very much a success, but the same cannot be said for the festivities to celebrate the majority of Lord Dunlo, the earl of Clancarty's son, two months earlier. Resentment against Lord Clancarty existed because of his proselytizing efforts among his tenantry as well as his refusal to allow the Sisters of Mercy to administer to the poor of the Ballinasloe Workhouse in the 1850s. As part of the festivities to celebrate the majority of Lord Dunlo, his heir, it was planned that the householders of the town would place lighted candles in their windows at darkness to honour his majority. One section of the town did not 'illuminate', however, and although Lord Clancarty stated that he respected their wishes to refuse and would not deny them access to his park, it must have rankled with him.[24]

22 *Western Star*, 16 June 1855.   **23** Ibid.   **24** *Tuam Herald*, 14 Apr. 1855.

At the Clonbrock festivities, the music and iconography had a mix of Gaelic and imperial flavours, suggesting that the two traditions could co-exist. 'Rule Britannia' was played alongside 'Rory O'Moore' and banners displaying 'God save the queen' were draped alongside others displaying Irish motifs like 'Erin go bragh'. This, however, was not the case at the festivities to celebrate the majority of Lord Bernard, the earl of Bandon's heir, in 1871. The festivities at Bandon, 'that most Protestant town',[25] featured marches of freemasons and Orangemen and there was no mention of the playing of Irish airs, but 'the strains of martial music (were not) wanting, for two bands were in attendance, the fine band of the 14th Hussars ... and that of the South Cork Light Infantry [also known as the Bandon Militia]'.[26] At Clonbrock, a festive atmosphere prevailed and, along with dancing and leaping, the choicest wines were supplied for the dinner. At Bandon, there was no mention of any dancing or the provision of alcohol at the tenants' dinner. During the after-dinner speeches, a clergyman referred to the 'sober men, like those he saw before him, met together in cordial friendship to pay compliment to their future landlord'.[27] Altogether, there was an austere and militaristic tone to the celebrations at Bandon, which reflects the siege mentality that pervaded in the town, not least with its principal resident, the earl of Bandon, who had held office in the Orange order.[28] Some weeks later, there was a further exhibition of this militarism when a banquet was given to the tenants on one of Lord Bandon's outlying estates at Durras Court. The day concluded with a display of fireworks 'accompanied by salvoes of artillery, which provoked many an echo in the surrounding mountains on the top of which bonfires were lit'.[29]

Coming-of-age rituals were celebrated in different ways by different families and provide insights into how landed families communicated with their tenantry. The success of the celebrations at Clonbrock indicates that the event was a well-managed affair that could permit a degree of high spirits while maintaining control. The *Galway Vindicator* reported that

> hilarity, order and regularity everywhere prevailed ... attended by nearly 3,000 spectators of all ranks and ages, no accident occurred. After a minute and painstaking inquiry, the only casualties we can record are the breaking of a couple of wine glasses, and the partial conflagration of a lady's dress.[30]

The *Irish Times*, a publication generally favourable to the landed class, reported such events regularly from 1859, communicating a message that property, hierarchy and tradition brought order. In Britain, as the new industrial and merchant class became wealthier and increasingly influential, they held similar celebrations when their eldest sons came of age, but these were seldom reported by the *Irish Times*. One exception

25 Ian d'Alton, *Protestant society and politics in Cork, 1812–1844* (Cork, 1980), p. 29. **26** *Cork Constitution*, 13 Sept. 1871. **27** *West Cork Eagle*, 16 Sept. 1871. **28** For a contemporary profile and history of the town, see George Bennett, *A history of Bandon and the principal towns in the west riding of County Cork* (Cork, 1869). **29** Ibid., 30 Sept. 1871. **30** *Galway Vindicator*, 16 June 1855.

in 1868 was the majority of the heir of a Staffordshire coal and iron magnate. This event surpassed any Irish coming-of-age in terms of magnitude. Entertainment was extended to between 4,000 and 5,000 people:

> 900 bottles of wine and 2,340 gallons of ale were consumed. The drunken orgies which marked the affair were most disgraceful. One reverend gentleman ... wandering he knew not whither, hatless and fighting with his friend and neighbour, was tumbled out of the pavilion. A gentleman of the press was discovered among the helpless at five in the morning in a field. Fights took place without number, and many, men, women, boys and girls were helpless through drink; others reeling home, and numbers lying in the fields and lanes, dead drunk. Sixteen men, felled by drink, helpless and prostrate, were counted within a radius of twenty yards, and scores scattered about, many bleeding, hatless, shoeless and coatless, incapable of movement or speech.[31]

The message here is clear, a man may accumulate wealth but that does not necessarily convey upon him the qualities of a ruler or one who could command order. The landed class considered this their birthright through generations of good breeding and superior education. Furthermore, this is given as an example of how society would disintegrate if the merchant and industry types ever replaced the landed class as the 'natural' rulers. The extent of the effervescence at coming-of-age festivities depended very much on the landed family hosting them and how comfortable they were with their tenants. As we have seen, there was a militaristic and austere atmosphere at Castle Bernard and the celebrations concluded there after a reception at 10pm. At Clonbrock, they continued until 1am, while at the coming-of-age of Lord Dunraven's heir at Adare in 1862, 'copious supplies of hot punch' were served at a supper to over one thousand people and dancing resumed afterward. 'At half past five o'clock [in the morning], his lordship was in the midst of his people throwing open his cellars to give his parting drink to his tenants and their families'.[32]

Newby argues that traditionally legitimized hierarchical organizations are capable of extreme stability because deference is granted to both the tradition itself and to the person holding the position of authority. Those deferring to the superordinate partner, however, cannot be taken for granted and to understand the social basis for deference it is necessary to understand the strategies by which rural elites legitimate their position. Deferential interaction consists of two opposing elements: *differentiation* and *identification*. It is by *differentiation* that the positions of domination and subordination are delineated, but acceptance of social hierarchies cannot be achieved unless the subordinate group identifies sufficiently with the superordinate partner in the relationship: 'It is the tension between these opposing elements of *differentiation* and *identification* from which contradictions arise that threaten the destruction of the

31 *Irish Times*, 21 Sept. 1868. **32** *Munster News*, 1 Feb. 1862.

relationship'. If the superordinate partner carries the process of *identification* with the subordinated group too far, then *differentiation* is not possible and 'deference to elite authority breaks down; thus, while elites attempt to retain the *identification* of those below them in the hierarchy, they must also operate certain mechanisms of social distancing which endorse their *differentiation*'.[33] At Clonbrock, the coming-of-age ritual provided an opportunity for this *identification* to be strengthened and if it is considered that the *Galway Mercury* reported that 'hilarity, order and regularity everywhere prevailed', then it appears that the balance between *differentiation* and *identification* had been struck perfectly, as the 'hilarity' of the occasion would have fostered *identification* while at the same time, unlike the debauchery witnessed in Staffordshire, there was sufficient *differentiation* to preserve 'order and regularity'.

While the opposing elements of *differentiation* and *identification* were well balanced at the Clonbrock coming-of-age, there was one narrative that challenged the legitimacy of Clonbrock's power. Popular tradition held that the Clonbrock estates were once owned by the O'Kelly clan and following their participation in a rebellion against the English crown they were confiscated and granted to an ancestor of Lord Clonbrock. The O'Kelly chieftain remained in the district, however, and paid clandestine visits to the site of his former power at Clonbrock, where a tannery had been established.

> On one of these occasions, having gone into the new tannery, he strongly excited the compassion of the workmen, who, through his rags, recognized their quondam chief, and one of them, perceiving the dilapidated condition of his shoes, gave him some of the leather to repair them. As he was going out with it, he chanced to encounter the new proprietor, who roughly handled him, overbearingly reproached him, and charged him with baseness and theft!!! At length, stung beyond endurance, the grey-haired chieftain knelt down and poured forth, in his native tongue, one of those aoirey maledictions [and] bound him under a spell that no father of his race should, for many generations, live to see his son come of age.[34]

In 1855, when Lord Clonbrock lived to see his heir come of age, the curse had, apparently, been broken, so reports like the one above appeared in numerous provincial publications. Similar reports, however, made it into the press many years before this. Daniel O'Connell made reference to the curse in 1843 and even those in far-flung Tasmania learned about it in 1851 through the *Hobart Town Courier*.[35] It is difficult to say, definitively, how long the curse or versions of it were in circulation, but if it is understood that the family's genealogy verifies that no father of the Dillon family had lived to witness a son's majority for over 150 years, then there was ample time and material for such narratives to develop.[36] What is important, however, is that the curse

---

33 Newby, 'The deferential dialectic', p. 152.   **34** *Galway Mercury*, 17 Mar. 1855.   **35** *Tuam Herald*, 15 Sept. 1843; *Hobart Town Courier*, 13 Aug. 1851.   **36** Lady Mahon, 'The Dillons of

can be viewed as a 'counter-public' at variance with the dominant paternalistic discourse expressed in the provincial press that, for the main part, constituted the ideological hegemony and legitimized the power of landlords such as Clonbrock.[37]

The foundation text for discussion of the public sphere is Jürgen Habermas' *Structural transformation of the public sphere*, which argued that, during the eighteenth century, the advent of salons in France and coffee shops in England, together with an increase in pamphlets and printed material, created a space that facilitated the reflexive circulation of discourse leading to the emergence of a bourgeois public sphere that challenged the power of church and state.[38] Habermas argued that this public sphere was open and inclusive, but Nancy Fraser, in her critique of his thesis, counter-argued that certain groups including women and the lower strata of society were excluded from this universal public sphere and formed their own 'subaltern counter-publics', which were 'parallel discursive arenas where members of subordinated social groups invent and circulate counter-discourses to formulate oppositional interpretations of their identities, interests and needs'.[39] The rhetoric that framed landlord–tenant discourse in the 1850s remained overwhelmingly paternalistic and even when landlords received criticism it was through this framework that they were accused of not fulfilling their duty. Therefore, the curse, with its narratives of dispossession and retribution, acted as a counter-discourse to the paternalistic *zeitgeist* that pervaded the provincial press through the 1850s.

The week of the coming-of-age was very significant in terms of the development of the public sphere in Britain and Ireland as Gladstone's bill to repeal the final stamp tax on newspapers was debated in parliament.[40] The conservative *Western Star* made its position clear on the issue and it provides insights into how small farmers were being excluded from the discourse of print culture. It argued that the bill 'would tend to produce a set of publications addressed only to the lower classes, and appealing in many cases to their worst passions and prejudices … the character of the newspaper press would be so lowered as essentially to bring it into collision with the public'.[41]

Clonbrock' (unpublished family memoir), genealogy and family tree appended to this volume; Bernard Burke, *A genealogical and heraldic dictionary of the peerage and baronetage of the British Empire*, 1 (London, 1853), pp 214–15; this volume provides dates of birth and death of the heads of the family from 1754, which confirm that neither the first or second barons had lived to witness the heir come of age.   **37** Curses by widows against landed families have been widely recorded in Irish folklore and many survive through oral tradition. Notable examples are those incurred by Lord Waterford and the Shirleys of Lough Fea in Co. Monaghan. For discussion of the curse in folkloric tradition, see Séamas MacPhilib, 'Legends of Irish landlords in their international context', *Béaloideas*, 62:3 (1994–5), 79–89; for gossip as a tool of resistance, see J.C. Scott, *Weapons of the weak* (New Haven, CT, 1985), p. 282. **38** Jürgen Habermas, Thomas Burger (trans.), *The structural transformation of the public sphere: an inquiry into the category of bourgeois society* (Cambridge, 1989). **39** Nancy Fraser, 'Rethinking the public sphere: a contribution to the critique of actually existing democracy', *Social Text*, 25 (1990), 56–80 at 67. **40** Marie-Louise Legg, *Newspapers and nationalism: the Irish provincial press, 1850–1892* (Dublin, 1999), p. 13. **41** *Western Star*, 24 Mar. 1855.

Lord Clonbrock did not vote on the issue in the House of Lords and does not appear to have been hostile to it as he toasted the press during the coming-of-age dinner. The press, he argued, 'exercised so potent an influence upon all communities. He believed it to be the one which, more than any other, guaranteed the freedom of a free people'.[42] The bill passed parliament that month and it is generally agreed that 'it was crucial for the growth of the newspaper industry on both sides of the Irish sea. But in Ireland the growth of a cheaper press coincided with the growth of nationalism'.[43] In the post-Famine period, increasing literacy and the growth of the provincial press facilitated the emergence of what might be called an 'agrarian public sphere' and the counter-public that articulated the narrative of dispossession and retribution embedded in the curse became part of this public which, by the time of the Land War, had no problems articulating those narratives. As Anne Kane has argued,

> the Land War provided the 'political field' on which a unified national iden-
> tity emerged from public discourse over landlordism and British domination,
> and collective action based on new symbolic understandings. At the core of
> both Land War ideology and the emergent national identity was a discourse
> of retribution, configured through the collective sharing of narratives,
> embodying central themes of the injustice of British and landlord domina-
> tion, and the rights of the Irish to the land and the country.[44]

When the next generation of the Dillon family came of age in 1890, the pater-nalistic rhetoric that, in the 1850s, had discussed the landlord–tenant relationship in terms of duties and responsibilities had become anachronistic. The rights of tenants had been enshrined in the land act of 1881 and it was the language of rights rather than the paternalist rhetoric of duty that had become the *lingua franca*. Furthermore, the settled land act of 1882 permitted the breaking of entailed estates, thus weakening the grip that the landed class had held on land for centuries. Entail had protected the interests of heirs and its abolition meant that it was less likely that the heir would inherit the estates. As such, the coming-of-age of an heir as a ritual of power had been divested of much of its significance. Despite this, in 1890, festivities to celebrate the coming-of-age of Robert Edward Dillon, the heir apparent, were staged in much the same fashion as they had been thirty-five years previously when Luke Gerald, his father, had come of age. A group of tenants formed a committee and commissioned an illuminated address and a portrait of Luke Gerald as gifts for Robert Edward. The content of this address differed in many ways from the one presented to Luke Gerald in 1855, however. It spoke of 'loyal hearts' but there was not a single mention of Robert Edward ever becoming their landlord or following in his father's or grand-

---

42 *Tuam Herald*, 16 June 1855.   **43** Legg, *Newspapers and nationalism*, p. 13.   **44** Anne Kane, 'Narratives of nationalism: constructing Irish national identity during the Land War, 1879–82', *National Identities*, 2 (2000), 245–64 at 245.

father's footsteps, as there had been in the 1855 address. A further difference between
the address of 1855 and that of 1890 was the absence in the latter of references to the
paternalist values of duties and responsibilities. There was little need for the tenants
to make reference to them, as Gladstone's land legislation had seen to it that landlords could not behave in an arbitrary fashion, as some had in former years, and
tenants had legal avenues by which they could assert their rights.

By now, the 83-year-old Lord Clonbrock, grandfather to Robert Edward, was
blind and confined to a wheelchair, yet he was still possessed of enough energy to
participate in the proceedings. He was brought out to the front steps of the house
and the *Western Star* reported that 'he literally electrified the whole audience and the
tenantry by delivering a speech which was throughout enthusiastically applauded'.
While the tenants' address neglected to mention the transmission of the estates from
one generation to the next, Lord Clonbrock did not; he spoke of how his place
would 'be filled by one far more capable of holding it than ever I have been myself'
and he urged the tenantry to 'stand to [his grandson], and when time and opportunity occur, my hand to you, he will stand to you'. Following tradition, a celebratory
dinner was held. One of those who eulogized Lord Clonbrock's treatment of the
tenantry during the Famine was Father Fahy, the local parish priest, who praised him
for giving up his hounds at this time. As in former years, the highlight of the event
was the fireworks display, after which a dance commenced in the servant's hall and
continued until the early hours of the following morning.[45]

The decline in importance of coming-of-age celebrations as rituals of power was
reflected in the relative disinterest that the provincial media displayed in reporting the
event. In 1855, Luke Gerald's attainment of majority was extensively covered by three
Galway newspapers as well as in minor reports in several others. In 1890, however,
the *Western Star* was the only Galway newspaper to devote any significant coverage
to his son's coming-of-age, and allocated only half a page, compared to almost a full
page when Luke Gerald had come of age in 1855. As a clear indication of its decline,
the address to and reply from Robert Edward were placed in the advertising sections
of both the *Western Star* and the *Athlone Times*, revealing that these once newsworthy
events now had to be paid for. A letter to Luke Gerald from a friend in the diplomatic service expressed the degree to which times had changed and lamented their
passing. This friend, on reading a newspaper account of the day's festivities, related
how he had felt both pleasure and pain:

> Pleasure ... at the grand sight suggested by the old man [Lord Clonbrock] on
> the steps of the house, speaking those beautiful simple words, transcendentally
> eloquent and thrilling one even at this distance ... The pain was the thought
> that this was an almost miraculous survival from a beautiful past never
> destined to return. Of a past that had not died a natural death but has been
> inhumanly murdered by the basest combinations of the very violent and

---

45 *Western Star*, 12 Sept. 1890.

vulgar political egotisms on both sides of the channel … Accursed army of murderers with the GOM [Gladstone] and Parnell at their head.[46]

In an increasingly democratic age, the rituals of paternalism and deference on the landed estate were losing their significance and Joseph Lee has argued that the Land League provided the stimulus 'to the struggle to emancipate tenants from the shackles of mental serfdom. It taught the tenants the simple but symbolic technique of not doffing their caps to landlords'.[47] Larry Geary has provided an example of this in action through a resolution passed by the Rossmore branch of the Land League, who did 'solemnly bind [themselves] not to take off [their] hats to any man in future except the priest'.[48] This illustrates that deference to landed authority was in decline and that, in certain cases, the power of the Catholic clergy at local level was in the ascendant. Although deference to the landed elite was on the wane, it had not yet disappeared as there was sufficient will to stage the coming-of-age at Clonbrock. The ritual did come under attack, however, and, had the author of letter quoted above been aware of how the event was criticized in the nationalist press or of a resolution passed by the local branch of the National League, his anguish, no doubt, would have been multiplied. Earlier, it has been explained how the folk-curse, with its narrative of dispossession and retribution, operated as a subaltern counter-discourse and an effective form of passive resistance to landed power. In 1890, however, and for many years beforehand, due to the growth of the nationalist press, these counter-discourses were being firmly expressed in print culture by those opposed to the landed interest. The *Tuam News* reported how the coming-of-age

> was taken as an occasion by some of the wealthiest of Clonbrock's tenants to show their flunkeyism. A committee was formed and a ticket sent to each of the tenants admitting one to lunch at Clonbrock, for which the modest sum of 3s. had to be paid. A couple of fat heifers and a fat sheep were killed for the feast, but the tenants paid smartly for it.[49]

A special meeting of the Ahascragh branch of the Irish National League was convened to discuss the event. The chairman, Andrew Manning, a poor law guardian for the Ballinasloe union, was a tenant on the neighbouring Mahon Estate and a veteran of the Land War. He had no objection to the celebrations at Clonbrock and stated that it was only natural that Robert Edward's parents 'should avail themselves of this opportunity to pay him this tribute of their affection'.[50] What he did find objectionable was that

46 Letter to L.G. Dillon, n.d. Clonbrock Papers, NLI MS 35,761/5. 47 Joseph Lee, *The modernisation of Irish society* (Dublin, 1973), p. 89. 48 Resolution passed by Rossmore branch of the Land League, in Laurence M. Geary, 'Anticipating memory', p. 127. 49 *Tuam News*, 12 Sept. 1890. 50 Ibid., 8 Oct. 1890.

> a Catholic priest should so far forget himself as to enter the camp of the polit-
> ical enemies of the people, and signalise his advent by an address that I feel
> bound to describe as nothing short of a tissue of the meanest and most
> crawling literary rubbish that ever came from the lips of the most servile
> hanger on or underscraper of an extensive landlord.

The branch unanimously adopted a resolution denouncing

> the language used by Father Fahy, of Fohenagh, at the Clonbrock festivities
> on the 9th inst., as being unworthy of an Irishman and a priest, and strongly
> calculated to resuscitate the dying institution of landlordism, and a most
> pernicious example to the members of his flock.[51]

While there may have been some transference of deference from the landed elite to
the Catholic clergy, it was very much dependent on the clergy behaving in an appropriate fashion, especially when the issues of landlordism and politics were a factor. As
J.H. Whyte has argued, 'it seems to be on the whole true that the Irish clergy could
lead their people only in the direction in which they wanted to go'.[52]

At some level, Manning and the other members of the National League understood the role of ritual in the legitimation of elite power and openly challenged it.
Newby identifies 'ideological hegemony' as one of the principle strategies by which
the landed elite maintained their positions of power, arguing that 'a crucial element
in the management of the tensions inherent in the deferential dialectic is the provision of a consistent and coherent set of ideas which interpret the power of the ruling
elite in a manner that reinforces their legitimacy'.[53] Until 1855, the landed elite's
influence over the press meant that paternalist rhetoric dominated the discourse of
landlord–tenant relations and ensured that the coming-of-age of heirs received sufficient coverage to buttress this ideological hegemony. The emergence and
development of the 'agrarian public sphere' from this point forward, however, undermined this hegemony and made the management of the deferential dialectic
increasingly difficult for landlords such as Clonbrock. With pressure from below,
these rituals became increasingly difficult to sustain in the face of popular opposition.
As the agrarian and mercantile classes began to establish their own hegemony, they
too began to assert themselves through different forms of ritual, from Land League
meetings to public statuary, as well as agrarian protests in the form of hunt sabotage
and 'cattle driving'.[54] With this increased pressure, coming-of-age rituals as expres-

---

51 Ibid.   **52** J.H. Whyte, 'The influence of the Catholic clergy on elections in the
nineteenth century', *English Historical Review*, 75 (1960), 239–59 at 248.   **53** Newby, 'The
deferential dialectic', 142.   **54** See Fergus Campbell, *Land and revolution: nationalist politics in
the west of Ireland, 1891–1921* (Oxford, 2005); Patrick J. Cosgrove, 'The Wyndham Land Act,
1903: the final solution to the Irish land question?' (PhD, NUIM, 2010); Anne Kane,
'Theorising meaning construction in social movements: symbolic structures and
interpretation during the Irish Land War, 1879–82', *Sociological Theory*, 15:3 (Nov. 1997), 249–

sions of power went into terminal decline and there were no further heirs to the Clonbrock title as Robert Edward Dillon, fifth Baron Clonbrock, died without issue in 1926. Denuded of much of their significance, reports of coming-of-age celebrations became less frequent and less spectacular. Some families continued to stage them, however, and they were reported by the *Irish Times* and the provincial press until at least the late 1930s. By this time, they were no longer used as opportunities to project power or affirm the position of the landed class at the apex of the social order. Their sole purpose was to try and maintain a bond of *identification* with their former tenants, as demesnes and their Big Houses increasingly became islands of isolation with the emergence of a new social and political order.

76; Heather Laird (ed.), *Subversive law in Ireland: from unwritten law to Dáil courts* (Dublin, 2005); Gary Owens, 'Nationalist monuments in Ireland, *c.*1870–1914: symbolism and ritual' in Raymond Gillespie and Brian P. Kennedy (eds), *Ireland: art into history*, pp 103–17.

Assuming control: elite women as household managers in late nineteenth-century Ireland

MAEVE O'RIORDAN[1]

Writing to her husband in 1874, Jane, Countess Bantry[2] (fig. 4.1) shared her delight at their future son-in-law's treatment of their eldest daughter:

> She is *perfectly* happy & the more I see of *Him* the more I feel he will be all we wish – he is so tender with and about her, and *quite* sees what a delicate plant she is, & what care & repose she requires a *very* rare quality in a man – men generally acting as if they believed women to be made of iron![3]

The 'care and repose' that Jane wanted for her daughter seems reflective of the sheltered existence of the clichéd Victorian lady, listlessly idling away the days on her couch. Jane's own life, however, which involved the management of numerous houses, demanded the qualities of a woman 'made of iron' rather than a stereotypical lady of leisure.

This essay focuses on the women of eight Munster families who owned estates

1 This research has been funded by the Irish Research Council. I wish to acknowledge the permission of the National Library of Ireland, and the Boole Library, University College Cork, to access material, and to use images held in their collections. Versions of this paper have been presented at conferences in Queen's University Belfast and Mary Immaculate College, Limerick. I would like to thank the organisers of these events, and of the SSNCI conference held in the Institute of Irish Studies, University of Liverpool, for their many useful comments and questions. I am grateful to Niall, Marie and Clare Cody for commenting on an earlier draft. I also wish to thank the School of History, UCC, for their assistance. A special word of thanks goes to Dr Clare O'Halloran for her continuous help and guidance in this, and other projects. Lastly, I want to thank my family for their unwavering support and encouragement; it is greatly appreciated. 2 Macroom Castle and Bantry House, Co. Cork; née Herbert of Muckross, Co. Kerry, 1823–98, m. 1845. I refer to women by their married names throughout, whether they were married at that time or not. Where possible I have included each woman's maiden name, parental home, marital seat and dates, at the first reference to their name. Biographical information was compiled using Sir B. Burke, *A genealogical and heraldic history of the landed gentry of Ireland* (London, 1904); Peter Townend (ed.), *Burke's genealogical and heraldic history of the peerage, baronetage and knightage* (105th ed., London, 1975). 3 Jane, Countess Bantry to third Earl Bantry, 12 May 1874, Bantry Estate Collection, Boole library, UCC IE/BL/EP/B/2395.

4.1 'Made of iron'; Jane, Countess Bantry, *c.*1870
(courtesy of the Boole Library, University College Cork).

with a minimum valuation of £1,000 in 1870, which placed them among the 2,500
wealthiest landowners in Ireland at the time.[4] The households discussed range from
those of titled magnates, with estates of over twenty thousand acres – such as the
earls of Bantry and the barons Inchiquin and Castletown – to Catholic country
gentry who owned less than three thousand – such as the Grehans of Cork and the
Ryans of Tipperary. Private letters, diaries and account books, supplemented by
published memoirs, from these landed families, over two generations, are used to
analyse the most local, practical application of power and influence: that of the
employer over her domestic servants. This is a study of power structures within the
homes of a provincial elite. In all of these homes, the landlord's wife, or a close female
relative, held the key role of house manager. This duty was one that contributed

---

4 D. Cannadine, *The decline and fall of the British aristocracy* (New Haven, CT, 1990), p. 9.

greatly to the family's success and was recognized as a valuable contribution to the estate.

The important role played by women in the management of the Big House has not been acknowledged in general research on this class. Terence Dooley reasoned, in the most important work on the Irish landed class to date, that this exclusion 'is merely a reflection of the non-status of women at the time', as 'they were confined to the role of mistress of the household and maid-servants'.[5] Cannadine's *The decline and fall of the British aristocracy* (which includes Ireland in its focus), has (by his own admission) 'almost nothing to say' about landed women.[6] These authors have acknowledged an 'urgent need', to address this 'glaring lacuna with regard to the role of women in Irish Big Houses'.[7] Maria Luddy has similarly appreciated the need for a 'study of landed women in nineteenth-century Ireland', and posed the questions: 'Did they play any role in the management of the estates? How did they manage their households?'[8]

In general, historians have failed to fully recognize the integrated nature of male and female duties on the estate. Women's roles as mistress of the household and hostess were essential for their families' prestige and social links. K.D. Reynolds has demonstrated that women in British aristocratic circles, during the first two-thirds of Queen Victoria's reign, had 'a natural role ... as promoters of the interests of their husbands and families' and that 'women had a series of roles and functions which gave content and meaning to their lives'.[9] Landed families did not epitomize the model Victorian family, as men's and women's roles overlapped, and were both centred on the family and estate, rather than on 'separate spheres'. The reality for the landed class during the period *c.*1860–1914 was that husbands and wives strived for the same ends. These women actively assisted their families through their position as household manager.

Some work on landed women and their household responsibilities has been carried out for Britain. Jessica Gerard has done seminal work in analysing country-house life in England and Wales.[10] This research is a very valuable point of comparison for Ireland, and clear similarities arise between the experiences of landed women living in Munster during the period *c.*1860 to 1900 and their counterparts in England and Wales. This is hardly surprising, as they had a shared culture, and many women moved between the two islands on marriage. Gerard has found that women's duties on the estate 'were conscientiously undertaken as recognized and valued duties' and that 'the stereotype of idle, useless ladies is clearly inaccurate and invalid'.[11]

5 T. Dooley, *The decline of the Big House in Ireland: a study of Irish landed families, 1860–1960* (Dublin, 2001), pp 16, 70. **6** Cannadine, *Decline and fall*, p. 7. **7** Ibid.; T. Dooley, *The Big Houses and landed estates of Ireland: a research guide* (Dublin, 2007), p. 178. **8** M. Luddy, 'Women's history' in Larry Geary and Margaret Kelleher (eds), *Nineteenth-century Ireland: a guide to recent research* (Dublin, 2005), p. 59. **9** K.D. Reynolds, *Aristocratic women and political society in Victorian Britain* (Oxford, 1998). **10** J. Gerard, *Country house life: family and servants, 1815–1914* (Oxford, 1994). **11** Ibid., p. 140.

The number of servants retained by Gerard's sample of one hundred families varied considerably, as life-stage and personal preference – and not just wealth – were influential in deciding the number of servants employed in landlords' homes. For families with incomes ranging from £1,000 to over £20,000, in the late nineteenth century, the average indoor staff size was ten.[12] Houses in this Munster sample employed similar, if slightly smaller, numbers of servants to those of the same income bracket in England and Wales.[13] The impact of the family's life stage on servant numbers can be seen in this sample. Nursery maids, schoolroom maids, governesses and tutors swelled the numbers engaged in houses with children.[14] In the 1901 census, (return for Bantry House (attached estate valued at £14,561)) only three servants were recorded, as the young landlord was away in Dublin. Ten years later, he was in residence with his wife, two daughters and eight indoor servants, including a nurse to attend to the children.[15]

So far, the only study of inter-class relations in the domestic setting in Ireland has been Mona Hearn's *Below stairs: domestic service remembered in Dublin and beyond, 1880–1922*.[16] Hearn utilized census data and interviews with surviving servants and employers. The chapter on the Big House discusses how house design minimized contact between the classes, and between the male and female servants. She described the experience of servants in the Big House, and focused on the reasons for rapid servant turnover; which included loneliness and harsh treatment at the hands of upper servants. Hearn's qualitative research has shattered the romantic illusion of the loyal retainer giving a lifetime of service to one family.[17]

Katherine Everett (née Herbert of Cahirnane, Co. Kerry, 1872–1951, m. 1901) noted a difference between Irish and English families' relationships with their staffs. She visited her cousin, Countess Ferrers (née White of Bantry, Co. Cork, 1852–1907, m. 1885), at her marital home at Staunton Harold, Leicestershire. Earl Ferrers ran his estate in the 'tradition of mutual obligations' and approved of a life that was 'dull and socially very formal'.[18] Katherine Everett found the 'pomp and formality', where three footmen and a butler laid out the tea, 'a little absurd' and there was no joking with the coachman as there might have been in a more 'casual and easy-going' Irish house.[19] For some landed women in Munster, there was little option but to know one's staff, as a housekeeper was not always employed to carry out a managerial role.

12 Ibid., p. 146. **13** Ibid., p. 146, Table 6.1; *Irish census*, 1901, http://www.census.nationalarchives.ie; Wage and meat account book, NLI MS/14,851. **14** *Irish census*, 1901, http://www.census.nationalarchives.ie, accessed 23 Nov. 2011; Wage and meat account book, NLI MS/14,851. **15** 'Residents of a house 3 in Seafield (Bantry, Cork)', *Irish census*, 1901, http://www.census.nationalarchives.ie/pages/1901/Cork/Bantry/Seafield/1091979/, accessed 23 Nov. 2011; 'residents of a house 1 in Seafield (Bantry Urban, Cork)', *Irish census*, 1901, http://www.census.nationalarchives.ie/pages/1911/Cork/Bantry_Urban/Seafield/374804/, accessed 23 Nov. 2011. *Irish Census*, 1901, http://www.census.nationalarchives.ie/pages/1901/Dublin/Trinity/Kildare_Street_Part/1310652/, accessed 23 Nov. 2011. **16** M. Hearn, *Below stairs: domestic service remembered in Dublin and beyond, 1880–1922* (Dublin, 1993), p. 78. **17** Ibid., p. 69. **18** K. Everett, *Bricks and flowers: memoirs of Katherine Everett* (2nd ed., Suffolk, 1951), pp 54, 44. **19** Ibid., pp 54, 46.

In most cases, employers preferred their staff, especially their upper servants, to share their religious affiliations. In Castlefreke, nine of the ten indoor servants employed by Lady Carbery (née Toulmin of St Albans, Hertfordshire, 1867–1949, m.[1] 1890, m.[2] 1902) in 1901 were Protestant; while in the Catholic Grehan home, only one of the seven indoor servants was Protestant.[20] As the landed class was predominantly Anglican, their servants were generally of the same denomination. In total, 68 per cent of servants employed in Irish country houses were Protestant. In all houses, staff members were more likely to come from outside the county, with many hailing from England. English servants were deemed to be more qualified than Irish ones, and so secured the more lucrative positions.[21]

Each house, therefore, had a wide catchment area for domestic staff, and might employ Irish, British and Continental European servants (the latter were mainly governesses). The fact that servants tended to be such a mixed group, both ethnically and religiously, suggests that, in this respect, each Big House was much like the others. New wives coming from another part of Ireland or, almost as commonly, from England did not face an alien workforce, but one of very similar make-up to that of their parental homes. This implied a sense of connection between the woman's old home and her new one, allowing her to step easily into her role as manager, and to appear in control.

Employers knew from experience that strong relationships could develop between children and their family's servants. One woman wrote of her childhood: 'All the servants, both indoors and outdoors, were our friends'.[22] Thus, employers chose servants who would help to mould their children into respectable members of the landed class. The kindly Mary O'Brien (Cahirmoyle, Co. Limerick; née Spring Rice of Mount Trenchard, Co. Limerick, m. 1863, d. 1868) was very definite about the type of environment she wanted in her children's nursery: 'a *good* Irish nurse wd be one's ideal – & the kind of badness that Irish women generally indulge in, untidiness &c, is compensated for in great measure by their being more attachable & less inclined to be fine or hard than the English'.[23] It was deemed important that children were surrounded by co-religionists, especially in the schoolroom and nursery, where servants contributed to the religious education of children. Katherine Everett was inspired with 'unquestioning faith' by her first nurse.[24] Even on their modest estate in Co. Kerry (£1,995 in 1878),[25] her mother employed successive Continental governesses to teach her children foreign languages, in an effort to stave off 'the native

20 'Residents of a house 2 in Castlefreke (Ruthbarry, Cork)', *Irish census*, 1901, http://www.census.nationalarchives.ie/pages/1901/Cork/Ruthbarry/Castlefreke/1162115/, accessed 23 Nov. 2011; 'residents of a house 13 in Gougane (Clonmeen, Cork)', *Irish census*, 1901, http://www.census.nationalarchives.ie/pages/1901/Cork/Clonmeen/Gougane/1148103/, accessed 23 Nov. 2011. **21** Hearn, *Below stairs*, pp 77, 80. **22** Everett, *Bricks and flowers*, p. 25. See also, for example, Emmeline Esdaile to Elizabeth White, Bantry Estate Collection, UCC IE/BL/EP/B/2454. **23** Mary O'Brien to her sister-in-law, Lucy Gwynn, 3 Feb. 1865, NLI MS/36,768. **24** Everett, *Bricks and flowers*, p. 17. **25** U.H. Hussey de Burgh, *Landowners of Ireland* (Dublin, 1876).

4.2 Ethel, Lady Inchiquin (wife of the fifteenth baron), on her presentation at court, May 1896 (courtesy of the National Library of Ireland).

brogue of which she had a horror'.[26] Girls received much, or all, of their education from governesses selected by their mothers. Ethel, Lady Inchiquin (Dromoland, Co. Clare; née Foster of Moor Park, Shropshire, m. 1896, d. 1940) (fig. 4.2) recognized the responsibility: 'will write to Mrs Hunt [employment agency] about the servants soon – I have a governess to get too – which is much more serious'.[27] Through their selection and control of nursery staff, these women greatly influenced the upbringing and education of the next generation of the landlord class.

Servants could also contribute to the image that their employer presented to the world in adulthood. Elizabeth MacKnight has discussed the complex ways in which nineteenth-century French aristocracy benefited from the employment of large retinues of servants. Using the concepts of 'theatre of rule' and 'cultural hegemony' discussed by E.P. Thompson in relation to eighteenth-century England, she has argued that the presence of deferential servants signalled how the rest of society should behave towards their employers, thus increasing aristocratic power.[28] Lady

---

26 Everett, *Bricks and flowers*, p. 18. **27** Ethel Lady Inchiquin to Lucius, fifteenth Baron Inchiquin, 29 June [1907], NLI MS/45,473(2). **28** E. MacKnight, 'A "theatre of rule"?

4.3 Ellen, Lady Inchiquin (second wife of the fourteenth baron), *c.*1880 (courtesy of the National Library of Ireland).

Carbery used her maids to demonstrate her own desired detachment from the 'squirrel cage of society': they were 'all alike in their black bonnets with strings, black coats and skirts, "as pretty as pinks". The visiting maids not half so attractive as mine are, in their "ladies" made-overs'.[29] When Ellen, Lady Inchiquin (Dromoland Castle, Co. Clare, née White of Annally, Dublin, b. 1854–6, m. 1874) (fig. 4.3) went to London, she would only get out of the carriage at her own house, as she had no footman with her.[30] For her, at least, the propriety and status provided by a manservant was important. Numerous servants were essential if women were to become lavish hostesses, or to travel and maintain critical links with other landed families. *The servant's practical guide* observed that, 'without the constant cooperation of well-trained servants, domestic machinery is completely thrown out of gear, and the best bred of hostesses placed at a disadvantage'.[31]

Domestic service in aristocratic households under the third republic', *French History*, 22:3 (1998), 316–36; E.P. Thompson, 'Patrician society, plebeian culture', *Journal of Social History*, 7 (1974), 382–405. **29** J. Sandford (ed.), *Mary Carbery's West Cork journal, 1898–1901* (Dublin, 1998), pp 123, 59. **30** Ellen to fourteenth Baron Inchiquin, July 1894, NLI MS/45,473. **31** *The servants practical guide* (1880), quoted in P. Horn, *The rise and fall of the Victorian servant*

The management styles of these women varied as a result of personality, wealth and training. Women did not receive any formal managerial training, but they learned from the example of their mothers and other female relatives. Esther Grehan (Clonmeen, Co. Cork; née Chichester of Runamoat, Co. Roscommon, 1860–1900, m. 1883) (fig. 4.4) won first prize in arithmetic at school, which may have helped her in accounts, Katherine Everett was trained by her mother to write references for servants, and Gertrude 'Bee' Foster, younger sister of Ethel, Lady Inchiquin, appears to have taken on much of the responsibility of finding, and refurbishing, a suitable house for the return of her sister and brother-in-law from honeymoon.[32] Living with an unmarried brother also allowed these women to run a home temporarily. After her parents' deaths and before her brother's marriage, Countess Ferrers acted as mistress of Bantry House, where she 'entertained all sorts of people'.[33] Nelly O'Brien also ran her brother's new Dublin house, but only until his marriage. While she impressed him in some ways, her lack of mathematical training was apparent: 'She, poor soul, is not over-strong in that line, either in accuracy of tots or in systematic jotting down of items'.[34]

Many women were diligent in their record keeping. The Viscountess Doneraile (Doneraile Court, Co. Cork; née Lenox-Conyngham, m. 1851, d. 1907) filed the receipts of wages paid to employees.[35] Esther Grehan had no housekeeper but kept her own accounts in coloured calligraphy. Ellen, Lady Inchiquin, initialled all payments to her servants, and supervised the meat account for the house. Such careful record keeping was essential, as the level of food production and catering activity in these houses was equal to that of a small business. In Dromoland, over four hundred servings of meat might be required on busy weeks.[36] Many of these houses regularly accommodated over twenty people; even in the more modest Grehan household, meals were rarely confined to the immediate family.[37] Furniture and goods, therefore, needed constant supervision.

Esther Grehan carefully listed all the silver given into the butler's care, and super-intended the purchasing and packing of stores herself.[38] When Ellen, Lady Inchiquin, noticed discrepancies in the meat account she searched for a new cook, who could be controlled more easily by Ellen's trusted housekeeper.[39] She would not be cheated by servants and knew how much she was willing to pay them: 'I would not get an expensive cook – £40 feeds you just as well as £60 in womankind'.[40] The Inchiquins were in financial difficulties, with as many as twenty-seven servants in the

(Dublin, 1975), p. 17.   **32** Esther Grehan, 'Red notebook', Grehan Estate Collection, UCC IE/BL/EP/G/845; Everett, *Bricks and flowers*, p. 20; Gertrude Foster to Ethel, Lady Inchiquin Mar. 1896, NLI MS/45,503(2).   **33** Everett, *Bricks and flowers*, p. 43.   **34** NLI MS/36,694 (p. 601).   **35** Wage receipts, NLI MS/34,124(11).   **36** Meat Account, NLI MS/14,851. **37** Esther Grehan, diary 1894, Grehan Estate Collection, UCC IE/BL/EP/G/839. **38** Wage account book, UCC IE/BL/EP/G/306; House account book, IE/BL/EP/G/406; Esther Grehan diary entry, 3 Oct. 1896, IE/BL/EP/G/841.   **39** Ellen, Lady Inchiquin to fourteenth Baron Inchiquin, 8–9 Dec. 1878, NLI MS/45,473(2).   **40** Ibid., 9 Dec. 1878, NLI MS/45,473(2).

1880s, and new servants were often paid less than their predecessors.[41] These women's careful management of employees, and of the house and its stores, was essential to the economic success of the estate.

As managers, these women were shrewd, but in the late nineteenth century, employer–employee relationships were not merely contractual; some paternal practices were retained. Throughout the period in Doneraile, employees were given an allowance for beer and laundry on top of wages.[42] In Dromoland, in the 1870s and 1880s, servants were allocated an equal share of meat to that of the family.[43] Mary O'Brien felt herself obliged to ensure that young servants in her household were trained correctly.[44]

An examination of the comments in Esther Grehan's wage account book show that, like many Big House employers, Grehan rarely if ever paid her servants on time; it was not uncommon for wages to be two months overdue.[45] Fines for damaged household items, such as a hair sieve from the cook, or for a 'smashed chair' from the housemaid, meant that wages could be reduced. Yet she was also willing to advance money to her employees, and gave out loans for medicine, clothes, travel expenses and telegrams.[46] She also provided payment in kind in the form of presents, such as that given to the nurse after 'baby' got her first tooth.[47] Esther Grehan knew her servants personally and supervised their work, reprimanding them when she felt it necessary.[48] She used what training she had to get the best from her workforce; the fines she extracted could be for something as small as a plate, but the contents of the house were her responsibility and she would not allow them to be damaged.

In spite of any informal perks or personal attention enjoyed by servants in these houses, few remained with their employers long. Mona Hearn, using census returns and estate account books, as well as interviews and newspaper advertisements, has found that during the period 1880 to 1922, the average Big House servant remained in each position for a short time, a pattern confirmed by this case study.[49] In the Grehan household, as many as two of about eight servants could give notice or leave per quarter.[50] Servants working in larger establishments did not necessarily stay for longer periods. Despite the fact that Ellen, Lady Inchiquin, generally paid her servants on time, servant turnover at Dromoland was considerable.[51]

41 See Meat and wage account books, NLI MS/14,851, NLI MS/14,848, NLI MS/14,849. **42** Account books, NLI MS/34,148(12) and NLI MS/21,514. **43** Meat book, NLI MS/14,850. **44** Mary O'Brien to Lucy Gwynn, 3 Feb. 1865, NLI MS/36 768. **45** Wage account book, Grehan Estate Collection, UCC IE/BL/EP/G/306. **46** Ibid. **47** House account book, Grehan Estate Collection, UCC IE/BL/EP/G/406. **48** See, for example, Esther Grehan, diary entry, 31 Aug. 1893, Grehan Estate Collection, UCC IE/BL/EP/G/838. **49** Board of Trade Labour Department, *Report by Miss Collet, on the money wages of indoor domestic servants*, BPP 1899 XCII [C. 9346], referenced in M. Hearn, *Below stairs*, p. 84. **50** See, for example, spring and summer entries 1894, Esther Grehan, wage account book, Grehan Estate Collection, UCC IE/BL/EP/G/306. **51** Wage account books, 1880–6, NLI MS/14,848–9. See also Hearn, *Below stairs*, p. 78.

4.4 Esther Grehan,
1898 (courtesy of the
Boole Library,
University College
Cork).

Much was written on the 'servant problem' as the nineteenth century drew to a
close, but Amanda Vickery has found that 'the servant problem was an "aging
chestnut", even in 1700'. The genteel women in Vickery's north of England study
needed to become 'impresarios of staffing', as they dealt with the problem of
absconding servants on a continuous basis.[52] The surviving correspondence of these
Munster women suggests that they accepted the conveyor-belt nature of their
servants' hall as 'tiresome' but unavoidable.[53] On one holiday in France, Esther
Grehan went through three cooks in one month: she thought the first was lying to
her, and the second, though well liked, fell ill, and so a third had to be found.[54]
Deference, competence and honesty in staff were essential qualities for the employer.
The landed class expected to employ the elite of domestic workers, as servants 'represented their families, much as receptionists do today.'[55] They could not retain
well-meaning servants who proved to be unqualified:

52 A. Vickery, *Gentleman's daughter*, pp 141, 135. **53** Gertrude Foster to Ethel, Lady
Inchiquin [1896], NLI MS/45,503(2). **54** Esther Grehan diary entry, 14–31 July 1897,
Grehan Estate Collection, UCC IE/BL/EP/G842. **55** Reynolds, *Aristocratic women*, p. 36.

I am going to part with Bell – but don't mention it, for I cannot as yet give her definite 'warning' … I am so very sorry to dismiss her, she is so very cheerful & willing & sweet-tempered; but the opportunities I have had since I came abroad of watching her day & night have convinced me that she is not fit to be *head* of a nursery.[56]

There is no evidence, in this sample, of women acting tyrannically towards their servants, but they were prone to lose patience with them, and, if they felt servants were not suitable, were quick to release them.[57] Some offences resulted in immediate dismissal. Esther Grehan recorded on one visit with friends that their footman and housemaid were 'to be packed off'.[58] Other offences required a more patient approach, however, as the prestige of the family was of paramount importance. Ethel, Lady Inchiquin, felt it would not be prudent to dismiss a potentially dishonest cook until after a visit from the duke of Marlborough, as she feared she 'might get a worse one'.[59]

Not all servant departures were the result of a relationship breakdown. Sometimes they left to marry, or were let go as their employer could no longer afford them.[60] Nursery servants and governesses were eventually laid off when children had grown up. Other servants were only employed on a temporary basis to staff a London house during the family's stay.[61] Surviving letters of recommendation show that servants who were dismissed could still get positive references. One letter from a Lady Scott in relation to an upper housemaid, whom she had dismissed over a row about the cleanliness of a carpet, found that her worst fault was that she was 'not very good about her looks'.[62] With such a high servant turnover, these women needed to be almost constantly recruiting if they were to present a well-run house to guests.

The responsibility of house and servants was a constant care for the landlord's wife. In 1887, Ellen, Lady Inchiquin, had bills and accounts, including the dairy accounts, sent to her while she was in England.[63] Even before Esther Grehan was married or mistress at Clonmeen, Viscountess Doneraile and others were inquiring what changes she would make to her new home. She found it stressful. 'It jars that I am expected to think of chopping and changing everything – before I am even married!'[64] Yet she advised her fiancé on ways to make the house neater, made plans

56 Mary O'Brien to Lucy Gwynn, 3 Feb. 1865, NLI MS/36,768.   **57** Sandford (ed.), *West Cork journal*, p. 76; Esther Grehan, diary entry, 26 June 1894, Grehan Estate Collection, UCC IE/BL/EP/G/839.   **58** Esther Grehan to Stephen Grehan, 7 Nov. 1882, Grehan Estate Collection, UCC IE/BL/EP/G/769.   **59** Ethel, Lady Inchiquin to fourteenth Baron Inchiquin, 9 Dec. 1878, NLI MS/45,473(2).   **60** Maraquita Grehan to George Grehan, 24 Sept. [n.d.], Grehan Estate Collection, UCC IE/BL/EP/G/627.   **61** Sandford (ed.), *West Cork journal*, p. 120.   **62** Lady Scott to George Lennox Conyngham (maternal grandfather of Lady Castletown), 10 Feb. 1861, NLI MS/34,148(12).   **63** Ellen, Lady Inchiquin to fourteenth Baron Inchiquin, 10 Dec. 1878, NLI MS/45,473(2); Emily A. Simpson to Ellen, Lady Inchiquin, 30 Aug. 1887, NLI MS/45,602(7).   **64** Esther Chichester to Stephen Grehan, 28 Oct. 1882, Grehan Estate Collection, UCC IE/BL/EP/G/670.

for the landscaping of the estate and advised him on 'the most economical sort of grate for burning coal'.[65] Jane, Countess Bantry, travelled to England to be with her daughter who was dangerously ill, having given birth to her second child. While there, Jane took over the house management, despite the presence of her son-in-law.[66] She hired wet nurses, ordered the doctor and 'inaugurated [a] regime of *strictest* quiet'.[67] Meanwhile, she was writing to her husband at home in Bantry about the potential visit, in her absence, of a duke.[68] On holiday in Tramore, Esther Grehan recruited staff for Clonmeen by mail.[69] Many families owned or rented additional residences, so women had to organize staffing for each house before the family travelled there, and managed lesser houses from afar.[70]

Of course inter-class relations were not only about wages and discipline. Personal servants, especially, were ever-present in their employer's lives. For some women, such as Lady Carbery, who was left a widow at a young age, employees were the only adults whom they were sure to meet every day. For others, trapped in an unhappy marriage, or suffering under the loneliness of widowhood or spinsterhood, a hired companion might be relied upon to alleviate the sense of isolation.[71] Governesses provided substitute companionship when no-one else was around.[72] Women, therefore, wanted positive, if unequal, relationships with their domestics. This was certainly the case with personal servants, such as lady's maids and nursery servants. When Esther Grehan died, her husband wrote that her maid had become 'more like a sister than a maid' in the final illness.[73] Lady Inchiquin's sister, Bee, wrote: 'I have got a new ladies [*sic*] maid … she seems a nice little thing & so far I like her'.[74]

Motherhood practices of the period demanded that the women of this class spent a good deal of time in the company of nursery servants. Neighbouring women, their children and nurses regularly visited each other. Nurses and governesses even entertained guests when their employers were away.[75] These servants were instrumental in the upbringing of their employers' children, so good relationships were preferable. Esther Grehan watched the children while the governess received a visit from her sister, and at another time she took the children while 'Mademoiselle' went to the dentist in Cork.[76] Sometimes, positive relationships led these women to trust upper servants with great responsibility. The countess of Bantry, who was travelling in

65 Ibid., and Esther Chichester to Stephen Grehan, 3 Nov. 1882, Grehan Estate Collection, UCC IE/BL/EP/G/677. **66** Countess Bantry to Earl Bantry, 12 May 1874, Bantry Estate Collection, UCC IE/BL/EP/B/2395. **67** Ibid., Friday [n.d.] 1876, Bantry Estate Collection, UCC IE/BL/EP/B/2400. **68** Ibid. **69** Esther Grehan, diary entry, 1–9 Aug. 1895, Grehan Estate Collection, UCC IE/BL/EP/G/840. **70** See, for example, Esther Grehan, diary entry, 18 July 1896, Grehan Estate Collection, UCC IE/BL/EP/G/841. **71** Everett, *Bricks and flowers*, pp 44, 27, 149, 156. **72** Sandford (ed.), *West Cork journal*, p. 76; Esther Grehan, diary entry, 10, 22 Nov. 1896, Grehan Estate Collection, UCC IE/BL/EP/G/841. **73** Stephen Grehan to Amy Chichester, 3 May 1900, Grehan Estate Collection, UCC IE/BL/EP/G/835. **74** Gertrude Foster to Ethel, Lady Inchiquin [1896], NLI MS/45,503(2). **75** Emmeline Esdaile to Countess Bantry, Bantry Estate Collection, UCC IE/BL/EP/B/2401. **76** Esther Grehan, diary entry, 4 Mar. 1893, Grehan Estate Collection, UCC IE/BL/EP/G/838.

Europe, allowed her children's governess to order other servants, entertain guests and even see to the funeral arrangements for the countess' late daughter, Emily.[77] Ellen, Lady Inchiquin, relied heavily on the advice of her housekeeper, even when hiring other staff.[78]

These women's view of their servants was influenced by nineteenth-century notions of hierarchy. Relationships could be quite jovial, as there was such a social gulf between employer and employee. Lady Carbery allowed herself to be scolded by her lady's maid, and, like Katherine Everett, she chatted to her coachman while driving.[79] Both of these women were nonetheless convinced of their own superiority, and approved of a hierarchical society.[80] Lady Castletown (née St Leger, childhood and marital home: Doneraile Court, Co. Cork, 1853–1927, m. 1874) obviously enjoyed laughter at the expense of the servant class, and kept comic cartoons of the foolishness of maids – along with derogatory depictions of Africans – in her scrapbook.[81]

These women did not just contribute to their family's economic security through careful management of the indoor servants; they were also involved in more recognizably commercial projects of their own. The dairy and farmyard were also under the remit of the landlord's wife. Esther Grehan's dairymaids were engaged in a form of bonded labour, as their wages were regularly deducted in part, or in full, for rent.[82] She was able to generate profit by selling butter, while helping her husband to collect rents. Ellen, Lady Inchiquin, monitored the price of butter before deciding when their stock should be sent to market.[83] In the early twentieth century, landed women became involved in even more overtly commercial activities. Esther Grehan's daughter, May (b. 1884, m. 1923), and many others, became involved in the cooperative movement. May attempted to improve local poultry-rearing practices.[84] The energetic Mabel O'Brien (Cahirmoyle, Co. Limerick; née Smyly, 4 Merrion Square, Dublin, 1869–1942, m. 1902), who had come from an urban background, set up the Ardagh Cheese business in the early twentieth century.[85]

As dairy maids were more likely than indoor staff to be recruited locally, the management of the dairy allowed landed women to forge links with tenants, thus strengthening the position of their family. Through their stewardship of house and farmyard, these women completed an important social and economic function, maintaining and even strengthening links with the local community, while contributing to their families' financial well being.

As many of the marriages in this study were companionate, women sometimes

77 Emmeline Esdaile to Countess Bantry, Bantry Estate Collection, UCC IE/BL/EP/B/2403 and IE/BL/EP/B/2401. **78** Ellen, Lady Inchiquin to fourteenth Baron Inchiquin, NLI MS/45,473(2). **79** Sandford (ed.), *West Cork journal*, pp 24, 65. **80** Everett, *Bricks and flowers*, p. 284; Sandford (ed.), *West Cork journal*, p. 121. **81** Lady Castletown's scrapbook, NLI MS/3,079. **82** Wage account book, Grehan Estate Collection, UCC IE/BL/EP/G/306. **83** Emily A. Simpson to Ellen, Lady Inchiquin, 27 June and 30 Aug. 1887, NLI MS/45,602(7). **84** 'Family Journal', no. 11, Sept. 1903, Grehan Estate Collection, UCC IE/BL/EP/G/1395. **85** NLI MS/36,821.

enlisted the assistance of their husbands to carry out managerial duties. While in Dublin, Esther Grehan's husband, Stephen, interviewed a cook for her and decided she would do.[86] He also called the police when a dismissed governess refused to leave without more money.[87] Ethel, Lady Inchiquin, told her husband to find a footman while in London.[88] Recruitment of men servants was technically the husband's responsibility, but Ethel knew what positions needed to be filled. She once recruited and tested a new chauffeur while her husband was away.[89] Ethel's step-mother-in-law, Ellen, Lady Inchiquin, did not withhold her domestic worries from her husband while he was away at parliament, but asked his advice on a cheating cook, discussed possible replacements and shared her difficulties in organizing a house party.[90]

At times, however, interventions by their husbands could be unwelcome. Mary O'Brien was a meek wife who usually did all she could to please her husband, and even asked his permission to attend church service.[91] Nonetheless, when (due to her having TB) he was searching for a new nurse for her, she would not heed his reservations about a potential candidate. She directed him as to who he should write to for references, and provided a list of questions for the interview. She preferred to trust in female opinion and directed him to include 'any other questions Mother can think of'.[92]

Not all families contained a husband and a wife to carry out their respective duties. The roles already discussed belonged to women who had a husband to perform the external management of the estate. Circumstances sometimes dictated that women took on the entire responsibility of the property. The widowed Lady Carbery had to act as employer to the outdoor as well as the indoor staff. Lady Castletown's husband was interned in an asylum with 'a form of melancholia' and so she was forced to take on all aspects of management; she examined their financial situation and tried to raise money to send him to South Africa on his release. These duties, along with her many other projects, may explain why she was so haphazard in her employment record keeping.[93]

When a mistress of the house predeceased her husband he had to replace her in some way. This was not just to satisfy desires for companionship and sexual fulfilment, but also to provide the home with a manager to replace the one it had lost. Viscountess Barrington believed that an older man's readiness to remarry illustrated his 'happiness under the first regime, and . . . his helplessness without a wife'.[94] When

---

86 Esther Grehan, diary entry, 28 Sept. 1895, Grehan Estate Collection, UCC IE/BL/EP/G/840. **87** Esther Grehan, diary entry, 4 Apr. 1895, Grehan Estate Collection, UCC IE/BL/EP/G/840. **88** Ethel, Lady Inchiquin to fifteenth Baron Inchiquin, 6 June [1909], NLI MS/45,504(4). **89** Ethel, Lady Inchiquin to fifteenth Baron Inchiquin, n.d. [July 1909], NLI MS/45,504(4). **90** Ellen, Lady Inchiquin to fourteenth Baron Inchiquin, 8–9 Dec. 1878, NLI MS/45 473 (2). **91** Mary O'Brien to Edward William O'Brien, 16 June 1867, NLI MS/36,752 (2). **92** Mary O'Brien to Edward William O'Brien, 25 and 28 June 1867, NLI MS/36,756 (2). **93** Numerous friends and relations to Lady Castletown, June to Sept. 1912, NLI MS/341664. Wage account book, Doneraile, NLI MS/21,514. **94** Charlotte, Viscountess Barrington, *Through eighty years* (London, 1986), p. 133, quoted in

Lady Elizabeth Leigh (High Leigh, Cheshire; née White of Bantry, 1847–80, m. 1874) died, her husband, Egerton, wondered how 'he shall ever get on without her'.[95] He would eventually remarry, but in the interim he relied on female family members. Egerton's sister-in-law, sister and mother all spent time at his home. They oversaw the laying out of the corpse and the care of his daughter – his son, Edward, was already living with his maternal grandparents – and organized his late wife's belongings.[96] An old widower, who knew he would never remarry, might invite an unmarried female relative to live with him, to partly fulfil his wife's role.[97] Similarly, a bachelor with his own establishment could rely on an unmarried sister to manage his home, until he replaced her with a wife.[98]

Some widowers took on their wives' tasks themselves. When Esther Grehan was dangerously ill, her husband Stephan closed up Clonmeen, sent the children to school or to stay with friends, and took her to the spa town of Davos.[99] When she eventually died in 1900, he was forty-one and young enough to remarry. He chose not to. He took on his wife's duties as manager and promoted a trusted maid to housekeeper. He had lived alone with his father at Clonmeen after his mother's death in his early childhood, and had assisted his wife over the years, so he had some experience of the necessary duties.[1] Grehan also had the benefit of grown-up, unmarried daughters, who took on some of their mother's responsibilities. Unfortunately, he appears to have inherited his wife's luck with cooks and his diaries are littered with references to disputes with women in that position.[2]

While both lived, spouses held complementary roles in relation to the estate. Household organization was just one of the wife's responsibilities, which also extended from maternal duties, to estate and garden management, and beyond the demesne walls to the wider society. However, apart from providing heirs, supervision of the household was the most important of the woman's duties. It was a position of power and influence in the family. As such, it increased these women's sense of self-worth. As a young, unmarried woman, Esther Grehan was asked her advice on 'some housekeeping'; she held her head 'an inch higher in consequence'.[3] During her married life, Esther contributed to the success of the family and estate, with her work in the home and farmyard. Stephen's sense of loss at her passing was evident in a letter to her sister, written shortly after her death: 'I don't know what I shall do

---

Gerard, *Country house life*, p. 113. **95** L.E. Leigh to Countess Bantry, Bantry Estate Collection, UCC IE/BL/EP/B/2414. **96** For example, see Gertrude Foster to Ethel Lady Inchiquin, 6 Mar. 1896, NLI MS/45,503. **97** Lord Castletown to Ethel St Leger, Apr. 1926–Mar. 1927, NLI MS/34,164(1). **98** For example, see Everett, *Bricks and flowers*, p. 43, and Dermod O'Brien to Mabel O'Brien, Oct.–Nov. 1891, NLI MS/36,694(1–2). **99** Esther Grehan, diary entry, 7 Dec. 1897, Grehan Estate Collection, UCC IE/BL/EP/G/842. **1** For example, Esther Grehan, diary entry, 3 Oct. 1896, Grehan Estate Collection, UCC IE/BL/EP/G/841; Esther Grehan, diary entry, 6 May 1898, IE/BL/EP/G/843. **2** For example, see Stephen Grehan, diary entry, Grehan Estate Collection, UCC IE/BL/EP/G/761. **3** Esther Chichester to Stephen Grehan, 2 Nov. 1882, Grehan Estate Collection, UCC IE/BL/EP/G/676.

without her ...You can have no idea what a terrible void she will create. I haven't
an idea how I'll manage'.[4] Wives contributed greatly to landed estates, and to their
husbands' careers as landlords, not just as loving companions, but as active partners.
Unfortunately, aside from a few 'great women', we know very little of the lives, or
the views, of the women of the landed class. Further new research needs to be
conducted on these women, if we are to move towards a more rounded understanding of the so-called leisured class – the elite of Irish society.

4 Stephen Grehan to Amy Chichester, 3 May 1900, Grehan Estate Collection, UCC
IE/BL/EP/G/835.

'Gentlemen practisers': solicitors as elites in mid-nineteenth-century Irish landed society

JOANNE McENTEE

In 1739, the refusal to admit solicitors as members to the Inns of Court resulted in the formation of 'The Society of Gentlemen Practisers in the Courts of Law and Equity'.[1] Although customarily solicitors were designated the title of 'gentlemen' once they received their licence to practice, by adopting this descriptor in the title of their newly inaugurated society, the lower branch of the legal profession seemed to unambiguously be asserting a professional claim to membership of elite society.[2] Yet, in reality, such social demarcations proved illusory. Old English elite society was never a static one and the barrier between the gentry and the classes immediately below them often was of a permeable nature. Entry into elite society was generally provided by the possession of wealth, property or a peerage. Professional standing, while perhaps not one of the primary criteria for entry into illustrious circles, nonetheless provided additional kudos to an individual who mostly likely 'belonged' in elite circles prior to receiving their licence to practice. W. J. Reader described how law, along with divinity and physic, were perceived as 'learned professions', and perhaps most significantly, were occupations that 'a gentleman might engage in without disgrace'.[3] While membership of the Bar was deemed respectable for a gentleman, the lower social standing of solicitors made this branch of the profession less attractive to those from high society.[4] Barnard commented how the lower branch of the profession occupied by solicitors was viewed with some disdain by members of the landed gentry. Specifically, he claimed how 'the propertied, although happy to have sons at the bar, remained at best ambivalent and at worst hostile to lawyers'.[5]

The nineteenth-century business relationship between solicitors as members of the legal profession grouping and other more entrenched elite groups, such as land-lords, requires more attention. In an age when tenant access to the courts appeared to be increasing, coupled with a series of land legislative changes that challenged the property rights of the landlord, a successful landlord–solicitor working relationship was of paramount importance. Although in 1963 David Spring called for further

---

1 R.J. Walker, *The English legal system*, sixth edition (London, 1985), p. 248. 2 Toby Barnard, *A new anatomy of Ireland: the Irish protestants, 1649–1770* (London, 2003), p. 122. 3 W.J. Reader, *The middle classes* (London, 1972), p. 7. 4 Ibid., p. 6; 24. 5 Barnard, *A new anatomy of Ireland*, pp 120–1.

research on the work of solicitor-agents, the relationship between landlord and solic-itor, especially within an Irish context, still requires study.[6] Through an analysis of legal correspondence and papers related primarily to three estates – namely the Farnham, Westport and Leitrim estates – this essay will examine the role of the solic-itor within a mid-nineteenth-century Irish landed estate context in order to determine on what basis the profession can claim to have been an elite during this period and ultimately to decide who had the real authority within the powerful part-nership of landlord and solicitor.

The relationship between members of the landed estate and the legal profession was a long and varied one. Although it is believed that approximately 800 to 1,000 barristers, solicitors and attorneys operated in eighteenth-century Ireland, many land-lords relied either on their own legal knowledge or on that of their estate employees in relation to estate related litigious matters.[7] Members of the gentry regularly received the rudiments of legal training as part of their general education. At the same time, a blurring and overlapping of steward duties with that of the agent, coupled with a frequent lack of distinction between the role of steward and legal advisor, resulted in a varied mix of legal knowledge and skill on each estate.[8] Some landlords employed attorneys as agents, although such a move was sometimes regretted by the landowner, who felt that their presence merely exploited and increased their own problems.[9] This quasi-legal role was increasingly diminishing in importance, however, with a greater reliance being placed on the employment of individuals with professional legal training.[10] It was during this time that legal profes-sionals relied significantly on the socially, economically, culturally and politically elite class of the landed gentry for employment. The social standing of the country lawyer proved rather inauspicious, however, occupying the same position in polite society as the country doctor and upper servants of the manor house.[11] Robson claimed that as the eighteenth century came to a close, solicitors in England were organized into two distinct groups; 'an elite of respectable solicitors and the less reputable majority'.[12]

Landlords continued to employ legal professionals on their estates well into the nineteenth century, with solicitors (and, less frequently, barristers) fulfilling the role of land agent, with some solicitor-agents even 'perpetuating themselves dynasti-cally'.[13] Early in the nineteenth century, the absentee landlord, third Viscount Courtenay, appointed London solicitor Alexander Hoskins as chief land agent on his 34,000-acre estate in Limerick, which triggered events that resulted in the emergence

6 Quoted in Sarah Webster, 'Estate improvement and the professionalisation of land agents on the Egremont Estates in Sussex and Yorkshire, 1770–1835', *Rural History*, 18:1 (2007), 47–69 at 49.   **7** Barnard, *A new anatomy of Ireland*, pp 115, 126.   **8** Webster, 'Estate improvement and the professionalisation of land agents', 48.   **9** Barnard, *A new anatomy of Ireland*, p. 124.   **10** Coral Lansbury, *The reasonable man: Trollope's legal fiction* (Princeton, NJ, 1981), p. 14.   **11** Reader, *The middle classes*, pp 8–9.   **12** Robert Robson, *The attorney in eighteenth-century England* (Cambridge, 1959), quoted in David Spring, *The English landed estate in the nineteenth century: its administration* (London, 1963), p. 60.   **13** Ibid., p. 15; 58.

of the infamous 'Captain Rock'.[14] Later in the century, in 1886, Lord Massereene appointed Athol Johnston Dudgeon, a partner in a Dublin firm of solicitors, as agent. In the eyes of the deputy inspector general of the Royal Irish Constabulary, such a move contributed significantly to continued disorder on the Massereene Estate.[15] Solicitor-agents, or lawyer-agents, also operated across the Irish Sea. Spring claimed that the majority of early nineteenth-century English estates employed a lawyer-agent on their holdings.[16] Contemporary estate administration handbooks frequently deplored the employment of solicitors as agents, claiming that both estate business and commitment to agricultural improvement suffered as a result.[17] This increasingly common development was viewed by some as contributing significantly to the oppression of Irish tenants. An 1847 pamphlet claimed that 75 per cent of Irish estates were managed by legal professionals 'employed, by "the squeezing, heartless and exterminating landlords" to superintend the *collection* of their rents, and the *scattering* of their tenants'.[18] Dooley claimed that this development signalled an increasing awareness among landlords of the legal ramifications involved in estate management.[19] Some land agencies even had a direct link to the legal profession. The land agency known as Stewart & Kincaid for most of the 1800s was established in the previous century by a member of the bar, Henry Stewart. Stewart's new business partner in 1809 was also a barrister named Graves Swan.[20] At the same time, land agents and even landlords, without any formal legal training, continued to fulfil a quasi-legalistic role with respect to matters related to last will and testaments. On the Shirley Estate, land agents were sometimes appointed both drafter and executor of wills.[21] Farnham landlords and agents also received requests with respect to the assets of the deceased and conflicts surrounding annuities.[22]

According to Walker, a distinctive feature of the English legal system was the division of the profession into two separate branches – solicitors and barristers. The division of the English legal system into serjeants and barristers – who operated in the common law courts – and attorneys, who were active in the preparatory stages of legal action, dated back to 1340. Solicitors, as distinct from attorneys, only emerged in the fifteenth century. Although initially perceived as inferior to attorneys, the

14 James S. Donnelly Jr, *Captain Rock: the Irish agrarian rebellion of 1821–1824* (Cork, 2009), p. 338. **15** Laurence M. Geary, *The Plan of Campaign, 1886–1891* (Cork, 1986), p. 43. **16** Webster, 'Estate improvement and the professionalisation of land agents', 48–50. **17** Spring, *The English landed estate*, p. 59. **18** *A letter from Peter Carroll to John Bull on the origin, nature, and conduct of the landlords of Ireland and on the best method of preventing them in future from starving 'Patrick' and robbing 'John'* (London, 1847), pp 16–17. **19** Terence Dooley, *The Big Houses and landed estates of Ireland: a research guide* (Dublin, 2007), p. 19. **20** Desmond Norton, *Landlords, tenants, famine: the business of an Irish land agency in the 1840s* (Dublin, 2006), p. 5. **21** Will of Mary Gillogly, witnesses Peter Ward, Thomas Reburn and Thos Carrole, 9 Feb. 1842, D3531/P/1; Last will and testament of Hugh Martin, 4 June 1839, D3531/P/2; Letter from Thomas Reilly and Moses Connor to George Morant esq., Jan. 1848, Shirley Papers, PRONI D3531/P/2. **22** Robt Black, respecting the assets of Robt Brady deceased, 1832; John Rayburn complains that he cannot get an annuity allowed him by his father-in-law from the Widow Montgomery, 1837: Farnham Papers, NLI MS 3,117–

distinction between solicitors and attorneys was finally abolished in 1877 following
the establishment of a single supreme court of judicature. Thereafter, the title 'solicitor' was deemed the most polite descriptor for a member of the profession.[23] While
both solicitors and barristers were recognized legal professionals, their training and
duties varied considerably, and this provided the distinction between the two groupings. Institutional learning was not a prerequisite for those desiring to receive training
as a solicitor. Recruits generally acquired the skills of the trade through apprentice-
ship. Regulations enacted in 1794 stipulated that benchers (senior members of the
Inn of Court) carry out more intently their role in considering the suitability of
masters for prospective new apprentices.[24] Once this part of their education was
complete, aspirants had to travel to their national capital for examination (which was
conducted orally and deemed merely perfunctory) and register before they could
practice.[25] One nineteenth-century commentator described the composite nature of
the role of a solicitor as follows:

> The modern solicitor combines in his proper person the functions of several
> professions. The duties of the ancient attorney, proctor and solicitor, and part
> of those formerly discharged by counsel and scriveners, are now performed
> by the solicitor. It was as an attorney that the solicitor was first known.[26]

Reader claimed that although solicitorship was a 'humble occupation', it proved
'invaluable to the landed gentleman, who referred to him, with a good deal of scorn
as "my man of business"'.[27] Barristers, in contrast, were held in greater esteem by the
landed gentry. Many new recruits to the bar came from the wealthier segments of
society, such as the landed gentry and contemporary prospering professions. Those
seeking to enter the barrister trade could spend from £1,000 to £1,500 in order to
obtain the appropriate qualifications. Although some landlords such as Richard
Edgeworth and Robert French received a legal training, once they inherited their
titles they ceased to practice.[28] Other landlords encouraged their sons to enter the
trade. An Irish barrister informed the 1846 Select Committee that many gentlemen
of property 'who wish not to allow their sons to spend a perfectly idle life send them
to the Inns of Court'.[29] Barristers, unlike solicitors, usually held a university educa-

18.   **23** Daire Hogan, 'The profession before the charter of 1852' in Eamonn G. Hall &
Daire Hogan (eds), *The Law Society of Ireland, 1852–2002: portrait of a profession* (Dublin, 2002),
p. 21.   **24** An attempt in 1836 to rule that masters had not only to be an attorney admitted
to all three common law courts, but also operate as a solicitor, was rejected along with a
repudiation of the society's 1852 proposal that only solicitors who were members of the
society were allowed to take on apprentices: Hogan, 'The profession before the charter of
1852', pp 33–8.   **25** Laurence Brockliss, 'The professions and national identity' in Laurence
Brockliss and David Eastwood (eds), *A union of multiple identities: the British Isles, c. 1750–c.
1850* (Manchester, 1997), pp 15–16; Barnard, *A new anatomy of Ireland*, p. 122.   **26** Edmund
Brown Viney Christian, *A short history of solicitors* (London, 1896), p. 1.   **27** Reader, *The
middle classes*, p. 8.   **28** Ibid., pp 118–20.   **29** Daire Hogan, *The legal profession in Ireland,*

tion, or its equivalent, along with a good knowledge of history, classical literature, rhetoric and logic – all of which were deemed essential for the role of advocate. It was also customary to spend a period in the London courts for practical experience before practicing in Ireland.[30] Barristers were also entitled to plead in court, while the role of the solicitor in this instance included giving instructions to barristers and aiding the preparatory work prior to the commencement of legal proceedings.[31] Barristers could also become judges, while members of the lower branches of the profession, such as solicitors, could not.[32]

Increased professionalization and organization of the legal trade occurred in 1830, with the establishment of the Law Society of Ireland at Inns Quay, Dublin. Initially, the society functioned as a club and membership was restricted only to those who had been approved of by the committee.[33] The society encouraged solicitors 'to raise and support themselves in the rank and estimation to which they are entitled'.[34] This perceived entitlement was founded on the contemporary assumption that the profession had evolved from a 'status professionalism' – that is, one based primarily on social class – to a specialty grounded in training and specific skills or 'occupational professionalism'.[35] As part of the expanding world of professions, solicitors appeared to fit into both Marshall's idea of the professions as 'gentlemanly occupations' (that is leisurely pursuits free from excessive labour), and Spring's argument that 'laborious activity' was the hallmark of newly emerging professions.[36]

A prerequisite to any analysis of solicitors as elites in mid-nineteenth-century Ireland is a discussion of the variety of 'legal' systems that were in operation at this time. Formal legal channels such as the petty sessions, quarter sessions and assizes followed the British common law code, while – in the eyes of the tenantry at least – estate legal processes operated according to notions of 'justice'. Both systems worked concurrently, sometimes even in collaboration, were accessible to all tenants and were often administered by members of the landed class. Landlords and agents alike functioned as magistrates during this period. Landlords such as Howe Peter Browne, second marquess of Sligo, William Sydney Clements, third earl of Leitrim, Evelyn Philip Shirley and Evelyn Charles Shirley occupied this powerful position alongside such land agents as Sandy Mitchell and John T. Gibbings on the Shirley Estate and Robert Powell on the Westport Estate. Through the official system, serious criminal offences, such as rape, murder and treason, were dealt with by the court of assize, while minor crimes remained under the remit of the petty sessions.[37] Within estate

1789–1922 (Naas, Co. Kildare, 1986), p. 5. **30** Brockliss, 'The professions and national identity', pp 16–17. **31** Hogan, 'The profession before the charter of 1852', p. 21. **32** Reader, *The middle classes*, p. 8. **33** Hogan, 'The profession before the charter of 1852', p. 31. **34** Hogan, *The legal profession in Ireland*, p. 7; Eamonn G. Hall & Daire Hogan, 'The law society of Ireland, 1852–2002: portrait of a profession', http://www.ehall.ie/ celebration.html, accessed 12 May 2011. **35** Phyllis S. Lachs, 'A study of a professional elite: Anglo-Jewish barristers in the nineteenth century', *Jewish Social Studies*, 44:2 (spring 1982), 125–34 at 125. **36** Spring, *The English landed estate*, pp 55–6. **37** Raymond Byrne and J. Paul McCutcheon, *The Irish legal system* (Dublin, 2002), pp 41–2.

boundaries, law and order was dispensed through the manor courts – consisting of the court baron and the court leet – and through the employment of an arbitration process. Although an overlapping of the remit of both courts occurred, the court baron primarily handled petty actions such as small debts and trespass cases, while the court leet had jurisdiction over criminal offences and issues related to the running of the estate.[38] Estate arbitration procedures were also used as a means of dispute settlement between tenants. In this instance, two or three tenants selected by the estate authorities as arbitrators determined the resolutions or 'awards' between the opposing parties, all of which had to be approved of by the land agent.[39] Arbitrations generally issued awards with respect to disputes over land and passes, family disagreements, and in instances where tenants disobeyed the previous orders of the land agent.[40] Although solicitors did not play a role in such primitive estate law and order arrangements, the simultaneous existence of two law-enforcement agencies partially diminished the elitism of solicitorship. As noted earlier, estate-authorized judicial tasks were frequently executed by the land agent and bailiff who adopted a similar role to a solicitor. Fundamentally, it was through their involvement with the estate as representatives of official legal channels that solicitors could assert a more credible claim to move within elite circles in nineteenth-century Ireland.

The estate employed a range of local, national and international solicitors for personal, familial and estate matters. Individual landed records not only contain correspondence from solicitors employed by the estate, but also solicitor correspondence for opposing parties. Estates frequently employed local solicitors for tasks such as ejectment proceedings and for cases brought against small tenants in the Petty and Quarter Sessions courts. On the Westport Estate, the marquess was represented locally by Manus Lewis O'Donel and Malachy Kelly, both of Castlebar; the Leitrim Estate by R.J. Slack, Carrick on Shannon, Co. Leitrim, and the Farnham Estate by Messrs Allen & Halpin, Cavan town.[41] Solicitors from the capital were also employed by provincial estates during this period. John William Browne, second son of the landlord Dominick Browne of Ashford, Cong and Kilskeagh, Co. Galway, not only operated as a solicitor for the Westport Estate from 16 Kildare St., Dublin; he also acted as the estate's agent on their Co. Galway holding and was a landlord in his own right, having bought the lease of Mount Kelly Estate, Galway.[42] The Leitrim Estate

38 Richard J. McMahon, 'The courts of the petty sessions and law in pre-Famine Galway' (MA, UCG, 1999), pp 14–15.   **39** Award in the case of Edward Gartlan and Phil McBride, 4 Sept.1843, Shirley Papers, PRONI D3531/P/2.   **40** 'Cases which require particular attention by new agent'; letter to Mr Morant Esq. from Michal [*sic*] Connor and Henry Reburn, 29 Jan. 1846 D3531/M/6/1; 'The award of James & John McCabe and promissory note for £6 9*s*.': Garret Byrnes & Michael Swinburn to W.S. Trench, 9 Apr. 1844 D3531/P/1; award to James and Francis McEntee by Mr Nathaniel Eakins of Shanco and Samuel Eakins of Mullycroghery, 5 Jul. 1845, Shirley Papers, PRONI D3531/P/2.   **41** The Leitrim estate also received correspondence from the following local solicitors: Osborne and Co., Milford, Co. Donegal, representing the Donegal estates.   **42** Estate: Browne (Coolaran, Kilskeagh and Mountkelly), Landed Estates Database, NUI Galway,

employed Dublin solicitors Johnston Teevan, 50 Middle Abbey St. and S.S. and E. Reeves and Sons, 51 Merrion Square East, the latter belonging to the Reeves landed family, Besborough, Co. Clare.[43] These examples reveal the intricate bond that frequently existed between the legal profession and landed families. Irish estates also employed legal teams from England. A firm of solicitors named Bray and Warrens, 57 Great Russell St., Bloomsbury, London, began to represent the Leitrim Estate in 1833. Consequently, landlords were oftentimes poised precariously between an old feudalistic world of manor courts and arbitration processes and a modern world dominated by an increasingly assertive British common law code. Prime players in bridging this gap were solicitors.

In accordance with the aphorism 'knowledge is power', solicitors' claims to elitism rested on their expertise of legal matters during a period in which Irish land-lords operated in, as Dooley suggested, a legal minefield.[44] In order to navigate more propitiously through such a precarious environment, many Big Houses had on their shelves a copy of Thomas De Moleyns Esq., QC, *The landowner's and agent's practical guide* (1858). An 1860 edition exists in the Westport Papers.[45] The book provided instruction on 'the new death duties – estate duty and settlement estate duty' (ch. 1); 'of leases generally' (ch. 7); 'minor tenancies and notices to quit' (ch. 14); 'claims for improvements and disturbance' (ch. 16); 'the Ulster tenant-right custom' (ch. 17); and 'ordinary actions between landlord and tenant' (ch. 20).[46] Oftentimes, the relation-ship between landlords and conventional law was a complicated one. Its course appears to have been influenced to some extent by the current landlord's own proclivity. A desire to avoid 'legal warfare' or simply a wish 'not to interfere' proved common place.[47] The seventh Baron Farnham customarily discouraged litigation among his tenants and a 'very litigious' individual would not be viewed favourably in the process of land applications.[48] Yet his predecessor, the fifth baron, frequently redirected tenants to attend the petty sessions during the 1830s.[49] He appeared to hold fast to a belief that certain matters must be settled by the law.[50] Ignorance of the

http://landedestates.nuigalway.ie:8080/LandedEstates/jsp/estate-show.jsp?id=1011, accessed 24 May 2011. **43** Estate: Reeves (Besborough), Landed Estates Database, accessed 24 May 2011. The Leitrim Papers also contain correspondence from the following Dublin-based solicitors: Beauchamp and Orr, 5 Foster Place, Dublin, representing Col. H.T. Clements (1879) and Newtown Gore estate; Thomas Tighe Mecredy and sons, 28 Westmoreland Street, Dublin, representing John Madden; John R. Peart, 38 St Stephen's Green, Dublin, representing the Irish Land Commission. **44** Dooley, *The Big Houses and landed estates of Ireland*, p. 69. **45** Westport Papers, NLI MS 41,030/3; Thomas de Moleyns esq. QC, *The landowner's and agent's practical guide*, ed. Albert W. Quill and F. Pollock Hamilton (8th ed. Dublin, 1899), p. viii. **46** de Moleyns, *The landowner's and agent's practical guide*, pp xi–xviii. **47** Letter from John Faris, Manorhamilton, to W.S. Clements, third earl of Leitrim, Sunday: Leitrim Papers, NLI MS 33,826(4). **48** Frans Hamilton, 1843; John Hogg, 1843; Alexd McDowell, 1858, Farnham Papers, NLI MS 3118. **49** John Heslip – to compel a person to give evidence relative to his horse which was stolen – 1832; Pat Magaghran – not paid for work done – 1835; Patrick Brady – violent attack – 1835, Farnham Papers, NLI MS 3117. **50** Geo. Trelford Jr – requesting advice having been unjustly distrained by the priest of

legalities of a range of matters may have propelled many landowners to adopt such a course. Even when acting as magistrates, confusion sometimes existed in landed circles with respect to official legal duties. In 1831, the second marquess of Sligo sought 'information of the magistrates' instructions as to the nature of offences which should be sent for trial to the quarter sessions'.[51] From a tenant viewpoint, pursuit of due legal process frequently required the financial backing and sometimes even the blessings of the landlord.[52] Consequently, it would appear that landlords increasingly turned to solicitors in the knowledge that they were the better trained and equipped persons to deal with pressing legal matters. At the same time, the law began to offer the tenant population increased rights. Therefore, it was imperative that the estate use official legal channels to the best of its advantage. It was in such instances that solicitors proved indispensible to estate authorities. Although averse to litigious tenants, Baron Farnham showed a distinct propensity himself towards official law, receiving ample advice from his 'law agent'.[53] Solicitors were perceived by the Shirley authorities as the 'proper persons' to have responsibility for serving processes and executing decrees.[54] With respect to estate management, solicitors were to the fore in the protection of long-established property rights. Malcomson noted how W.S. Clements 'spent an unascertainable, but large, amount on lawsuits to defend and enforce his property rights'.[55]

The solicitors' knowledge of the law, and hence his claim to intellectual elitism, ultimately came to the fore in the rudimentary, banal, yet pertinent legal procedures and protocol that occupied the professional's daily life. While solicitors were involved in a range of tasks with respect to the estate, such as the construction of marriage settlements and the enfranchisement of property, it was above all in the area of dispute resolution that they made their mark. An examination of the solicitor's role in estate dispute resolution not only reveals much with respect to the solicitor's working relationship with the landlord, but also sheds significant light on the landed estate's role with respect to order in its hinterlands. It was the responsibility of the solicitor to find errors in legal papers in order to provide a stronger case for his client. The negotiation, construction and copying of leases in particular occupied a significant amount of the solicitor's time. Baron Farnham's rights were protected with respect to the lease of Derryheen due to the solicitor noting how 'the document of the 5

Cavan – I can not interfere ... 1832; John Sheridan – for justice – cannot interfere as the matter is referred to the petty sessions, 1838; Rev [Eugene?] Reilly (p.p.) – In favour of Terence Boylan & Delaney ... I cannot interfere in the case as it involves much legal difficulty, 1845. Farnham Papers, NLI MS 3,117–18. **51** Marquis of Sligo's correspondence, 173–216 (1830–4), letter from E.G. Stanley, Dublin Castle, to Howe Peter, second marquess of Sligo, 18 Jan. 1831, Trinity College Dublin [TCD] MS 6403. **52** Farnham Papers, NLI MS 3,117–18, David Galligan, 1836; Judith Stratford, 1837; Noble Paget, 1843; Pat Brady, 1836; George Lee, 1839. **53** Farnham Papers, NLI MS 3,118, John Browne, 1840; Thomas O'Connor, 1852; Mr Lindsay, 1858. **54** 'Copy of part of Mr Smith's letter', 5 May 1843, Shirley Papers, PRONI D3531/C/3/5. **55** A.P.W. Malcomson, *Virtues of a wicked earl: the life and legend of William Sydney Clements, third earl of Leitrim, 1806–78* (Dublin, 2008), p. 367.

April 1823 is not signed or sealed nor does it purport to be delivered by the granting party, each of these matters is an essential requisite to its validity as a deed'.[56] Consequently, solicitors through their mastery of the law could dismantle the credibility of a significant legal document and in turn maintain estate order. Solicitors were also required to disseminate pertinent knowledge to estate authorities in order to strengthen their chances of success in the courts. Information on ejectment procedures, such as the document entitled 'instructions for the due and correct service of the ejectments', was circulated to estate officials on the Westport Estate. This important script outlined the exact terminology to employ when serving such a document.[57] Express emphasis was noted to 'observe particularly that to give a copy to anyone else save to the tenant himself, anywhere or to his wife ... son, daughter (over sixteen) or servant in the dwelling house of the tenant' was legally required for the law to take its course.[58] The solicitor was also responsible for the censure and phraseology of written correspondence between opposing parties. At first glance, this role may appear somewhat trite. Yet its magnitude was revealed much to the chagrin of James Dombrain and his solicitors Messrs Barrington in 1853.[59] Dombrain had written a letter in jest to the third marquess of Sligo, which he forwarded to his solicitor as was customary practice. In error, this letter was passed on by his solicitor to the marquess, who received the correspondence with much ire. He blamed both Dombrain and his solicitor for the unfortunate event, adding that 'when he & you correspond in such terms you should both be careful how to address the letters'.[60] Although it was subsequently claimed that the letter had been written in a 'jocular manner' and was not intended for the recipient, the controversy that arose from its circulation merely underlined the importance of vigilance and care required in legal correspondence.[61]

Although seeming to occupy an elite position with respect to their clientele, it would appear that oftentimes the solicitor had to defer to Queen's Counsel for advice and recommendations before proceeding with certain cases.[62] As one solic-

56 Copy opinion of John Brooke, Esq. (Queen's Counsel), 3 Feb. 1864: Farnham Papers, NLI MS 41,148/6. **57** Westport Papers, NLI MS 40,978/8. **58** Ibid. **59** Ibid., NLI MS 40,968/1, letter from Sir James Dombrain, 36 Leeson Street, Dublin, to the third marquess of Sligo, 14 May 1853; Westport Papers, NLI MS 40, 968/1, letter from Sir James Dombrain, 36 Leeson Street, Dublin, to the third marquess of Sligo, 1 Jun. 1853. **60** Westport Papers, NLI MS 40,968/1, Letter from the third marquess of Sligo, London, to [James Dombrain?], 6 Jul. 1853. **61** Westport Papers, NLI MS 40,968/1, Letter from Sir James Dombrain, Dublin (solicitors: Messers Barrington, 10 Ely Place) to the third marquess of Sligo (solicitor: F. Sutton esq.), 5 Jul. 1853. **62** Westport Papers, NLI MS 41,003/12, letter from Frederick Sutton, solicitor, 22 Harcourt Street, Dublin, to J. Sidney Smith esq., Westport, 14 Dec. 1859; Farnham Papers, NLI MS 41,148/6, Letter from Jas. Armstrong, 160 Lower Gloucester Street, Dublin, to Henry Maxwell, seventh Baron Farnham, regarding lease of Derryheen, parish of Urney, 4 Feb. 1864; Westport Papers, NLI MS 40,976/13, petitioner the marquis of Sligo and respondent Revd Brownlow Lynch, cause petition under the Court of Chancery Ireland Regulation Act (1850), instructions to accompany draft petition in this case, on behalf of Lord Sligo (coupled with a noted signed John Sidney Smith, Westport, 24 Oct.

itor told a select committee of the House of Commons in 1846, 'if there are deeds of very great magnitude, such as marriage settlements and wills ... we then have the aid of counsel'.[63] John William Browne, the marquess of Sligo's solicitor, claimed how he did 'nothing but with the advice of counsel and nothing discreditable to you'.[64] However, the advice of counsel was not always blindly followed by solicitors. On the Drapers' estate, counsel's opinion was sought in relation to the refusal of the dismissed agent to hand over 'all letters addressed to him in his official capacity by the clerk of the company, on the ground that they were his private property'.[65] The case was accordingly submitted to Colquhoun, QC, whose conclusion that the agent was legally justified in removing the letters was met by 'surprise' by both the deputation and Mr Glover, the solicitor. They subsequently arranged a further inquiry into the matter.[66] This example reveals how landlords sometimes resorted to the law in employee disputes. The marquess of Sligo also sought professional legal assistance with respect to the behaviour of two of his land agents, namely George Clendining Junior in 1847 and George Hildebrand in 1851. Both agents were dismissed over monetary issues – Clendining's bankruptcy to the tune of £3,500 and Hildebrand's poor account keeping. With respect to the latter, the court of chancery found that Hildebrand was overcharging the marquess through the concealment of loans from various persons and payments made on the land improvement account.

An exploration of elitism inevitably includes an examination of human relations. Business relationships not only revolve around and are influenced by social markers such as status, wealth, religious affiliation and educational levels attained, but are also shaped by the temperament and character of the prime players involved. This reality, coupled with the competency and ability displayed by the legal professional, would have significantly influenced and altered the dynamic in the dialogic relationship between the representative of the landed estate and the solicitor. Regarding solicitor–land agent relations, many solicitors felt frustrated by what they perceived as incompetence displayed on the part of land agents. Ignatius Kelly, Castlebar, and solicitor to the Westport Estate, was wont to highlight to the agent J. Sidney Smith how informalities and inattention to detail were to be avoided.[67] Solicitors often had to provide land agents with simple legal training to ensure that proper procedures were adhered to. Yet surviving correspondence between solicitors and agents also suggests a more equal social footing between the two groups of estate employees.

1857, to apply at once for an injunction to restrain tenant), plus note by Buchanan, 23 North Frederick Street, 3 Nov. 1857. **63** Hogan, *The legal profession in Ireland*, p. 1. **64** Marquis of Sligo's correspondence, 173–216 (1830–4), Letter from John William Browne, 16 Kildare Street, Dublin, to Howe Peter, second marquess of Sligo, 23 Dec. 1839. TCD MSS 6403. **65** Report of the deputation of the court of assistants of the Drapers' Company appointed to visit the company's Irish estates in the year 1881, Microfilm, acc. 16727, mic617, reel 24, D3632/D/1/13, Drapers' Hall, London, p. 9. **66** Report of the deputation of the court of assistants, D3632/D/1/13, pp 9–10. **67** Westport Papers, NLI MS 41,003/12, letter from Ignatius Kelly, solicitor, Court House Ballina, to J. Sidney Smith esq., 8 Jan. 1859; 24 May 1859.

Some agents, like Charles Magee on the Whyte Estate in Co. Down, even implored the landlord not to be so hard, exacting and even suspicious of the solicitor's motives with respect to estate affairs, claiming how he always sought to save the landlord expense and trouble at every opportunity.[68] Solicitors had to receive final approval from the land agent before acting (though, of course, such consent may have been subtly influenced by the solicitor himself).[69] For example, permission was required from the land agent prior to obtaining warrants.[70] Whether this behaviour pointed more towards the niceties of protocol and tradition, or if the solicitor was actually at the behest of the agent, however, is unclear. An examination of solicitor–landlord relations may shed some light on the matter.

The professional relationship between landlords and solicitors fundamentally revolved around trust, with landlords frequently placing important estate decisions in the hands of these men. In turn, a collaborative business relationship appeared to exist between the two. In 1853, the third marquess of Sligo left the decision to his solicitor, Sutton, to 'send or not as you think fit' correspondence he had drafted to his legal opponent.[71] Landlords often deferred to their learned friends on specific legal matters. Leitrim's solicitor, John Faris, Manorhamilton, advised the landlord

> to postpone the service of notice to quit on Rogan, until after the election, as if now served, Rogan would make use of it with the Roman Catholic tenants of your lordships as an argument to induce them to vote against your candidate.[72]

Solicitors also worked hard on behalf of the estate, amending, reworking and rewording legal documents to ensure the best possible scenario for their clients should issues arise in the future.[73] Solicitors respected the decisions made by their employers on certain issues, such as refraining from enacting legal proceedings should peaceful possession of a holding be possible and avoiding legal recourse during periods not deemed 'judicious'.[74] These instances also highlight reluctance on the part of the estate to pursue redress through official legal channels. Ultimately, the decision and power whether to act legally or not appeared to rest with the landlord. John William Browne asserted to the marquess of Sligo: 'I have hitherto followed your instructions and I will continue to do so until I receive your orders to the contrary' and 'I will not stop without your orders'.[75] In 1859, solicitor Kelly claimed

68 Whyte Papers, D2918/3/7/101–75, letter from Charles Magee, Banbridge, to N.C. Whyte esq., 27 Jan. 1844. **69** Westport Papers, NLI MS 41,003/12, letter from Ignatius Kelly, solicitor, Castlebar, to J. Sidney Smith esq., 29 Apr. 1859. **70** Ibid., 30 Apr. 1859. **71** Westport Papers, NLI MS 40,968/1, letter from the third marquess of Sligo, London, to Sutton, 6 Jul. 1853. **72** Leitrim Papers, NLI MS 33,826(4), letter from John Faris, Manorhamilton, to W.S. Clements, third earl of Leitrim, Sunday. **73** Westport Papers, NLI MS 40,969/2, Lord Sligo and Peter D. Browne, copy of notice respecting lease, Frederick Sutton, 22 Harcourt Street, 24 Aug. 1858. **74** Report of the deputation of the court of assistants, D3632/D/1/12, p. 24; D3632/D/1/13, p. 10. **75** TCD Special Collections; MSS

how he owed 'a deep debt of gratitude to every member of Westport House, which I feel I never can repay'.[76] Therefore, the balance of power in business transactions between the estate as represented by the landlord and land agent and the solicitor branch of the legal profession appeared to rest with the former during the period under study.

As noted earlier, the relationship between the estate and the law – played out most notably in relations between landlord and solicitor or solicitor-agent – was an intricate, multi-layered and constantly evolving one. Changes initiated from Westminster also contributed to the complexity of the relationship. Landlords' control of local legal official systems through the role of magistrate, which was of immense significance in the early part of the century, was beginning to wane following the introduction of stipendiary magistrates.[77] Crossman found that 'the number of stipendiaries rose from 11 in 1831 to 54 in 1839 and continued to increase, reaching a total of 73 in 1860', remaining at this level until the turn of the century.[78] The tendency to appoint lawyers and solicitors to vacant land agent positions on Irish estates appeared to continue right up to 1870.[79] At the close of the century, however, this trend seemed to be diminishing, with H.H. Smith, agent to the marquess of Lansdowne, noting in 1898 how solicitor-agents had begun to decline in number from 1870. He attributed this reduction to the marked growth in estate business and the establishment of the Institution of Surveyors in 1868. The latter served as a training ground for professional land agents.[80] The cessation of the dual role of land agent and solicitor meant that landlords lost the power they exerted over these individuals in their capacity as estate employees. The job of the solicitor to defend the property rights of the landlord was gradually diminishing following the introduction of a series of pieces of legislation specifically directed at the estate. The Encumbered Estates Acts of 1848 and 1849 – which legally made the process of selling heavily indebted estates more straightforward – and the tenant purchase initiatives in the 1870, 1881 and 1885 land acts provided the incentive for many landed proprietors to sell their estates. Consequently, the solicitor's fundamental role in the management of estate relations through assisting the landlord maintain his landed rights and negotiating tenurial terms with the tenantry was no longer required.[81]

As a professional grouping, by the mid-nineteenth century, solicitors on the whole appeared to have risen in the ranks of English society with some members receiving knighthoods, novelists proclaiming their respectability and commendations

6403, marquis of Sligo's correspondence, 173–216 (1830–4), letter from John William Browne, 16 Kildare Street, Dublin, to Howe Peter, second marquess of Sligo, 23 Dec. 1839. **76** Westport Papers, NLI MS 41,003/12, letter from Ignatius Kelly, solicitor, to J. Sidney Smith esq., 24 Aug. 1859. **77** Virginia Crossman, *Local government in nineteenth-century Ireland* (Belfast, 1994), p. 21. **78** Ibid., p. 22. **79** Terence A.M. Dooley, 'Estate ownership and management in nineteenth- and early twentieth-century Ireland', 1–14 at 1–4, http://www.aughty.org/pdf/estate_own_manage.pdf, accessed 28 Nov. 2011. **80** Spring, *The English landed estate*, p. 67. **81** Namely the Landlord & Tenant (Ireland) Act (1870); the Land Law (Ireland) Act (1881), and the Purchase of Land (Ireland) Act (1885).

appearing in such notable publications as *Saturday Review* and *The Times*.[82] With an expansion in the number of new entrants to the profession, along with a growing repertoire of duties to perform, it would seem as if the presence and power of solicitors was to become a permanent fixture of modern society. In 1896, such developments were even believed to suggest 'the operation of natural law, so that now a solicitor may be called upon to advise on any incident affecting the person, the property, or the reputation of men'.[83] An increasingly socially diverse legal clientele – including members of the tenantry – which also was expanding in number – signalled a growing public perception in the indispensability of the solicitor.[84] A comment made in 1887 revealed how pervasive the solicitor's presence had become in the countryside: 'we are sure to meet clients on the road, and seldom return from one of these expeditions without having picked up some new business or advances some matter already in hand'.[85]

Although fulfilling some of the criteria of new model professions, being 'a formal qualifying and disciplinary association, [possessing] specialized knowledge [and] a self-conscious professional identity', solicitorship during this period continued to function within the realm of proto-modern professions.[86] Consequently, if a solicitor's claims to membership of elite society rested solely on the advantage of professional training, it would appear a rather tenuous one indeed. Changes in the legislature from the 1870s, such as 'the nullification of the principle that a barrister's fee is an honorarium and not a wage', also undermined the elitism of this branch of the legal professional with respect to their clients.[87] In *The Irish establishment, 1879–1914*, Fergus Campbell argued that the Irish establishment corresponded more readily with the classical elite model rather than with its democratic counterpart. The former characterized elite society as 'all-powerful, "closed", homogenous, wealthy, and not representative of the society which it dominates', while the latter recognized elite society as 'diverse, recruitment is open, and absolute power is restricted by various constraining factors'.[88] Solicitors, it seems, fall into the democratic elite theory's category of sub-elite in its three-tiered division of society. Campbell highlighted how democratic elite theory 'takes into consideration the influence of middle-ranking members of elite groups (sub-elites) on the leadership, and also recognizes the potential influence of the public on elite decision-making'.[89] At the level of the estate at any rate, the law, which provided solicitors with perhaps a façade of elitism, in practice operated as a nexus of power between landlords, land agents, solicitors and Queen's Counsel. As part of the 'rising middle class', solicitors began

82 Ibid., p. 61.   **83** Christian, *A short history of solicitors*, p. 236.   **84** Daniel Duman, 'Pathway to professionalism: the English bar in the eighteenth and nineteenth centuries', *Journal of Social History*, 13:4 (summer 1980), 615–28 at 617, http://www.jstor.org/stable/3787436, accessed 28 May 2011. **85** Alfred B. Major (solicitor), *Legal sketches* (Montreal, 1887), pp 38–9, http://www.archive.org/stream/legalsketchesoomajouoft#page/n5/mode/2up, accessed 30 Nov. 2011.   **86** Duman, 'Pathway to professionalism', 615.   **87** Ibid., 622.   **88** Fergus Campbell, *The Irish establishment, 1879–1914* (Oxford, 2009), pp 312–13.   **89** Campbell, *The Irish establishment*, pp 11–12.

to embody and represent a more equitable, accessible and increasingly powerful common law system in contrast to estate-controlled systems of justice. In mid-nineteenth-century rural Irish society, 'gentlemen practisers' or solicitors operated primarily as sub-elites; but, as alluded to earlier, such categorizations never remain static.

'The most perfect specimen of civilised nature': the Shannon Estuary Group – elite theory and practice

MATTHEW POTTER

The purpose of this essay is to examine a small but influential group within the Irish landlord caste with reference to elite theory. During Hobsbawm's 'long nineteenth century' (1789–1914), Limerick and Clare produced a remarkable and closely knit coterie of enlightened gentlemen who practiced *noblesse oblige* on a large scale, over several generations in a wide geographic area. In 1988, David Fitzpatrick first drew attention to them and they formed the subject matter of a dissertation by Jennifer Ridden in 1998.[1] As they were without a useful collective term, and as they generally had their principal residences at the mouth of the River Shannon, they have been recently dubbed the 'Shannon Estuary Group' by the present author.[2] The principal families of the group were the Perys of Dromore; the Wyndham-Quins of Adare; the Spring Rices of Mount Trenchard; the Monsells of Tervoe; the de Veres of Curragh Chase; the O'Briens of Dromoland and the O'Briens of Cratloe Woods House. This circle may have represented the Irish landlord class at its best, at least according to some observers. In 1840, the English author, educationalist and cleric, William Sewell, who had become a close friend of leading members of the group, wrote that 'an Irish gentleman, well born, well educated, and with his natural tendencies modified by English associations is perhaps one of the most perfect specimen of civilised nature'.[3]

The origins of the Shannon Estuary Group (SEG) as a progressive and reforming circle can be traced to the careers of Edmond Sexton Pery (1719–1806), MP for Limerick city (1760–85), and John Jebb (1775–1833), Church of Ireland bishop of Limerick (1822–33). Georgian Limerick was ruled by successive ascendancy families that dominated the corporation by excluding most Protestants as well as all Catholics from the political life of the city. However, the eighteenth-century economic boom created a prosperous Catholic and Nonconformist mercantile elite, which battled the Smyth and Vereker family (the most powerful and durable of the ruling cliques) for many decades. Pery, a patriot who supported legislative independence for Ireland and

1 See David Fitzpatrick, 'Thomas Spring Rice and the peopling of Australia', *The Old Limerick Journal*, 23 (spring 1988), 39–49; Jennifer Ridden, 'Making good citizens: national identity, religion and liberalism among the Irish elite, *c.*1800–1850' (PhD, U. London, 1998). 2 Matthew Potter, *William Monsell of Tervoe, 1812–94: Catholic Unionist, Anglo-Irishman* (Dublin, 2009), p. 6. 3 William Sewell, 'Romanism in Ireland', *Quarterly Review*, 67:133 (Dec. 1840), 121.

Catholic relief, allied himself with the local 'popular' elements as much to disoblige the Smyth and Vereker clique as for ideological reasons. After 1800, these disputes were framed by the emergence of a new two-party system in Britain and Ireland, with Limerick Corporation, led by Lord Gort, adhering to the Tories, while the Pery family, Thomas Spring Rice and the merchant elite supported the Whigs. The question of Catholic Emancipation also divided the parties, with the Smyths and Verekers against and their opponents largely in favour.[4]

If Sexton Pery was the political founder of the SEG, Bishop John Jebb may be described as its religious exemplar. Within the group was a sub-division sometimes known as the Tervoe convert set, consisting of William Monsell, the third earl of Dunraven and the three de Vere brothers. All of them had been followers of the Oxford Movement, whose members wished to restore and revive the Church of England by emphasizing the elements in it that would justify its claim to be the ancient, apostolic and Catholic Church. They emphasized the importance of Apostolic Succession, the sacraments and the central position of communion in the church service.[5] These tenets were the elements in Anglicanism that most resembled the Roman Catholic position, but after working so diligently to revive Anglicanism, many of its leaders, including the most prominent, John Henry Newman, eventually became Roman Catholics.[6] The Oxford Movement in Ireland was very weak, because the Church of Ireland, surrounded by a sea of Catholicism, was predominantly Low Church and more inclined to stress its Protestantism than the relatively more confident and secure Church of England.[7] However, there was also an old High Church tradition within the Church of Ireland which had revived in the early nineteenth century. Its best known exponent was Bishop Jebb, under whose rule 'the diocese of Limerick became a High Church centre for both clergy and laity'.[8] Though opposed to Catholic Emancipation, Jebb was a political and religious moderate who enjoyed good relations with his Catholic colleagues and opposed the Second Reformation and it is due to this heritage that Co. Limerick saw such a positive response to the Oxford Movement.[9]

The exercise of a local hegemony by the SEG was not an exceptional experience, or so elite theory would have it. Geraint Parry writes that 'the core of the elitist doctrine is that there exists in any society a minority of the population which takes the major decisions in the society'.[10] The Italian or classical school of elitists founded by Gaetano Mosca and Vilfredo Paredo did not merely assert that every society is divided between a small dominant minority and a large dominated majority but that

4 See Matthew Potter, *The government and the people of Limerick: the history of Limerick Corporation/City Council, 1197–2006* (Limerick, 2006), pp 258–79.   5 Olive Brose, *Church and parliament: the reshaping of the Church of England, 1828–1860* (Oxford, 1959).   6 David Newsome, *The convert cardinals: Newman and Manning* (London, 1993).   7 Peter Nockles, 'Church or Protestant sect? The Church of Ireland, high churchmanship and the Oxford Movement, 1822–1869', *Historical Journal*, 41 (1998), 457–93.   8 Alan Acheson, *A history of the Church of Ireland, 1691–1996* (Dublin, 1997), p. 153.   9 For Jebb, see Desmond McCabe, 'John Jebb (1775–1833)', *DIB*.   10 Geraint Parry, *Political elites* (London, 1969), p. 30.

this was an inevitable and unalterable situation; what Robert Michels called the 'iron law of oligarchy'.[11] Different assets were held to explain the ascendancy of elites: organizational abilities (Mosca and Michels); a particular psychological profile leading to high achievement (Pareto); control of economic resources (James Burnham); and control over important institutions such as government, big business and the armed forces (C. Wright Mills). Classical elite theory postulated that an elite must be united and self-aware, possessing what James Meisel described as the 'three Cs': consciousness of being part of a group; coherence; and conspiracy, defined in this instance as a 'common will to action'.[12] Democratic or pluralist elite theory modified classical elitism by positing the existence of several groups, competing in a democratic system and thus dependant on the masses for support in much the same way as discussed by Kevin Mc Kenna earlier in this volume in relation to the 'deferential dialectic'. This pluralist elite need not be homogenous; it can accommodate conflicting views in many areas (while adhering to certain basic beliefs); and must be able to renew itself by recruiting new members or even entire sub-groups, often on merit from a wide socio-economic base. However, failure to do so could result in the gradual or even violent displacement of the old elite by a new one. All elites survived due to the apathy and deference of the majority as well as the latter's acceptance of (or at least acquiescence in) elite ideology, while few could prevail against a loss of legitimacy in the eyes of the majority.[13]

Before 1800, the Perys had been the most politically powerful family of the SEG and possessed the most senior peerage (their principal title, earl of Limerick, dated to 1803), but became largely peripheral figures in the nineteenth century. In the 1870s, their estates consisted of 4,083 acres in Co. Limerick, 1,550 acres in Co. Clare and 76 acres in Co. Cork. In addition, the Perys owned the largest estate within the borough boundary of Limerick, later known as Newtown Pery, which yielded a large income and made them one of the most influential families in the city. The head of the family in the mid-eighteenth century was Edmond Sexton Pery, who has been described as 'the most notable Limerickman of all time, and also its greatest benefactor'.[14] This accolade is due to his influence on the history of the city, arguably greater than that of any other single individual, as he was largely responsible for the creation of the present Georgian core of Limerick, named Newtown Pery in his honour. In addition to his local primacy, Pery's period as Speaker of the House of Commons (1771–85) made him one of Ireland's most powerful men.[15] His nephew,

11 See T.B. Bottomore, *Elites and society* (2nd ed., London, 1993) and John Scott, *The sociology of elites: the study of elites* (Cheltenham, 1990). **12** Parry, *Political elites*, pp 30–63. **13** Eva Etzioni-Halevy, *Classes and elites in democracy and democratization: a collection of readings* (London, 1997); Ilkka Roustetsaari, 'Coexistence of elites and democracy in an information society' at http//www.Hicsocial.org/Socia12003Proceedings. **14** Kevin Hannan, 'The rich inheritance of a Limerick mayor' in David Lee (ed.), *Remembering Limerick: historical essays celebrating the 800th anniversary of Limerick's first charter granted in 1197* (Limerick, 1997), p. 112. **15** For Speaker Pery, see A.P.W. Malcomson, 'Speaker Pery and the Pery Papers', *North Munster Antiquarian Journal*, 21 (1973–4), 33–60; David Huddelston, 'Edmond Sexton

Edmond Henry (1758–1844), also sat for Limerick city (1785–94) and in 1803 was created the first earl of Limerick. After the Act of Union, the Perys ceased to be resident in Ireland, and became unpopular absentees for over sixty years, though the first earl sat as an Irish representative peer (1800–44). Even after they made Ireland their principal residence again in the 1860s, with the construction of Dromore Castle near Pallaskenry, Co. Limerick, they continued to be relatively inactive politically until the 1890s, when the third earl (1840–96) served as a Conservative whip and member of the British Privy Council.[16]

The Wyndham-Quins held the title earl of Dunraven for nearly two centuries (1822–2011) and were the wealthiest family in the group. In the 1870s, the fourth earl was reputed to be one of the richest earls in the United Kingdom, with estates totalling 39,755 acres, of which 23,751 were in Glamorganshire, and 14,298 were in Co. Limerick. Their principal Irish seat was Adare Manor, set in the picturesque village of Adare, about ten miles from Tervoe. Besides their immense estates in Limerick and Glamorganshire, they owned land in Kerry, Clare and Gloucestershire. Their other principal residences were Dunraven Castle, near Bridgend in Glamorganshire (from which they took their principal title), and Clearwell Court, Gloucestershire. The most significant members of the family were the third earl, Edwin Richard Windham Wyndham-Quin (1812–71) and his son the fourth earl, Windham Thomas Wyndham-Quin (1841–1926).[17]

The Spring Rice family resided at Mount Trenchard, just outside Foynes, Co. Limerick, and since 1839 have held the title of Baron Monteagle of Brandon. In the 1870s, the family estates consisted of 6,445 acres in Co. Limerick and 2,310 acres in Co. Kerry. The most prominent member of the family was Thomas Spring Rice (1790–1866), who was one of the most significant Irish political figures of the nineteenth century. Married to a daughter of the first Lord Limerick, he sat successively as MP for Limerick city (1820–32) and Cambridge (1832–9) and was later created the first Baron Monteagle. He was one of the leading members of the Whig Party for over a decade, and held a number of senior government posts (parliamentary secretary to the treasury 1830–34; secretary of state for war and the colonies 1834), before his career culminated in a term as chancellor of the exchequer (1835–9).[18]

The Monsells resided at Tervoe House (fig. 6.1), about five miles from Limerick city, and in 1876 their estates in Cos Limerick and Clare comprised 2,710. The family

Pery, Viscount Pery (1719–1806)', in *ODNB*. **16** Malcomson, 'Speaker Pery and the Pery Papers', 55, n. 44. **17** The Dunravens have been the subject of much recent research: Odette Clarke, 'Caroline Wyndham-Quin, countess of Dunraven (1790–1870): an analysis of her discursive and material legacy' (PhD, Limerick, 2010); Theresa Hereward-Ryan, 'An examination of the life of Edwin Wyndham Quin, third earl of Dunraven, 1812–71' (PhD, Limerick, 2010); Michael Spillane, 'The fourth earl of Dunraven, 1841–1926: a study of his contribution to the emerging Ireland at the beginning of the twentieth century' (PhD, Limerick, 2002). **18** Charlotte Mary Murphy, 'The life and politics of Thomas Spring Rice, first Baron Monteagle of Brandon, 1790–1866' (MA, UCC, 1991); Bridget Hourican, 'Thomas Spring Rice (1790–1866)', *DIB*.

6.1 Tervoe House, residence of William Monsell, and one of the principal centres of the Shannon Estuary Group (courtesy of Limerick Museum).

held the title Baron Emly of Tervoe from 1874 to 1932. The most prominent member of the family was William Monsell (1812–94) (fig. 6.2), who in the 1840s moved from being Church of Ireland and Conservative to being Roman Catholic and Liberal. His political career lasted for sixty years (1835–94), during which time he sat as MP for Co. Limerick (1847–74) and in the Lords (1874–94) and became one of the leading political figures in Ireland, serving under four prime ministers in a succession of offices between 1853 and 1873. One of the most prominent lay Catholics in Britain and Ireland, he was a lifelong unionist, a Liberal Catholic and a friend of such giants as Gladstone and Pius IX; cardinals Newman and Cullen; and Acton and Balfour.[19] The English branch of the family was also significant. Bolton Meredith Eyres Monsell (1881–1969) had the most brilliant political career of any Monsell, culminating in a seat in the cabinet as first lord of the admiralty (1931–6).[20]

The de Vere family were cousins of the Monsells through a common Pery ancestry and their country seat was at Curragh Chase, on the main road from Limerick to Askeaton. They held the baronetage of Curragh from 1784 to 1904. In the 1870s, their estate consisted of 4,166 acres, all situated in Co. Limerick. Sir Aubrey de Vere (1788–1846) and his wife, Mary Spring Rice, had five sons and three daughters. Three of their sons were Sir Vere (1808–80), Sir Stephen (1812–1904) and

19 For Monsell, see Potter, *William Monsell of Tervoe*. **20** See Stuart Ball, 'Bolton Meredith Eyres Monsell, first Viscount Monsell (1881–1969)', *ODNB*.

6.2 William Monsell, one of the leading members of the Shannon Estuary Group (courtesy of Limerick Museum).

the poet Aubrey (1814–1902). Stephen was an enlightened landlord and social reformer who travelled to Canada on a so-called 'coffin ship' in 1847 to experience the privations of Irish emigrants, and later campaigned for reform of the conditions under which they travelled to North America.[21]

North of the Shannon, the O'Briens lived at Dromoland Castle, Newmarket-on-Fergus, Co. Clare. Among the titles held by the family were Baron Inchiquin (from 1543), earl of Inchiquin (1654–1855), marquess of Thomond (1800–55) and baronet of Leaghmenagh (from 1686). In the 1870s, the family estates consisted of 20,321 acres in Co. Clare. Sir Edward O'Brien (1773–1837) and his wife had five sons and four daughters. His most famous son, William Smith O'Brien (1803–64), resided at Cahirmoyle House, near Ardagh, Co. Limerick, and his estate there consisted of

21 For brief profiles of the most important figures in the family, see Elizabeth Lee, revised M.C. Curthoys, 'Sir Stephen Edward de Vere (1812–1904)'; Robert Welch, 'Aubrey Thomas de Vere (1814–1902)', both in *ODNB*; Desmond McCabe, 'Sir Aubrey de Vere (Hunt) 1788–1846'; Desmond McCabe, 'Sir Stephen Edward de Vere (1812–1904)'; Tom Kelley and Linde Lunney, 'Aubrey Thomas de Vere (1814–1902)', *DIB*.

4,997 acres. A commanding figure in the Repeal Movement in the 1840s, O'Brien led the abortive 1848 Rebellion, for which he suffered transportation to Tasmania and consequently became a significant figure in the apostolic succession of Irish nationalism.[22]

A distant cousin was Augustus Stafford O'Brien (1811–58) who lived at Cratloe Woods House, across the Shannon estuary from Tervoe House, and also at Blatherwicke House, Northamptonshire. In the 1870s, the estates comprised 27,394 acres in Ireland (Cos Clare, Limerick and Tipperary) and England (the shires of Rutland and Northampton).[23]

The SEG reached the peak of their influence in the mid-nineteenth century, but continued to produce prominent figures into the early twentieth century. The fourth earl of Dunraven became one of the leaders of constructive unionism, and a supporter of land purchase and devolution. He was instrumental in the establishment of the 1902 Land Conference composed of representatives of landlords and tenants, whose report led to the enactment of the Wyndham Land Act of 1903. The second Lord Emly (1858–1932) became a fervent though eccentric convert to Irish nationalism and the labour movement, while his cousin Elinor Mary Monsell (1879–1954) became a celebrated portrait painter and engraver, and was a close friend of Lady Gregory and the Yeats brothers.[24] Monteagle's grandson was the prominent diplomat, Sir Cecil Spring Rice (1859–1918), British ambassador to the USA from 1913 to 1918, while a great-granddaughter was Mary Spring Rice (1880–1924), a noted Irish nationalist and social reformer.[25] Smith O'Brien's daughter Charlotte Grace O'Brien (1845–1909) was a literary figure and social reformer who campaigned tirelessly to improve the lot of Irish female emigrants, and also supported land reform and the Gaelic League. David Fitzpatrick has rightly pointed out that 'few regions of Ireland could have boasted of so dense a concentration of liberal-minded and educated patrician families'.[26]

The central research questions of this essay are: what kind of elite was the SEG and, consequently, how successful was it as an elite? To begin in the field of organization, identified by Mosca and Michels as essential to elite power, the group was bound together by several informal but powerful ties. In the first place, its members were closely related, both by birth and by marriage, as can be demonstrated by a few examples. Thomas Spring Rice's sister was married to Sir Aubrey de Vere, making him the uncle of the brothers Vere, Stephen and Aubrey de Vere. In turn, Spring Rice was married to Theodosia Pery, a daughter of the first earl of Limerick. One of Edmund Sexton Pery's sisters, Dymphna, was married to William Monsell of

22 Grania R. O'Brien and Hugh Weir, *These my friends and forebears: the O'Briens of Dromoland* (Whitegate, Co. Clare, 1991). 23 All of the data concerning landed estates is taken from John Bateman (ed.), *The great landowners of Great Britain and Ireland* (Leicester, 1971; facsimile reprint of the edition of 1883). 24 For Elinor Darwin, see Theo Snoddy, *Dictionary of Irish artists, 20th century* (Dublin, 1996), pp 93–4. 25 See Bridget Hourican, 'Mary Ellen Spring Rice (1880–1924)', *DIB*. 26 Fitzpatrick, 'Thomas Spring Rice and the peopling of Australia', 42.

Tervoe, and their great-grandson was William Monsell, first Lord Emly. The latter's first wife was Lady Anna Maria Wyndham-Quin, daughter of the second Lord Dunraven and sister to the third Lord Dunraven. One of William Smith O'Brien's sisters, Harriet, was married to Charles Monsell, a first cousin of the first Lord Emly. Secondly, members of the SEG enjoyed the benefits of an elite education, often at public school followed by Oxbridge or Trinity College Dublin. Again, a few examples will suffice. Thomas Spring Rice and William Smith O'Brien both attended Trinity College, Cambridge; William Monsell, Oriel College, Oxford; and the third earl of Dunraven, Trinity College Dublin. Thirdly, members of the SEG were united by ties of deep friendship. Thus, Monsell, the third earl of Dunraven, and the three de Vere brothers were bound together by their common adherence to the Oxford Movement and later conversion to the Roman Catholic Church; all five sympathized with Smith O'Brien when he was transported, while deploring his 'folly' in leading the 1848 Rebellion; Stafford O'Brien detested the religion of the Tervoe convert set, while continuing to have warm feelings for them personally.[27]

With regard to Pareto's concept of an elite consisting of high achievers, the SEG included significant cultural figures. Generally, members of the group self-identified as Irish patriots, but defined their Irish nationality 'in cultural and territorial terms' while 'rejecting political nationalist aspirations'.[28] Thus, the two leading literary figures of the SEG, Aubrey de Vere and the third earl of Dunraven were 'cultural nationalists', indeed major figures in the Celtic Revival, while remaining political unionists. Aubrey de Vere became a celebrated poet whose greatest work was *Inisfail: a lyrical chronicle of Ireland* (1861), and was a close friend of Wordsworth and Tennyson. Indeed, *Inisfail* is considered an important precursor of the Irish Literary Renaissance and his *Ballad of Athlone* long enjoyed high status in nationalist circles.[29] The third earl of Dunraven studied astronomy for three years under his friend Rowan Hamilton, and his vast range of intellectual activity included archaeology, architecture, theology and even spiritualism. He was also a leading figure in the earlier stages of the Celtic Revival and his magnum opus, *Notes on Irish architecture*, was published posthumously in 1875–7.[30] In addition, Sir Aubrey de Vere, Stephen de Vere and William Smith O'Brien were all minor poets, and William Monsell, though he published comparatively little, was a man of wide intellectual interests. The SEG were also local cultural leaders and made a large contribution to the built environment. The Perys inspired the construction of Georgian Limerick and were later responsible for building Dromore Castle (one of the most dramatic buildings of the Celtic Revival); the earls of Dunraven created the beautiful mansion and village of

---

27 For the offices held by group members, see *Thom's Irish almanac and official directory* (Dublin, 1844–80); *Thom's official directory of the United Kingdom of Great Britain and Ireland* (Dublin, 1881–1922), hereafter referred to as *Thom's directory*, passim.   28 Ridden, 'Making good citizens', p. 218.   29 Sr M. Paraclita Reilly, *Aubrey de Vere: Victorian observer* (Dublin, 1956).   30 Edwin Richard Wyndham-Quin, third earl of Dunraven (ed. Margaret Stokes), *Notes on Irish architecture* (London, 1875–7).

Adare; the O'Briens built Dromoland and Cahermoyle and the Monsells constructed Tervoe House and the nearby estate village.[31]

Nevertheless, their elite status was not based on possession of outstanding talents; on the contrary, it was their wealth and leisure which enabled them to develop their talents and abilities (later to be eclipsed by the achievements of individuals from much less affluent backgrounds, such as Yeats, Shaw and Joyce). Here, Burnham's location of elite power in the control of a disproportionate amount of economic resources comes into play and it is difficult to avoid the Marxian conclusion that the SEG owed their elite position to their ownership of landed estates, mostly acquired in the Plantations and augmented during the era of the Penal Laws. From the Dunravens' 40,000-acre estate to the Monsells' 2,000 acres, their status as landowners gave them a massive advantage over all other interest groups in society before the 1880s. Indeed, the Dunravens, O'Briens of Dromoland and O'Briens of Cratloe Woods were part of the exclusive club of 305 landowners with Irish estates of 10,000 acres or more each. Ownership of land did not merely bring economic power, but also conferred much greater prestige than fortunes made in business or trade, and carried with it social hegemony in the locality. It was regarded as part of the natural order that society should be controlled and led by the landed elite. The connection between economic, social and political hegemony is demonstrated by the fate of the Irish landlords after the 1880s, when all three forms of social control slipped simultaneously from their grasp as a result of the disestablishment of the Church of Ireland, the Land Acts and the creation of a democratic local government system in 1898–9.[32]

In accordance with Wright Mills' location of elite power, the SEG and their allies controlled most of the important local institutions and offices until the Land War. The principal offices in an Irish county were the lord lieutenant (not to be confused with the chief governor of the entire country) and the high sheriff. The lord lieutenant was the chief civil and military official in his county and, though a ceremonial figure, he was also granted significant powers. He commanded the county militia, appointed deputy lieutenants, was head of the magistracy and recommended to the lord chancellor for appointments of all local magistrates. In Co. Limerick, this office was filled by the third Lord Dunraven (1864–71), the first Lord Emly (1871–94) and the fourth Lord Dunraven (1896–1922) and in Co. Clare by the thirteenth Lord Inchiquin (1843–72) and the fourteenth Lord Inchiquin (1879–1900). The high sheriff was an annual appointment, whose main functions were the selection of the grand jury (forerunner of the county council, an unelected committee chiefly composed of landlords, which administered each county) and the organization of parliamentary elections. Holders of the office in Co. Limerick included William Monsell (1835), Vere de Vere (1836), Stephen Spring Rice (1837) and Stephen de Vere (1870). Members of the SEG also served as magistrates and sat on grand juries and

---

31 For more details on these buildings, see the website of the Irish Architectural Archive, http://www.iarc.ie.   **32** Bateman, *The great landowners of Great Britain and Ireland*, passim.

poor law unions; indeed, William Monsell was chairman of Limerick Board of Guardians from 1857 to 1882.

Members of the SEG also sat in both houses of parliament for long periods, particularly before the 1880s. The 1850s and 1860s, framed by the two great nationalist movements of O'Connellism and Parnellism, were marked by a strong revival of the power of the Irish landed elite, who benefited from the mid-century economic boom, the absence of a major nationalist agitation and the dominance of localist and deferential politics. Even the Irish Tory Party flourished at this time.[33] This Indian summer of the landlords enabled the SEG to enjoy a political prominence unimaginable after the 1880s, which witnessed the creation of a mass Irish electorate and a powerful agrarian-nationalist political machine.[34] The group included four significant political figures – Edmond Sexton Pery, Thomas Spring Rice, William Smith O'Brien and William Monsell, but many more were also parliamentary representatives, such as the third earl of Dunraven, who, though not primarily a politician, was MP for Glamorgan (1837–51) and, on being created a peer of the United Kingdom, a member of the Lords (1866–71).[35]

The SEG also had Meisel's three Cs. In the first place, they possessed self-consciousness of being part of a coterie. Cultured, wealthy, politically active and related by blood and marriage, they also shared a common social, religious and intellectual background. Secondly, they were a cohesive group, socially and (with important exceptions) in their general political ideology. Most of them were liberal in the broadest sense and supported moderate, peaceful, piecemeal reform rather than radical revolution. Accordingly, the Catholic converts in the SEG can be classed as Liberal Catholics, followers of the French ideology that opposed the reactionary tendencies of Ultramontanism and strove to reconcile the Church with modern doctrines, such as parliamentary government, individual freedom, equality before the law and protection of private property, which they regarded as positive, and to be compatible with the teachings of the Church.[36] Additionally, most of the SEG espoused a dual Irish and British identity, in that they were passionately attached to Ireland, but were also conscious of an overarching British loyalty. They 'saw themselves as British, but not English' and 'found it necessary to claim Irish identity, in order to maintain and reinforce their legitimate leadership within Ireland'. They cast themselves as mediators, representing the needs and desires of the Irish people to the British state.[37] Thirdly, they possessed a common will to action centred on *noblesse*

---

33 Andrew Shields, *The Irish Conservative Party, 1852–1868: land, politics and religion* (Dublin, 2007).   **34** For the economic revival of the landlords, see W.E. Vaughan, *Landlords and tenants in mid-Victorian Ireland* (Oxford, 1994). For their political position in this period, see D. George Boyce, *Nineteenth-century Ireland: the search for stability* (Dublin, 1990), pp 124–53; K. Theodore Hoppen, *Elections, politics and society in Ireland, 1832–85* (Oxford, 1984), pp 89–170.   **35** *Thom's directory*, passim.   **36** For the Liberal Catholics, see also Josef Altholz, *The Liberal Catholic movement in England:* the Rambler *and its contributors, 1848–62* (London, 1962); Hugh A. MacDougall, *The Acton–Newman relations: the dilemma of Christian Liberalism* (New York, 1962).   **37** Ridden, 'Making good citizens', p. 204.

oblige and a strong social conscience.[38] They were nearly all resident and improving landlords, exemplified by Thomas Spring Rice, who wrote in 1815 on the 'elevated duties of the Irish country gentleman'.

> It is a sphere of personal privation and of personal exertion. But when a mind is awake to that first of all delights, the power of becoming extensively and permanently useful, all privations are forgotten, all labour is well repaid. A peasantry capable of improvement and grateful for every benevolent assistance, look up to the landlord as to a protector and friend. He may not only assist their distresses, but may enable them to assist themselves.[39]

This may be regarded as the common ideology (Meisel's 'conspiracy') of the SEG.

In the language of pluralist elite theory, the SEG was self-recruiting and 'closed', as membership was based on the two criteria of hereditary possession of landed wealth and relationship by birth and marriage. However, it was not immune from the influence of public opinion and the masses (indeed it is a moot point whether any elite in history operated in such a purely autonomous fashion). Even in the restricted political system of the late eighteenth and early nineteenth centuries, members of the SEG had contested parliamentary elections, which, though conducted on the basis of a limited franchise, were still influenced by non-voters, such as urban and rural 'mobs'. Additionally, they were divided politically, ranging from conservatives, like the first earl of Limerick and Sir Edward O'Brien, to an armed insurrectionary like William Smith O'Brien (though, as revolutionaries go, even he was comparatively moderate). With the gradual widening of the franchise, the SEG's responsiveness to public opinion increased, and many of them, such as William Smith O'Brien (whose political position evolved from Liberalism to Repeal and beyond), William Monsell (who converted from Conservatism to Liberalism) and the fourth Lord Dunraven (a Conservative who eventually supported Home Rule), modified their political views accordingly. In this manner, the SEG, while remaining 'closed', took on some of the traits of an 'open' elite.[40]

Consequently, the group succeeded in maintaining their position with at least the acquiescence of the non-elite majority, until the cataclysm of the 1880s brought about its demise as part of Irish landlordism's general collapse. Elite theory usually accounts for the displacement of elites in two ways: 'structural factors' and 'socio-psychological factors'. In the case of the Shannon Estuary Group, the structural factor that brought about their displacement was the loss of their landed estates, which undermined the economic basis of their hegemony and left them in possession of large houses and assets without the wherewithal to support them.[41] The major socio-

---

38 See Horace Plunkett, *Noblesse oblige: an Irish rendering* (Dublin, 1908). **39** Thomas (Spring) Rice, *An inquiry into the effects of the Irish grand jury laws* (London, 1815), p. 12. **40** A number of books chart Smith O'Brien's political evolution: see, for example, Robert Sloan, *William Smith O'Brien and the Young Irelander rebellion of 1848* (Dublin, 2000). **41** Parry, *Political elites*, pp 58–60.

psychological factor was the rise of the two-headed monster of Irish nationalism and land agitation, which threatened the entire social system of which they were part. Irish nationalist ideology excluded the Anglo-Irish from the Irish nation and the governing myths of twentieth century Irish nationalism – of an Ireland Gaelic, peasant, Catholic – took shape in the 1880s and 1890s. This was completely antagonistic to the belief of the SEG in an Ireland that was anglicized, ruled by enlightened gentry, made up of all classes and creeds, and above all part of the United Kingdom.

Fundamentally, the SEG was an example of a classic closed elite sub-group that was unable to make the transition to a democratic open elite. While there were often political differences within their ranks, the bulk of the group were unionists who supported the social and political system within which they had always operated. Irish patriots and advanced reformers until the 1870s and 1880s, they were later regarded as being both socially and politically conservative. Yet, it was not their ideology that had altered but rather political circumstances had forced them, like so many of their fellow landlords, into a more strident and self-conscious espousal of unionism and the ascendancy of the Anglo-Irish. Unable to co-opt or recruit the rising Irish bourgeoisie, which had colonized local government and parliamentary representation, they found themselves squeezed between nationalism and unionism; gradually excluded from the emerging sense of Irishness; and derided for their identity of being both Irish and British. Some of the SEG did attempt to engage with the 'new Ireland'. Senior figures such as the fourth Lord Dunraven, second Lord Emly and second Lord Monteagle successfully contested seats on Limerick County Council, but their involvement ceased in the early 1920s. The curious involvement of Mary Spring Rice and Conor O'Brien (grandson of William Smith O'Brien) in the Howth gun-running was a more picturesque episode but had little lasting impact. Although the fourth earl of Dunraven sat in the Free State Senate from 1922 to 1926, the SEG as a whole held aloof from independent Ireland. By the mid-twentieth century, many of its constituent families had become extinct (the de Veres) or non-resident in Ireland (the Perys and the Monsells), though the earls of Dunraven and barons Inchiquin continued to be popular residents in their respective localities to the time of writing.[42]

The Shannon Estuary Group are of interest for many reasons: their particular combination of religious and political views representing an ideological strand in Irish political life obliterated from the 1880s onwards; their status as a microcosm of the doomed Irish landlord elite; and perhaps most of all the inclusion in their ranks of some of the most idealistic, high-minded and interesting figures produced by the Anglo-Irish, several of whom aspired to Sewell's idyllic vision of the Irish gentleman as 'the most perfect specimen of civilised nature'.[43]

---

42 Ridden, 'Making good citizens', pp 18–21 and 238–40.   **43** William Sewell, 'Romanism in Ireland', 121.

Double helix: two elites in politics and journalism in Ireland, 1870–1918

FELIX M. LARKIN[1]

I

The concept of an elite is not one that readily springs to mind when we think about journalists and the press. Sir Walter Scott, writing in 1829, thought that 'nothing but a thorough-going blackguard ought to attempt the daily press' – and still today journalism is scarcely seen as a dignified or reputable profession.[2] Nevertheless, in the lively world of Irish political journalism at the end of the 'long' nineteenth century, there are two groups that, by virtue of their numerical strength and the prominence of many of their members, may validly be regarded as elite. These groups – discrete but interrelated, entwined together as in a double helix and linked by some notable persons who straddle both – were part of the fabric of nationalist Ireland from the 1870s until the 1918 general election.

During that period, the press reached the zenith of its influence in political and social life in Great Britain and Ireland. The words and actions of politicians and others clearly illustrate the power that the press had, and few attested more eloquently to it than the dominant Irish nationalist figure of the time, Charles Stewart Parnell. Speaking at a public meeting in Dublin in August 1891, just weeks before his death, he said:

1 I am particularly grateful to Ian d'Alton for his valuable contribution to this essay, for reading and commenting upon successive drafts of it and for his constant encouragement while it was in preparation. Philip Hamell, John Horgan, Peter Lacy, Mark O'Brien and Robert P. Schmuhl (Notre Dame University, Indiana) also read the essay in draft and I thank them for their insightful criticism. Michael Foley gave me good advice at an early stage, and I am grateful to him for that. I am grateful also to Pauric Travers for alerting me to one journalist-MP whom I had overlooked. Various participants in the 2011 SSNCI conference, at which a shorter version of the essay was delivered, commented on it either in the open forum afterwards or privately to me later – my thanks to all who did so, but especially to Ciara Breathnach, Tom Garvin, Patrick Maume and Colin Reid. My thanks also to Honora Faul, of the National Library of Ireland, for facilitating my use of the image reproduced on p. 128. Finally, I am grateful to the editor of this volume, Ciaran O'Neill, for his assistance.
2 *The journal of Sir Walter Scott* (2 vols, Edinburgh, 1890), ii, p. 262 [3 Apr. 1829], quoted in A. Aspinall, 'The social status of journalists at the beginning of the nineteenth century', *Review of English Studies*, 21:83 (1945), 216–32 at 216.

> The profession of journalism is a great and powerful one in these days. It is likely to become more influential as the years go by. The readers of newspapers increase from time to time, and the press is becoming even mightier than the politician ... In these days politics and journalism run very much together, and a tendency is more and more to combine the two.[3]

This reference to a tendency to combine politics and journalism reflects the fact that the power of the press was by no means confined to its capacity to sway public opinion. Journalists and others associated with newspapers were often actively involved in politics, or were aspirant politicians or politicians *manqué*. Nowhere was the tendency more evident than in the Irish Parliamentary Party. The journalists and other newspapermen who were Irish party MPs with Parnell and afterwards represented a particularly important segment of the nationalist political class in Ireland, the first of the two elites that are the subject of this essay. These journalists-cum-politicians included many of the leaders of the Irish party and some of its most radical and militant members.

My main purpose in this essay is to identify the individuals in question, briefly noting their principal journalistic endeavours – a tabulation that draws on a wide range of sources and is the first comprehensive list of such persons to be published.[4] I will also suggest some reasons why so many combined careers in journalism and politics, and why the journalist-in-politics became a much rarer phenomenon in post-independence Ireland. The essay will accordingly provide historical context for further work on the inextricable links between politics, journalists and the press. Moreover, I will discuss the curious fact that many of the foremost Irish journalists in the period from the 1870s until 1918 – those who did not become MPs, as well as those who did – were natives of Co. Cork and had begun their working lives on Cork newspapers. The Cork contingent was a pivotal element in Irish political journalism in this period, the second of the two elites with which this essay is concerned.

II

The importance of journalists within the Irish parliamentary party was acknowledged by Roy Foster in his characterization of the party as 'a curious blend of Trollopian fixers, political journalists, respectable ex-Fenians and closet imperialists'.[5]

3 *Freeman's Journal*, 29 Aug. 1891. Quoted by Frank Callanan in his introduction to Edward Byrne, *Parnell: a memoir*, ed. F. Callanan (Dublin, 1991), p. 4. **4** The sources in question include the following: A. O'Day, *The English face of Irish nationalism: Parnellite involvement in British politics, 1880–86* (Dublin, 1977); M. Stenton & S. Lees, *Who's who of British members of parliament: a biographical dictionary of the house of commons based on annual volumes of Dod's parliamentary companion and other sources* (4 vols, Hassocks, Sussex, 1978), ii (1886–1918); Patrick Maume, *The long gestation: Irish nationalist life, 1891–1918* (Dublin, 1999); M.-L. Legg, *Newspapers and nationalism: the Irish provincial press, 1850–1892* (Dublin, 1999); *DIB*. **5** R.F.

This is a much too irreverent dismissal of men who fought the good fight for Home Rule in unpromising circumstances and came close to winning it, but Foster was right to highlight the ubiquity of political journalists in the ranks of the Irish nationalist parliamentarians. Thus, for example, nearly two-thirds of the party's most prominent MPs shown in a cartoon entitled 'Parnell Party Portraits' published with the *Weekly Irish Times* on 17 March 1883 (fig. 7.1) were journalists or otherwise associated with newspapers. They are: Justin McCarthy, deputy leader of the party; two of Parnell's principal lieutenants in the Land War, William O'Brien and Thomas Sexton; his nemesis, T.M. Healy, and Healy's uncle, T.D. Sullivan; Edmund Dwyer Gray, owner of the chief nationalist daily newspaper in Ireland, the *Freeman's Journal*, and of the *Belfast Morning News*; Timothy C. Harrington, founder of the *Kerry Sentinel* and later manager of the *United Ireland* newspaper in its final years; J.J. O'Kelly, who had been a war correspondent for the *New York Herald* and became London editor of the *Irish Daily Independent* after he lost his seat in parliament to fellow journalist Matthias McDonnell Bodkin in 1892; T.P. O'Connor and Frank Hugh O'Donnell, both prominent in London journalism, the latter – incongruously for an Irish nationalist – with the reactionary *Morning Post*; and Edmond Leamy, editor of *United Ireland* in the 1890s.

To these names should be added the following newspapermen who, though not in parliament in 1883, were at other times members of the Irish party at Westminster: William Martin Murphy, creator and owner of the modern *Irish Independent*; Michael Davitt, who derived his income for many years mainly from freelance journalism; T.P. Gill, editor in the 1880s of the *Catholic World* in New York and later of Dublin's *Daily Express* when the latter was owned by Sir Horace Plunkett; A.M. Sullivan and Donal Sullivan, brothers of T.D. Sullivan; Edward Harrington, brother of Timothy C. Harrington; Justin Huntley McCarthy, son of Justin McCarthy; William O'Malley, brother-in-law of T.P. O'Connor and associated with O'Connor's *Sun* newspaper in London and later with the *Connacht Tribune*; Daniel McAleese, prominent in Belfast journalism and then editor and proprietor of the Monaghan *People's Advocate*; eight other well-known provincial newspaper editor-proprietors – James L. Carew of the *Leinster Leader*, Jasper Tully of the *Roscommon Herald*, P.A. McHugh of the *Sligo Champion*, J.P. Farrell of the *Longford Leader*, John O'Donnell of the *Connaught Champion*, Daniel Sheehan of the *Southern Star*, John P. Hayden of the *Westmeath Examiner*, and his brother, Luke Hayden, of the *Roscommon Messenger*; the aforementioned Matthias McDonnell Bodkin, chief leader-writer of the *Freeman's Journal* from 1895 to 1907; John Hooper, editor of the *Cork Daily Herald* and later of the Dublin *Evening Telegraph*; J.P. Nannetti, a foreman printer with the *Freeman* who also wrote

Foster, 'Thinking from hand to mouth: Anglo-Irish literature, Gaelic nationalism and Irish politics in the 1890s' in Foster, *Paddy and Mr Punch: connections in Irish and English history* (London, 1993), p. 265. In an astringent review of *Paddy and Mr Punch* (*Irish Times*, 9 Oct. 1993), Frank Callanan wrote that this characterization 'will simply not do. Here, as too often elsewhere in these essays, the historian is submerged in the litterateur … [and] there is an implicit disdain for the stuff of politics'.

7.1 Parnell, without his customary full beard, with seventeen other leading members of the Irish Parliamentary Party – eleven of whom were journalists or otherwise associated with newspapers (supplement to the *Weekly Irish Times*, 17 March 1883).

on labour matters for the *Evening Telegraph*; Charles Diamond, who established the London *Catholic Herald* and a number of other Catholic newspapers in England and Scotland; Daniel Crilly, a journalist with the *Nation* before entering parliament in 1885; James O'Connor, who had been on the staff of Charles Kickham's *Irish People*; John T. Donovan, editor of the Belfast *Northern Star* and author of the 'Stargazer' column in that newspaper;[6] Arthur Lynch, who worked for several British popular newspapers in the 1890s, including the *Daily Mail*; Stephen Gwynn, more litterateur than journalist, but he described himself as a journalist and was Irish correspondent of the *Observer* in the 1920s; and Henry Harrison, Parnell's trusted confidant who pursued a career in journalism after the First World War.[7]

That gives a total of thirty-eight MPs with journalistic connections, of which eleven – or 30 per cent – came from Co. Cork. They are: William O'Brien from Mallow; Justin McCarthy from Dunmanway; Daniel Sheehan from Kanturk and later of Skibbereen; John Hooper from near Millstreet and later of Cork city; and T.M. Healy, the Sullivan brothers, William Martin Murphy and the Harrington brothers – all from around the Bantry area. These MPs were, of course, members of both elites under consideration in this essay – the journalists-cum-politicians *and* the Cork-born journalists – but there are many additional figures who fall within the second category only. The most important include: James Tuohy, long-time London correspondent of the *Freeman's Journal*; Patrick Hooper, son of John Hooper and the *Freeman's* last editor from 1916 to 1924; T.R. Harrington, editor of the *Irish Independent* from 1905 to 1931; and John Fergus O'Hea and Thomas Fitzpatrick, two political cartoonists whose work appeared as a supplement to the *Weekly Freeman* in the 1880s and 1890s.[8] T.R. Harrington was not related to the Harrington brothers, Timothy and Edward – though, like them, he was born in Castletownbere, near Bantry.

How do we account for this ascendancy of Corkonians? They themselves, especially those who hailed from Bantry, tended to regard it as a phenomenon of nature. Serjeant Sullivan, son of A.M. Sullivan, wrote that 'there was something in the air and atmosphere of Bantry that stimulated the growth of Irish nationalism' and that it was 'the native genius of the place' that gave rise to so many notable careers in journalism and politics.[9] A similar view was expressed by the eminent president of Queen's

---

6 A.C. Hepburn, *Catholic Belfast and nationalist Ireland in the era of Joe Devlin, 1871–1934* (Oxford, 2008), p. 63, n. 124. **7** Of the thirty-eight journalists-cum-politicians listed here, all but three – John O'Donnell, Luke Hayden and John T. Donovan – merit entries in the *DIB*. **8** Tuohy, Hooper, Harrington and O'Hea have entries in the *DIB*. **9** Serjeant [A.M.] Sullivan, *Old Ireland: reminiscences of an Irish K.C.* (London, 1927), pp 11–12. A recent essay by Ian d'Alton may be relevant in attempting to come to an understanding of what was 'in the air and atmosphere of Bantry that stimulated the growth of Irish nationalism'. He argues that the unusually high level of sectarian violence in Cork in the period 1920–3 may be explained by reference to 'a theory about the visibility of minorities – the "Goldilocks postulation" ... Too small a minority, and the majority is indifferent; too large a minority, and the majority is reluctant to take on its rivals. West Cork appears to have been

College Cork, Bertram Windle, in 1906 – and he was an Englishman, then only newly arrived in Cork. He said:

> One would expect to find that a very large proportion of the Irish pressmen ... came from or about Cork. The nimble wit, the ready grasp of a subject, the quick intelligence, the rhetorical or poetical pen – the peculiar natural gifts of the Southerner – are exactly the kind of things which find a ready market in journalism.[10]

In reality, the explanation is probably more prosaic: many, though certainly not all, of the Cork pressmen owed their success in journalism and politics – either directly or indirectly – to the Sullivan brothers, proprietors of the *Nation* weekly newspaper in Dublin from the mid-1850s until 1890.[11] Though now largely forgotten, the Sullivans played a central role in shaping the politics and culture of nationalist Ireland in the second half of the nineteenth century. They were good at spotting and fostering talent, particularly in fellow countrymen from Cork.

A.M. Sullivan ran the *Nation* until 1876, after which his elder brother T.D. Sullivan took over. T.M. Healy was their nephew and he married T.D.'s daughter (who was, in fact, his double first cousin), while William Martin Murphy was taken under A.M. Sullivan's wing when he came to Dublin at a young age to attend Belvedere College for his secondary education. Murphy, while still a schoolboy, often visited the *Nation*'s offices in Middle Abbey Street and helped out with copy-editing, proof-reading and other tasks – and no doubt picked up there his lifelong love of the newspaper industry in which he was to play such an important part. Murphy looked on A.M. Sullivan as a father figure, and wrote this tribute in a letter to Sullivan's widow shortly after his death:

> I often think my success in life was largely due to the happy inspiration of A.M. in getting my father to send me as a schoolboy to Dublin, and I have never forgotten A.M.'s night journey to Bantry the day after my father was buried, when, as a forlorn boy, he gave me counsel and encouragement at the most critical period of my life.[12]

"just right", it seems': see I. d'Alton, '"A vestigial population"? Perspectives on southern Irish protestants in the twentieth century', *Éire-Ireland*, 44:3 & 4 (fall/winter 2009), 9–42 at 28.   **10** M. Taylor, *Sir Bertram Windle: a memoir* (London, 1932), p. 185. I am indebted to Ian d'Alton for bringing this book to my attention.   **11** The sale of the *Nation* was announced in its issue of 19 Apr. 1890, and the following issue (26 Apr. 1890) carried a letter from T.D. Sullivan expressing his continued 'feelings of affection for the *Nation*, of fraternity with its workers and of warm regard for its friends'. It was merged with the *Irish Catholic* in July 1891.   **12** Quoted in an address by Dr Lombard Murphy to the staff of Independent Newspapers Ltd, 29 June 1941 (Murphy Papers; I am grateful to the late T.V. Murphy for access to these papers). For an insightful account of Murphy's early years, see T.J. Morrissey, *William Martin Murphy* (Dundalk, 1997), pp 4–7.

Thomas Sexton, though a Waterford man, was likewise a protégé of A.M. Sullivan and got his start in journalism on the *Nation* newspaper. Following a period as an occasional correspondent for the *Nation*, he joined its staff in 1869 and was subsequently editor of its sister papers, the *Weekly News* and *Young Ireland*, before entering parliament in 1880. He ran the prestigious *Freeman's Journal* newspaper from 1893 to 1912, replacing – albeit after an interval – Edmund Dwyer Gray, who had died at an early age in 1888.[13] Murphy and Sexton were the most powerful newspapermen in Dublin in the last decade of the nineteenth century and the first decade of the twentieth – and, through them, the strong Cork influence in Irish nationalist journalism, which had been established by the Sullivan brothers, lived on long after the *Nation* ceased publication in 1891.[14]

This Cork influence was also evident within the Irish Parliamentary Party. So many members of the party had roots in West Cork or were otherwise linked to the Sullivan-Healy dynasty that they were known collectively as the 'Bantry band'.[15] All of the 'Bantry band', with the exception of the Harrington brothers, took the anti-Parnell side in the split – and it has been suggested that their uncompromising opposition to Parnell may have been fuelled, at least in part, by a sense that the Sullivans and T.M. Healy had a claim on the leadership of nationalist Ireland which had been, as they saw it, usurped by Parnell.[16] Their opposition to Parnell was not limited to the political sphere. They also mounted a press campaign against him, which caused a bitter newspaper war in Dublin – a sidelight on the nexus between politics and journalism in Ireland at this time. The vehicle for the anti-Parnell press campaign was a new daily newspaper, the *National Press*, launched – largely through Healy's efforts – in the early months of the split to counter the influence of the *Freeman's Journal*, which initially supported Parnell. The *Freeman* responded to this unaccustomed competition by changing sides, and eventually it was merged with the *National Press* – with, however, the *Freeman's* more venerable title being retained. That did not settle the newspaper war. When the *Freeman* abandoned him, Parnell founded the *Irish Daily Independent*, which was later acquired by William Martin Murphy and transformed in 1905 into the modern *Irish Independent*. The *Freeman* and the *Independent* were rivals until the former went out of business in 1924.[17] The more

---

13 See F.M. Larkin, 'Two gentlemen of the *Freeman*: Thomas Sexton, W.H. Brayden and the *Freeman's Journal*, 1892–1916', C. Breathnach and C. Lawless (eds), *Visual, material and print culture in nineteenth-century Ireland* (Dublin, 2010), pp 210–22.   **14** The *Nation* title was revived briefly in 1896 for a new Healyite organ, and it continued as the *Daily Nation* from June 1897. The *Daily Nation* was absorbed by the *Irish Daily Independent* in 1900. In the 1920s, a Fianna Fáil organ – the precursor of the *Irish Press* – was also called the *Nation*; it had no connection with the earlier newspaper of the same name.   **15** The 'Bantry band' (also sometimes referred to as the 'Bantry gang') comprised the three Sullivan brothers, T.M. Healy and his brother Maurice, the two Harrington brothers, John Barry (a distant relation of the Healys), James Gilhooly and William Martin Murphy.   **16** See, for example, Frank Callanan's essay on Serjeant (Alexander Martin) Sullivan in *DIB*.   **17** See F.M. Larkin, 'Mrs Jellyby's daughter: Caroline Agnes Gray (1848–1927) and the *Freeman's Journal*', Larkin (ed.),

prominent of the Harrington brothers, Timothy C. Harrington, was briefly a director of the Parnellite *Independent* before becoming manager of the *United Ireland* newspaper.

The most significant of the Cork journalists-cum-politicians who were not part of the 'Bantry band' was William O'Brien. He had much in common with T.M. Healy and ended his political career in a loose alliance with him – though whether they ever agreed on anything other than their disaffection with the Irish party leaders post-1900 is doubtful. Both were mavericks, adamantly opposed to what O'Brien once called 'the modern juggernaut of so-called party discipline'.[18] O'Brien had worked on the *Cork Daily Herald* and on the *Freeman's Journal* in Dublin before becoming editor of *United Ireland*, the weekly newspaper that Parnell established in 1881 in order to have a personal organ independent of the *Freeman* and *Nation* newspapers.[19] With this pedigree, O'Brien was not an obvious ally of the 'Bantry band' – and, in the words of F.S.L. Lyons, he 'drifted into close relations with Healy' only after he fell out with almost everyone else in the Irish party over the 1903 Land Act.[20] He ultimately retreated to his Cork hinterland, where his 'All-for-Ireland' League remained a force until 1918 and he ran a succession of newspapers – most notably the *Cork Free Press* – catering principally for his local supporters.

O'Brien's rise from obscurity without the benefit of wealth or connections shows why so many in this period in Ireland combined careers in politics and journalism. As Niamh O'Sullivan has noted in her biography of Aloysius O'Kelly, brother of J.J. O'Kelly, 'journalism, both print and illustrated, provided a high level of social mobility'.[21] It was thus a means by which bright, able young men could establish themselves solely on merit in a world where the distinction between journalism and politics was ill-defined – and their lowly origins explain their often radical politics and militant ways. Moreover, if they succeeded in entering parliament, the fact that they would not be paid a salary as MPs meant that another source of income was necessary and journalism was a convenient job compatible with parliamentary work.[22] Several politicians even found work as parliamentary correspondents: for instance, Justin McCarthy was parliamentary correspondent for the London *Daily News* for almost all of his time as an MP.

Such double-jobbing offends against modern notions of the independence of the press and the profession of journalism. These concepts were only beginning to gain currency in the late nineteenth and early twentieth centuries. In an important recent essay, Michael Foley identifies some green shoots of professionalism just then

Librarians, poets and scholars: a Festschrift for Dónall Ó Luanaigh (Dublin, 2007), pp 121–39. **18** *Cork Free Press*, 19 Mar. 1912; quoted in *Times* (London), 20 Mar. 1912. **19** The then owner of the *Freeman*, Edmund Dwyer Gray, had had ambitions to lead the Irish party himself and – like the Sullivans and Healy – tended to regard Parnell as a usurper; Parnell could not count on his support (see Larkin, 'Mrs Jellyby's daughter'). **20** F.S.L. Lyons, *The Irish Parliamentary Party, 1890–1910* (London, 1951), p. 122, n. 2. **21** N. O'Sullivan, *Aloysius O'Kelly: art, nation, empire* (Dublin, 2010), p. 54. **22** MPs were not paid a salary until 1911: see 'House of Commons factsheet M5: members' pay, pension and allowances' (May 2010).

emerging in Irish journalism – such as 'the use of shorthand to ensure accuracy' and 'a belief in objectivity or impartiality, and the professional skills to deliver it'.[23] Irish journalists also participated in the National Association of Journalists, later renamed the Institute of Journalists, a professional body founded in London in 1884; and a Corkman – Thomas Crosbie, editor and proprietor of the *Cork Examiner* – became the first Irish president of that body in 1894–5, further evidence of the ascendancy of Corkonians in Irish journalism. Moreover, in 1909 University College Cork – the former Queen's College, now a constituent college of the new National University of Ireland – began offering 'a special course for journalists who propose to proceed to the BA degree', with a wide range of subjects 'which have a special bearing on the daily work of writers for the press' and with 'opportunities to attend lectures on the professional aspects of journalism'.[24] This course – the first of its kind in Britain or Ireland – was introduced on the initiative of the president of the college, Bertram Windle, whose views on the peculiar aptitude of Corkonians for journalism have been quoted earlier. Nevertheless, there were at that time very few Irish journalists, especially among the journalists-cum-politicians, who would pass muster as genuinely professional by today's standards – and this was particularly true of those who worked for Irish, as distinct from British, newspapers. Such journalists tended to be unashamedly partisan in their writing, and it was rare for any of them to work for a newspaper with whose editorial position he did not agree.[25] Nor did Irish newspapers easily tolerate journalists in their employment who openly disagreed with editorial policy: Andrew Dunlop, an acknowledged unionist, was thus dismissed from the reporting staff of the nationalist *Freeman's Journal* in 1884 on political grounds.[26]

One noteworthy exception to the norm of the partisan journalist was James Tuohy, born in Cork city in 1857 and London correspondent of the *Freeman's Journal* from 1881 to 1912. He was – like the *Freeman*, his employer – loyal to Parnell at the beginning of the split, but he remained with the *Freeman* after it switched sides and later when it merged with the anti-Parnellite *National Press*. This is in marked contrast to the actions of others on the *Freeman* staff – for example, the editor Edward Byrne – who jumped ship to join the new pro-Parnell *Irish Daily Independent* when the *Freeman* abandoned Parnell. It is evidence of professionalism in a journalist unusual for this period, though another factor may have been Tuohy's growing disillusionment with Parnell.[27] Tuohy's reporting skills were so highly regarded that he was entrusted with covering the Irish party's protracted debate in Committee Room

23 M. Foley, 'Colonialism and journalism in Ireland', *Journalism Studies*, 5:3 (2004), 373–85 at 379, 383. **24** Taylor, *Sir Bertram Windle*, p. 202. See also Ann Keogh and Dermot Keogh, *Bertram Windle: the Honan bequest and the modernisation of University College Cork, 1904–1919* (Cork, 2010), p. 68. **25** See F.M. Larkin, 'Parnell, politics and the press in Ireland', the Parnell Lecture at the 2010 Parnell Summer School (Avondale, Co. Wicklow), 11 Aug. 2010 (publication forthcoming). **26** A. Dunlop, *Fifty years of Irish journalism* (London, 1911), pp 250–1. **27** J.M. Tuohy, 'Parnell at bay', with an introduction by F. Callanan, *The Recorder: the Journal of the American Irish Historical Society*, 17:2 (fall 2004), 59–66.

15 on the question of Parnell's continued leadership in December 1890. No journalists other than Tuohy and five colleagues from the *Freeman* staff chosen by him
and working strictly under his direction were allowed to attend, so his reports were
the only first-hand contemporary record. Despite complaints by T.M. Healy, it is
generally accepted that the reports are accurate and objective.[28] Tuohy also had a very
distinguished international journalistic career – for he combined his post on the
Freeman with that of London correspondent and European manager of Joseph
Pulitzer's *New York World*. When he died in 1923, the London *Times* hailed him as the
'doyen of American correspondents in Europe' – a remarkable accolade for a
Corkman, and from a most unlikely source.[29]

The restructuring and modernization of the *Independent* by William Martin
Murphy in 1905 involved a major advance in professional standards in journalism in
Ireland. He appointed a new editor, T.R. Harrington, who was – like Murphy
himself – a native of Castletownbere, Co. Cork, and whose prior experience had
been on the reporting staff of the newspaper. The usual route into an editorial chair
had been through the leader-writing staff – the commentators, not the reporters, got
the job. Before coming to Dublin, Harrington had learned his trade on the *Cork
Daily Herald* under the editorship of John Hooper – one of the journalists from Cork
who became an Irish party MP. As editor of the *Independent*, Harrington prescribed
a new style of reporting for his staff, instructing them 'to approach the work with a
perfectly open mind … and confine themselves as a rule to reporting facts or
speeches in a fair and impartial way, following our usual practice of not giving things
fully'.[30] Brevity, like objectivity, was unusual in Irish journalism at the time.
Moreover, he fought for and secured an unprecedented degree of editorial independence, with Murphy agreeing to remain at a distance from day-to-day
operations. These were huge innovations – and, with the phenomenal success of the
Independent under Harrington's editorship, other newspapers in Ireland gradually
followed suit. If they didn't, they went under – and such was the fate of the *Freeman's
Journal*.[31] The last editor of the *Freeman* was another Corkman, Patrick Hooper – son
of Harrington's early mentor, John Hooper. After the *Freeman's* closure, he served as
an independent member of the Senate of the Irish Free State and was vice-chairman
of the Senate when he died in September 1931 – one more journalist of the Irish
Parliamentary Party tradition who went on to have a career in politics.

III

With less political bias and greater professionalism in Irish journalism, it follows that
the high representation of journalists in the Irish Parliamentary Party has not been

28 F.S.L. Lyons, *The fall of Parnell, 1890–91* (London, 1960), pp 119–21. **29** *Times*, 8 Sept.
1923. **30** NAI, T.R. Harrington Papers, MS 1052/3/4. **31** For a full account of the
Freeman's last years, see F.M. Larkin, '"A great daily organ": the *Freeman's Journal*, 1763–1924',
History Ireland, 14:3 (May/June 2006), 44–9.

replicated in Dáil Éireann. Relatively few journalists have been elected to the Dáil: Arthur Griffith, of course;[32] J.J. O'Kelly ('Sceilg'), editor of the *Catholic Bulletin* – and no relation of his namesake, the Irish party MP; Piaras Béaslaí, whose journalistic endeavours included a daily Irish language column for the *Freeman's Journal* in the early 1900s and the weekly 'Moods and memories' feature in the *Irish Independent* in the 1960s; Martin Roddy, editor and proprietor of the *Sligo Champion*; Frank McDermot, who worked for the *Sunday Times* after his Dáil career ended; Patrick J. Little, who edited various advanced nationalist newspapers between 1915 and 1926, and was Minister for Posts and Telegraphs from 1939 to 1948; Garret FitzGerald and Conor Cruise O'Brien, both of whom were lots of other things as well as being journalists; John Horgan and Geraldine Kennedy, both of the *Irish Times*; Ted Nealon, news editor of the *Sunday Review*, a 'brash and breezy Sunday tabloid' published by the *Irish Times* from 1957 to 1963;[33] Conor Lenihan, a reporter with the Dublin radio station 98FM before he was elected to the Dáil; George Lee, RTÉ's economics correspondent before his brief sally into politics; and Shane Ross, long-time business columnist with the *Sunday Independent*. In addition, a handful of TDs had been television presenters.[34] The special position of the *Irish Press* as the organ of the Fianna Fáil party should also be noted in this context: Eamon de Valera and his son, Major Vivion de Valera, were successively editors-in-chief of the *Press* – and Seán Lemass was its managing director from 1948 to 1951, and in that capacity wrote a regular 'Political commentary' column from March 1948 onwards. Moreover, Seán T. O'Kelly was editor of the weekly *Nation* newspaper, the precursor of the *Irish Press*, in the late 1920s; O'Kelly's *Nation* had no connection with the nineteenth-century newspaper of the same name.[35]

Not one of the journalists-cum-politicians in Dáil Éireann was born in Co. Cork, and there is only one with Cork antecedents – John Horgan, currently Ireland's first press ombudsman and a native of Tralee, Co. Kerry. His grandfather and namesake was the notable Cork city solicitor, J.J. Horgan, who was deeply involved at grassroots level in the Irish party in its final years and later wrote regularly about Irish affairs for the influential British journal *The round table*. His book, *Parnell to Pearse* (first published in 1949; re-issued, with a biographical introduction by the younger

---

32 For assessments of Griffith *qua* journalist, see F.M. Larkin, 'Arthur Griffith and the *Freeman's Journal*' and C. Meehan, '"The prose of logic and scorn": Arthur Griffith and *Sinn Féin*, 1906–1914', both chapters in K. Rafter (ed.), *Irish journalism before independence: more a disease than a profession* (Manchester, 2011), pp 174–85, 186–99.   **33** The *Sunday Review* is so described in Dermot James, *From the margins to the centre: a history of the* Irish Times (Dublin, 2008), p. 158. See also M. O'Brien, *The Irish Times: a history* (Dublin, 2008), pp 159–61.   **34** The TDs in question were David Thornley, Justin Keating and Pat Cox. Ted Nealon, after his stint with the *Sunday Review*, was also a television presenter before his election to Dáil Éireann in 1981.   **35** Griffith, J.J. O'Kelly, Béaslaí, Roddy, McDermot, Little, de Valera *père et fils*, Lemass and Seán T. O'Kelly have entries in *DIB*. For information on Lemass' 'Political Column', see M. O'Brien, *De Valera, Fianna Fáil and the* Irish Press (Dublin, 2001), pp 82–3 and B. Evans, *Seán Lemass: democratic dictator* (Cork, 2011), pp 161–7. Regarding the *Nation* newspaper, see n. 14 above.

John Horgan, in 2009), makes a strong case for the old Irish party, and his explanation of why it ultimately failed is persuasive: the party was betrayed by their allies, the British Liberals, in the face of armed Ulster unionist resistance to Home Rule. He concludes with these words:

> We constitutionalists had been wisely prepared to make large concessions in order to avoid the division of our country which we believed to be the final and intolerable wrong. The price of our successors' triumph was Partition – an Ireland divided into a state which is not coterminous with the country, and a province which is itself dismembered. They sacrificed Irish unity for Irish sovereignty and attained neither.[36]

This perceptive comment – a fairer and broader assessment than Foster's curt dismissal of the Irish party as 'Trollopian fixers, political journalists, respectable ex-Fenians and closet imperialists' – comes from a man who, had Sinn Féin not triumphed in the 1918 general election, might have sat in Westminster as an Irish party MP and so would now be counted among those who straddle the two elites that helped define the character of Irish politics and journalism between the 1870s and 1918.[37]

36 J.J. Horgan, *Parnell to Pearse: some recollections and reflections*, with a biographical introduction by J. Horgan (Dublin, 2009), p. 354.   **37** J.J. Horgan's first wife (d. 1920) was a daughter of Bertram Windle, the president of University College Cork who has been quoted above on the Corkonians' peculiar aptitude for journalism. Windle, however, strongly disapproved of their marriage – see Keogh and Keogh, *Bertram Windle*, pp 83–92.

The three Fs – founders, fellowship and finance: the influence of book club members on Belfast's civic identity in the nineteenth century

PAMELA EMERSON

> There were no football matches, but there were cock-fighting and bull-baiting for the poor, and fox hunting for the rich, and much card playing by the ladies in the late afternoon, and by the gentlemen in the early morning.[1]

For the citizens of nineteenth-century Belfast, diversions such as cock-fighting and bull-baiting were not the only means of occupying leisure time. The analysis of leisure activities shows that pastimes fall into two camps, the rough and the respectable.[2] This essay focuses on the overtly respectable pastime of reading by examining the membership of some of Belfast's book lending institutions. Intellectual development was also important, as Robert Marshall tells us it 'was a period of great desire for knowledge, for culture, and for social betterment. The middle classes were thrifty and prosperous, and formed societies for their mutual improvement'.[3] This desire for knowledge and improvement manifested itself in Belfast by, among other things, an increase in the number of reading clubs and library societies established from the 1780s onwards. We can only speculate as to what motivated this proliferation of book club activity at this particular time, though Mary Casteleyn attributes this 'revival in scholarly interests' to the Volunteer movement that led to 'the mingling of people from different sectors of the community' and states that 'reading, at first a fashion, turned to being a favoured occupation'.[4] It would therefore appear that involvement in this pastime seems to have been adopted by the politically motivated as a vehicle to further their aims. A quantitative study of Ulster book clubs and library societies has never been attempted, but it is estimated that at least fifty societies connected with book lending existed within the town of Belfast during the nineteenth century. Literacy levels varied depending on the amount of

---

1 Robert Marshall, *The book of Belfast compiled for the 105th annual meeting, in 1937, of the British Medical Association* (Belfast, 1937), p. 11. 2 H. Cunningham, 'Leisure and culture' in F.M.L. Thompson (ed.), *People and their environment: the Cambridge social history of Britain, 1750–1950*, 2 (Cambridge, 1996), p. 289. 3 Marshall, *The book of Belfast*, p. 11. 4 Mary Casteleyn, *A history of literacy and libraries in Ireland: the long traced pedigree* (Aldershot, 1984), p. 89.

schooling received, and many people faced social and economic problems. There were strong political interests in the city, while science and exploration were expanding the average citizen's knowledge of the world. In an unequal society, reading could address concerns of specific social groups by providing knowledge to help improve their lives, whether for societal progression, improved personal status or ideological advancement. Technology also meant that there were more newspapers and books printed, and improved transportation made for wider distribution. This essay takes a prosopographical approach, identifying the people who belonged to local reading societies, especially the dominant mercantile class, and establishes what other public organizations they were involved in before assessing their role in the development of Belfast's civic identity in the nineteenth century.

The reasons for establishing or belonging to a particular book club were often determined by class and personal interests. Marie-Louise Legg has identified six motives for founding library-based associations. Firstly, there were self-serving clubs where members of the local gentry and the urban middle classes created 'new centres for sociability'. Secondly, they were established to create places for improvement and education of the artisans that were accessible outside working hours. Thirdly, paternalistic clubs were set up by landlords or employers for their staff. The fourth motive was commercial, as people would pay to read books that they could not afford to buy outright. Her fifth reason was a desire to 'encourage civic pride' and, aligned to this, the final motive was 'education for the masses in order to inculcate a spirit of virtue and social conformity allied with nationalism'.[5] These motivations led to the creation of book clubs and other book-lending associations that catered for the needs of the different social groups, with printed materials appropriate to the interests, status and literacy levels of the intended membership. For example, the collections of a small lending library would be of a different nature to those of a library of the medical society.

TYPES OF BOOK CLUBS AND OTHER BOOK-LENDING FACILITIES

For comparative purposes, the literary based societies of Ulster have been sub-divided into four groups depending on the way in which the club or association originated, the reading materials they provided and the method of operation. These groups are book clubs, commercial circulating libraries, newsrooms, and libraries built up by organizations initially set up for another purpose. The foundation motives outlined by Legg will also be considered.

The first category is made up of those with 'self-serving' attributes, which have been variously described as book clubs, reading societies, subscription libraries or literary societies. However, the overarching term 'book club' has been used for this

---

5 Marie-Louise Legg, 'Libraries' in James H. Murphy (ed.), *The Irish book in English, 1800–1891*, The Oxford history of the Irish book, 4 (Oxford, 2011), pp 243–61 at p. 244.

section for clarity. These voluntary clubs were set up by locals who each paid a membership fee that was initially used to offset the cost of book purchases. Later, as the membership grew and collections increased, funds were also used to employ staff and to rent or purchase premises. The books, selected and agreed by the members or elected committee, were read by the members and either auctioned to become the personal property of a member or alternatively kept by the club to build up a library collection. Some clubs welcomed anyone able to pay the subscription, while others had a ballot or recommendation system to limit membership to known persons. The Belfast Reading Society (1788) and the Belfast Literary Society (1801) were two of the earliest book clubs to be established in Belfast. Many of the influential figures in Belfast's development and nineteenth-century history were members of these book clubs. As the name implies, commercial circulating libraries were established for commercial reasons and not driven by a desire to disseminate information. A 1797 instruction manual on how to set up such an enterprise suggests that book lending on its own was 'insufficient to support a family' and suggested that suitable partnerships were: 'haberdashery, hosiery, hats, tea, tobacco and snuff, perfumery and the sale of patent medicines'.[6] Legg discovered Irish examples that were run in conjunction with stationers and patent medicine vendors.[7] The proprietors set aside a shelf or small area for book storage and lent from their stock for a small fee. In the long term, they probably received more income through multiple loans of the one book than would have been generated by the sale of one copy of the book. Commercial circulating libraries had a shop front and were open to any citizen in the area able to pay the fee to borrow books. Although Mary Casteleyn identified circulating libraries in Belfast run by Eliza Archer, John Hodgson and Francis Lamont, contemporary sources show that other concerns were run by Hugh Warrin from 1794, Isabella Drummond's library was in existence in 1805, Henry Greer operated one from 1820 to 1824, Robert Graham ran a library in his book shop in 1824, Morgan Jellett's establishment ran from 1830 to 1833, George Phillips and Sons was in existence between 1832 and 1870, while Cornelius Hassen ran his circulating library from 1836 to 1838.[8] The commercial circulating libraries contained a high proportion of novels and, as the constitution of the Belfast Reading Society did not

---

6 *The use of circulating libraries considered; with instructions for opening and conducting a library either upon a large or small plan* (London, 1797), p. 35.   **7** Legg, 'Libraries', p. 244, based on her research in *Newspapers and nationalism: the Irish provincial press, 1850–1892* (Dublin, 1998), pp 177–222.   **8** Casteleyn, *A history of literacy and libraries in Ireland*, pp 60–1. *Northern Star,* 9 Jan. 1794, 26 June 1794 and 27 Oct. 1794; *Belfast Commercial Chronicle*, 16 Mar. 1805 and 18 May 1805; *The Commercial Directory of Ireland/Scotland for 1820–21 and 1822* (Manchester, 1820), p. 137; *Northern Whig*, 1 Jan. 1824 and 23 Dec. 1824; James Pigot, *Pigot and Co. Provincial Directory of Ireland for 1824: Ulster*, p. 332. *Belfast News-Letter*, 5 Nov. 1830, 1 Nov. 1831, 5 Oct. 1832, 8 Sept. 1835, 8 July 1856, 5 Nov. 1864, 7 June 1866, 27 June 1870, 10 July 1838 and 27 July 1838. William Matier, *Matiers's Belfast Directory for 1835–6* (Belfast, 1835), p. 64. The dates given are those where an advertisement or entry has been located in a primary source not exact dates of establishment or closure.

permit it to obtain 'any common novel or farce or other book of trivial amusement', members may have used these commercial establishments to borrow this type of reading material.[9] The ban on novels was not unique to this institution; Marsh's Library and the Dublin Literary Society also operated this policy.[10]

Regarding the third type, newsrooms, it appears that 'Ireland's first newsroom opened in Belfast in 1782'.[11] Newsrooms supplied local and national newspapers for communal reading on the premises. The title of some newsrooms gave an indication of their location, such as Brookfield News Room, the Waring Street News Room and the Coal Exchange News Room at Ballymacarrett. Others were prefixed by Belfast in their title; for example, the Belfast Athenaeum, the Belfast Commercial News Room or the Belfast People's News Room. These were considered to be open to all, irrespective of their political or religious views. In some instances, however, the newsroom title reflected the political or religious interests of the organizations that established the facility. Casteleyn and Higgins both consider the effect of Repeal Reading Rooms in their research, but neither mentioned that one was set up by this movement in Belfast.[12] Oliver Rafferty made reference to the Belfast Repeal Reading Room that 'was housed in Chapel Lane near to St Mary's Church'.[13] References to a Whig News Room, a Nelson Club News Room and the Belfast Catholic Institute News Room have been discovered. These newsrooms fall under Legg's motives of 'civic pride' and the espousal of 'virtue and social conformity', although I would add that membership of such defined organizations was also a badge of identity and a public declaration of their principles or opinion. These facilities attracted individuals who supported the ideology of the club or adhered to a specific way of life and the clubs therefore had a select membership. The Northern Whig club was set up by Alexander Haliday, 'a medical doctor who had been an officer in the Second Belfast Volunteers' and, more importantly, 'Charlemont's link with Belfast Volunteering'.[14] The establishment of newsrooms by interested parties furthered their aims and the facilities were possibly used to recruit members who showed empathy by joining. As there are few records relating to membership of commercial newsrooms, it has been difficult to trace who made use of these facilities. There is evidence to suggest that the Commercial News Room set up prior to 1819 was patronized by some of the radical members.[15]

The fourth category includes churches, workplaces, the Mechanics Institute and charitable organizations that set up library facilities, often for benevolent reasons,

9 John Killen, *A history of the Linen Hall Library, 1788–1988* (Belfast, 1990), p. 12. **10** Richard Cargill Cole, *Irish booksellers and English writers, 1740–1800* (London, 1986), p. 36. **11** Roisín Higgins, 'The *Nation* reading rooms' in Murphy (ed.), *The Irish book in English, 1800–1891*, pp 262–73 at p. 263. **12** Mary Casteleyn, *A history of literacy and libraries in Ireland*, pp 140–50. Higgins, 'The *Nation* reading rooms', pp 262–73. **13** Oliver P. Rafferty, *Catholicism in Ulster, 1613–1983: an interpretive history* (Columbia, 1994), p. 129. **14** Allan Blackstock, *Double traitors? The Belfast Volunteers and Yeomen, 1778–1828* (Belfast, 2000), p. 8. **15** *Northern Herald*, 7 Dec. 1833 included Robert Grimshaw and William Pirrie in the committee list. They are mentioned in connection with other establishments in the text.

although this was not their primary function. These library service providers, for the most part, correspond with two of Legg's motives; by adopting a 'paternalistic' system of provision for the 'the improvement of artisans'. In this instance, the person was firstly a member or employee of the original organization and, as such, was then eligible to join the book club or library set up under their auspices. The local business owners, ministers and educationalists were involved in the organizing committees of these libraries rather than being members. The Belfast Mechanics Institute, set up in 1825, had as one of its objects the formation of a library. William Tennent and Robert Grimshaw were two of the five trustees elected for life.[16] The Medical Society Library was set up by leading medics who considered it important that medical knowledge was disseminated to practitioners.

The establishment of book club and library facilities may have stemmed from the desire of individuals to acquire reading material without great expense or, alternatively, the facility was imposed by an individual or group of influential citizens who felt that reading books and newspapers would be beneficial to the people. For this reason, each of the book clubs and other lending facilities established in Belfast was unique. They served different geographical areas, the reading requirements of the clientele differed, the size of the collections varied from a few hundred to several thousand volumes, some had a limited subject range, some stocked novels while others refused to stock these and the membership costs and requirements varied. Agreements were entered into by Queen's College and Belfast Society for Promoting Knowledge that prevented the duplication of stock.[17] This variety allowed the fifty plus establishments to co-exist within the town of Belfast over the course of the nineteenth century and in some instances much longer. As Ronnie Adams stated, 'the social importance of this proliferation of small local libraries (many of which have vanished from the record) should not be overlooked'.[18]

FOUNDERS

The book club members were also involved in setting up committees and establishing organizations to improve Belfast and put it on a par with British towns such as Liverpool and Manchester. British institutions served as models for Belfast literary associations. An Athenaeum had been established in Liverpool in 1797.[19] A Belfast Athenaeum was proposed in 1811 and a detailed description of its intentions was printed in the *Belfast News-Letter*.[20] Nothing seems to have transpired as the idea was again mooted in the 1840s, when a proposal was circulated to fifty-nine interested

16 'Constitution and laws of Belfast Mechanics Institute 1825', PRONI D1769/24/2.
17 Mary Casteleyn, *A history of literacy and libraries in Ireland*, p. 131; T.W. Moody and J.C. Beckett, *Queen's, Belfast, 1845–1949: the history of a university*, 1 (London, 1959), p. 129.
18 J.R.R. Adams, 'Books and libraries in Bangor and Holywood', *Linen Hall Review*, 2:1 (spring 1985), 14–15 at 15.   19 http://www.theathenaeum.org.uk, accessed 19 Sept. 2011.
20 *Belfast News-Letter*, 17 Dec. 1811.

citizens.[21] The wealthy business owners were not as forthcoming with subscriptions on this occasion. On the 1845 document, only nine people had signed up as subscribers. Of these, only Robert J. Tennent was already a book club member. A Belfast Athenaeum was established in 1867 at 22 Castle Place, but it was a scaled down version of the original vision.[22]

Other improvements to the town included the creation of public spaces, parks and gardens, the provision of recreational facilities, the development of cultural and musical skills as well as the establishment of centres for progressive medical and scientific study. The forward-thinking book club members also used their influence, interests and connections to further the development of the Botanic Gardens, the Ulster Gaelic Society, the Belfast Harp Society and the People's Library and News Room, to name a few examples.[23]

One of the earliest specialist libraries was the Belfast Medical Library, established in 1806. It was regarded as a valuable resource that contributed 'to the improvement of medical science, as it affords an opportunity of consulting books too expensive for many individuals to purchase'.[24] The Medical Library committee members in 1808 were listed as Samuel S. Thompson, William Halliday, Robert McGee, Robert McCluney and Andrew Marshall.[25] These medical practitioners were also actively involved in other book clubs. Although this library later fell into disuse, it was revived in 1822 by the efforts of Dr James McDonnell.[26]

The pro-active McDonnell, as well as belonging to libraries and re-establishing a specialist medical library, wanted to promote the Irish language. When the Ulster Gaelic Society was set up in 1830, McDonnell, at the age of sixty-eight, was its chairman. Fellow Belfast Society for Promoting Knowledge and Belfast Literary Society members, Robert MacAdam and Reuben Bryce, were co-secretaries. Perhaps it was through their influence that the Belfast Society for Promoting Knowledge held Gaelic books in its collections.[27] Irish, at this time, was a functioning language, spoken in Belfast and in rural Ulster and was compulsory for those who intended to become Presbyterian ministers.[28] A.G. Malcolm paid tribute to the endeavours of McDonnell thus: 'It would seem, indeed, that so great and varied was his intellectual capacity, that he was enabled, almost single-handed, to stamp a literary

21 Prospectus for the Belfast Athenaeum, PRONI D4191/1. Handwritten date Nov. 1845 at the top of the document; 'Miscellaneous scraps including … names of persons to whom prospectuses of the Athenaeum had been furnished', PRONI D1748/G/811/5. **22** *Belfast News-Letter*, 21 Mar. 1868. **23** *Catalogue of books contained in the People's Library with the rules and regulations, office bearers, patrons and a list of the periodicals and newspapers supplied to the news room* (Belfast, 1863). **24** John Dubourdieu, *Statistical survey of the county of Antrim* (Dublin, 1812), pp 536–7. **25** Joseph Smyth, *Belfast directory, for 1808; or a list of names and places of the merchants, traders and co.* (Belfast, 1808, repr. 1991), p. 83. **26** Ulster Medical Society, *Transcript of the minutes of the Belfast Medical Society, 1822–1828* (Jan. 1995, July 2005), p. 1. **27** Roger Blaney, *Presbyterians and the Irish language* (Belfast, 1996), pp 33–4; Anderson, *History of Belfast Library and Society for Promoting Knowledge* (Belfast, 1888), p. 24; Killen, *A history of the Linen Hall Library*, p. 65. **28** A.J. Hughes, *Robert Shipboy MacAdam (1808–95): his life and Gaelic proverb collection* (Belfast, 1998), pp 19, 20, 27–9.

face upon the locality'.[29] It is thanks to the sustained efforts of enthusiastic men like McDonnell that Belfast had a well developed literary and cultural identity.

Membership of a club was, and still is, a social pastime, which allows people with similar interests to meet together to share their leisure pursuits, learn from each other and converse with others holding a similar outlook, all in the spirit of fellowship. The underlying purpose of many of these clubs was comradeship and sociability. Clubs were a place to relax and enjoy activities with others, but they were also centres that 'served as a vector for new ideas, new values, new kinds of social alignment, and forms of regional and national identity'.[30]

One of the earliest and certainly the best known book clubs to be established in Belfast was the Belfast Reading Society. It was later renamed the Belfast Society for Promoting Knowledge (1792) and, in 1837, the Belfast Library and Society for Promoting Knowledge. The society was successful in attracting members and through their protracted efforts the collections were expanded and premises were obtained. As the Linen Hall Library, it is the last remaining example of a subscription library in Ireland and it continues to 'improve the mind and excite the spirit' nearly 225 years later.[31] John Killen, the current librarian, has used the minutes of the club to record its history up to the bi-centenary. He records the foundation thus:

> It would appear from the minute books of the Belfast Reading Society that there were some fifteen founding members, as no record of their later joining the society can be traced. They were: William McCleery, tanner; Robert McCormick, gunsmith; his brother James McCormick; Roger Mulholland, architect and builder; John Rabb, printer; Robert Cary, the society's first librarian; William Hamilton; Arthur Quinn; Hugh McNamara; James Burges; James Woodburn; James De Butts; Maurice Spottiswood; James Potts and Richard Murdock . . .[32]

Killen has identified the occupations of a few of these founders as skilled tradesmen: tanner, gunsmith, printer and builder. Robert Cary rented out rooms in his house to store the books of the society in and to facilitate the meetings. Cary was involved in this club for six years, from its inception until 1794, when he emigrated.[33] James McCormick and John Rabb 'espoused the most advanced and radical political views' so the society's rules had to be clarified to specify that there was to be no political

---

29 Malcolm, *The history of the General Hospital* (1851), cited in Marshall, *The book of Belfast*, p. 21.   **30** Peter Clark, *British clubs and societies, 1580–1800: the origins of an associational world* (Oxford, 2000), p. ix.   **31** John Anderson, *History of the Belfast Library and Society for Promoting Knowledge*, p. 9.   **32** Killen, *A history of the Linen Hall Library*, p. 9.   **33** Ibid., pp 14, 213.

discussion in the club.[34] This action ensured that the club attracted members from all shades of political opinion and none. Prominent personalities within the Society of United Irishmen, such as Thomas Russell, who was elected librarian in 1794, were members.[35] While this could have alienated people, the membership remained broad. Gerard Long said that 'This radicalism among the membership was counterbalanced by conservative elements, which served to protect the society from reprisals'.[36]

A particularly acerbic comment on the membership of this club was made by Martha McTier around 1792 and it is often quoted: 'there was not among them one of higher rank than McCormick the gunsmith, or Osborne the baker'.[37] It suggests that McTier, and possibly others, considered that the Belfast Reading Society was most appropriate for the lower classes. McTier herself indulged in the leisure pursuit of gambling, an activity that was apparently deemed appropriate for her middle-class status.[38] Although her 'worthy plebians' comment is frequently quoted in isolation, she did continue by qualifying that '... of late some gentlemen [who] wished to take advantage of a valuable collection of books have deigned to enrol themselves'.[39] But the club was in financial difficulty. Killen noted the change in the class of new members and the emergence of some influential citizens of the nineteenth century.

> Around that time, the faltering steps of the society were noticed by other residents of Belfast ... members of Belfast's professional and merchant classes who gave the fledgling society a new impetus and direction. This influx of new members occurred in the latter part of 1792, when (among others) men like the Rev. Dr William Bruce (principal of Belfast Academy and minister of the First Presbyterian Church), Narcissus Batt (merchant and banker), Waddell Cunningham (merchant and banker), Robert Getty (merchant), Nicholas Grimshaw (cotton manufacturer), Dr Alexander Haliday (physician and scholar), the Rev. Hugh O'Donnell (parish priest of St Mary's) and William Tennent (merchant and banker) all joined.[40]

34 Ibid., p. 16.   **35** C.J. Woods (ed.), *Journals and memoirs of Thomas Russell, 1791–5* (Dublin and Belfast, 1991), p. 140.   **36** Gerard Long, 'Institutional libraries and private collections' in Murphy (ed.), *The Irish book in English, 1800–1891*, pp 281–97 at p. 290.   **37** Quoted by Johanna Archbold, 'Book clubs and reading societies in the late eighteenth century' in James Kelly and Martyn J. Powell (eds), *Clubs and societies in eighteenth-century Ireland* (Dublin, 2010), pp 138–62 at p. 146; Eoin Magennis, 'Clubs and societies in eighteenth-century Belfast' in Kelly and Powell (eds), *Clubs and societies*, pp 466–83 at p. 479; Killen, *A history of the Linen Hall Library*, p. 7; John Killen, 'The reading habits of a Georgian gentleman, John Templeton, and the book collections of the Belfast Society for Promoting Knowledge' in Bernadette Cunningham and Máire Kennedy (eds), *The experience of reading: Irish historical perspectives* (Dublin, 1999), pp 99–108 at p. 99; Helen Maloney Davis, 'The library tradition' in Neil Buttimer, Colin Rynne and Helen Guerin (eds), *The heritage of Ireland* (Cork, 2000), p. 282. **38** Kate Newmann, *Dictionary of Ulster Biography* (Belfast, 1993), pp 172–3.   **39** Jean Agnew (ed.), *Drennan McTier letters*, p. 419. Letter written by Martha McTier to William Drennan, 360, Sunday 28 Oct. [1792].   **40** Killen, *A history of the Linen Hall Library*, p. 13. He cites his source as the register of the members of the Belfast Society for Promoting Knowledge,

The change in membership to educators, clergy and business owners brought new skills and served to strengthen the club and expand its collections. By 1819, the club, now renamed the Belfast Society for Promoting Knowledge, had a collection of 'between three and four thousand volumes ... many of them scarce and expensive books, seldom found in public libraries' – a real treasure trove for dedicated readers whatever their social class.[41] The avid reader may have been encouraged to join to borrow books, but the society at this time was ostensibly a front for reform. Radical members of the Belfast Society for Promoting Knowledge passed a resolution supporting Catholic Emancipation, thereby linking the book club to political affairs.[42]

By 1844, an unnamed subscriber to the Belfast Library and Society for Promoting Knowledge wrote to the editor of the *Belfast News-Letter* complaining that the high annual subscription cost had rendered the society 'an exclusively aristocratic corporation'.[43] The radical United Irishmen would have used a Francophile interpretation of the term 'aristocratic'. Considered as hereditary spongers, 'aristocratic' was used as a form of denigration and the opposite of 'citizen', which was considered to carry a connotation of virtue and democracy. In less than fifty years, the perception of the social status of the membership had changed from 'plebian' to 'aristocratic'. This should not come as a surprise, as the society was then organized and run by 'middle-class professionals and dissenting Christians'. Indeed, an examination of the names shows that the members were 'a closely knit group of families, linked by marriage and kinship'.[44] It should be noted that as the landlords were absentee, the local power and influence was in the hands of this business community, many of whom were 'prepared to give generously of their time and money to philanthropic and cultural activities'.[45] For this reason, the business owners, educators and clerics can be regarded as an elite, rather than aristocratic, as they were not titled or landlords, but little happened in the town without their involvement.

Casteleyn noted that 'forty-five members, predominately Presbyterian, signed the original rules of the society, but Catholics were not excluded from membership'.[46] Only twenty-three of the early members have been mentioned here as a snapshot of the membership, but as Killen records, in 1828 there were 152 members, this dropped to 109 in 1830 but by 1849 there were 192 members.[47] In researching *A history of the Linen Hall Library*, Killen included biographical information on those who had served as the society's presidents or librarians, but he did not analyse the wider membership, their interests and the effects the members had on society outside the club. Magee noted that 'ministers were particularly influential', as 'they were largely responsible for

1792–1829, which is held at the Linen Hall Library.   **41** Thomas Bradshaw, *Belfast general and commercial directory for 1819* (Belfast, 1819), xxxv.   **42** Killen, *A history of the Linen Hall Library*, pp 11–12.   **43** *Belfast News-Letter*, 18 June 1844.   **44** Juliana Adelman, *Communities of science in nineteenth-century Ireland* (London, 2009), p. 12; John Magee, *The Linen Hall Library and the cultural life of Georgian Belfast* (Belfast, 1982), p. 5.   **45** Magee, *The Linen Hall Library*, p. 5.   **46** Casteleyn, *A history of literacy and libraries in Ireland*, p. 10.   **47** Killen, *A history of the Linen Hall Library*, p. 232.

shaping public opinion in the town'.[48] As this essay principally concerns Belfast's social and mercantile elite, it is worth examining a few of the other 'enterprising, enlightened, philanthropic and self-improving' citizens who were members of this organization in the early nineteenth century and how they contributed to the growth of Belfast.[49]

Edmund Getty, born in 1799, educated at Belfast Academical Institution, was also a member of the Belfast Literary Society and served as secretary of the Belfast Mechanics Institute. He was involved in the Natural History and Philosophical Society and Botanical Gardens. He was Ballast Master of the Belfast Ballast Board, Secretary of Belfast Harbour Board and constructed Belfast's 'Crystal Palace'. His interests were antiquary and linguistic and he published *Chinese seals in Ireland*, *History of the Harbour Board* and *Last king of Ulster*, as well as contributing to the *Ulster Journal of Archaeology*.[50]

William Thompson was treasurer of the Scientific Fund of the Belfast Society for Promoting Knowledge set up in 1837 by twenty-one subscribers who wanted to purchase works 'on science, chiefly foreign'.[51] He later served as its vice-president on two occasions. Thompson was also a member of the Belfast Literary Society and its president from 1838 to 1839. He was a naturalist and published *The natural history of Ireland* and is known to have corresponded with Charles Darwin.[52]

John Stephenson Ferguson, born in 1763, was a committee member in 1798. He was a linen merchant who founded the firm J.S. Ferguson and Co., which had offices located within the White Linen Hall. His business concerns also included ownership of bleach greens at Ballysillan and a paper mill at Antrim, so he would have been a major employer at the time. He supported different causes, serving as a volunteer in the 1790s, holding the position of president of the Chamber of Commerce for eleven years and was involved on the committee of the Belfast Charitable Society.[53]

Born in Scotland in 1780, William Pirrie had a varied career as a ships' captain, a merchant and then a ship-owner. He settled in Belfast, residing at Donegall Street. As well as membership of the Belfast Society for Promoting Knowledge, he was also on the committee of the Commercial News Room. As one of the first Belfast Harbour Commissioners, he had the honour of opening the Victoria Channel in 1849, which was beneficial for the industrial development of Belfast.[54]

48 Magee, *The Linen Hall Library*, p. 7.   **49** Killen, *A history of the Linen Hall Library*, p. 5. **50** Kate Newmann, *Dictionary of Ulster biography*, pp 85–6; *Belfast Literary Society, 1801–1901: historical sketch with memoirs of some distinguished members* (Belfast, 1902), p. 165; Edmund Getty, *Chinese seals in Ireland* (Dublin, 1850); Edmund Getty, *History of the Harbour Board* (Belfast, 1852); Edmund Getty, *Last king of Ulster* (London, 1841).   **51** Killen, *A history of the Linen Hall Library*, p. 139.   **52** Geoffrey V. Morson, 'Thompson, William (1805–1852)' in *ODNB*; Anderson, *The history of the Belfast Library and Society for Promoting Knowledge*, pp 94, 96; *Belfast Literary Society, 1801–1901* (Belfast, 1902), p. 187; William Thompson, *The natural history of Ireland*, 1 (London, 1849).   **53** Anderson, *The history of the Belfast Library and Society for Promoting Knowledge*, p. 95; A.C.W. Merrick and R.S.J. Clarke (eds), *Old Belfast families and the new burying ground from gravestone inscriptions, with wills and biographical notes* (Belfast, 1991), pp 87–8.   **54** Merrick and Clarke, *Old Belfast families and the new burying ground*, p.

These four men served on the committee of the Belfast Library and Society for Promoting Knowledge and were notable for their personal achievements within science, civic architecture, natural history and the development of Belfast as an industrial centre and commercial port. They were distinguished in the positions that they held, their research was published and thus brought to a wider audience, their skills contributed to the development of port and leisure facilities and their social network was impressive.

It is also necessary to examine the membership of the Belfast Literary Society as a friendship element was involved with its members opening their homes to fellow book club members in order to facilitate club meetings. It was said that the Belfast Literary Society was 'private in its form, but public in its tendency and importance. The meetings were held in the houses of members in rotation'.[55] Indeed, this practice continued for over twenty years. According to Dr William Bruce, the fellowship element was an important aspect within the organization.

> We cannot boast of having contributed much to enlighten or entertain the public, but we have enlightened and entertained ourselves and one another ... We have now the satisfaction to observe that other societies, enlightening different branches of literature and science, have sprung up, stimulated, perhaps, by our example.[56]

The *Historical sketch of Belfast Literary Society* records that between 1812 and 1818 the meetings were held in the homes of James McDonnell, Henry Joy, John Knox, Ross Jebb, William Bruce, Mr Comines and Samuel Martin Stephenson. The extent of the host's hospitality was also established: 'no refreshment shall be introduced except tea or coffee'.[57] The location of these meetings has a bearing on their significance. It has been observed that the 'intellectual, professional and industrial elite would have been highly visible ... many of the wealthy merchant families lived in grand town houses dotted in or around Donegall Square'.[58] The residences where the meetings were held were all in this vicinity: Dr McDonnell lived at 13 Donegall Place, Henry Joy lived at 5 Donegall Square North, William Bruce had a residence at the Belfast Academy and Dr Stephenson lived at 6 Waring Street.[59] The addresses of the book club members were therefore in keeping with their social status and the close proximity of the members meant they were known to each other.

Although members of the Belfast Literary Society had commercial and business

233; *Belfast News-Letter*, 7 Dec. 1833, 7 Dec. 1838, 6 Dec. 1839, 4 Dec. 1846. **55** A. Hume, *The learned societies and printing clubs of the United Kingdom* (London, 1847), p. 210; Hugh Adair, *Adair's Belfast street directory for 1860–61* (Belfast, 1860), p. 403, also records this practice. **56** Bruce Papers, National Library of Ireland, MS 20,898. **57** *The Belfast Literary Society, 1801–1901*, p. 6. **58** John Bew, *The glory of being British: civic unionism in nineteenth-century Belfast* (Dublin, 2009), p. 11. **59** www.ums.ac.uk/mcdonnell_j.html, accessed 21 June 2011; Thomas Bradshaw, *Belfast and general commercial directory for 1819* (Belfast, 1819), p. 40; Pigot, *Directory of Ireland, 1824*, pp 348, 77.

connections, mixed socially and belonged to the same churches, all was not harmonious within this organization. In 1803, Mrs McTier told Mrs Drennan in a letter 'I hear J. Templeton has withdrawn from the Literary Society to avoid his former friend, McD'.[60] Members held conflicting political attitudes that occasionally surfaced within the associational context. As already mentioned, many carried with them memories of the events of the 1790s. Within Belfast Literary Society, William Drennan was a member of the Society of the United Irishmen, while William Bruce, originally a Volunteer, became a loyalist and 'took the Yeomanry oath'.[61] Thomas Robinson immortalized some of the book club members by including them in his painting *Review of the Belfast Yeomanry by the lord lieutenant, the earl of Hardwicke, 27 August 1804*.[62] Portraits of Dr Bruce, William Sinclaire, James McDonnell and Henry Joy were incorporated into the scene.[63] William Drennan, styled as a 'doyen of the politically radical literati', was originally included in the painting but was later removed as he wanted to distance himself from the incidents.[64]

Meanwhile, some well-to-do merchants felt that the Belfast Academy did not offer a 'complete uniform, and extensive system of education'.[65] William Drennan recorded that he had attended a meeting of the Belfast Literary Society in 1807 where he 'heard a report read from the committee appointed to draw up a sketch of the proposed [Academical] Institution. About 60 were present … The report appeared well drawn up'. The Belfast Literary Society members reacted to this proposal positively and 'a committee was appointing to call for subscriptions'.[66] Drennan became actively involved in the foundation of the Belfast Academical Institution along with fellow book club member John Templeton. At the formal opening in 1814, he announced that to 'diffuse useful knowledge, particularly among the middling orders of society, was a necessity, not a luxury of life'.[67] Perhaps it was this attitude that instilled a love of reading in the alumni of this establishment.

The list of staff of the Belfast Academical Institution in *Pigot and Co. provincial directory of Ireland* of 1824 shows that there was a strong link between the school and book club membership.[68] Out of the fourteen staff, ten were members of the Belfast book clubs under consideration. Six of these learned gentlemen belonged to both

60 D.A. Chart, *The Drennan letters, being a selection of the correspondence which passed between William Drennan MD and his brother-in-law and sister, Samuel and Martha McTier, during the years 1776–1819* (Belfast, 1931), p. 332. McD indicating Dr James McDonnell. **61** A.T.Q. Stewart, *Belfast Royal Academy: the first century, 1785–1885* (Belfast, 1985), pp 12, 22, 31. **62** Eileen Black, *Art in Belfast, 1760–1880: art lovers or philistines?* (Dublin, 2006), p. 8: pl. 6 shows the painting. Allan Blackstock examines this painting in relation to loyalist association membership in his chapter 'Loyalist associational culture in Ireland' in Jennifer Kelly and Vincent Comerford (eds), *Associational culture in Ireland* (Dublin, 2010), pp 47–66. The painting is in the collection of the Belfast Harbour Commissioners. **63** Stewart, *Belfast Royal Academy*, p. 86. **64** Black, *Art in Belfast*, pp 222–3; Nancy Curtin, *The United Irishmen: popular politics in Ulster and Dublin, 1791–1798* (Oxford, 1994), p. 212. **65** Royal Belfast Academical Institution, www.rbai.org.uk, accessed 21 June 2011. **66** Chart, *The Drennan Letters*, p. 379. **67** www.rbai.org.uk, accessed 21 Jun. 2011. **68** *Pigot and Co. provincial directory of Ireland of 1824*, p. 349.

the Belfast Society for Promoting Knowledge and the Belfast Literary Society: Thomas Dix Hincks, James Thomson, James L. Drummond, John Young, William Cairns and William Bruce. Two of the educationalists were only members of the Belfast Society for Promoting Knowledge (Samuel Hanna and John Stevelly), while a further two members of staff belonged to Belfast Literary Society (Adelbert D'Oisy and Henry Montgomery). All eight of the Belfast Literary Society members mentioned served as its president for at least one year.[69] The fact that these men were members of more than one club paints a distinctive picture of membership of Belfast book clubs, as in England membership of 'two clubs concurrently' was regarded as 'uncommon'.[70]

It can be seen that the membership of these book clubs was not mutually exclusive. People belonged to more than one book-lending association and within these clubs new friendships and alliances were made and often these were beneficial to the development of social and educational facilities in Belfast.

FINANCE

As well as accessing reading materials for their own yearning and intellect via the book clubs, however, the members also had a desire to use their influence to improve the social and cultural facilities that were available to Belfast citizens. As the second marquis of Donegall had heavy debts and was unable to fund projects in the town, the philanthropic and entrepreneurial citizens made 'energetic attempts to improve the town'.[71] Williams stated that 'in Ireland it was not possible to command as large a membership of scholars and bookmen, nor to find an equivalent number of moneyed supporters' compared to England and Scotland.[72] The members of Belfast book clubs defied this generalization, however, and were financially involved in the expansion of public resources and significantly influenced the development of the town. They patronized and supported institutions both financially and in kind. They were particularly generous in supporting the establishment or extension of educational, medical and cultural facilities.

William Bruce, principal of Belfast Academy, a member of both the Belfast Literary Society and the Belfast Society for Promoting Knowledge, promoted the benefits of reading and education, stating that 'when the labour of education is over ... they are prepared to study the finest authors with facility and pleasure'.[73] Belfast Academy was established in 1785 and several book club members such as Henry Joy and William Sinclaire were included among the original subscribers and designated as patrons. The patrons could not meet the financial demands involved in running

69 See *The Belfast Literary Society, 1801–1901*, pp 151–3.   **70** Paul Kaufman, *Libraries and their uses: collected papers in library history* (London, 1969), p. 64, n. 36.   **71** Jonathan Bardon, *Belfast: an illustrated history* (Belfast, 1984), p. 66.   **72** Harold Williams, *Book clubs and printing societies of Great Britain and Ireland* (London, 1929), p. 50.   **73** William Bruce, 'On the advantages of classical education', *Select papers of the Belfast Literary Society* (Belfast, 1808), 40.

the school, however, and Bruce, who 'had considerable private means', took on the payments of leases, amounting to 'about £470'.[74] Belfast Academy played an important role as numerous book club members were educated there.

Writing about the Belfast Literary Society, the *Belfast Monthly Magazine* noted that 'the name of this society would seem to indicate that its discussions were confined to polite literature only. This is by no means the case'.[75] Indeed, by 1814 the same publication reported that Mr Comines, a surgeon, had spoken to the members of the Belfast Literary Society about various hospitals, 'plans of which he laid before the society, with a view to promote the erection of the intended General Hospital'.[76] Following this promotion, various members of the Belfast Literary Society became involved in the foundation of medical institutions within the town.

During 1813, 1817 and 1819, subscriptions towards the building of the Fever Hospital were collected. Of the forty-six individual subscribers, sixteen belonged to book clubs. Twelve were members of the Belfast Society for Promoting Knowledge, five belonged to the Medical Society Library, four were connected to the Belfast Literary Society and four were subscribers to the Commercial News Room. Seven were members of two or more societies. The sixteen book club members donated a total of £256 10s. to the building of the Fever Hospital. William Clarke and James McDonnell each donated £50. James Cunningham, John McCrum, Robert Tennent, W. Simms, J.S. Ferguson, S.S. Thompson, W. Halliday, John Vance, H. Joy, W. Park, Andrew Marshall and Robert McCluney each donated £11 7s. 6d., and William Cairns and Lawson Annesley each donated £10.[77]

The members of Belfast book clubs did not limit their combined efforts to education and medical facilities. They were also influential in the development of cultural facilities in the town. George C. Hyndman, secretary of the Belfast Natural History Society, wrote to the Belfast Literary Society in 1831 thanking them for the £50 contribution for the establishment of a museum in the town and, in return, the Literary Society members were allowed the privilege of visiting the museum, the use of a room and the establishment of a communal library.[78] There was considered to be an 'intimate connection by membership'[79] between the Natural History Society and the Belfast Literary Society. In 1831, out of the twelve committee members of the Natural History Society, ten were also involved in the Belfast Literary Society.[80] Those holding double memberships were James L. Drummond, Edmund Getty, Robert Patterson, James MacAdam, Robert S. MacAdam, George C. Hyndman,

---

74 Stewart, *Belfast Royal Academy*, pp 32–3, 102. **75** *Belfast Monthly Magazine*, 10:54 (Jan. 31 1813), 23. **76** *Belfast Monthly Magazine*, 13:76 (Nov. 30 1814), 416. **77** A.G. Malcolm, *The history of the General Hospital and other medical institutions of the town* (Belfast, 1851), appendix p. xiv. **78** *The Belfast Natural History and Philosophical Society: centenary volume, 1821–1921* (Belfast, 1924), p. 20. This publication also records that the Literary Society books 'remained on the shelves of our library in the museum up till comparatively recent times', p. 21. **79** *The Belfast Natural History and Philosophical Society: centenary volume*, p. 20. **80** James L. Drummond, *Address of the president of the Natural History Society on the occasion of the opening of the Belfast Museum, 1st November 1831* (Belfast, 1831), appendix p. 44.

William Thompson, William Patterson, James D. Marshall and James Bryce jun. Of these ten committee members, eight were also members of the Belfast Society for Promoting Knowledge. The remaining two members of the Natural History committee, William Webb and William Sinclaire, were members of the Society of Promoting Knowledge only.

CONCLUSION

This essay has identified sixty-eight book club members who primarily belonged to the Belfast Society for Promoting Knowledge and the Belfast Literary Society. They also made their mark on the social and cultural character of Belfast during the nineteenth century. Their love of reading and desire to acquire reading materials may have initially brought them in contact with each other, but this was not just for mutual improvement or social purposes. These book club members were pro-active and formed other networks and thus became involved in the development of public healthcare, the improvement and increase in educational facilities and the establishment of museums and other facilities that became familiar landmarks in the developing town, many of which are still in existence today. They not only instigated these facilities but they motivated other citizens to follow their example and thus gave Belfast the title 'Athens of the north'. McTier's oft-quoted comments about the artisan nature of book club membership can be negated in light of the examples included in this brief examination. Many of the personalities involved in the various book clubs, circulating libraries and reading rooms in nineteenth-century Belfast had vision, aspiration, an enlightened outlook and a real desire for societal improvement. The following statistics should emphasize the important contribution that these sixty-eight book club members made to Belfast and the wider world. Twenty-three, or a third, received an entry in the *Dictionary of Ulster biography*, although only seven of the entries mentioned their membership of a book club. Sixteen achieved significant renown to be included the *Oxford dictionary of national biography* and two are known to have been members of the Royal Irish Academy.[81]

McTier mentioned the occupations of gunsmith and baker in her comments. McTier was a sister of William Drennan, and her husband, Samuel, was a United Irishman, yet she takes an elitist stance that points to how middle-class the core United Irishmen were. Involvement in the Volunteer and United Irish movements suggests that many of the book club members 'resented the dominance of the Anglican landed interest in the economic, social and political arrangements of Ireland, and thought that the time had come for a redistribution of power'.[82] The membership profile was not aristocratic but comprised 'a new thrusting middle-class'

---

81 Newmann, *Dictionary of Ulster biography*; *ODNB*. Membership of the Royal Academy was noted in the individual biographies in the *ODNB*.   **82** Curtin, *The United Irishmen*, p. 40.

that, while 'seeking to replace existing establishments' and influenced by Enlightenment ideas, became 'a layer of society' that was 'radical, outward looking and tolerant'.[83] In addition to their involvement in reading societies, these people were involved in developing educational and healthcare institutions and used their money to finance community leisure facilities around the town. Of the book club members mentioned in this text, Presbyterian ministers connected to the First Congregation in Rosemary Street form a distinctive group. They included Revd Dr William Bruce, Revd Thomas Dix Hicks and Revd Samuel Hanna. This congregation was non-subscribing or 'new light', which, according to A.T.Q. Stewart, was appropriate, as the ministers connected to this tradition 'were in general more erudite and intellectually more inquisitive than their orthodox brethren'.[84] Other book club members included foundry owners, naturalists, harbour commissioners, newspaper proprietors, geologists, timber merchants, inventors, insurance agents, auctioneers and a gentleman. They were prepared to invest time and money in the improvement of their town and many received recognition outside Ireland for their endeavours. They wrote numerous books and contributed scholarly articles to journals, animal species were named in their honour and they made significant discoveries and advances in scientific and medical knowledge, and considered themselves part of the rising social and civil elites of nineteenth-century Belfast. Harold Williams wrote of these men in 1929 that 'the intrinsic worth and wide range of all that they have done is not commonly appreciated'.[85] It is hoped that this essay has accorded the movers and shakers of early nineteenth-century Belfast some appreciation for the foundation of the civic institutions that they established in the Ulster capital.

83 Jack Magee, 'The Linen Hall Library: the first two hundred years', *Linen Hall Review*, 5:2 (summer 1988), 9. **84** Stewart, *Belfast Royal Academy*, p. 9. **85** Williams, *Book clubs and printing societies of Great Britain and Ireland*, preface.

The Big House at play: archery as an elite pursuit from the 1830s to the 1870s

BRIAN GRIFFIN

Any worthwhile study of Ireland's nineteenth-century landed elite invariably focuses on the central importance of field sports, particularly fox-hunting, as recreational and associational activities for the class that stood at the apex of rural society.[1] The hunt was integral to the lifestyle of the landed elite, even if the extravagance involved was a major contributory factor to landlord indebtedness.[2] For the landed elite, regardless of whether they were wealthy aristocrats or minor gentry, fox-hunting was an 'essential compound' that bound them together and set them apart from other groups in Irish society; it 'regenerated and re-energized the community on an annual basis', periodically bringing together the different strands of the elite and helping to reinforce its collective sense of identity and exclusiveness.[3] Fox-hunting functioned on a number of levels, then: as sport, as status symbol, and as bonding agent. A strong argument can be made that archery – a subject hitherto overlooked by historians – performed a similar multiple role in the lives of the Irish landed elite in the early and mid-Victorian decades. From the 1830s to the 1870s, enthusiasm for archery affected all levels of the landed elite, as they adopted it as a sport and pastime exclusively for themselves. Some of the archery meetings in this period were of purely local significance, expressions of status by a small number of families in a particular community, often involving only the minor gentry, but it was also common for the minor gentry and the aristocracy of particular counties or, occasionally, the country as a whole to mingle at archery meetings. An examination of their participation in archery adds an important further dimension to our knowledge and understanding of the social history of the landed elite in this period: archery, like hunting, not only allowed all ranks of the elite to socialize together, it also served as an important assertion of status and of separation from the rest of Irish society.

In the 1860s, a Westmeath lady, Mrs Smyth of Gaybrook, near Mullingar, a member of one of the 'leading landed families in the county', was credited with having introduced archery to Ireland in the early 1830s.[4] Although this pioneering

---

1 For just some examples, see Mark Bence-Jones, *Twilight of the ascendancy* (London, 1987), pp 1–6, 61–2; Terence Dooley, *The decline of the Big House in Ireland: a study of Irish landed families, 1860–1960* (Dublin, 2001), pp 56–9; Tom Hunt, *Sport and society in Victorian Ireland: the case of Westmeath* (Cork, 2007), pp 10–38; L.P. Curtis, 'Stopping the hunt, 1881–1882: an aspect of the Irish land war' in C.H.E. Philpin (ed.), *Nationalism and popular protest in Ireland* (Cambridge, 1987), pp 139–62. 2 W.E. Vaughan, *Landlords and tenants in mid-Victorian Ireland* (Oxford, 1994), p. 132. 3 Hunt, *Westmeath*, pp 37–8. 4 Tom Hunt, 'Women and

lady certainly played an important role in the early development of Irish archery, it is an exaggeration to say that she introduced the sport to the country. For instance, there is evidence to show that 'a society of gentlemen and eminent citizens' practised archery in Dublin in the first half of the eighteenth century, before finally giving up their pastime in 1745,[5] while at Ballynahinch Spa in the latter part of the century special archery contests for ladies formed part of the amusements that were provided for the resort's fashionable clientele.[6] Archery also featured in the recreational activities of Theobald Wolfe Tone's circle of acquaintances at Rathcoffey in the 1790s, with the future rebel leader recording in his diary that he attended archery shooting there on three occasions in September 1792.[7] It is likely that archery was practised in various parts of Ireland before Mrs Smyth and two Meath landlords, Gustavus Lambert of Beauparc and James Naper of Loughcrew, established an archery society, the Meath Archers, in 'about' 1833.[8] The evidence is, admittedly, sketchy, but the fact that the viceroy, the duke of Northumberland, had an official bowyer named Blang in 1830, and that Blang conducted the archery department of the 'Royal Shooting Saloon' at Horne's Hotel on Usher's Quay in Dublin, is suggestive of at least some interest in archery in the capital in the period leading up to the establishment of the Meath Archers.[9] Stronger evidence of archery's appeal to sections of the Irish elite at this time comes from Sligo in 1832. In August, at Markree Castle, Joshua Cooper hosted an archery meeting that attracted much of the elite of Sligo society, including the owners of the Hazelwood, Portland, Temple House, Lissadell, Annaghmore, Castle Neynoe, Cooper's Hill, Newpark and Castle Dargan estates and their families, as well as the bishop of Ossory's family.[10]

Although Mrs Smyth and her collaborators among Meath's landed elite were not the first Irish archery enthusiasts in the nineteenth century, they were among the first Irish people to adopt the new approach to the sport that had taken hold of much of fashionable society in the neighbouring island. In Britain, by the 1830s, archery was no longer an ad hoc pastime of the landed elite but was being promoted on a semi-regular basis by numerous clubs that organized frequent competitions during the summer months for their members, which were almost invariably followed by dinners and dances. The British landed class was attracted to archery for a number

sport in Victorian Westmeath', *Irish Economic and Social History*, 34 (2007), 29–46 at 34–5. **5** *New Annual Register* (1788), 151; *The European Magazine, and London Review*, 15 (May 1789), 375; Joseph Cooper Walker, *Historical memoirs of the Irish bards* (2 vols, Dublin, 1818), ii, p. 151n. **6** Peter Somerville-Large, *The grand Irish tour* (London, 1982), p. 298. **7** William Theobald Wolfe Tone (ed.), *Life of Theobald Wolfe Tone* (2 vols, Washington DC, 1826), i, pp 181–2. Unfortunately, the diary entries do not state whether Tone participated in the shooting or not. **8** Hunt, 'Women and sport', 34, n. 39. Lambert and Naper were deputy lieutenants for Meath. **9** *Freeman's Journal*, 20 Nov. 1830. The 'Saloon' also catered for those who wished to engage in rifle and pistol shooting. **10** *Freeman's Journal*, 18 Aug. 1832. Cooper's nephew, the Tory MP for Sligo and famous astronomer, Edward Joshua Cooper, who succeeded to Markree in 1837, was prominent in the establishment and promotion of archery in Sligo: *Lady's Newspaper*, 4 Sept. 1852.

of reasons. Not only did the sport represent a fashionable and romantic form of conspicuous consumption, adding a colourful new dimension to the obligatory displays of hospitality that were important elements in the upper class' affirmation of its own status,[11] but archery's pre-industrial associations meant that it was easily absorbed into the enthusiasm, sometimes verging on an obsession, for neo-medievalism that swept much of landed British society in the nineteenth century; an obsession that was partly fuelled by Walter Scott's writings, especially his hugely popular *Ivanhoe* (1820).[12] Increasingly, Britain's archers organized themselves in clubs in the decades after the Napoleonic wars, a process that culminated in the establishment of one of sport's first national championship competitions, the annual Grand National Archery Meetings, the first of which was held at York in 1844.[13]

The Meath Archers were the first archery club to be established in Ireland in the nineteenth century, and the Westmeath Archers, formed in January 1834, were the country's second toxophilite club. They followed the template of their British counterparts by adopting uniforms, admitting new members by ballot, and encouraging sociability by holding shooting competitions at the houses of different members. The Westmeath Archers had four male patrons, including Sir Percy Nugent, and four 'lady patronesses', including Lady Nugent and Mrs Smyth of Gaybrook. Only the families of members were allowed to attend the club's competitions, which were to alternate between the houses of the male patrons and lady patronesses, and then at the homes of any members who wished to host them; in every case, a 'collation' had to be provided after the archery.[14] One gets a better sense of the scale of some of these occasions from the fact that at one of the Meath Archers' meetings, in July 1838, which was hosted at Headfort House, Kells, by the marquis of Headfort, 'upwards of 180 persons' sat down to dinner in a marquee erected for the occasion.[15] An example of a less lavish Meath Archers affair was the meeting hosted by John Tisdall of Charlesfort in June 1844, when 'a party of seventy of the *elite* of the county' attended to participate in or observe the archery competitions. After dinner, the 'Lady Paramount', the countess of Bective, distributed the prizes, one of which she herself had won. After this, 'In the evening the company adjourned to the house for dancing,

11 E.G. Heath, *A history of target archery* (Newton Abbot, 1973), pp 63–4, 68, 71; Martin Johnes, 'Archery, romance and elite culture in England and Wales, *c*.1780–1840', *History*, 89:294 (Apr. 2004), 193–208 at 193–7, 202; Martin Johnes, 'Archery' in Tony Collins, John Martin and Wray Vamplew (eds), *Encyclopedia of traditional British rural sports* (London and New York, 2005), pp 25–6. **12** Johnes, 'Archery and elite culture', 200, 205–6; Johnes, 'Archery', pp 27–8; Mark Girouard, *The return to Camelot: chivalry and the English gentleman* (New Haven, CT, and London, 1981). **13** John Burnett, 'Sport and the calendar: archery and rifle shooting in Scotland in the nineteenth century', *Scottish Studies*, 33 (1999), 110–30 at 120. **14** Hunt, 'Women and sport', 35; *Rules of the society of the Westmeath archers* (Mullingar, 1834), p. 5 (Westmeath County Library, Mullingar, Small Collections). **15** *Freeman's Journal*, 10 July 1838. For accounts of Meath Archers' meetings at various members' demesnes, see *Bell's life in London and sporting chronicle*, 12 Aug. 1838, 2 Sept. 1838, 4 Sept. 1838, 18 July 1852; *The Era*, 4 Sept. 1842, 10 Aug. 1845; *Freeman's Journal*, 22 July 1844.

which was kept up until a late hour, when they separated highly delighted with the day's amusement and the hospitality of their kind host and hostess'.[16]

Generous hospitality to one's guests was an early and enduring feature of Irish archery meetings, as, indeed, it was a feature of landed elite life throughout the nineteenth century.[17] This was evident at one of the first recorded archery meetings in Ireland, a 'grand archery Fête' that was held at Rathfarnham Castle in June 1835, where some 'two hundred of the *haut ton* sat down to dinner', following the competitions and prize giving. After a promenade through the castle park, refreshments were served to the guests and then dancing was 'kept up until a late hour', the music being provided by the band of the 15th Hussars and a quadrille band.[18]

Not even the Famine put an end to such convivial gatherings, although their number appears to have decreased during the years of the catastrophe. A particularly interesting meeting was held in 1847 at Ballynahinch Spa, under the auspices of Lady Selina Ker, who was keen to have an archery society inaugurated in Down along the lines of the Meath Archers, 'the ladies of which headed by Lady Fanny Herbert, annually distinguish themselves at the use of the bow'.[19] This took place on 13 July; there were some 150 guests, and around 800 people attended altogether, when one includes the local peasantry who were attracted by the novelty of the event, as well as by such side attractions as a donkey race and foot race in which they could compete, and a 'mock tournament'. The latter involved the gentlemen guests engaging in a tilting competition, in which they had to negotiate a specially laid out course on horseback, spearing suspended rings of various sizes, 'balls in imitation of faces', and 'a wooden man in armour, on a pivot, with arms extended' while they did so.[20]

In addition to these planned amusements, the proceedings were further enlivened by the arrival of Revd C. Boyd, 'the loyal vicar of Magheradroll', mounted upon a spirited horse and 'decorated with orange insignia', who was 'loudly cheered by the assembled multitude'. The needs of the thirsty guests were well provided for:

> There was a cow on the grounds, ornamented with garlands of flowers, for the purpose of affording milk for syllabub, and from the number who partook of that beverage, she was as able and willing to exercise the virtues of hospitality as her kind and generous owners. She was attended by a 'lady in waiting' dressed in a grotesque cap, petticoat and skirt 'a la Suisse'.

The proceedings finished, as was usual, with a dinner, 'which consisted of everything the season could afford, or hospitality devise'; this was followed by a quadrille dance in the pleasure grounds, and then a larger dance later in the evening, which lasted into the early hours of the morning 'until papa and mama interfered' and 'this most agreeable entertainment' finally came to a close.[21]

16 *Freeman's Journal*, 22 June 1844. **17** Dooley, *Decline*, pp 44–7, 52–6; Bence-Jones, *Twilight*, pp 11–12. **18** *The Court Journal*, 13 June 1835. **19** *Downpatrick Recorder*, 10 July 1847. **20** Ibid., 17 July 1847. **21** Account by 'Correspondent' in *Downpatrick Recorder*, 17

In August 1846, the Meath Archers held their second meeting of the year at Oakley Park, the seat of George Bomford, 'a modern place, tastefully laid out by Mr McNevin'. After the shooting, which took place under the direction of 'the popular lady paramount for the year', the guests commenced dancing at 9pm, and 'the dancing kept up with great spirit till three o'clock, when the party broke up delighted with their day's amusement, and anxiously looked forward to their next meeting, which was to take place at Beauparc'.[22] Three years later, the Meath Archers held an enjoyable meeting at Naper's demesne at Loughcrew, which was 'most fashionably attended'. The band of the 35th Regiment, from Mullingar, played during dinner, which was served 'in the ornamental grounds attached to the splendid mansion, in a spacious marquee', while the shooting took place on the lawn in front of the mansion. In the evening, there was a ball in the mansion, 'where dancing was kept up with unabashed spirit till daylight, to the music of Hanlon's band'.[23] In November of the same year, the Wexford Archers held their annual ball, described as 'this brilliant reunion of the nobility and gentry composing the members of the Archery Club', in Wexford's Assembly Rooms. The fact that they held their ball suggests that they also had a full season's shooting.[24]

After the Famine, the elite of Wexford society – and much of the landed gentry and aristocracy throughout the rest of Ireland – continued with their sociable archery meetings.[25] The second meeting of the Wexford Archers' 1850 season was held at Ballinkeeffe, 'the beautiful residence of John Maher, Esq'. After the shooting, some 140 guests sat down to 'a very elegant collation' in 'a spacious and beautiful tent' that was furnished by Hynes' of Silver Street, Dublin; the proceedings were watched over by the club's vice-president, C.H. Cliffe, in the absence of the president, Lord Carew. According to the *Wexford Independent*, 'the amusements of this delightful and social *reunion* were concluded by dancing in the beautiful suite of rooms in the mansion house, which were thrown open for the purpose by the hospitable proprietor'.[26] While clubs continued to be important in the organization of archery contests in this period, there is also evidence that some aristocratic families included archery as part of other amusements for their guests. For example, in August and September 1853, the earl and countess of Erne put on a fortnight's entertainment for a large number

July 1847. 'Magheradroll' is today spelled 'Magheradrool'. For a discussion of the Famine in Down, see Trevor McCavery, 'The Famine in County Down' in Christine Kinealy and Trevor Parkhill (eds), *The Famine in Ulster: the regional impact* (Belfast, 1997), pp 99–127. **22** *Bell's life in London and sporting chronicle*, 30 Aug. 1846. **23** *Anglo-Celt*, 24 Aug. 1849. For a discussion of the Famine in Meath, see Noel E. French, 'The impact of the Great Famine on the population of County Meath', *Ríocht na Midhe*, 18 (2007), 156–69. **24** *Freeman's Journal*, 13 Nov. 1849. For a discussion of the Famine in Wexford, see Anna Kinsella, *County Wexford in the Famine years, 1845–1849* (Dublin, 1995). **25** For an anonymously authored fictional account of an archery fete in the grounds of 'Ballyhowley Castle', which was written by somebody who apparently had pleasant experience of the largesse at these kind of gatherings, see 'An archery fete', *Irish Metropolitan Magazine*, 34:16 (July 1858), 410–17. **26** Undated *Wexford Independent* report in *Freeman's Journal*, 8 Aug. 1850.

of visitors to their Crom Castle Estate in Fermanagh, which included an archery fete, the first prize in which was won by their daughter, Lady Louisa Crichton.[27] A year later, the Ernes put on another archery fete for the visit of the lord lieutenant, the earl of St Germans, to Crom Castle.[28]

According to Alfred Perceval Graves, son of the bishop of the united diocese of Limerick, Ardfert and Aghadoe, the 1860s in Limerick were halcyon days for 'we young people', with fishing, boating, archery and picnic parties by day and dances and concerts by night ensuring that 'socially our Limerick days in the sixties were delightful ones';[29] archery also constituted one of the few amusements for daughters of Church of Ireland clergymen in rural Munster in the same decade.[30] Most of the evidence suggests that clubs were the mainstay of archery in the post-Famine period, with a marked growth in their number from the late 1850s to the 1860s. These clubs were, in many respects, typical of the myriad associations that sprang up in eighteenth- and nineteenth-century Ireland for the purposes of providing opportunities for socializing with people of similar background or interests:[31] what distinguished the archery clubs from most contemporary recreational associations was, of course, that their membership was drawn from the upper tiers of Irish society.

Army officers and their families played a leading role in some of these clubs. As early as July 1856, archery formed the principal attraction in the field day and exercises of the officers at the Curragh. Some thirty marquees were pitched for the comfort of the spectators and competitors, who consisted of a 'large number of fashionables of both sexes'. By 1858, weekly archery competitions formed part of the regular routine at the camp, and by 1861 a Curragh Archery Society was in existence, holding competitions for officers and civilian gentlemen and ladies.[32] Officers and their families were to the fore in the archery competitions and balls that formed the principal amusements of the Templemore and Ormond Archery Clubs in the late 1850s and early 1860s, with the officers of the Templemore garrison often hosting these affairs and inviting large numbers of 'the elite of North Tipperary' to attend.[33] The officers of the Belfast garrison were so keen on archery that they formed the Belfast Military Archery Club in 1862, with the officer-commanding as president. The five 'lady patronesses' included Lady Donegall and Lady Massereene. By 1864, there were some eighty members in the club, who practiced on Tuesdays, Thursdays and Saturdays in the Royal Botanic Gardens, with a monthly prize meeting in June and July and a major prize meeting in September.[34] At the other end of the country,

27 *The Lady's Newspaper*, 3 Sept. 1853. **28** *Morning Chronicle*, 7 Aug. 1854. **29** Alfred Perceval Graves, *To return to all that: an autobiography* (London and Toronto, 1930), p. 147. **30** Anonymous, 'Recollections of an Irish home', *Blackwood's Magazine*, 161:978 (Apr. 1897), 578–91 at 578. **31** James Kelly and Martyn Powell (eds), *Clubs and societies in eighteenth-century Ireland* (Dublin, 2010); Jennifer Kelly and R.V. Comerford (eds), *Associational culture in Ireland and abroad* (Dublin, 2010), pp 11–47, 105–27. **32** *Freeman's Journal*, 11 July 1856, 16 July 1861; *Belfast News-Letter*, 1 July 1858. **33** *Nenagh Guardian*, 12 May 1858, 5 June 1858, 9 Oct. 1858, 11 June 1859, 18 Aug. 1860, 29 Aug. 1860. **34** J. Sharp (ed.), *The archer's register: a yearbook of facts for 1864* (London, 1864), p. 128.

the membership roll of the Doneraile Archery Club, founded on 11 June 1863, varied considerably, depending on the number of 'military gentlemen' who were stationed nearby. In 1865, there were some forty-nine members in the club, which was much smaller than in previous years, when the garrison – and the pool of potential officer members – had been larger.[35]

The attractions of archery for gentlemen officers had almost nothing to do with its potential military usefulness. Most contemporaries recognized that the longbow had long outlived its usefulness as a weapon in war: indeed, in 1860 the lord lieu-tenant, the earl of Carlisle, caused amusement in some of his audience when he gave a speech at a Joneswell archery fete, in which he praised the Kilkenny Archers for being ready 'to furnish a fair band of defenders who showed so much skill and effi-ciency in those formidable weapons of our ancestors, the bow and arrow'.[36] However, a few people persisted in believing that archery potentially served a useful military purpose. In a letter to the *Belfast News-Letter* in June 1865, a Bangor corre-spondent, while complaining of the dangers which one 'son of Mars' posed to the public by practising his archery in an area that was frequented by passers-by, suggested nevertheless that he and other nuisance archers could put their skill to good use against the Fenian threat[37] – it is difficult to believe that even the Fenians, ill-equipped and poorly trained as they were, would have had much difficulty in overcoming opponents who were armed with bows and arrows. At the Exhibition grounds in Dublin in 1866, where the Grand Leinster Archery Society held their annual prize competition, Captain John Norton of the County of Dublin Archers demonstrated to his fellow toxophilites his 'percussion shell arrow', which exploded on contact with the grass; Norton explained to his audience that 'it would also explode on striking a ship's sail, and might be found useful against pirates'. A few years previously, he had also argued that the same arrow 'might be used effectively against wild animals, such as lions, tigers, buffaloes &c., even when shot from a lady's bow'.[38]

It is unlikely that many officers had thoughts of shooting either Fenians, tigers or pirates when they participated in archery: it is possible, however, that in their imagi-nation many of them – and their civilian counterparts – pictured themselves as latter day Robin Hoods or other mythical or real figures from the medieval past. The widespread popularity of archery among the landed elite allowed them to sustain their romantic role-playing as medieval heroes. The setting of many archery contests helped to maintain the sport's neo-medieval trappings. Ruined castles, such as the King's Castle at Ardglass[39] and Monkstown Castle, the evocative setting for the

---

35 J. Sharp (ed.), *The archer's register: a yearbook of facts for 1865* (London, 1865), pp 160–1. **36** *Freeman's Journal*, 13 Sept. 1860. **37** Letter from 'Douzenberry' in *Belfast News-Letter*, 17 June 1865. **38** *Belfast News-Letter*, 11 Sept. 1866; John Norton, *A list of Captain Norton's projectiles, and his other naval and military inventions: with original correspondence* (Gravesend, 1860), p. 136. Like many Irish officers, Norton spent part of his military service in India. While stationed there in 1823, he developed a percussion rifle shell. **39** *Belfast News-Letter*, 5 Sept. 1837.

County of Dublin Archers' meetings,[40] or mock Gothic castles, such as Markree Castle in Sligo,[41] easily lent themselves to this kind of illusion. The landed elite's fascination with a romanticized vision of the medieval past[42] was not revealed solely by their indulging in archery, but also by the construction of hundreds of 'Big Houses', either built as neo-medieval castles or featuring such neo-medieval features as castellations and turrets.[43] As in Britain, where archery meetings 'had the cultivated feel of a medieval tournament',[44] Irish toxophiles created a neo-medieval atmosphere by such means as erecting tents and marquees at their archery competitions, employing buglers to announce the entry of competitors or the attainment of 'gold' scores,[45] or decorating archery grounds and ballrooms with flags and banners displaying heraldic devices.[46] The occasional awarding of such prizes as a golden arrow, which was presented to the best female competitors at the Meath Archers' meetings of June 1844 and August 1845 and at the Royal Irish Grand National Archery Club's meeting at Bray in August 1863,[47] or a statuette of Robin Hood, which was presented to the best female shooter at the Grand Leinster Archery Club's competition in September 1865,[48] further helped to achieve the desired effect.

The rhetoric employed in the sporting and general press to describe Irish archery meetings also frequently emphasized the neo-medieval character of these occasions. For example, one observer commented that the archery competition at Ballynahinch Spa in July 1847 'might remind one of the happy days of "Merry England"',[49] while the excellent shooting of the ladies and gentlemen at the Royal Irish Grand National Archery Club competition at the Rotundo Gardens in Dublin in July 1861 was deemed 'worthy of the brightest days of "merry Sherwood" itself'.[50] An effort was

40 G.R. Powell, *The official railway handbook to Bray, Kingstown, the coast and the county of Wicklow* (Dublin, 1860), p. 47; *Freeman's Journal*, 14 Sept. 1864.   **41** *Freeman's Journal*, 13 Aug. 1832.   **42** This is further evidenced by the participation of a number of Irish aristocrats in the extravagant Eglinton tournament of 1839: *Downpatrick Recorder*, 7 Sept. 1839. For a full treatment of the Eglinton tournament, see Girouard, *Return to Camelot*, pp 88–110. See also the photograph of Sir Charles Barrington wearing medieval armour, in his guise as 'deputy warden of Glenstal Castle' in Bence-Jones, *Twilight*, p. 179.   **43** For good discussions of two of these neo-medieval 'Big Houses' – Gosford Castle in Co. Armagh, the construction of which began in 1819, and Glenstal Castle in Co. Limerick, which was designed in 1836 – see Lindsay Proudfoot, 'Placing the imaginary: Gosford Castle and the Gosford estate, *ca.*1820–1900' in A.J. Hughes and William Nolan (eds), *Armagh, history and society: interdisciplinary essays on the history of an Irish county* (Dublin, 2001), pp 890–9; Marion D. McGarry, 'Creating a noble past: the design of Glenstal Abbey, 1836–1861', *Old Limerick Journal*, 42 (2006), 20–3. For photographs of some of the neo-Gothic houses that were built in the nineteenth century, see Bence-Jones, *Twilight*, pp 33 (Killeen Castle, Co. Meath), 35 (Mitchelstown Castle, Co. Cork), 218 (Gurteen le Poer, Co. Waterford).   **44** Johnes, 'Archery', p. 27.   **45** Anonymous, 'An archery fete', 412; *Freeman's Journal*, 13 Sept. 1860, 27 Aug. 1867.   **46** *Downpatrick Recorder*, 17 July 1847, 9 Nov. 1872; *Freeman's Journal*, 13 Sept. 1860, 10 Sept. 1874; *Belfast News-Letter*, 15 May 1865, 8 Aug. 1867, 2 Oct. 1873.   **47** *Freeman's Journal*, 22 June 1844; *The Era*, 10 Aug. 1845; *Belfast News-Letter*, 15 Aug. 1863.   **48** *Freeman's Journal*, 21 Sept. 1865.   **49** *Downpatrick Recorder*, 17 July 1847.   **50** *Freeman's Journal*, 27 July 1861.

made to entice the Bray public to attend the competition of the latter club in August 1863 with an announcement that they would be treated to a display of 'that "annciente and ryghte nobile pastime" of archery' should they attend.[51] The *Freeman's Journal* was particularly prone to this kind of rhetoric. In September 1874, it informed its readers that

> Archery has attractions altogether and peculiarly its own. There is no sport or science which has been so long known and so universally practised, and there is none with which so many pleasant and interesting associations are connected. In every age of the world's history the bow has been the favourite weapon of every nation in every corner of the globe. [...] From [Homer's] day to our own bows and arrows have done wonderful execution in the hands of verse makers and romance writers. They play a particularly prominent part in the metrical and non-metrical, but equally fascinating romances of the 'Great Wizard of the North' [...] In the story of 'Ivanhoe', perhaps the most fascinating passages are those in which the doings of Robin Hood and his merry men are so delightfully detailed. Indeed, the memory of the jovial band of outlawed archers ought, in itself, to be sufficient to popularise the sport, for it is hard to look upon a bow and arrows without being reminded of the waving leaves, and glancing deer, and groups of merry outlaws in the shady forests of Nottingham.[52]

On a number of occasions, the newspaper evoked images of Robin Hood, and reminded readers that the sport 'is associated more with history, poetry and romance than any other', in its coverage of Irish archery contests.[53]

A British officer serving in Ireland in the 1830s commented on the obsession of what he called 'the Anglo-Irish party' with the myths and legends of England, an obsession which was nurtured from childhood and which formed an important element of the revival of interest in archery in the nineteenth century:

> The mythic heroes of their childhood are King Arthur and 'the knights of the round table' – Sir Lancelot, Sir Tristram, Sir Percival, Sir Gawain and the rest of that fair throng. Merlin is their wizard. Robin Hood and Little John are of their familiar acquaintance from the first; and the old glories of English archery swell their little hearts from the moment they can draw a tiny bow.[54]

---

51 *Freeman's Journal*, 8 Aug. 1863. **52** *Freeman's Journal*, 22 Sept. 1874. For a recent discussion of Walter Scott and Ireland, but which, unfortunately, does not focus on *Ivanhoe*, see R.F. Foster, *Words alone: Yeats and his inheritances* (Oxford, 2011), pp 14–21. **53** *Freeman's Journal*, 13 Aug. 1863, 15 June 1864, 17 Sept. 1865, 17 Sept. 1869, 21 Sept. 1872, 2 June 1875. **54** Anonymous ('An officer in a marching regiment'), 'Of Ireland in 1834', *Fraser's Magazine for Town and Country* (Feb. 1835), 193–217 at 202.

Although there were some traditions connecting Robin Hood and his associates with Ireland,[55] these do not appear to have been particularly important in sustaining the Irish elite's interest in archery. Instead, it is likely that it was the perceived essential *Englishness* of the Robin Hood legends, rather than their reputed Irish episodes, which appealed to at least some sections of the Irish landed gentry. This was also a factor in the vogue among some of the landed elite for neo-medieval 'Big Houses', allowing their builders to emphasize their Norman or alleged Norman ancestry.[56] In England, as Stephanie Barczewski has argued, the cult figure of Robin Hood, as a Saxon hero, was an ideal tool to exploit in a project for bolstering a sense of Englishness in the multicultural and partly 'Celtic' United Kingdom.[57] Hood was also used to bolster the Irish elite's sense of separateness from the rest of Irish society, as well as their sense of shared values with their counterparts in Britain. This sense of separateness was made apparent to a British tourist in Co. Tipperary in 1869, who congratulated a young woman on winning an archery contest that he had witnessed. On explaining to her how glad he was 'to see an Irish girl carrying all before her', the victor insisted that she was not Irish: her response was: 'I'm a Tipperary girl, if you like; but Irish I am not'.[58] Abbé Emanuel Domenech, a French priest who visited Ireland in the 1860s, considered the efforts of female archers to be wasted, commenting that:

> Had I to give advice to the young women of Erin, it would be to recommend them to found, not archery clubs, but a vast patriotic association, the first statute of which should be that not one of them would consent to marry a man who spoke anything but Celtic, and to obstinately reject all who did not speak it.[59]

Such advice is unlikely to have appealed to the victorious Tipperary archer, or to many of her sister toxophilites. The various archery clubs, then, helped to reinforce the elite's sense of separateness and to strengthen its unique sense of collective identity. As we have seen, some of these clubs were closely associated with the army officer corps – which was itself largely drawn from the ranks of the aristocracy – but most Irish archery clubs were organized and joined by civilian members of Ireland's landed elite, with the result that archery made a pleasant addition to their social round in the summer.[60] Some of these clubs appear to have been more select than others. The South Tipperary Bowmen, 'an aristocratic archery club',[61] for example,

55 *Irish Shield and Monthly Milesian*, 1 (1829), 401; 'Little John in Ireland', *Dublin Penny Journal*, 1:2 (7 July 1832), 13–14; *Mirror of Literature, Amusement and Instruction*, 20:568 (Sept. 1832), 204; *All The Year Round* (20 Nov. 1869), 584; *Freeman's Journal*, 2 June 1875.
56 Proudfoot, 'Placing the imaginary', pp 895–9; McGarry, 'Glenstal Castle', 20–3.
57 Stephanie L. Barczewski, *Myth and national identity in nineteenth-century Britain: the legends of King Arthur and Robin Hood* (Oxford, 2000), pp 99–105, 107–8, 124–34, 137–41.
58 *Fraser's Magazine for Town and Country* (Aug. 1869), 185.   59 *Times*, 4 Jan. 1867.
60 Dooley, *Decline*, p. 53.   61 *Belfast News-Letter*, 20 Sept. 1862.

were considered to be particularly exclusive, and James Mason, the Confederate States of America's special commissioner for Europe, probably felt at home when he was entertained at the club's fete at Knocklofty, the seat of the earl of Donoughmore, in September 1864. Mason donated a prize of 'a valuable jewelled brooch' to the club and Donoughmore, when presenting it, 'took occasion to allude in kindly terms to the sympathy felt for his countrymen in their struggle for independence'. The earl, who also received Mason as a guest in the previous year, was considered 'one of the South's staunchest supporters' in Europe.[62] Another relatively exclusive club was the Ulster Archers, founded in 1865 by 'the nobility and leading gentry' of Ulster. Among its patrons were the marquis and marchioness of Donegall, the marquis and marchioness of Downshire, the earl and countess of Charlemont, the countess of Caledon, the earl of Dartrey, Lord and Lady Dufferin, Lord Edwin Hill-Trevor, Viscount Massereene and Ferrard and Lord and Lady Lurgan.[63]

While no other Irish toxophilite club could match the Ulster Archers for the eminence of its members, what all these clubs shared was a relatively select membership, which was drawn almost entirely from the country's landed elite. One club, the Castleconnell Archery Club, founded in 1859, initially took the idea of exclusion to the extent of limiting membership to just twenty-four families; however, on 1 May 1865, at a meeting at Captain Vansittart's house at Coolbawn, the club wound itself up and decided to reconstruct itself as the Munster Archers, and to base itself in Limerick city, as this would facilitate 'encouraging the practice of archery in this and the adjoining counties'.[64] There were at least thirty-two archery clubs in Ireland in the 1860s, the decade when the sport was at its most popular (see table 9.1). These clubs performed a dual role: they enabled their members to associate in agreeable surroundings with people of similar background while participating in or observing archery competitions,[65] while also excluding people who were not of the desired sort.

The clubs' balloting mechanism ensured that undesirable candidates for membership could be blackballed,[66] while prohibitive membership and entry fees had a similarly excluding effect. Although in 1860 the Kilkenny Archers had what was considered a low annual subscription of 10s., with a 5s. entrance fee,[67] even these charges would have been prohibitive for most strata of Irish society. In 1865, the Sligo Archers had an annual subscription of 7s. for an individual member and 10s. for a family membership, with entrance fees of £1 for an individual member and £1 10s.

---

62 *Freeman's Journal*, 21 Aug. 1863, 4 Sept. 1863, 8 Sept. 1864; *Morning Post*, 6 Sept. 1864; Gerald M. Garmon, *John Reuben Thompson* (Boston, 1979), p. 117. For accounts of South Tipperary Bowmen's archery meetings, see *Freeman's Journal*, 23 June 1863, 31 Aug. 1866. 63 *Belfast News-Letter*, 8 Aug. 1866, 9 Aug. 1867. 64 Sharp (ed.), *Archer's register for 1864*, p. 132; Sharp (ed.), *Archer's register for 1865*, p. 163. 65 Archery clubs consisted of shooting and non-shooting members. 66 Mike Huggins, *The Victorians and sport* (London and New York, 2004), p. 34; *Rules of the Society of the Westmeath Archers* (Mullingar, 1834), p. 11 (Westmeath County Library, Mullingar, small collections); *The Sligo Archers: rules* (Sligo, 1865), p. 8; *Belfast News-Letter*, 15 Aug. 1877. 67 *Freeman's Journal*, 13 Sept. 1860.

Table 9.1 Archery clubs in the 1860s.[68]

Club name	Founded	Membership
Archers of the Bann		
Armagh Archers	17 November 1863	'upwards of 200' (1864)
Belfast Military Archery Club	1862	82 (1864)
Buttevant Archery Club		
Carlow Archers		
Castleconnell Archers	1859	24 families (1864)
County of Dublin Archers	*c.*1845; re-founded 14 June 1857	60 (1864)
Curragh Archery Society		
Doneraile Archery Club	11 June 1863	49 (1865)
Fermoy Archery Club	1860	*c.*100 (1864)
Fingall Archers		
Grand Leinster and Munster Archery Society	1863	68 (1864)
Inishannon Company of Archers	1861	24 (1864)
Kildare Archers		
Kilkenny Archers	*c.*1857	
King's County Archers		
Kinsale Archers		
Mallow Archers	2 May 1863	60 (1865)
Meath Archers	*c.*1833	
Munster Archers	1 May 1865	'upwards of 100' (1865)
North Tipperary Archers		
Ormond Archers	*c.*March 1859	
Queen's County Archers		
Queenstown Archers		
Rathkeale Archers		
The Rock (Cashel) Archers		
Royal Irish Grand National Archers	May 1861	100 (1864)
Sligo Archers		
South Tipperary Bowmen		
The Ulster Archers	20 July 1865	'exceeds 100' (1865)
Waterford Archers	1860	*c.*200 (1864)
Wexford Archers	1845	195 (1864)

for a family membership.[69] Essential equipment such as bows, quivers, arrows, tassels, arm guards and targets added to archery's expense.[70] Attending archery clubs' annual

---

68 Information from *The Era*, 31 Aug. 1845; *Nenagh Guardian*, 5 Mar. 1859; *Freeman's Journal*, 13 Sept. 1860, 12 Oct. 1860, 16 July 1861, 13 Aug. 1863, 28 July 1864; *Sporting gazette*, 15 Aug. 1863; *Bell's life and London and sporting chronicle*, 23 Aug. 1863; J. Sharp (ed.), *Archer's register for 1864*, pp 125, 128, 131–5; J. Sharp (ed.), *Archer's register for 1865*, pp 160–3, 165. With thanks to Tom Hayes and Patrick Bracken for information on the Rathkeale and Rock (Cashel) clubs, respectively.   **69** *Sligo Archers*, p. 7.   **70** For the cost of these and other archery items,

balls involved further expenditure: in the 1870s, ladies and gentlemen paid 12*s*. 6*d*. and 15*d*., respectively, for tickets to the Downshire Archers' annual ball.[71] The Downshires, founded in 1870, principally through the efforts of Mrs Jane Blakiston-Houston of Orangefield, were considered 'by far the most aristocratic and select' sports club in Co. Down.[72]

The uniforms sported by most archery clubs were a further expense and were signifiers of both belonging and exclusion: the uniforms heightened members' sense of collective identity, while distinguishing them from the common herd; their cost also helped increase clubs' exclusive nature.[73] Archery uniforms varied in design and appearance: the Westmeath Archers required lady members to wear a uniform of 'White dress, of any material, with green ribbon; white chip, or straw hat, trimmed with green ribbon, feather or flower', while men had to wear a dark green coat and white trousers;[74] the Meath Archers wore white and crimson uniforms.[75] The ladies who participated in Lady Selina Ker's archery competition at Ballynahinch Spa wore striking uniforms: according to one observer, these consisted of 'green jackets, white skirts and straw hats, with broad brims, turned up at the right side', while another described their uniforms as 'Polka jackets of green velvet, and silver buttons, black muslin dress, with black boots; large leaved straw hats, looped on the right side with a rosette of green and white ribbon under the chin with the same, together with a bow and a quiver of arrows'.[76] The ladies' uniform of the County of Dublin Archers consisted of 'white petticoats, green jackets and turned-up straw hats, decorated with ostrich feathers', while the men wore Lincoln green velvet caps and uniforms. The Kilkenny Archers also sported green uniforms.[77] The ladies of the Armagh Archers wore a uniform consisting of 'a white lustre skirt, with a rich green light-colo[ur]ed trimming, and a cashmere jacket of the same colo[u]r' (fig. 9.1).[78] One enterprising bootmaker, Mr Butler of Nassau Street in Dublin, even produced a 'royal archery shooting boot', which was showcased at the Dublin International Exhibition in 1864. Reaching halfway up the wearer's leg, this leather boot was 'composed of fine green cloth, massively worked out with shamrocks and turned over at the top with a hand-

see 'J.T.H.' (ed.), *John Lawrence's handbook of cricket in Ireland, and record of athletic sports, football &c. Fourteenth number, 1878–79* (Dublin, 1879), p. 213. A number of shops catered for archers' various needs, including John Lawrence's sports goods shop on Grafton Street and Barrett's archery warehouse on St Stephen's Green, both in Dublin, and Henry Greer's archery warehouse on High Street in Belfast: *Freeman's Journal*, 13 Apr. 1854, 27 July 1861, 22 June 1864, 5 Sept. 1866, 29 Aug. 1867; J. Sharp (ed.), *The archer's register: a year-book of facts for 1866–67* (London, 1867), p. 160. **71** For accounts of the Downshire Archers' annual ball, see *Belfast News-Letter*, 29 Oct. 1870, 28 Sept. 1871, 2 Oct. 1873, 22 Sept. 1874, 18 Oct. 1879; *Downpatrick Recorder*, 9 Nov. 1872, 30 Nov. 1877, 30 Nov. 1878, 11 Dec. 1880. **72** *Belfast News-Letter*, 10 Sept. 1874; *Downpatrick Recorder*, 30 Nov. 1877. **73** On this aspect of clubs' uniforms, see Jennifer Kelly and R.V. Comerford, 'Introduction' in Kelly and Comerford (eds), *Associational culture*, p. 6. **74** Hunt, 'Women and sport', 35n41; *Rules of the Society of the Westmeath Archers*, p. 11. Uniforms were optional for non-shooting members. **75** *Freeman's Journal*, 22 July 1844. **76** *Downpatrick Recorder*, 17 July 1847. **77** *Freeman's Journal*, 9 Aug. 1860, 13 Sept. 1860. **78** *Belfast News-Letter*, 10 Aug. 1867.

9.1 The Armagh Archers, 1874 (courtesy of the Armagh County Museum).

some gauntlet'.[79] Regardless of the kind of uniform favoured by Irish archers, their appearance made a favourable impression on many observers of archery contests in this period,[80] which was undoubtedly the wearers' aim.

Creating a favourable impression at archery meetings was a particularly important consideration for many female archers: as many contemporary observers commented, mingling and cutting an attractive figure at archery contests enhanced unmarried women's chances of finding a husband.[81] This is not to say that archery was not important as a sports activity in its own right for female participants; indeed, archery in the post-Famine decades was the sport with the highest female participation, and was often a majority female affair.[82] The evidence suggests that Irish female toxophilites were often keen competitors[83] and that their level of skill equalled, and sometimes surpassed, that of male competitors.[84] Indeed, Ireland's first female inter-

79 *Freeman's Journal*, 15 June 1864.   **80** *Freeman's Journal*, 13 Aug. 1863; *Belfast News-Letter*, 21 Sept. 1865, 23 Sept. 1865; *Our Boys and Girls*, 1:14 (6 Apr. 1867).   **81** For the case of British women, see Johnes, 'Archery and elite culture', 199; Hugh D.H. Soar, *The romance of archery: a social history of the longbow* (Yardley, 2008), p. 142.   **82** Henry Parkinson and Peter Lund (eds), *The illustrated record and descriptive catalogue of the Dublin International Exhibition of 1865* (Dublin and London, 1866), p. 531; *Belfast News-Letter*, 28 Aug. 1867; *Times*, 14 Sept. 1869; Tom Hayes, '"God save the queen, God save the green, and the usual loyal toasts": sporting and dining for Ireland and/or the queen' in Peter Gray (ed.), *Victoria's Ireland? Irishness and Britishness, 1837–1901* (Dublin, 2004), p. 82.   **83** *Times*, 6 July 1863; *Freeman's Journal*, 13 Aug. 1863, 18 June 1869; *Belfast News-Letter*, 10 Aug. 1866, 10 Sept. 1874. **84** *Freeman's Journal*, 20 Aug. 1850, 14 Sept. 1864; *Belfast News-Letter*, 21 Sept. 1865.

national sports champion was an archer, Cecilia Maria Eleanor Betham. Betham, the daughter of the Cork herald and captain of the County of Dublin Archers, Molyneux Cecil John Betham, took the archery world by storm when she won the British championship for the first time at Alexandra Park, London, in 1864, setting a record score in the process. She won further British championships in 1865, 1866 and 1868,[85] as well as the Irish championship in 1864, 1865 and 1867.[86] Such was her fame that she even had a dance named in her honour (fig. 9.2).[87]

Betham was the most notable of the hundreds of Irish women from landed families who availed of the opportunities that archery provided for physical exercise in this period; opportunities that were otherwise rare for most women of this class. Mid-Victorian Ireland shared the attitudes of mid-Victorian Britain concerning what constituted appropriate physical activity for men and women: robust physical exertion by women was frowned upon as not only physically dangerous but also posing a threat to women's essential femininity.[88] Archery, however, could safely be participated in by women, without prevailing norms of gender behaviour being challenged; while the sport benefited women's health – according to the *Freeman's Journal* in 1869, women's archery was 'worth all the croquet in the world'[89] – the amount of physical exertion involved was well within acceptable limits. The *Belfast News-Letter* approved of women's archery, claiming in 1870 that 'its healthy effect can hardly be over-estimated', especially as it 'gives an erect and graceful bearing to the entire body, which no other out-door exercise for ladies can lay claim to'.[90] The sport was unusual in this period in that it allowed not merely for female participation, but also for female competition,[91] which probably added to its attractions in the eyes of many women from Ireland's landed families.

Despite Betham's remarkable victories at archery competitions in Ireland and Britain, sporting success was not necessarily uppermost in the minds of most Irish women who joined archery clubs in the Victorian period; indeed, the same point may be made about men who attended archery meetings. As Martin Johnes explains, 'archery, complete with the romantic associations of Cupid and his bow and arrows, offered men and women an opportunity to meet, view and enjoy their social equals'.[92] A lovelorn Belfast correspondent recognized that archery involved more than the mere winning of such prizes as jewellery, money, bracers or bows and arrows

85 Parkinson and Lund (eds), *Dublin International Exhibition*, p. 531; *Gentleman's Magazine*, 13 (July–Dec. 1874), 167. **86** *Bell's life in London and sporting chronicle*, 6 Aug. 1864; *Belfast News-Letter*, 2 June 1865; *Freeman's Journal*, 17 Aug. 1867. **87** Richard F. Harvey, *The Irish archers: Valse, dedicated to Miss Betham and the archery clubs of Ireland* (Dublin, c.1866). **88** For a good discussion of these fears, see Kathleen E. McCrone, *Playing the game: sport and the physical emancipation of English women, 1870–1914* (Lexington, KY, 1988), pp 7–8. **89** *Freeman's Journal*, 17 Sept. 1869. **90** *Belfast News-Letter*, 26 Aug. 1870. **91** Jennifer Hargreaves, *Sporting females: critical issues in the history and sociology of women's sports* (London and New York, 1994), p. 88; Arthur G. Credland, 'The Grand National archery meetings, 1844–1944, and the progress of women in archery', *Journal of the Society of Archer-Antiquaries*, 43 (2000), 68–104. **92** Johnes, 'Archery and elite culture', 199.

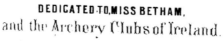

9.2 Dance dedicated to Cecilia Betham, *c.*1866 (courtesy of the National Library of Ireland).

– to itemize just some of the prizes awarded at Irish archery meetings – when he called in 1862 for the establishment of an archery club in the northern city. He explained that,

> Once started, you may depend upon it the amusement would be most popular, besides giving young men, like myself, in search of a wife an opportunity for seeing the beauties of the Northern Athens, now only seen on such

rare occasions as a lord lieutenant's visit, or through the opening of an Ulster Hall.[93]

The *Freeman's Journal* pointed out that archery 'is at once the most graceful as well as the most healthful of outdoor amusements', and 'almost the only one in which we enjoy the privilege of ladies' society', where 'they not only compete with honour to themselves, but add largely to the beauty and interest of the scene'.[94] Archery contests allowed women from the elite of society to display their figures without causing scandal,[95] and flirting with male archers and spectators was often integral to the proceedings.[96] The opportunities that archery meetings provided for meeting or attracting members of the opposite sex are described vividly in Nicholas Gannon's *Above and below*, a novel of 1864 that was praised for the accuracy of its depiction of Irish archery contests.[97] Set in the fictional Grangemore Hall, 'the wood-studded domain of the de Lacys', a 'great archery meeting' is organized by Rosamond de Lacy, the novel's heroine:

> It was a gathering of the county gentry, and its rank and fashion were well represented. As the eye ranged along those benches, rich in parti-coloured silks and shawls of varied pattern, it was impossible to avoid being struck with the aristocratic appearance of the assemblage, and the beauty of many of the ladies who composed it. Exceptions of course there were as in all meetings of the kind, but the general appearance of those around was decidedly such as to impress one strongly with the conviction that Ireland yields to few countries in the loveliness of its daughters.[98]

The narrator continues:

> All are unanimous in admitting that woman is the most beautiful object in creation; but many differ in their opinions as to the costume or attitude which makes her look most to advantage. Some there are who maintain the invincibility of the ball dress; others are dazzled by the witcheries of a riding habit; many, and with much justice, express indomitable faith in the attitude formed when [women are] sweeping the strings of the harp; but it is difficult to conceive how anything can render woman more attractive than the pose of her figure, as dressed in appropriate attire, with the most becoming of little hats upon her head, she gracefully bends the bow, and sends the feathered arrow on its flight.

93 Letter from 'Toxopholite' (sic) in *Belfast News-Letter*, 27 May 1862.   **94** *Freeman's Journal*, 8 Aug. 1863.   **95** *Freeman's Journal*, 13 Aug. 1863, 20 Sept. 1873; *Times*, 5 June 1865; *Belfast News-Letter*, 10 Aug. 1867, 26 Aug. 1870.   **96** *Our Boys and Girls*, 1:14 (6 Apr. 1867); *Fraser's Magazine for Town and Country* (Aug. 1869), 185; Oliver Optic, *Shamrock and thistle: or, Young America in Ireland and Scotland* (Boston, 1868), pp 174–5.   **97** *Freeman's Journal*, 21 Oct. 1864.   **98** Nicholas J. Gannon, *Above and below* (2 vols, London, 1864), i, pp 132–3, 134–5.

9.3 Robert Edward Dillon and Georgina Dillon playing at archery at Clonbrock
lawn, Co. Galway, *c*.1883 (courtesy of the National Library of Ireland).

> The costume itself does wonders for the wearer, provided she have a good
> figure and a pretty face; but when to this be added the kindling eye, flushed
> cheek and indescribable grace imparted by such elegant exercise, a combina-
> tion of unrivalled fascinations are formed which would melt the heart of the
> most strong-hearted gunosymist [misogynist] that ever lived.[99]

Predictably, Rosamond, who 'seemed, as she glided, rather than walked ... the very
embodiment of grace and loveliness', wins the heart of a young aristocrat, one Arthur
O'Leary of Benbow Castle, with her graceful display at the archery contest.[1]
Newspaper accounts of archery contests also describe how ladies' arrows metaphor-
ically struck the hearts of male observers.[2]

Archery clubs, which formed such a vibrant part of the social round of Ireland's
elite in the 1850s and 1860s, went into decline in the 1870s. Notwithstanding the
romanticizing of the sport in newspapers, poetry and fiction, unless one were actually taking part in the sport as a contestant, archery was not a particularly exciting
pastime, a fact that was admitted on a number of occasions by both archers and journalists.[3] Archery went into inevitable decline as an organized sport once alternative

99 Gannon, *Above and below*, i, pp 140–1. This idealized image of the female archer
displaying her figure while wearing 'becoming' headgear is captured well in William Powell
Frith's 1872 painting, 'The fair toxophilites'.   **1** Gannon, *Above and below*, i, pp 142–3.   **2**
Downpatrick Recorder, 17 July 1847; *Freeman's Journal*, 13 Aug. 1863.   **3** Sharp, *Archer's register*

attractions grew more popular, such as croquet[4] and hunting, the latter of which attracted increasing numbers of female adherents from the 1860s onwards.[5] Lawn tennis also grew in popularity among the landed class from the 1870s onwards,[6] to the detriment of archery. One of Ireland's first lawn tennis clubs, the Monkstown club, was started by the County of Dublin Archers in 1877,[7] the same year in which the Downshire Archers also started playing lawn tennis.[8]

Lawn tennis quickly displaced archery in the affections of the Downshire and other Irish toxophilites. Archery did not disappear entirely as an elite pastime in the late nineteenth century, however. It remained as a largely private pursuit, conducted without the neo-medieval pageantry that had characterized the sport in its mid-century heyday:[9] no longer an organized sport, but a pastime, enjoyed by parents and siblings on the lawns of country estates (fig. 9.3) or the back gardens of city mansions.[10] Before its eventual displacement by more popular pursuits, however, archery played an important role in the lives of Ireland's landed elite, providing opportunities for enjoyable socializing and group bonding as well as displays of conspicuous consumption, generous hospitality and social status at a local and wider level, and offering rare opportunities for women from the landed elite to compete in sports contests.

for 1866–67, p. 12; *Freeman's Journal*, 2 June 1875, 29 July 1876. **4** For the increasing popularity of croquet as a pastime among Ireland's landed elite, see Hunt, *Westmeath*, pp 76, 80–1, 85–6. **5** Hunt, *Westmeath*, pp 17–19. **6** Ibid., pp 76–84; N.D. McMillan, *One hundred and fifty years of cricket and sport in County Carlow* (Dublin, 1983), p. 13; Patrick Bracken, '*Foreign and fantastic field sports': cricket in County Tipperary* (Thurles, 2004), pp 44–5. **7** Caoimhín Kenna, *A glance back: a brief history of Monkstown Lawn Tennis Club* (Dublin, 1978), p. 3. **8** *Belfast News-Letter*, 15 Aug. 1877. **9** As an example of archery as a private affair of the landed classes in the 1870s, rather than a club activity, it is instructive that when W.E. Gladstone visited the earl of Meath at Kilruddery, Co. Wicklow, in 1877, he was able to engage in archery there as a substitute for cutting down oak trees, 'as an outlet for his excessive muscular power': see *Funny Folks*, 3 Nov. 1877. **10** See the photograph of the Guinness family practising archery at Iveagh House in Dublin, in Laurence O'Connor, *Lost Ireland: a photographic record at the turn of the century* (London, 1984), p. 33.

The ruins of Youghal: Canon Samuel Hayman, antiquarianism and the decline of Irish Anglican ascendancy

PATRICK MAUME[1]

The history of nineteenth-century Ireland was shaped by a contest of elites, as defenders of the Protestant ascendancy installed by the victors in the wars of the seventeenth century fought a long retreating battle against the Catholic strong farmers, priests and professionals seeking local and national leadership. The 'Protestant ascendancy' is popularly viewed as referring to the rural landlords defeated in the Land War of the 1880s, but some of its stoutest early defenders came from urban Protestant elites who dominated town corporations until the Municipal Corporations (Ireland) Act of 1840,[2] and the concept was also intimately bound up with the struggle to persuade the British state to continue to officially recognize the (Anglican) Church of Ireland as the true national church – an official recognition which ended with the coming into force of Gladstone's 1869 Irish Church Act.

The subject of this essay, Canon Samuel Hayman (1818–86), belonged to these overlapping Protestant elites. From the late seventeenth century, his family had been prominent among the civic elites that dominated Youghal Corporation; they also had a small landed estate near Youghal – whose inhabitants Hayman attempted to convert to Protestantism. As a clergyman of the Established Church, Hayman participated in its pastoral work and sought to promote devotional renewal, missionary work (especially through the Irish language) and church building and restoration. Hayman is best remembered as an antiquarian writing on the history of Youghal; but a sketch of his wider career illuminates how these explorations of the past derived from a wider attempt to defend the position of the Anglican elite as civic and religious leaders, and how Hayman could maintain confidence in the prospect of victory for what in hindsight can be seen as an inevitably lost cause.

---

1 This paper draws on research done for the *DIB*. Thanks to Paul Bew, Derval Fitzgerald, Patricia Maume, James McGuire, Brian S. Murphy. References to *Handbook for Youghal with annals of Youghal* are to the 1896 edition published by W.G. Field of Youghal. Field added entries for the period after Hayman's original text concludes in 1852 and possibly revised earlier entries (though O'Flanagan's 1885–6 articles on Hayman state that he was revising the text shortly before his death). Though most of the 1896 text is by Hayman, catalogues usually list Field as author – earlier editions are attributed to Hayman.   2 Jacqueline Hill, *From patriots to unionists: Dublin civic politics and Irish Protestantism, 1660–1840* (Oxford, 1997).

In 1816, St Mary's Church at Youghal was renovated. An Italian stuccadore decorated the interior; upon completion it was discovered that the decorative motifs included crosses. The Youghal-born Whig historian and social theorist William Cooke Taylor recalled the response:

> Had the pope come in person to celebrate high mass in the church, greater indignation could not have been displayed by the pious Protestants of Youghal. They averred that the image of Baal had been erected in the sanctuary ... After a brief struggle between common sense and bigotry, the crosses, which really looked very pretty, were effaced, and in their place, two unmeaning lumps of plaster erected, with the words 'Holy Bible' beneath ... There were a few who defended the crosses, and they were at once set down as Papists. Some others laughed at the entire proceeding, and were of course stigmatized as infidels.[3]

Youghal's Protestant community in the early nineteenth century saw itself as besieged; its medieval and early modern buildings were reminders of its past as a major urban centre in the estate of the earls of Desmond, and the struggles of the early modern period when Raleigh, Spenser and Cromwell walked its streets, still seemed painfully alive.[4] The port's hinterland in the diocese of Cloyne and the Blackwater valley experienced recurring agrarian violence[5] as the political, social and economic structures implanted by the Munster plantation and the wars of the seventeenth century weakened.[6] During the mini-famines of 1819 and the early 1820s[7] and the Great Famine of 1845–9[8] Youghal witnessed riots against food exports; the entrenched Tory municipal oligarchy that controlled Youghal Corporation under the auspices of the earl of Shannon from 1744[9] was displaced in 1822 by Whig supporters of the duke of Devonshire; in 1832 a campaign led by the future Chartist Feargus O'Connor captured the parliamentary seat for Daniel O'Connell's son John (an event described by a local historian in 1945 as ending '700 years of alien ascendancy');[10] the corporation experienced drastic reform in the 1830s under Whig legislation passed at O'Connell's behest. The town retained a parliamentary seat until 1885, but its role as a port was undermined as the growth of road and rail transport extended the sphere of Cork and other ports; it became a resort town.[11]

3 William Cooke Taylor, *History of the civil wars of Ireland* (Edinburgh, 1832), II, n. 16. 4 *Handbook,* p. 44 recalls demolition of Cromwell's Youghal residence in 1835. Raleigh discussed pp 16–18, 26–27, 28–29. 5 *Handbook,* pp 67–68 (under 1762) describes Whiteboys near Youghal; pp 82–83 'infestation by banditti' in 1815 and 1817; p. 86 imprisonment of three Youghal inhabitants for refusal to pay tithes, 1832. 6 *Handbook*, p. 82 ascribes beginning of decline to peace after Waterloo, competition with Fermoy, and growth of Queenstown and Monkstown as resorts. For the wider context see David Dickson, *Old world colony: Cork and south Munster, 1630–1830* (Cork, 2005). 7 *Handbook*, p. 83. 8 *Handbook*, p. 94 (24 Sept. 1846). 9 *Handbook*, p. 63 (under 1744). 10 *Handbook*, pp 86, 88; John V. Condon, 'The Borough of Youghal', *Journal of Cork Historical and Archaeological Society* (July–Dec. 1945), 112–17. 11 *Handbook*, p. 74 (contrast description of

One response by the traditional Protestant elite is represented by Cooke Taylor, who became a Broad Churchman in religion, a Whig-Liberal Unionist in politics, and believed Archbishop Richard Whately's programme of Broad Church religious reformism, nondenominational state education, abolition of traditional social, religious and economic restrictions and dissemination of political economy could create a happy and prosperous Ireland, and reconcile rival creeds within the Union.[12] Another response was represented by Isaac Butt, editor of the *Dublin University Magazine* (hereafter *DUM*) and MP for Youghal in the 1840s and 1850s, who wished the Protestant elite to recover the underlying principles of enlightened conservatism in religion and politics, reclaiming the historical heritage of Ireland as expressed through its venerable institutions – above all the Church of Ireland, to be rescued from eighteenth-century scepticism and corruption by recapturing a true religious sensibility.[13]

Samuel Hayman's descent from Youghal's traditional elite gave him a lasting fascination with its history, and he is remembered for such works as the multi-edition *Annals of Youghal* and *Notes and records of the ancient religious foundations at Youghal, County Cork, and its vicinity*. He was a contributor on antiquarian and literary subjects to the *DUM*, and a close friend of Charles Lever; he inhabited a network of antiquarians such as the Catholic Whig lawyer James Roderick O'Flanagan (1819–1900) and Richard Caulfield (1823–87), editor of the municipal records of Cork boroughs.[14] Hayman was also a devotional writer for the *Christian Examiner* (founded by Caesar Otway, also part of the *DUM* circle) and studied the Irish language for missionary as well as antiquarian purposes. Even Disestablishment did not shake his belief in the triumph of evangelical truth over Popish heathenism, and as a builder of churches and rectories and an activist in missionary societies, he exemplifies the reforming spirit within the Victorian Church of Ireland as much as its embattled conservatism.

Hayman was born at Youghal on 27 July 1818.[15] The Haymans, who came to Ireland in 1629 from Minehead in Somerset, claimed illustrious Norman ancestry. They first appeared in Youghal during the Commonwealth when Samuel Hayman

flourishing trade in 1791). **12** D.H. Akenson, *A Protestant in purgatory: Richard Whately, archbishop of Dublin* (South Bend, IN, 1981); William Cooke Taylor, *Reminiscences of Daniel O'Connell* (Dublin, 2004; notes and intr. Patrick Maume); Patrick Maume, 'The natural history of society: the Orientalism of William Cooke Taylor' in Robert Blyth & Keith Jeffrey (eds), *The British Empire and its contested pasts* (Dublin, 2009), pp 77–94. **13** Wayne E. Hall, *Dialogues in the margin: a study of the Dublin University Magazine* (Washington DC, 1999). **14** T.A. Lunham, 'Memoir of the late Richard Caulfield', *Journal of the Royal Historical Association of Ireland*, 8 (1887–8), 171–5. **15** The principal biographical sources for Hayman are T.A. Lunham, 'Memoir of the late Canon Hayman', *Journal of the Royal Historical Association of Ireland*, 8 (1887–8), 165–70 (Lunham was churchwarden in Hayman's last parish); James Roderick O'Flanagan, *Fermoy Monthly Illustrated Journal of Instruction and Amusement*, 1:9 (Dec. 1885), 'Munster Literary Celebrities: no. vii – Revd Canon Hayman', continued in 1:10 (Jan. 1886), journal unpaginated. See also entries in *ODNB* by Marie-Louise Legg and *DIB* by Patrick Maume.

of Minehead acquired the former Franciscan friary (which the family still owned in the early nineteenth century). The building known as Sir Walter Raleigh's house (also known as Myrtle Grove; built for the wardens of a college founded in 1464 by the earls of Desmond) was their main residence throughout the eighteenth century. The connection began in 1670 when it was purchased by John Atkin, who in 1705 bequeathed it to his grandson John Hayman, MP for Youghal.[16]

Richard Caulfield's edition of *The council book of the Corporation of Youghal* (1878), for which Hayman supplied illustrations and manuscript sources as well as a list of sovereigns, mayors and bailiffs,[17] features numerous Haymans. In 1654, burgesses stand surety for a colleague's debts to George Hayman of Minehead;[18] in 1721, a Samuel Hayman is permitted to block the walk on the town walls;[19] in 1773, the corporation pays rent to Elizabeth Hayman for built-up ground near the clock tower.[20]

The first Hayman municipal official appears in 1666 (Samuel Hayman, bailiff that year, mayor 1670). They are admitted freemen and serve on the Common Council. Hayman monuments in St Mary's (on the north side of the nave near the choir arch) are described in Hayman's *Notes and records of the Ancient religious foundations at Youghal...* (pp 23–4) and *Illustrated guide to St Mary's Church* (1861 ed., p. 15).[21] In 1689, John Hayman – later MP for Youghal in the early eighteenth century[22] – executed a promissory note for four guineas, to be paid if Youghal did not submit to William III by 1 May 1690.[23] Four Haymans (two Johns and two Samuels) were Mayors in 1704, 1705, 1742 and 1750–1;[24] but the most prominent municipal Hayman was our Samuel's grandfather, William Atkin Hayman (whose father was Revd Atkin Hayman, rector of Ballyclogh in Cloyne, a sign of the family's clerical connections).[25] William Atkin Hayman was a bailiff as early as 1774 and mayor in 1788, 1792 and 1798[26] and again in 1805.[27] He was prominent in organized loyalism among the self-consciously embattled Youghal Protestant community, which implicated him in such repressive measures as the hanging of four suspected United Irishmen from the clock

---

16 Richard Caulfield (ed.), *The Council Book of the Corporation of Youghal* (Guildford, 1878), p. xxiii. **17** Caulfield, *The Council Book*, p. xii. **18** Ibid., p. 300. **19** Ibid., p. 417. **20** Ibid., p. 485. **21** Also in *Handbook*, pp vii–viii. The Hayman family presented the church with an antique sword-rest displaying the arms of the borough in 1788 after the borough arms in St Mary's were defaced by an intruder (ibid., p. 54 under 1684, when the sword-rest was originally made). **22** *Handbook*, p. 58, 1703 and 1707. **23** *Handbook*, pp 55–6. Youghal surrendered 2 Aug. 1690, so Hayman lost his wager. **24** *Handbook*, p. 63 mentions that in 1743 Samuel Hayman was elected churchwarden but successfully declined because of his mayoral duties. 'He was appointed one of the Commissioners of Arrays, on the apprehended invasion of the Pretender.' Under 1751 (p. 64) it emphasizes the honour paid to John Hayman by unanimous re-election as mayor: 'He was an efficient magistrate, collecting the public rates himself and performing a variety of useful undertakings'. **25** O'Flanagan, 'Canon Hayman'. **26** *Handbook*, p. 70n notes him taking advantage of a 1769 parliamentary grant to improve the harbour by leasing sections of the strand from the corporation and reclaiming it from the sea. **27** Not in Caulfield; *Handbook*, p. 8 records his salvaging the cargo of a wrecked Liverpool brig and receipt of an inscribed silver vase from the owners and underwriters.

tower at Youghal in 1798.[28] 'Surely universal feeling will now turn with horror from these dreadful scenes and will breathe the prayer that they be never again enacted in our native country.'[29] (This passage may have been added by the publisher W.G. Field after Hayman's death, but it is unlikely that Hayman, and other inhabitants of Youghal, were unaware of the darker side of his grandfather's activities.)

The family's connection with Raleigh's house ended with the death of Walter Atkin Hayman on 5 June 1816,[30] but a sense of illustrious family history (reinforced by a collection of family deeds, wills and letters dating back to Charles I) may have encouraged Hayman's antiquarianism. At his birth, his father, Matthew Hayman, lived at South Abbey, Youghal, amid the ruins of the medieval Franciscan friary. (Hayman notes that when building a new dwelling in the friary precincts in 1820 his father turned up skeletons and decorated gravestones; the last remnants of the friary buildings were demolished between 1817 and 1826 to build a chapel of ease and the building which subsequently became the Devonshire Arms Hotel. Some years later numerous medieval graves were uncovered during the building of a Presentation convent and school nearby; a Magdalene asylum was also erected there.)[31]

Hayman was educated at the classical and English school of Revd Thomas Nolan at Youghal, at Clonmel endowed school and at TCD, which he entered as a Fellow Commoner on 18 October 1835. He was a bright student, shy and frail in health. Hayman graduated BA on 2 July 1839. He was ordained deacon on 19 September 1841 and priest on 14 August 1842, and became curate of Glanworth, near Fermoy. When his attempts to evangelize local Catholics encountered more or less polite rebuffs, he realized that his ignorance of the people's language made him an outsider. He took Irish lessons from a local hedge-school teacher employed by the proselytizing Irish Society. Although the teacher abandoned the lessons under 'sacerdotal pressure' because of (correct) suspicions about Hayman's motives, the clergyman had acquired sufficient foundation to perfect his idiom by speaking with the people. Hayman later heard that many famine emigrants from the area converted to

---

28 On 8 Jan. 1793 (as mayor), he formed 'The Youghal and Barony of Imokilly Association ... for the purpose of discouraging and suppressing all seditious publications and for promoting loyalty and obedience to the constituted authorities' (*Handbook*, p. 74). On 6 Feb. 1793 Mayor Hayman suppressed a meeting at Youghal 'to demand emancipation and Reform ... John Hall, secretary of (Lodge 900) the Youghal Orangemen presented an address to the mayor, thanking him for his hereditary loyalty' [ibid. p. 74; as the Orange Order was founded in 1795, this must refer to some other loyalist society]. In 1799, he entertained Youghal yeomanry corps 'officers and men' at Myrtle Grove after a review at Castlemartyr (p. 78). **29** *Handbook*, p. 78. **30** *Notes and records*, p. 59; Hayman writes wistfully of the house in *Handbook for Youghal* (1896 ed., xiv) 'Like all Old English domestic architecture, it forms a picturesque appearance from the variety and artistic play of its outlines, with light and shade brokenly contrasted on them, so grateful to the initiated eye, and so seldom realized in our modern monotonous erections'. **31** *Notes and records of the ancient religious foundations at Youghal, County Cork, and its vicinity* (1854 ed.), p. 46; *Handbook*, p. 84.

Protestantism in America – he believed this was a long-term product of his Irish-language evangelization.[32]

By the time he came to Glanworth, Hayman had begun to write for the *Patrician*, a London-based genealogical publication run by Sir Bernard Burke, for the *DUM*, chief platform of the new Irish Toryism – he was recruited by its publisher James McGlashan – and for Caesar Otway's *Christian Examiner*. (In 1843, displaying local patriotism, he reviewed and promoted a book by Cooke Taylor, which used new discoveries in Egyptology to elucidate Biblical society and idioms.)[33] Hayman produced *DUM* pieces with such titles as 'Air bubbles' and 'Fragments of a dreamer's notebook' modelled on the German Romantic aphorist Jean-Paul Richter.[34] Hayman also formed a close friendship with Charles Lever, who occasionally visited him while editing the *DUM* (from 1842).[35] As Lever prepared to leave Ireland in the late 1840s, he spoke of Hayman as one of his three intimate Irish friends – 'a shamrock of friendship'.[36] They corresponded regularly and after Lever's death Hayman was asked to write the official life. Hayman refused, but he assisted W.J. Fitzpatrick – who completed the work – with correspondence and reminiscences.[37] Hayman preferred Lever's earlier novels – notably *Arthur O'Leary* – to the later works;[38] he also told Fitzpatrick that Lever, even in his early career, possessed stronger religious convictions than casual readers might have suspected.[39]

In 1846, with the vicar of Glanworth incapacitated by illness, Hayman organized the parochial famine relief committee and became its secretary, working himself to exhaustion.

> Letters to kinsfolk and other friends brought us generous supplies from England. A provision depot was opened. Flour and meal were brought within reach of the villagers, being retailed to them at prices proportioned to their slender means. The Committee gave daily attendance. Thus passed with us the dreadful winter of 1846.
>
> 'And the famine was sore in the land'; and in its train came the fever, that swept away unnumbered victims. Medical men and ministers of different denominations succumbed in numbers to the pestilence; yet none flinched, for the people clung to us as their preservers. The work of relieving distress went on; but, after a time, the misery outgrew human help. We toiled continually, and when we had done our best were lost in bewilderment. In some

---

32 Hayman, 'A reminiscence' in Charles Bullock et al., *What Ireland needs: the Gospel in the native tongue* (London, n.d. [*c.*1880]), pp 54–66. **33** James Roderick O'Flanagan, *An octogenarian literary life* (Cork, 1896), p. 75. **34** O'Flanagan, 'Canon Hayman'. **35** W.J. Fitzpatrick, *Life of Charles Lever* (rev. ed. Dublin, 1884), pp 38, 107, 120, 130, 208–10. **36** Ibid., pp 241, 280. **37** Ibid., p. vii. **38** Ibid., pp 182–3, 197–8, 211–12, 238, 243–4, 257. **39** Ibid., p. 233n. Hayman recalled to Fitzpatrick that Lever was denounced by the *Christian Examiner* for commenting in one novel that parsons never spoke piety in convivial company; Hayman reassured the novelist that he enjoyed the joke and found it truer than he liked (p. 178n.).

instances whole families died, and they lay unsepulchred until we pulled down their homes over them for entombment. I cannot, however, even at this lapse of time, describe these horrors.[40]

In 1847, his curacy at Glanworth was terminated by the death of the rector. Hayman then served as curate of Glanmire, Co. Cork, but decided that this prosperous suburban parish gave insufficient opportunity for evangelization. He therefore returned to his native Youghal (25 March 1849)[41] as a curate at St Mary's Church, and soon found himself ministering to the sick and dying during a cholera epidemic.[42] His humanitarian labours did not restrain Hayman from suggesting, in a later devotional article, that the Famine was divine punishment for the spread of Mariolatry. Hayman quotes approvingly some anonymous verses that presented the failure of Marian prayers to ease the Famine as proving the futility of idolatry.[43]

In his antiquarian publications, Hayman mentioned superstitious beliefs and observances in passing.[44] In a publication promoting the work of the proselytizing Irish Church Missions, Hayman provides a scathing account of the 'pattern' in honour of St Declan at Ardmore, Co. Waterford, in the early 1850s.[45] 'The scenes here enacted could be surpassed only before Juggernaut's car or among the fetish-tribes of the Congo River ... "rounds" were observed by creeping a certain number of times around the reputed holy place like a four-footed beast, and sometimes proceeding on the knees only'. The skull of St Declan was venerated and earth brought into contact with it credited with supernatural powers, after which 'a carnival took the place of penitential observances. Scenes occurred over which I must draw a veil. Rioting and drunkenness, with their concomitant evils, reigned paramount'. Hayman recounts with some glee claims that the original skull disintegrated during repairs to its metal shrine in the early seventeenth century and had been replaced by the (Protestant) craftsman responsible with the skull of John Dromada, executed for murder and piracy, itself allegedly replaced some years later (when the priest discovered the truth) with an anonymous skull from a local graveyard.[46]

Hayman arranged for an Irish-speaking scripture-reader to be employed on a small estate that his father owned in the parishes of Youghal and Clonpriest,[47] and

---

40 Hayman, 'A reminiscence', pp 62–3. Hayman also suggests the famine represented divine interposition to save Ireland from civil war precipitated by O'Connell's Repeal campaign and Young Ireland. **41** *Memorials of Youghal, ecclesiastical and civil* (Youghal, 1879), p. 28. **42** Hayman, 'A second reminiscence' in Bullock et al., *What Ireland needs*, pp 67–84. **43** *Looking upward*, p. 45n. **44** For example, *Notes and records*, p. 10 (Ardmore). **45** Hayman, 'A second reminiscence', pp 76–80; Stiofán Ó Cadhla, *The holy well tradition: the pattern of St Declan, Ardmore, County Waterford, 1800–2000* (Dublin, 2002) cites many accounts, including antiquarian descriptions and arguments over the carnivalesque aspects of the devotion, but overlooks Hayman. **46** Hayman, 'A second reminiscence', pp 78–9n; *Memorials of Youghal, ecclesiastical and civil* (1879 ed.), p. 34 reproduces a 1681 map including Dromada's head displayed on the exchange and a brief account of his crimes. **47** NUI Galway Landed Estates database http://landedestates.nuigalway.ie:8080/LandedEstates/jsp-

happily received reports that this employee dissuaded tenants from card-playing by reciting Bible passages in Irish.[48] Hayman retained a lifelong connection with the Irish Society; some verses he wrote on Jesus as the only true priest were translated into Irish by Canon James Goodman (now best-remembered as a folksong collector) and distributed in Irish-speaking districts.[49]

Hayman remained at Youghal until 13 May 1863,[50] living with his parents (his mother died in 1851, his father in 1867) and a sister. He had been offered livings in both Britain and Ireland, but his independent means allowed him to remain where he felt most needed. In 1854, he married Emily Cassidy, whose father was incumbent of Newtownards while her mother was an heiress (also of Co. Down). They had one daughter, who later married and settled in England. Hayman frequently discourses on the blessings of clerical marriage, the evils of Romish celibacy, and the role of a clergyman's wife as parochial helpmate,[51] and illustrates the growth of the Christian soul by reference to his own child.

This period saw the appearance in several editions of Hayman's antiquarian writings on Youghal; they were published by a Youghal printer, J.W. Lindsay, and directed at the developing tourist trade encouraged by the new Cork–Youghal railway. *The annals of Youghal: the handbook for Youghal* appeared in four editions (1848, 1851, 1854 and 1858 as well as the posthumous 1896 revision); a guide to the ancient religious foundations at Youghal (also in the form of an annal and drawing on exploration of the sites, originally published in the *Journal of the Royal Historical Association of Ireland*) in different versions in 1850, 1854, 1861, 1863 and 1879, and an illustrated guide to the Blackwater region in 1860, 1861 and 1875 (reprinted 1896 by W.G. Field, updating the ownership of various gentlemen's houses). The medieval and early modern sections of the annals (from Edward I) reproduce many references to Youghal in the plea, patent and close rolls and other state papers then preserved in Dublin.[52] We know Hayman used the duke of Devonshire's papers at Lismore and other local archives and that friends looked up source material in Dublin.

One friend was James Roderick O'Flanagan, a Catholic lawyer and son of the barrack-master of Fermoy, whom Hayman had encouraged to produce an illustrated guide to the Blackwater after O'Flanagan lectured on the subject at an 1843 British Association meeting in Youghal (organized by Cooke Taylor).[53] O'Flanagan made Hayman's acquaintance in the early 1840s; they became lifelong friends, and Hayman helped O'Flanagan in compiling his works on Irish legal history.[54] Hayman was noted for his generosity in sharing his research material among the networks of nineteenth-century Irish antiquarianism. His contacts stretched farther afield; on the foundation of the Harleian Society for the study of genealogy in 1860 Hayman

/estate-show.jsp?id=3013 (accessed 5 Sept. 2011). I owe this reference to Dr Brian S. Murphy. **48** Hayman, 'A second reminiscence', pp 69–75. **49** Ibid., pp 81–4. **50** *Memorials of Youghal, ecclesiastical and civil* (Youghal, 1879), p. 28. **51** For example, *Papers from a parsonage*, pp 1–5; *Criteria; or, The Divine Examen*, p. 33. **52** For example, *Handbook*, p. 6 (14 Feb. 1301), pp 7–8 (1347). **53** James Roderick O'Flanagan, *An octogenarian literary life* (Cork, 1896), p. 75. **54** O'Flanagan, 'Canon Hayman'.

became a council member, and he wrote for antiquarian publications including the *Cork Magazine* of the 1840s, the *Journal of the Royal Society of Antiquaries of Ireland*, *Notes and Queries*, and a London journal called the *Reliquary*. Much of his research remains scattered in such journals or reappeared in fascicule format, as with his work for the *Reliquary* on the history of the East Cork family of Greatrakes. Even his work on the first part of the *Geraldine Papers*, published in 1870–81 (the only part he edited, though he is conventionally listed as co-editor of the whole series), was reprinted from the *Journal of the Royal Historical Association of Ireland*, as was his 1854 work on the ancient religious foundations of Youghal and Ardmore.[55]

As late as 1885, when O'Flanagan edited the short-lived *Fermoy Monthly Illustrated Journal*, Hayman, though in declining health, contributed articles on local place-names and supplied other material;[56] O'Flanagan dedicated the bound volume to Hayman.[57] Even though O'Flanagan was an inveterate name-dropper, it is clear from the letters he publishes that their friendship was personal as well as antiquarian; in view of Hayman's religious and political attitudes, it is striking that he could maintain such a friendship with a devoutly Catholic acquaintance of Newman and (conservative) O'Connellite, later a Parnellite Home Ruler.

In Youghal, Hayman participated in a 'restoration' of St Mary's Church that re-emphasized its Gothic character under the direction of his rector, Revd Pierce Drew; his writings praise 'the noble Gothic', denounce the 'vandalism' of eighteenth-century restorers, lament that the early nineteenth-century 'restoration' left Youghal's medieval church 'as conventicle-like as possible', and criticize 'pagan' classical symbols on gravestones as no more Christian than 'the old heathen practice of combustion'.[58]

In 1863, Bishop John Gregg, whom Hayman revered and who shared his desire for Irish-language missionary activity,[59] appointed him rector of Glenville, which Hayman called by its Irish name of Ardnageehy. He loved its romantic mountain setting and 'acquired and beautified' a rectory for future incumbents[60] (a devotional essay states that the rectory had views of five counties and the distant sea), but it proved too remote for the family's convenience and in 1867 he became rector of Doneraile.[61]

Hayman attributed the disestablishment of the Church of Ireland to the legacy of eighteenth-century corruption and scepticism, which had already been remedied by the revival of evangelical religion;[62] he hoped disestablishment might cause the laity to take a greater share of pastoral work (he wanted to revive the permanent

55 Hayman's equivocal comment that Dominick Collins, soldier-turned-Jesuit executed in Youghal (15 June 1601) 'met his death, with what some would deem heroism, and others impenitence and contumacy' may accommodate the mild ecumenism of the antiquarian world: *Handbook*, p. 16. 56 The place-name articles appear Sept. 1885–May 1886; see also May 1885, Sept. 1885, Nov. 1885, May 1886, June 1886. 57 O'Flanagan, *An octogenarian literary life*, pp 195–6. 58 *Notes and records*, pp 29–30. 59 Miriam Moffitt, *The Society for Irish Church Missions to the Roman Catholics, 1849–1950* (Manchester, 2010), esp. p. 231; Hayman, 'John of the Golden Mouth'. 60 *Papers from a parsonage*, pp ix–x. 61 *Looking upward*, pp 90–3. 62 *Ministrations*, pp 90–3; *Criteria*, pp 9–11.

diaconate) and improve relations with other Protestant denominations on the basis of scriptural religion (he thought the Church of Ireland too suspicious of contemporary revivalism).

> The state for centuries sought to make of the Church of Ireland a political tool; and, when such degradation could no longer be endured, punished her by confiscation. So be it! Better to have things as they are, than as they were. Our political Balaam [that is, Gladstone] will be found in God's goodness, not to have cursed but to have blest us altogether.[63]

In 1872, he became rector of Carrigaline with Douglas, and a canon of Cork diocese. In 1875, the parish was divided; Hayman retained Douglas and built a new church and rectory, raising a large portion of the money himself. The church spire was completed after his death as a memorial to him; he is buried in the cemetery which he laid out. This was in line with the general policy of Bishop Gregg, who oversaw the construction of many handsome churches, most famously St Finn Barre's Cathedral. In a memorial article, Hayman emphasized that the bishop's activities did not reflect sacerdotalist tendencies; he simply desired appropriately dignified settings for church services.[64]

Hayman zealously supported Sunday schools.[65] He was secretary to the Cork auxiliaries of the Church Mission Society, the Bible Society and the Mission to the Jews, and 'active in Irish missionary societies generally'.[66] He was secretary to the Cork Protestant Home for Incurables, which he assisted Bishop Gregg in founding. His health was always frail (he had a near-fatal illness in 1852) and after a decline lasting about a year he died on 15 December 1886.

Hayman could easily be presented as an Old Mortality figure, child of a declining oligarchy brooding over the ruins of a vanished past as a metaphor for his own caste's demise. There was, however, another side to his literary work. Although Hayman is chiefly remembered as an antiquarian, he was widely read in his own day as a devotional writer, consciously drawing on the tradition of the Anglican literary parson meditating on the lessons of parish life. He occasionally published sermons from quite early in his career (*The Bible: the wisdom of a nation* (London, 1846) – a sermon on behalf of the Irish Church Education Society, which tried to create a system of Church of Ireland schools to rival the National Schools;[67] *A farewell sermon, preached in Glanmire* (Cork, 1849); *To-day, its duties and supplies, a lecture delivered before the Cork Young Men's Association* (Dublin, 1857) – all reprinted in *Ministrations: or feeding the flock of God* (1875)).[68] In the late 1860s and early 1870s, probably in response to the looming disestablishment of the Church of Ireland, Hayman collected many papers from the *Christian Examiner* and its successor the *Irish Ecclesiastical Gazette* (precursor

---

63 *Ministrations*, p. 93.   **64** Hayman, 'John of the Golden Mouth' in Bullock et al., *What Ireland needs*, pp 135–6, 141.   **65** *Ministrations*, pp 15–31.   **66** *Cork Constitution*, 18 Dec. 1886.   **67** *Ministrations*, pp 61–82.   **68** Ibid., pp 34–60.

of the *Church of Ireland Gazette*) in a series of books, most in a uniform format from the Dublin publisher George Herbert (*Looking upward: a country pastor's reveries* – 1871; *Papers from a parsonage* – 1872; *Passages from a Commonplace Book* – 1873; *Criteria, or the Divine Examen* – 1874). *About footsteps, in twelve chapters* appeared from the London publisher James Nesbit in 1869. Some papers were clearly written earlier than their appearance in book form – four *Papers from a parsonage* were written at Youghal and the rest date from Ardnageehy.[69]

These papers emphasize that Hayman's Gothic enthusiasm did not translate into sympathy for the Church of Rome (though one wonders how he squared his complaint about St Mary's having been transformed into a conventicle[70] with his disquisitions on the contrast between the garish ornaments of Romanism and Ritualism and the noble simplicity of true Protestant churches,[71] and there is incongruity in his evocation of a ruined abbey in Somerset as emblematic of fallen man retaining traces of his creator's workmanship).[72] He denounces the display of the crucifix, even of the cross, as violating the Second Commandment and denying the Resurrection of Christ by emphasizing his death.[73] He is dismissive of the doctrine of apostolic succession even as held by Anglicans.[74] He calls forcefully for different Protestant bodies to work together as parts of the army of Christ, adding that Popery is the army of Antichrist.[75] He laments, obliquely but unmistakably, over the impending prospect of disestablishment.

Hayman sometimes deploys his antiquarian researches. A description of the site of the mediaeval leper hospital near Youghal develops into an extended description of the world as leper hospital, the Bible as sole cure, and Éire as a particularly pain-suffused ward, long abused by religious quacks but soon to see the light when Popery becomes as extinct as leprosy.[76] Musings over an old Templar preceptory at Rhincrew near Youghal (discussed in *Notes and records...*)[77] develop into a denunciation of the Crusades as a parody of the spirit of Jesus, and a sign of the eternal persecuting spirit of Popery (though Hayman also states that Crusaders genuinely loved and suffered for God and exemplify true Christian warfare against sin).[78] Meditating on an antique communion cup in St Mary's, he rejoices that it dates from the Reformation:

> No shaveling priest of the old College ever defiled this Cup with his idolatrous ordinances. No Caenobite, that despised the pure love of woman, yet indulged himself with things forbidden, of which it were a crime to speak, ever handled it. No! the freemen of Christ prepared and fashioned it; and over it the simple Scriptural forms only of a holy worship were administered by those who love the truth as it is in Jesus.[79]

69 *Papers from a parsonage*, pp ix–x.   **70** *Handbook*, p. 23n.   **71** *Papers from a parsonage*, pp 218–33.   **72** *Looking upward*, pp 78–89.   **73** *Ministrations*, pp 161–2; *Criteria*, pp 13–14. **74** *Papers from a parsonage*, p. 224.   **75** *Ministrations*, pp 83–98.   **76** *Papers from a parsonage*, pp 144–52.   **77** *Notes and records* (1854 ed.), pp 39–40.   **78** *Papers from a parsonage*, pp 34–42.   **79** *Papers*, pp 24–33.

The same piece suggests a major source of Hayman's antiquarianism; fascination with the past as reminder of those who went before and of a future when Hayman and his generation would have departed, while new generations worshipped at St Mary's. (He calculated that the dead in St Mary's churchyard outnumbered the living inhabitants of Youghal by eight to one.)[80] Criticizing the sceptical 'modern Sadducee', Hayman states that their arguments against Jesus, God and an afterlife logically present as unreliable all historical knowledge and all evidence of the past (or of remote parts of the world, not beheld with one's own senses, in the present).[81] This fascination with the transience of life and the intangible reality of memory as paralleling the supernatural world may partly reflect the fact that these *Christian Examiner* selections are predominantly the work of an older man.

The motive of Hayman's apparently unclerical zeal for writing tourist guides is also suggested here; his writings are suffused by the Romantic sublime and a sense that nature displays the wonders of God. Convalescing by the seaside, he walks the sands, watches the ships, and broods on the piety of sailors and the biblical promise that in the New Jerusalem there will be no more sea;[82] contemplating the mountains of North Cork, he reflects on Biblical high places, on Ararat, Sinai and Sion.[83] Hayman loved the Lake District (he spent his honeymoon there, corresponded with Wordsworth in the old poet's later years and quotes his later, more explicitly Christian verse)[84] and compares the Galtees and Comeraghs to the landscapes of Cumbria and of his ancestral Somerset so frequently that he seems hardly to recognize the Irish scenery in its own right.[85] His love of creation is underpinned by certainty that God constantly intervenes in myriad ways; we may not recognize the numerous special providences that shape our lives, but if accepted as God's will we will see them in hindsight.

This faith underpinned Hayman's confidence that Anglican missionary work would inevitably triumph in Ireland – was triumphant already. A contrast with that other literary clergyman of Doneraile, Canon Patrick Augustine Sheehan (coincidentally also an admirer of Jean-Paul Richter), is striking; although a representative of the majority faith when it was increasing in influence and status, Sheehan appears more gloomy and isolated than the representative of the former Established Church. In part, this reflects personal temperament (Sheehan was depressive and lost his parents and all but one sibling in early life), in part the isolation of the celibate; but Sheehan is a self-conscious provincial haunted by fear that he will lose his people's love, and they will lose their souls, to unbelieving metropolitan modernity, while despite his denunciations of 'the sceptic', 'the modern Sadduccee', and Roman 'Babylon', the older cleric remains blithely – almost delusionally – confident that the Church of Ireland, with God on its side, will defeat Popery.

---

80 *Papers*, pp 277–82. **81** *Papers*, pp 57–67, 107–8; *Looking upward*, pp 119–31. **82** *Papers*, pp 175–91; *Looking upward*, pp 63–4. **83** *Looking upward*, pp 99–102; *Papers*, pp 262–7. **84** *Looking upward*, p. 91; *Papers*, pp 12–13, 169–70. Hayman also loved the poetry of George Herbert and the sermons of John Donne and Charles Wolfe. **85** *Papers*, pp 10–11; *Ministrations*, pp 1–2, 4–5.

His career, then, in its antiquarianism and its ecclesiastical journalism, in its missionary work and its church-building represents the Janus-faced self-image of the Victorian Church of Ireland elite. It is easy in hindsight to note their regrets over eighteenth-century missed opportunities and their fears that the progressive collapse of traditional bastions of Protestant ascendancy before Whig reformers and a resurgent Catholicism heralded the coming of Antichrist and the Biblical Apocalypse;[86] it is harder to evoke the sense shared by many of them that they were recapturing a deeper inward spirituality, and that as their church rediscovered its historical and doctrinal roots, God would surely grant victory and fill its new Gothic churches with worshippers.

86 *Criteria*, p. ix.

Lady Gregory's fans: the Irish Protestant landed class and negotiations of power

ANNA PILZ

'[I]f we are considering Lady Gregory's rise in the world', suggested George Moore in his third volume of autobiography, *Vale*, in 1914, 'we must admit that she owes a great deal to her husband'.[1] Leaving aside Moore's generally negative portrayal of Lady Gregory in *Hail and farewell*, this is a perceptive remark. With her marriage to Sir William Henry Gregory of Coole Park, Co. Galway, Augusta Persse entered the high stratum of society on both sides of the Irish Sea, and was introduced to an established circle of friends including eminent politicians, artists and writers of the British elite. Indeed, becoming Lady Gregory proved to be the first stepping stone to a career as a prolific writer of the Irish Literary Revival and co-founder of the Abbey Theatre. Reflecting on her life in the summer of 1928, she expressed gratitude: 'If he had not given me his name[,] his position, I should not have had so good standing'.[2] Such an idea of elitism and tradition reveals an awareness of her privileged position within society. The remark suggests a continuity of high social standing in a period of time associated with a decline in wealth and power of that echelon.

Both Moore and Lady Gregory seem to agree that Sir William's renown and name guaranteed continued access to privilege. However, this essay will demonstrate the complexity of Lady Gregory's status within society, as her roles as landlord, widowed mother and cultural nationalist led to tensions with the established elite in both Ireland and England. Thus, her attitude towards the elite as well as the elite's perception of her was under strain, and power or privilege had to be negotiated. From the beginning of her marriage in 1880, Lady Gregory showed concern for the reputation of the Gregory family, in part to further the future career of her son, Robert Gregory (1881–1918), but also with regard to the reputation of the landed class at a time when Irish nationalism gained momentum. With her move towards cultural nationalism in the 1890s, Lady Gregory relied on the support of the same elite circles both to assist her son Robert, whom she wished to become an influential member of the Irish elite, and to support her cultural projects, mainly the founding of the Abbey Theatre in 1904. This period raises questions concerning how the landed elite viewed their position at the end of the Victorian age, whether their power diminished and what methods were employed to retain their elite status.

---

1 George Moore, *Vale* (London, 1914), pp 174–5.   2 Lady Augusta Gregory, diary entry for 22 June 1928, in Lady Augusta Gregory, *Lady Gregory's journals: volume two, Books 30–44, 21 February, 1925–9 May 1932*, ed. Daniel J. Murphy (Gerrards Cross, 1987), p. 281.

The last two decades of the nineteenth century in Ireland were characterized by agrarian unrest in the midst of the Land War, a diversification of Irish society with a rising Catholic middle class, the franchise reforms of 1884–5 and increasing questioning of British imperialism. These changes were of particular importance to Ireland's elite, advancing the gradual decline of that social stratum in wealth and power. As pointed out by D. George Boyce, 'the decline of deference was particularly marked in the Land War'.[3] Thus, a major pillar of power for the landed class began to dismantle with incoming rents dwindling and estates shrinking in size. Yet the Gregorys' landed wealth was already diminishing prior to the land agitation of the 1880s. In 1847, Sir William inherited 15,000 acres and an annual income of more than £7,000. However, this was largely absorbed by up to £50,000 of encumbrances due to mortgages and losses during the Famine. His ardent interest in horse racing added to the already substantial debt. In 1857, he sold about two-thirds of his land in the encumbered estates court and Coole Park was only saved when his mother bought 5,000 acres of land and he took another mortgage from his cousin, Charles Gregory, in 1867.[4] According to W.E. Vaughan, an estimated 700 landlords owned land of 5,000 acres or above in the 1870s and, by that standard, Sir William could still be considered above average.[5]

Despite a decline in landed wealth, Sir William's leverage in elite circles of London society was founded on a rising political career. After entering the Irish Privy Council in 1871, he was appointed governor of Ceylon the following year. The latter position was secured by Lord Granville's recommendation, which he had gained through his friendship with Lady Waldegrave, prominent hostess of a political salon.[6] The governorship came with an annual salary of £7,000, which, by the standards of the late 1860s, settled him comfortably among those 30,000 families of Britain with an income of £1,000 or higher.[7] Yet it was mainly due to the substantial fortune of his first wife, Elizabeth Bowdoin, that Sir William gained financial stability.[8] After her sudden death in 1873, only a year after their marriage, Sir William wrote to Bess Gregory with relief: 'The legacies are £2,000 to other people and £9,000 to me – besides the life income. […] I am now so extremely well off that I often doubt whether it is worth while to stay on here and save money'.[9] With the sale of their house in Eaton Square and the trust fund, his inheritance amounted to

3 D. George Boyce, *Nineteenth-century Ireland – the search for stability* (rev. ed. Dublin, 2005), p. 278.   **4** See Brian Jenkins, *Sir William Gregory of Coole: the biography of an Anglo-Irishman* (Gerrards Cross, 1986), pp 84–108.   **5** W.E. Vaughan, *Landlords and tenants in mid-Victorian Ireland* (Oxford, 1994), p. 6. Vaughan notes that a minimum of 500 acres entitled 'its owner to be considered a landlord' and the official returns for the 1870s show that there was an estimated 6,500 landowners: ibid.   **6** See Jenkins, *Sir William Gregory of Coole*, p. 211. **7** See Stefan Collini, *Public moralists: political thought and intellectual life in Britain, 1850–1930* (Oxford, 1991), pp 36–7.   **8** See Jenkins, *Sir William Gregory of Coole*, p. 219.   **9** Letter from Sir William Henry Gregory to Bess Gregory (17 Aug. 1873), Gregory Papers, Emory University, quoted in Brian Jenkins, 'The marriage' in Ann Saddlemyer and Colin Smythe (eds), *Lady Gregory: fifty years after* (Gerrards Cross, 1987), pp 71–2.

almost £50,000.[10] Knighted in 1875 by the Prince of Wales, Sir William continued to serve as governor for a further year. He resigned in 1876 and returned the following year to Ireland, where he first met Augusta Persse of the neighbouring estate, Roxborough. After their marriage in March 1880, Augusta entered society as Lady Gregory, travelled extensively to Continental Europe and Britain's overseas colonies, attended dinner parties and gradually developed her talent as a hostess and conversationalist among the British elite.

Described as 'an Irish landlord but an English gentleman', Sir William enjoyed spending the social season of the year in London and bought a townhouse at the fashionable address of 3 St George's Place, just off Hyde Park.[11] His life is summed up by his friend F. Standish: 'A pretty house, pretty [*sic*] decorated, with artistic surroundings – a good cook and cellar, pleasant friends, and ample income and good health'.[12] It was there that Lady Gregory gained her first experiences as a hostess and was introduced to the art of conversation at dinner tables and tea parties. 'In her drawing-room were to be met men of assured reputation in literature and politics', George Moore wrote, 'and there was always the best reading of the time upon her tables'.[13] Lady Gregory quickly adapted to the social seasons in London and rose to host 'one of the most agreeable [salons] in London', as Frank Lawley, a friend of Sir William, remarked.[14]

Lady Gregory, deeply impressed by the importance of their societal circle, started to collect the autographs of selected acquaintances on an ivory fan soon after her marriage, a practice that invited the scorn of George Moore.[15] Arriving at St George's Place as the historian William Lecky was about to leave, Moore recalled 'the look of pleasure on her face when she mentioned the name of the visitor'. On Lecky's exit, Sir Edwin Arnold, poet laureate candidate in 1892, made an entrance and, Moore remembered, 'when Sir Edwin rose to go, she produced a fan and asked him to write his name upon one of the sticks'. It is in his subsequent comment, however, that Moore revealed the reason for his mockery: 'she did not ask me to write my name', he wrote with a recognizable sense of disappointment, 'though at that time I had written not only *A modern lover*, but also *A Mummer's wife*, and I left the house feeling for the first time that the world I lived in was not so profound as I had imagined it to be'.[16] The fan included the signatories Sir John Millais, Sir Alfred Lyall, Lord Tennyson, Lord Dufferin, Lord Randolph Churchill, Sir Edward Malet, Sir Arthur Sullivan, Wilfrid Scawen Blunt, Ahmed Arabi, W.E. Gladstone, A.W. Kinglake, Sir G.O. Trevelyan and Sir Henry Layard.[17] Significantly, the list is formed mainly by politicians of high social standing, all friends or acquaintances of Sir William. It was not Moore's turn yet, but he would eventually be asked to sign his

10 See ibid., p. 71.   **11** Mary Lou Kohfeldt, *Lady Gregory: the woman behind the Irish renaissance* (New York, 1985), p. 45.   **12** Letter from F. Standish to Sir William Henry Gregory (20 Mar. 1878) quoted in Jenkins, 'The marriage', p. 72.   **13** George Moore, *Ave* (London, 1911), p. 275.   **14** Frank Lawley quoted in Kohfeldt, *The woman behind the renaissance*, p. 53.   **15** Ibid.   **16** Moore, *Vale*, pp 175–6.   **17** Colin Smythe, *A guide to Coole Park, Co. Galway, home of Lady Gregory* (4th ed. Gerrards Cross, 2003), p. 57.

name to the same fan, as was Sir Edwin Arnold, their names representing what was to become Lady Gregory's increasingly Irish-based and literary social circle.

With some pleasure, Moore informs his readers that Sir William 'looked a little distressed at her want of tact' as she proudly showed him the newly gained addition.[18] This habit of collecting appears to have been an important tradition for Lady Gregory, however, as she also arranged letters, photographs and articles of English and Irish politicians in a large autograph book. This included not only contemporary letters, but also older ones associated with previous generations of the Gregory family, such as those by the duke of Wellington, Sir Robert Peel and Daniel O'Connell. Notably, most entries date from the period of her marriage. A signed note by the first Viscount Wolseley, an Irish army officer, for instance, reads 'I hope the enclosed photographs may please your young son'.[19] Equally, Sir Edgar Boehm, sculptor of a statue of Sir William for the Museum of Colombo, wrote in 1883, enclosing 'the photograph you did me the honor to ask for'. With this statue, Boehm contributed to Sir William's stature abroad and, hence, helped Lady Gregory's project of continuing a tradition of a good name and reputation. That she wrote with the future of her son in mind, in part arguably designing the book for him, is exemplified in Sir Edgar remarking 'I wish with all my heart he may yet give you all the happiness & pride a good & talented son is to parents'.[20] Thus, both the fans and autograph book functioned as the location for a common heritage and tradition. These artefacts, with their embedded shared memories through photographs and personal letters, provided a basis for future support for her son – an address book in a different format.[21]

Thus endowed by Sir William with a privileged position, Lady Gregory entered early widowhood in 1892. The death of her husband marked as important a moment in her life as did her marriage to him. Showing a sense for practicality, she wrote to Wilfrid Scawen Blunt, one of her closest friends, from St George's Place only a few weeks after Sir William's death:

18 Moore, *Vale*, pp 175–6.   **19** Viscount Wolseley to Lady Augusta Gregory (undated), Autograph Book, NLI MS 25639.   **20** Sir Edgar Boehm to Lady Augusta Gregory (30 July 1883), Autograph Book, NLI MS 25639.   **21** In 1914, as demonstrated by L.P. Curtis, Irish Catholics 'were under-represented in the professions'. For detailed percentages by profession in the context of the 1911 census returns, see L.P. Curtis Jr, 'Ireland in 1914' in W.E. Vaughan (ed.), *A new history of Ireland, vi: Ireland under the Union, II, 1870–1921* (1996; Oxford, 2003), p. 156. According to Fergal Campbell, the Irish civil service, for instance, was still dominated by Protestants in 1911. Despite the introduction of open competitive examination in 1870, the high positions within the civil service were filled by nomination and appointment well into the twentieth century. See Fergal Campbell, 'Who ruled Ireland? The Irish administration, 1879–1914', *Historical Journal*, 50:3 (2007), 637. Thus, it needs to be emphasized that the decline of the Irish elite was a gradual process, and privileged positions within the professions, for instance, are arguably due to networks based on shared traditions and memories, a system of patronage that Lady Gregory emphasizes through her collecting of autographs.

> I want to sell this house & to let Coole. To live at either cd swallow up all I
> have, & I want to get things straight for Robert before he grows up. I will
> always take him to Galway for the summer though, that he may keep good
> friends with the people.[22]

Although she considered it to be of great importance to keep contact with tenants
in Ireland, Lady Gregory realized the particular importance of London's social elite.
Her role as both guest at and hostess of dinner parties gave her 'a feel of independence & *power*'.[23] It was more important, however, to keep in contact with friends and
acquaintances of Sir William. Her entry for 19 April 1894 sums up the urgency of
maintaining a residence in Britain's capital:

> I [...] had come to the conclusion, that, money permitting, it would be
> unwise to give up London – I have at present many friends, but there of all
> places one must keep one's friendship 'in constant repair' [...] And I might
> probably lose that & become dull in society, whereas now I have the name of
> brightness & agreeability – I should lose sight of William's friends by staying
> away & they may in 8 or 9 years time be of great use to Robert, as I see from
> Paul [Harvey] & others the difference made to a lad by a good start & influ-
> ential friends.[24]

Lady Gregory revealed a sense of practicality, whereby the social connections she
gained through her marriage provided an important platform to further the career
of her son in the future. Giving up St George's Place, she rented rooms at Queen
Anne's Mansion in London for £95 per year and was thankful for its independence
and 'absence of housekeeping & servant troubles'.[25] Left with a jointure of £800 and
the still unpaid mortgage from 1867, Lady Gregory had to economize and was glad
for the support of friends who helped with the furnishing.[26] With a modest income
and a mortgaged estate in Ireland, wealth no longer offered security and access to
privilege. More than ever, friendships and social networks provided the means by
which to ensure both her own position within society, and that of her son.

In order to maintain the social connections already established, it was again

---

22 Letter from Lady Augusta Gregory to Wilfrid Scawen Blunt (31 Mar. 1892), 233 A.L.S.
2 A.L., 17 T.L.S., 1 A.N. to Wilfrid Scawen Blunt [June? 1882]–18 June 1922. 50 folders,
Lady Gregory collection of papers, the Henry W. and Albert A. Berg Collection of English
and American Literature, New York Public Library, Folder 23 (hereafter: Berg). Quotation
from Lady Gregory's correspondence by permission of Colin Smythe Ltd. James Pethica
acknowledges Lady Gregory's emphasis on the importance of patronage for the benefit of
her son. See James Pethica, 'Patronage and creative exchange: Yeats, Lady Gregory and the
economy of indebtedness' in Deirdre Toomey (ed.), *Yeats and women: Yeats annual no. 9* (2nd
ed., London, 1997), p. 171.   23 Entry for 30 Jan. 1894 in Lady Augusta Gregory, *Lady
Gregory's diaries, 1892–1902*, ed. James Pethica (Gerrards Cross, 1996), p. 19.   24 Entry for 19
Apr. 1894 in ibid., p. 26.   25 Entry for 19 April 1894 in ibid., p. 27.   26 James Pethica,

crucial to work on a collective memory and enhance the reputation in elite circles. Thus, Lady Gregory started editing her husband's autobiography, which he had written with her encouragement from 1886 onwards. However, as she admitted in her preface, his memoir was 'first intended only for me and our boy, but he after-wards showed them in part to one or two old and dear friends'.[27] Lady Gregory took great care in her editorial work not to cause offence. Particularly in the political climate of the time, with the Second Home Rule Bill introduced in 1893, she was careful with regard to the subject of her own country. Writing to Sir Henry Layard in the final stages of the editing process in October of that year, Lady Gregory noted that she would not 'give any of the passages about Ireland [...], as the language is often incisive & I don't want to make enemies for Robert over here'. Keen to emphasize Sir William's liberalism, she was 'anxious it should be known how much he did in his lifetime, & what a kindly nature, & liberal mind he had'.[28] On 30 January 1894, she wrote in her diary that she had 'sent the MS to [John] Murray'. Murray agreed to make an offer after further editing and shortening and his propo-sition was greatly received:

> he wd publish at his own risk & expense, giving me half profits – this was an immense relief to my mind, I was anxious, for Robert's sake, to publish, that his father's name might be kept alive a little longer – but the risk & expense wd have been an anxiety to me – though 'a good name is better than riches' & I would if necessary have laid the money out.[29]

The importance placed on achieving and maintaining a favourable standing cannot be overestimated, especially with a lack of financial security. '[H]e wont have that poor little man', Lady Gregory regretfully wrote to Sir Henry Layard, informing him that she was saving to pay off the mortgage as 'when that is done we shall be easier'.[30] Consequently, the publication of the autobiography has to be seen as a deliberate method by a representative of the elite, supposedly in decline, to restructure power from the realms of wealth and land to the realm of social networking. Lady Gregory expressed this most eloquently when outlining that her 'hope in publishing them is that [Sir William's] name [...] may be kept alive a little longer, and that for his sake a friendly hand may sometimes in the future be held out to his boy'.[31] In addition, her work as family editor raised her own profile in society and offers a further example of her sense of practicality and political manoeuvring.

'Introduction' in ibid., p. xiii; Lady Augusta Gregory, *Seventy years*, ed. Colin Smythe (New York, 1974), p. 269.   **27** Sir William Henry Gregory, *Sir William Gregory KCMG – formerly Member of Parliament and sometime Governor of Ceylon – an autobiography*, ed. Lady Gregory (2nd ed. London, 1894), p. iii.   **28** Letter from Lady Augusta Gregory to Sir Henry Layard (29 Oct. 1893), 17 A.L.S. to Sir Austen Henry Layard, 6 Mar. 1892–3 Feb. 1894, 4 folders, Berg, Folder 4.   **29** Entry for 30 Jan. 1894 in Gregory, *Diaries*, p. 18.   **30** Letter from Lady Augusta Gregory to Sir Henry Layard (29 Oct. 1893), 17 A.L.S. to Sir Austen Henry Layard, 6. Mar. 1892–3 Feb. 1894, 4 folders, Berg, Folder 4.   **31** Gregory, *Sir William Gregory*, p. iii.

Importantly, Lady Gregory proved very conscious of her audience and sent presentation copies to a selected, yet diverse, group of people. Among these were members of parliament such as George Russell and Henry Labouchere, Sir William's long-time friend Lord Dufferin and Lord Rosebery. Moreover, Father Fahey, parish priest of Gort, received a copy, as did Baron Clonbrock, lieutenant of Co. Galway. Dr James Edward Welldon, headmaster of Harrow School, where Robert continued the Gregorys' family educational tradition, was also sent a copy.[32] Surely the selection is not mere coincidence and Lady Gregory presumably was thinking about Robert's future career in parliament, the civil service or academia. Moreover, with the two representatives from Co. Galway, she reminded the local community, both religious and governmental, of the Gregorys' liberalism. It conveniently demonstrated to the local nationalist community a positive example of a representative family from the landed class.

Showing an increasing awareness of the profits patronage would bring to her family and herself, Lady Gregory maintained a full calendar of social engagements and constant correspondence, as her diary attests. She received favourable comments after the publication in 1893 of her anonymous anti-Home Rule pamphlet entitled *A phantom's pilgrimage, or home ruin*, which, she would note with pride, had 'been a success'. Among 'those who knew me to be the writer', she added, were Lord Randolph Churchill (1849–95), Sir Henry Layard, Sir Frederic Burton and W.E.H. Lecky.[33] Significantly, her initial antagonism towards the possibility of Home Rule was well received, mainly by members of Sir William's generation – a generation that petered out with the end of the nineteenth century. Lady Gregory, having married a man thirty-five years her senior, found that Sir William's friends were equally part of an older generation. His central companions, Alexander Kinglake and Sir Henry Layard, died in 1891 and 1894 respectively. The death of her husband and some of his closest friends underlined the need for her to establish her own social network. The witnessing of the end of a generation that had been not only her support, but also the means through which she had gained access to the elite, and the changing political and social climate of the time, resulted in a sense of nostalgia, as is evidenced in her autographed book and fans.

Such nostalgic practice, it can be argued, had a particular function. Maurice Halbwachs argues in his chapter on the 'Social classes and their traditions' that 'whilst a society may be broken down into a number of groups of people serving a variety of functions, we can also find in it a narrower society whose role, it may be said, is to preserve and maintain the living force of tradition'. With the diversification of the social stratum in Ireland, society did indeed break down. Lady Gregory would belong to that 'narrower society', and her two fans and autograph book functioned as artefacts in which a collective memory for an elite group was located and stored for future generations. Halbwachs states that 'whether that society is directed toward the past or toward what is a continuation of the past in the present, it participates in

---

32 Entry for 18 Oct. 1894 in Gregory, *Diaries*, pp 39–40.   **33** Entry for 17 June 1893 in ibid., pp 13–14.

present-day functions only to the extent that it is important to adapt these functions to traditions and to ensure the continuity of social life throughout their transformations'.[34] This can be equally applied to Lady Gregory, as her second fan was decorated with autographs by Henry James, W.E.H. Lecky, J.A. Froude, Sir William Orpen, Mark Twain, Thomas Hardy, Antonio Mancini, Augustus John, Rudyard Kipling, Bernard Shaw, J.M. Synge, George Moore, John Eglinton, Sean O'Casey, Douglas Hyde, Jack B. Yeats, George Russell, Edward Martyn and W.B. Yeats. While the tradition of creating a collective memory in an artefact continued, the frame of reference had changed: the representatives here are mainly Lady Gregory's new circle of friends who would become associated with the Irish Literary Revival. The second fan marks the shift from the political to the cultural.

Throughout her marriage, Lady Gregory had learned the importance of patronage for her own benefit, yet when Edward Martyn visited her at Coole Park in the summer of 1897 with his guest, the young poet William Butler Yeats, she soon became a prominent patron herself. Following her meeting with Yeats, Lady Gregory quickly developed a keener interest in the literary movement, which was not always perceived in positive terms. For instance, on a visit to the judge Lord Morris, she discussed the recent developments in Ireland with her host, who referred to the Irish Literary Society as 'a set of schemers', and she confided in her diary that she 'did not like to say I have just been elected to it!'[35]

After the death of her husband, Lady Gregory, through her responsibility as landlord of Coole Park, rediscovered Ireland, took up Irish lessons and supported Horace Plunkett's cooperative movement. She developed an interest in local Irish folklore and her political stance of anti-Home Rule was moving towards Irish nationalism. This would result in increasing tensions between her and the elites in Ireland and England, as shown by Lord Morris' remark. In 1898, Lady Gregory published *Mr Gregory's letter-box*, continuing her work as family editor in order to uphold the reputation of the Gregorys.[36] By the end of the year, her friend Frederic Burton 'reproved me for having become a red hot Nationalist!'[37] From the late 1890s onwards, her previous focus on the family reputation and concern to endow her son with the necessary contacts for a political career among the elite became difficult to uphold due to her nationalist sympathies and her support for the Gaelic League and Irish Literary Society. Yet she retained both concerns simultaneously and proved able to negotiate in both the political and cultural sphere through continued use of patronage.

Not only did she secure the publication of a number of articles on Irish folklore she worked on with Yeats in the 1890s through her contacts with editors of magazines such as the *Nineteenth Century* and the *Fortnightly Review*, but she also supported the poet financially. Yeats wrote in 'Dramatis Personae' of his *Autobiography* in 1934

34 Maurice Halbwachs, *On collective memory*, ed. and trans., Lewis A. Coser (Chicago, 1992), p. 129. 35 Entry for 12 Apr. 1897 in Gregory, *Diaries*, p. 146. 36 Sir William Gregory, *Mr Gregory's letter-box: 1813–1830*, edited by Lady Gregory (London, 1898). 37 Entry for 16 Dec. 1898, in Gregory, *Diaries*, p. 195.

that he was 'ashamed' to find out that the debt to his life-long friend and patron had come to £500.[38] James Joyce equally owed his position as a reviewer for the *Daily Express* to Lady Gregory. Most importantly, however, the first list of guarantors for the Irish Literary Theatre in 1897 consisted mainly of names of Lady Gregory's acquaintances such as Lecky, Lord Dufferin, Aubrey de Vere, Lord Castletown, Lord Morris, Lord and Lady Ardilaun and Count de Basterot.[39]

Lady Gregory's diary entries demonstrate how she kept both interests simultaneously. While she dined at Horace Plunkett's, where she met supporters of the Irish Literary Theatre such as Edward Martyn, Sarah Purser, Lady Balfour and Lord Lytton, she was also attending parties with a more political audience including Lord Robert Cecil, son of Lord Salisbury, Lord Balfour and Grant Duff.[40] Dining at John Murray's, she sat between the editor of *The Times*, George Earle Buckle, and Lord Eustace Cecil, Lord Salisbury's brother. Her diary entry 'if there was any friend I cd give a lift to' demonstrates her awareness of favours and possible opportunities to converse about her projects.[41]

Considering Robert's educational development at Oxford in 1899, Lady Gregory discussed her son's career options in either the House of Commons or the foreign office with William Peel and her protégé Paul Harvey.[42] Her ambitions for her son to enter the political elite explain her continued efforts to sustain her contacts. As she stated,

> I keep my purpose in mind, Robert's good – & have been kept in mind of it
> by various things – E. Martyn said the other day 'You are right to go to
> London – you have nice friends there – I never had any friends there' – & I
> don't want R. to have to say that.[43]

Lady Gregory expressed strong assurance that her social network would bear fruits as she noted a few months later that she felt 'that Robert will have good houses open to him, whether I am here or not'.[44] However, her increasing movement towards political nationalism heightened the already existing tensions between her and her elite circles.

In 1900, she published an article entitled 'The felons of our land' in which she

---

38 W.B. Yeats, *Autobiographies* (London, 1977), p. 408. Lady Gregory provided substantial financial help to the young poet from the late 1890s onwards, buying for him furniture, clothes and food. In addition, she paid for Yeats' medical bills when he underwent treatment for his teeth and eyes. Yeats eventually repaid the sum in 1914. See Pethica, 'Patronage', pp 174, 189. **39** *Times*, 11 May 1899. **40** Entry for 22 Feb. 1899, 23 Feb. 1899 in Gregory, *Diaries*, pp 205, 206. **41** Entry for 23 Feb. 1899 in ibid., p. 206. **42** Entry for 25 Feb. 1899 in ibid., p. 208. Robert started at New College, Oxford, in the autumn of 1899. His move to England provided a vital component in Lady Gregory's continued efforts to sustain her London circle of friends. She noted in her diary on 2 Mar. 1899: 'I get a sort of passion to keep going in society now Robert's appearance here is comparatively near': ibid., p. 212. **43** Entry for 12 Feb. 1899 in ibid., pp 202–3. **44** Entry for 6 Mar. 1899 in ibid., p. 214.

wrote in favour of Irish ballads of rebellion and defeat. Considered as her most political piece, the article almost certainly was inspired by the Boer War, which radicalized
Irish nationalism. Lady Gregory notes in her diary in April of that year that Count
de Basterot, a neighbouring landlord, 'read it & gave me a talking to in the evening
– complimentary as to style, but thinks I am going too far away from the opinions
of my husband & my son'. She assured him in their conversation that she had already
decided 'not to go so far towards political nationalism in anything I write again as in
"Felons", partly because I wish to keep out of politics & work only for literature, &
partly because if Robert is Imperialist I don't want to separate myself from him'.[45]
She would have been equally aware that the overt declaration of her political opinion
might alienate vital contacts among her friends, thus endangering Robert's future
career paths. However, once Robert decided to become an artist, his mother's own
interest appeared to merge with her son's and strengthened Lady Gregory's ambition
to keep the family name in high esteem in the cultural realm.

In 1903, she was keen to make use of her social network to find the best possible
education in art for Robert. As she wrote in her diary, '[h]e would have tried for
H[ouse] of C[ommons] clerkship to please me, but his heart was on art – I told him
he shd choose as he liked'.[46] Her preference for a career in the civil service is possibly
linked to a desire to continue the tradition of Gregory men in great political offices.
However, as she was considerably involved in the Irish Literary Revival at the time,
with her success in collaborating with Yeats on the famous nationalist play *Cathleen
ni Houlihan*, Lady Gregory more willingly supported her son's entrance into the
cultural sphere. Writing to Blunt, she enquired 'whatever place is best, Paris or
London. I should think Paris. Do you know where the best teaching is?' She also
explicitly asked Blunt to get in contact with Lord Lytton, whom she believed

> could answer [more] satisfactorily than any of my artist friends of an older
> generation who may be a little out of date. I had a nomination for a House
> of Commons clerkship, if Robert cared to try for it, but his heart is in art –
> & I must say I am very glad he should have chosen for himself, he is sure to
> work better at what he cares for.[47]

The letter suggests that, whatever Robert's ambition in life, she would be able to
provide him with the necessary contacts to support his choice. By the end of 1903,
she expressed in a tone of relief that '[i]t is such a blessing not having to attend to
politics, now I am sure Robert wont take to parliament'.[48] Her efforts to maintain a
prominent and diverse social network had left him in a privileged position, although
she did acknowledge that some of her acquaintances were no longer of use. Again,
working on new connections was crucial to keep up with the changes of time. Of

45 Entry for 30 Apr. 1900 in ibid., p. 267.   **46** Entry for 26 Apr. 1903 in ibid., p. 314.
47 Letter from Lady Augusta Gregory to Wilfrid Scawen Blunt (17 Apr. 1903), Berg, Folder
30.   **48** Letter from Lady Augusta Gregory to Wilfrid Scawen Blunt (29 Dec. 1903), Berg,
Folder 31.

even more importance was the necessity to create a narrative of continuity in a period of change, which guaranteed the Gregory family, and by extension the landed class of Ireland, a persistent claim to their elite status.

Writing retrospectively on the founding of the Abbey Theatre in *Our Irish theatre* (1913), Lady Gregory quotes Aubrey de Vere's letter as the first response to the subscription for the Irish Literary Theatre:

> Whatever develops the genius of Ireland must in the most effectual way benefit her; and in Ireland's genius I have long been a strong believer. Circumstances of very various sorts have hitherto tended much to retard the development of that genius; but it cannot fail to make itself recognised before very long, and Ireland will have cause for gratitude to all those who have hastened to the coming of that day.[49]

The 'genius' de Vere referred to was a cultural one, and Lady Gregory's use of that quotation reflects her shift from the political to the cultural sphere. Subtly, Lady Gregory positioned herself at the top of the list of those Ireland should be grateful for – next to William Butler Yeats and John Millington Synge – her co-founders of the Abbey. Thus, the continuity of the Gregory family's stature would be maintained and lead as an example of the continuous importance of that social stratum for Irish culture – if not for Irish politics.

In accordance with Halbwachs, the publication of *Our Irish theatre* marked a link between past and present, a link that would bind together the political tradition of the Gregory family and the emerging cultural tradition with herself as patentee of Ireland's national theatre, the Abbey, and her son as an artist. Aubrey de Vere (1814–1902) was the quintessential link of past and present as his support was 'carrying as it were the blessing of the generation passing away to that which was taking its place'; and he was a poet.[50] Indeed, Lady Gregory underlined the continuity from past to present in her second chapter, entitled 'The blessing of the generations'. Here, she remembered her friend Sir Frederic Burton and stressed, importantly, that despite his unionist politics 'his rooted passion for Ireland increased', adding that 'all politics seem but accidental, transitory, a business that is outside the heart of life'.[51] Thus marginalizing politics, culture took centre stage. In some detail, she continued to dwell on Burton's interest in the Irish language movement. Lady Gregory closes the chapter with Douglas Hyde, whom she considered to be instrumental in the establishment of the theatre, with his 'disclosure of the folk-learning, the folk-poetry, the folk-tradition' that so greatly influenced the writers of the revival. Thus she described him as one who

---

49 Lady Augusta Gregory, *Our Irish theatre* (New York/London, 1913), p. 10.   **50** Ibid.   **51** Ibid., p. 56.

tells what he owes to that collaboration with the people, and for all the attacks, he has given back to them what they will one day thank him for. … The return to the people, the re-union after separation, the taking and giving, is it not the perfect circle, the way of nature, the eternal wedding-ring?[52]

Thereby closing the gap between her husband's generation and her son's, Lady Gregory created a new framework in a time when the social order in Ireland started to change to ensure a continuous claim to an elitist status.

Writing in 1895 in an article about Sir William's friends, Sir Henry Layard, Sir Alfred Layall and Alexander Kinglake, Lady Gregory bemoaned the demise of her husband's generation: 'many have been the changes within the last decade', she observed nostalgically as she looked on those who entered and left the building of the Athenaeum Club at 107 Pall Mall, London. 'Without, the building has become a whited sepulchre; within, to many, many, as to me, it is "peopled by ghosts"'.[53] As has been argued, these 'ghosts' of a lost generation were kept alive through established patterns of collective memory, thereby linking the past with the present and leading a way into a future in which the elite status of the members of the subsequent generations might still be secured.

After her husband's death, carrying the responsibility for her son's legacy, it became pivotal for Lady Gregory to find new methods of upholding the social standing she and her family had previously enjoyed. During the 1890s, she thus found herself working tirelessly on her three central concerns: providing her son Robert with the necessary social network for a career as a member of the elite, maintaining and enhancing the Gregory name, and supporting Irish cultural nationalism. These at times conflicting aims resulted in tensions between Lady Gregory and the British elite on both sides of the Irish Sea. As a result, she began to operate on three fronts. Firstly, she kept a regular residence in London with a full social calendar to uphold old connections and establish new ones, both among the political and cultural elite. Secondly, she edited and published the Gregory family history to sustain a favourable reputation for the benefit of her son, herself and her class. And thirdly, by using arte-facts such as the fans, an autograph book and, ultimately, the famous autograph tree in the grounds of Coole Park, she embraced the idea of a collective memory that would link the past with the present and bridge the gap between the political and the cultural realm. Eventually, Lady Gregory would attain her most enduring cultural legacy by becoming the patentee of the Abbey Theatre – a project supported by a financially and socially privileged elite. As such, it acted precisely in the way that Lady Gregory required: as a means not only of maintaining, but also of extending, her family's and her class' position of leadership and power well into the twentieth century.

---

52 Ibid., pp 76, 77.   **53** Lady Augusta Gregory, '"Eothen" and the Athenaeum Club', *Blackwoods Edinburgh Magazine*, 158:962 (Dec. 1895), 797.

A diasporic elite – the emergence of an Irish middle class in nineteenth-century Manchester

NEIL SMITH AND MERVYN BUSTEED

In the crafting of popular and academic images of Irish migrants in urban Britain, Manchester occupies an intriguingly significant position. The events following the rescue of Kelly and Deasy in September 1867 produced the iconic 'Manchester Martyrs', an anthem and a stream of songs and ballads.[1] Equally long lasting was the legend of 'Little Ireland'.[2] This small, short-lived district inhabited in 1841 by just over 1,100 Irish-born people was written up in vivid and almost voyeuristic fashion by, in quick succession, the local Board of Health, Dr James Phillips Kay, Frederich Engels and a procession of visiting commentators.[3] The result was to establish an enduring image of Irish migrants in British cities as a uniformly proletarian marginalized group. Yet, the *Catenians*, a fraternal Catholic organization, were founded in Manchester in 1908 because, alongside the aristocratic native Catholics and the working class Irish, 'there were signs of an emerging Catholic middle class which was unsure of its place'.[4]

In the nineteenth century, Irish people travelled for many reasons – some strategic. This essay seeks to challenge the perception of the Irish abroad as typically forlorn and desperate. It briefly reviews existing writings on the class structure of the Irish migrant population in nineteenth-century Britain and traces the emergence of an elite in Manchester and their multiple roles in relation to the Irish community and the wider civic life of the city. It shows how the pre-Famine Irish in the city produced leaders, both clerical and lay. While the Famine influx was marked by a high level of poverty, in the latter half of the nineteenth century an active middle class re-emerged, both second-generation and Irish-born, and three personalities are

1 Mervyn Busteed, 'The Manchester Martyrs: a Victorian melodrama', *History Ireland*, 16:6 (2008), 35–7.   2 Mervyn Busteed, '"The most horrible spot"? The legend of Manchester's Little Ireland', *Irish Studies Review*, 13 (1995/6), 12–19.   3 *Proceedings of the Special Board of Health, Manchester*, 1, 10 Nov. 1831–15 Aug. 1832; meeting of 19 Dec. 1831, 52–3. Archives Department, Manchester Central Library, M 9/3/36/1; J.P. Kay, *The moral and physical condition of the working classes employed in the cotton manufacture in Manchester* (London, 1832); Friedrich Engels, *The condition of the working class in England* (London, 1892); Lawrence Bradshaw, *Visitors to Manchester: a selection of British and foreign visitors' descriptions of Manchester from c.1538 to 1866* (Manchester, 1985).   4 www.thecatenians.com/history & organization; accessed 4 June 2011.

discussed, involved in industry, politics, medicine and finance, serving the Irish population and in two cases also active on the broader civic stage.

THE IRISH IN MANCHESTER

The earliest efforts by Irish commentators to survey the Irish in nineteenth-century Britain strained to challenge the image of a single class influx. In his series of articles for the *Nation* newspaper in the latter half of 1872, the Irish journalist Hugh Heinrick, a keen nationalist and Catholic, was pulled in two directions. Where he found prosperous Irish people, Heinrick eagerly applauded their achievements. In Manchester, he noted that, 'though the great body of the [Irish] people are labourers and artisans and factory hands, there is a considerable number whose positions would entitle them to aspire to representative [electoral] honours.'[5] But, alongside the pride in material achievement, there was a recurring fear that their aspirations to middle-class respectability as defined by English society would lead them to abandon faith and fatherland. Twenty years later, John Denvir, another Irish journalist and nationalist, was equally gratified by the number of Irish who had 'got on', but he too lamented that there were 'many who disclaim both our creed and our nationality'.[6] In Manchester and Salford, he discerned signs of partial progress, though he had a curiously narrow definition of middle class: 'a fair number are in trade ... we are well represented in the humbler walks of life, and fairly among the professional classes, but among the middle classes – the traders who possess the solid wealth of the country – we make but a poor figure'.[7]

Subsequent academic studies have dwelt at length on the overwhelmingly unskilled nature of the Irish population in Britain and the fact that they reinforced the working-class nature of certain sectors of nineteenth-century British cities.[8] While some did note the presence of the Irish in the ranks of the professions and commercial life, and signs of upward mobility in the late nineteenth century, these were passing asides.[9] R.F. Foster (1993) was the first to focus on 'Micks on the make' in Britain as a central concern, noting in particular those who left Ireland to further their careers.[10] Subsequent work by Foster and Fintan Cullen (2005) focused on the Irish in the arts, theatre, journalism and politics, but not in industrial or commercial

5 Hugh Heinrick, *A survey of the Irish in England* (London, 1872), p. 84.   6 John Denvir, *The Irish in Britain* (London, 1892), p. 392.   7 Ibid., p. 431.   8 John Werly, 'The Irish in Manchester', *Irish Historical Studies*, 18 (1973), 345–58.   9 Richard Lawton, 'Irish immigration to England and Wales in the mid-nineteenth century', *Irish Geography*, 4:1 (1959), 45–52; J.A. Jackson, *The Irish in Britain* (London 1963), pp 91–3; W.J. Lowe, *The Irish in mid-Victorian Lancashire: the making of a working-class community* (New York, 1989), pp 81–90; Graham Davis, *The Irish in Britain, 1815–1914* (Dublin, 1991), p. 117; Don MacRaild, *Irish migrants in Modern Britain, 1750–1922* (Basingstoke, 1999), p. 72.   10 Roy Foster, 'Marginal men and Micks on the make: the uses of exile, *c.*1840–1922' in R.F. Foster, *Paddy and Mr Punch: connections in Irish and English history* (London, 1993), pp 281–305.

life and exclusively in London.[11] John Belchem (1999, 2000) explored the development of an Irish middle class in the commercial, financial and political life of Liverpool and their role in the dense network of Irish-oriented organizations, clubs and mutual aid groups that constituted the rich 'associational culture' of the city.[12] More recently, there has developed a trend to unravel the details of this development by focusing on individual narratives of local personalities.[13]

The economic structure of Manchester was in sharp contrast to that of Liverpool, so long dominated by commerce and dock work. Despite its popular image as 'cottonopolis' dependent on textiles, the city was at the centre of a network of canals, roads and eventually railways, which made it a regional service, commercial, financial and warehousing centre.[14] There was also a thriving 'street economy' in the buying and selling of low-priced consumer goods. This wide range of employment possibilities at various skill levels made it particularly attractive to immigrants. Until the large-scale arrival of Jews in the late nineteenth century, escaping the pogroms of imperial Russia in east and central Europe, the Irish were the most exotic population group in Manchester, marked out by their religion, politics, accent and in many cases their language.[15] Early commentators set a pattern by simultaneously focusing on Irish poverty while implying the presence of a more prosperous element. In the seventeenth and eighteenth centuries, there had been dissatisfaction at the presence of Irish vagrants and 'poor Irish' Catholics in the city at various times, and yet the importation of Irish linen yarn by the cotton industry had led to the presence of Irish merchants and highly skilled Irish weavers.[16] This element was reinforced from the late 1780s when spinning was widely mechanized and the resulting production bottleneck led Manchester entrepreneurs to send recruiting agents for hand loom weavers throughout Britain and Ireland. The result was a notable increase in the numbers of Irish in the city. This was boosted by the end of the French wars in 1815, when Ireland's population grew rapidly, Irish economic conditions deteriorated, the fast-growing industrial cities of Britain proved increasingly attractive and travel links across the Irish Sea became cheaper, safer and more regular.[17] By the early 1820s, the

11 Roy Foster, '"An Irish power in London": making it in the Victorian metropolis' in F. Cullen and R.F. Foster (eds), *Conquering England: Ireland in Victorian London* (London, 2005), pp 12–15; Fintan Cullen, 'Conquering England', *Irish Arts Review* (spring 2005), 64–9. **12** John Belchem, 'Class, creed and country: the Irish middle class in Victorian Liverpool' in R. Swift and S. Gilley (eds), *The Irish in Victorian Britain: the local dimension* (Dublin, 1999), pp 128–46; 'The Liverpool enclave' in D. MacRaild (ed.), *The Great Famine and beyond: Irish migrants in modern Britain in the nineteenth and twentieth centuries* (Dublin, 2000), pp 128–46; *Merseypride: essays in Liverpool exceptionalism* (Liverpool, 2000), pp 129–51. **13** Philip Bull, 'William O'Brien MP: the metropolitan and international dimensions of Irish nationalism', *Immigrants and Minorities*, 27:2/3 (2009), 212–25; Elaine McFarland, 'The making of an Irishman: John Ferguson and the politics of identity in Victorian Glasgow', *Immigrants and Minorities*, 27:2/3 (2009), 194–211. **14** Alan Kidd, *Manchester* (Keele, 1993), pp 30–6. **15** Bill Williams, *The making of Manchester Jewry, 1740–1875* (Manchester, 1985). **16** Anon., *Manchester vindicated: being a compleat collection of the papers lately published in defence of the town in the Chester Courant* (London, 1749), p. 6. **17** Frank Neal, 'Liverpool, the Irish Sea

Irish dominated the Catholic population of the city in terms of both numbers and preoccupations.[18]

There were various efforts to estimate Irish numbers, including guesses of 5,000 in 1787, between 10,000 and 15,000 in 1804 and in early 1834 figures from 17,000 to 40,000 were offered to the parliamentary commissioners investigating the state of the Irish poor in Great Britain.[19] There is also evidence that in addition to the hand loom weavers there were other Irish who were quite prosperous and prominent in the life of their community and the city, being especially notable in the milling industry and there are indications that some were doing well in the textiles trade.[20] John Casey, an Irish-born textile merchant and manufacturer who died in 1792, left £840 in his will 'to assist the poor Catholics of Manchester' and the Casey Charity remained active until 1848.[21] Patrick Lavery, an Irish-born silk merchant who died in 1821, left £2,000 to establish a school for girls and a convent of Presentation nuns, opened in 1836.[22] The steady growth in the numbers of Catholic churches – seven by 1847 – and the associated infrastructure of presbyteries, parochial halls and schools also suggests plentiful capital in a Catholic population now overwhelmingly Irish. St Edward's Church in the strongly Irish Hulme district on the south-western side of the city was largely financed by the two O'Connor brothers, Irish-born merchants and warehouse owners.[23] The 1841 census revealed that among the Irish born in the city, 876 (2.89 per cent) could be considered 'middle class', including teachers, clerks and police officers.[24] This compares to 3.6 per cent of income receivers for the total population for England and Wales.[25]

LEADERSHIP: CLERICAL AND LAY

From quite early on, there were indications of the emergence of an active lay leadership and a growing network of organizations and associations. In the late eighteenth century, local Catholics seem to have shared much the same outlook and

steamship companies and the famine Irish', *Immigrants and Minorities*, 5:1 (1986), 82–111. **18** Gerard Connolly, 'Catholicism in Manchester and Salford, 1770–1850' (PhD, University of Manchester 1980), p. 410. **19** J. Holt, *General view of the agriculture of the county of Lancashire with observations on the means of improvement* (London, 1795), p. 213; Anon., *The Manchester guide: a brief historical description of the towns of Manchester and Salford, the public buildings and the charitable and literary institutions* (Manchester, 1804), p. 123; *Report of the Royal Commission on the state of the poorer classes in Ireland; Appendix G: report on the state of the Irish poor in Great Britain* (London, 1836), pp 42–83 at pp 42, 61. **20** Connolly, 'Catholicism in Manchester', p. 24. **21** Ibid., p. 241. **22** Anon., *Souvenir of the one hundred and fiftieth anniversary of the arrival of the Presentation Sisters in England* (Manchester, 1986), p. 18. **23** Anon., 'Daniel Moncrieff O'Connor', *The Harvest*, 24:285 (1911), 129. **24** W.A. Armstrong, 'The use of information about occupations' in E.A. Wrigley (ed.), *Nineteenth-century society: essays in the use of quantitative methods for the study of social data* (Cambridge, 1972), pp 191–8. **25** John Burnett, *A social history of housing, 1815–1985* (London, 1978), p. 98.

organizations as the rest of the population, but with the growing influx of Irish, the advent of the French wars from 1793 onwards, the growing sense of Irish nationalism and the emergence of Catholic emancipation as an issue, by the early nineteenth century there was an increasing tendency for the organization of societies distinctly Catholic and strongly Irish in nature. Some, such as the Board of the Catholic Day and Sunday Schools of Manchester and Salford, founded in 1813, were concerned with the preservation and transmission of the Catholic faith. Others, such as the Manchester and Salford Catholic Total Abstinence Society (1838), were concerned with Catholic self-discipline, and some, such as the Manchester and Salford Catholic Ladies Clothing Society (1823), aimed at relief of distress, while the Manchester Catholic Literary Society (1842) aimed to broaden cultural horizons. But one of the most notable developments followed the societal trend towards locally based mutual aid groups. In 1823, the Barton-upon-Irwell Catholic Friendly Society was founded, and by the 1840s virtually every parish had its sick and burial club.[26]

The multiplication of these groups was clearly dependent upon the presence of individuals capable of leadership and administration. Throughout the period, Catholic clergy were an integral, active element in the leadership cadre, especially in those groups with a specifically spiritual purpose or aimed at the defence of Catholic interests. Fr Daniel Hearne, the redoubtable Waterford-born priest of St Patrick's, serving the large Irish neighbourhood of Angel Meadow on the north side of the city from 1832 to 1846, ran at least two sick and burial clubs, campaigned against the Corn Laws and, like several other local clergy, was actively involved in local repeal agitation. He also acted as broker between his flock and the authorities. During the cholera outbreak of September 1832, angry crowds gathered at the gates of the local hospital following rumours of mistreatment of a sick child, but Fr Hearne succeeded in pacifying them just as troops arrived.[27] When several parishioners were in court following clashes with local Orangemen in July 1834, he provided character references.[28] However, his close identification with political issues had long troubled Catholic Church leaders and, following a public dispute with a curate, he was removed in 1846.

It is equally clear that from the earliest times the Irish migrant population was contributing to lay leadership and by the early nineteenth century the Catholic Irish in Manchester had developed 'an authentic voice of their own, with their own leaders, and ... no regard for the traditional niceties of the wealthy English Catholic laity'.[29] Among the emerging elite, certain families of Irish background constantly recur. Examples include the prosperous O'Connor brothers noted earlier, the Mallons, a family of Irish linen merchants, and the Lees, prominent in the calico trade and civic life. Daniel Lee gave £1,000 for construction of a chapel in St John's Cathedral, Salford, and brought the Sisters of Charity to Manchester in 1848. He was

---

26 Connolly, 'Catholicism in Manchester', pp 250–68.   **27** *Manchester Guardian*, 5 Feb. 1832.   **28** Ibid., 19 July 1834; *Manchester Courier*, 19 July 1834.   **29** Connolly, 'Catholicism in Manchester', p. 441.

one of the city's earliest Catholic magistrates and was held in such high regard that he chaired the meeting of Catholic laity that gathered in the Free Trade Hall in February 1851 to acclaim the restoration of the Catholic hierarchy of England and Wales and pledge their allegiance to the Queen.[30]

The rapid build-up of this Irish Catholic element, so different in history and cultural traditions, was a considerable challenge to the indigenous Catholic population, whose leadership, both clerical and lay, was mostly derived from ancient gentry families.[31] Lancashire was one of the few regions of England where a significant native Catholic community had survived the sixteenth-century Reformation. The county contained over 40 per cent of all the English Catholics listed in the 1767 Returns of Papists and 69 of the 139 significantly termed 'Missions' in Britain.[32] Originally, this population consisted of rural dwellers living quietly in remote areas under the protection of Catholic landlords, but by the mid-eighteenth century there was a notable drift into urban areas.[33] At the same time, the inflow of Irish was steadily accelerating, transforming the Catholic population and placing the church infrastructure under considerable strain. By 1830, the Catholic population of Manchester was predominantly Irish in numbers and preoccupations.[34] The class-based tensions are suggested by the fact that they 'met together, albeit after a fashion, for religious worship', but tended to favour particular churches.[35] The English element patronized St Augustine's, Granby Row, on the southern side of the city, consecrated in 1820, while the Irish concentrated at St Chad's (1776) and St Mary's (1795) in the city centre and later at St Patrick's (1832) on the northern side close to Angel Meadow.[36] By 1830, it has been argued that the English element was 'fast becoming irrelevant'.[37]

In the mid-1840s, therefore, there was clearly a well-established Irish population in Manchester. They were bound together by the migration experience, a dominant Catholic religion and a close network of religious and secular organizations with a vigorous leadership. The clergy were notable in this leadership cadre, but there was also a significant number of lay leaders active in church, charitable, cultural and political activities.

From 1845 to the early 1850s, the influx of refugees from the Famine transformed the numbers and socio-economic structure of the Irish population in British cities,

30 *Manchester Guardian*, 22 Feb. 1851.   **31** Sheridan Gilley, 'Roman Catholicism and the Irish in England' in D. MacRaild (ed.), *The Great Famine and beyond: Irish migrants in Britain in the nineteenth and twentieth centuries* (Dublin, 2000), pp 147–67 at p. 150; 'English Catholic attitudes to Irish Catholics', *Immigrants and Minorities*, 27:2/3 (2009), 226–47.   **32** *Returns of Papists 1767 Diocese of Chester*, transcribed under the direction of E.S. Worrall (London, 1980); Peter Doyle, *Mitres and missions in Lancashire: the Roman Catholic Diocese of Liverpool, 1850–2000* (Liverpool, 2005), p. 12; chapter two is entitled 'The Irish Invasion'.   **33** Doyle, *Mitres and Missions*, p. 13.   **34** Connolly, 'Catholicism in Manchester', pp 229–30.   **35** Ibid., p. 149.   **36** Mervyn Busteed, 'Irish migrant settlement in early nineteenth century Manchester', *Manchester Geneaologist*, 32:1 (1996), 21.   **37** Connolly, 'Catholicism in Manchester', p. 422.

including Manchester. The evolution of the Irish total in the city followed the general pattern for England and Wales, reaching a peak of 52,000 or 15.4 per cent of the population in 1861 and thereafter declining to 20,070 or 3.7 per cent in 1901, though by then there were second and subsequent generations (Table 12.1).

Table 12.1 Irish in Britain and Manchester, 1841–1901.[38]

Year	Britain	Per cent	Manchester	Per cent
1841	289,404	1.8	30,304	12.5
1851	519,959	2.9	45,136	15.2
1861	601,643	3.8	52,000	15.4
1871	566,540	2.5	34,006	8.6
1881	562,374	2.2	25,442	7.8
1891	458,315	1.6	23,180	4.6
1901	426,565	1.3	20,070	3.7

The geography of immigrant Irish in the cities of this period has been the subject of some academic debate. Much early work tended to accept the image of deep poverty and sharp segregation established by Kay and Engels, but subsequent research has suggested that the degree and intensity of residential segregation varied with the size and socio-economic structure of the urban question, the dimensions, rate and timing of the Irish influx and the spatial scale of study and that, 'if they were segregated in some towns, the Irish were never pressed back into ghettos'.[39] Initial work on Manchester unquestioningly accepted the traditional picture, but subsequent research on the 1851 census suggests that, while there was a tendency for the Irish to reside in distinct neighbourhoods within working-class areas, it is equally clear that separation was by no means total, that non-Irish neighbourhoods were close by and that the Irish moved out in search of work and were actively engaged in the broader life of the city. The largest Irish neighbourhoods were the long established Angel Meadow area and nearby Ancoats on the north side and Hulme on the south-western side of the city.[40] Significantly, even in 1851 the census returns for Angel

38 David Fitzpatrick, '"A peculiar tramping people": the Irish in Britain, 1801–70' in W.E. Vaughan (ed.), *A new history of Ireland, v: Ireland under the Union, II, 1801–70* (Oxford, 2010), pp 623–60; 'A curious middle place: the Irish in Britain, 1871–1921' in Roger Swift and Sheridan Gilley (eds), *The Irish in Britain, 1815–1939* (London, 1989), pp 10–59. **39** E.P. Thompson, *The making of the English working class* (London, 1968), p. 480; C.G. Pooley, 'The residential segregation of immigrant communities in mid-Victorian Liverpool', *Transactions, Institute of British Geographers*, 2 (1977), 364–82; 'Segregation or integration: the residential experience of the Irish in mid-Victorian Britain' in R. Swift and S. Gilley (eds), *The Irish in Britain, 1850–1939* (Dublin, 1999), pp 60–83; 'Residential segregation in Victorian cities: a reassessment', *Transactions, Institute of British Geographers*, 9 (1984), 131–44; Graham Davis, *The Irish in Britain, 1815–1914* (Dublin, 1991), ch. 2: 'Little Irelands'. **40** Werly, 'The Irish in Manchester', 350; Mervyn Busteed, 'The Irish in nineteenth-century Manchester', *Irish*

Meadow, an intensely working class area, yielded traces of skilled and lower class elements. In that year, there were eighty-one people in the district employed as power loom weavers, an occupation then regarded as at the cutting edge of technology. Of these, forty-two were Irish born. There were also Irish publicans, shopkeepers, policemen, teachers and clerks.[41]

As the nineteenth century wore on and the Irish population settled down in the city, an Irish middle-class elite became more perceptible. It emerged from two sources. One was upward mobility among second and subsequent generations of Irish migrants, taking advantage of the expanding educational provision by the Catholic Church and the British state, and the growing diversity of the British economy. Another source was the continuing, though declining, immigration from Ireland. One of the notable developments in Ireland in this period was the emergence of an educated, qualified professional middle class in numbers that, though perhaps modest, may have been more than Ireland could employ, it has been argued that at the very topmost level there were still obstacles to the upward mobility of nationalistically minded Catholics.[42] For some, the greater employment opportunities and wider cultural horizons of British cities proved attractive.

By the second half of the nineteenth century, Manchester had graduated in British popular perception from its earlier role as the frightening pioneer city of the industrial revolution.[43] Its dynamic wealth-producing economy and its embrace of the radical economic and political tenets of classical liberalism had given rise to a confident and inclusive civic ethos, a numerous wealthy middle class and a remarkably dense network of voluntary organizations, associations and clubs.[44] There was a notable Irish presence on this lively urban scene, some second-generation, some part of the ongoing if diminishing inflow from Ireland. As three personal narratives will now demonstrate, they were to be found across the entire spectrum of activity, some in public service, some in the professions and some in more than one sphere.

TEXTILES, POLITICS, MEDICINE AND BANKING

The career of Charles O'Neill demonstrated that it was possible to combine an Irish, an international and a local dimension. O'Neill was second-generation Irish, born in Manchester in 1831 and educated locally. He became an analytical chemist with a local textile print works, specializing in bleaching, dying and printing, in which he soon became an acknowledged expert, publishing books on the subject in 1860 and 1862. In 1863, he was head-hunted by a calico printing firm in Moscow and spent ten years in Russia, becoming fluent in Russian, German and French. Returning to

Studies Review, 18 (1997), 8–13.   **41** Busteed, 'Irish migrant settlement', 26–7.   **42** Joe Lee, *The modernisation of Irish society* (Dublin, 1973); Catriona Clear, *Social change and everyday life in Ireland, 1850–1922* (Manchester, 2007); Fergus Campbell, *The Irish establishment* (Oxford, 2009).   **43** Asa Briggs, *Victorian cities* (London, 1968), ch. 3: 'Manchester, symbol of a new age'.   **44** Kidd, *Manchester*, pp 72–9.

Manchester, he and his four sons set up their own business. He resumed writing, publishing a six-volume work on textile printing, contributing regularly to the *Textile Recorder*, the trade journal, and occasionally to local newspapers. He became a Fellow of the Chemical Society and the Institute of Chemistry and taught at the Manchester Technical College, where he served as 'an admirable and successful teacher'.[45] He had wide cultural and literary interests, helping to establish the Arts Club in 1878 and frequently attending the Manchester Philosophical Society.

O'Neill also publicly identified with the Irish Catholic community and its concerns. An enthusiastic advocate of Catholic education, when Bishop Vaughan established St Bede's College in 1876, O'Neill taught classes in chemistry and natural philosophy. At a public meeting held in September 1884 to express dissatisfaction with government policy on church schools, he was the only layman among the major speakers, proposing a motion that after the next election Irish members should be well placed to pressurize the administration.[46] From 1879 to 1891, he was elected to the Manchester School Board as one of the Catholic members, he was one of the city's earliest Catholic magistrates and its first Catholic councillor in modern times, elected as a Liberal for the strongly Irish St Michael's ward in Angel Meadow from 1885 to 1891. He was a strong supporter of Home Rule, an impressively cogent public speaker and was approached to stand for parliament but declined. He was a regular participant in St Patrick's Day events, chairing the banquet in 1889, proposing the first toast and expressing his belief that after their long struggle, Irish prospects for self government, peace and happiness were at last brightening.[47] Taken ill on a trip to Russia, he died in 1894.

One observer noted his ability to combine strong personal convictions with wider civic responsibilities:

> It was less his strong Liberal views than his Irish sympathies and his religious belief which gained him the seat for St Michael's ward ... but there was no member of the Council ... who more clearly grasped than he did the broad clear obligation of the city's representatives to legislate and to act for the general good; or who was more easily able than he was to free himself from the dictation of feelings, however cherished, that were entitled to no voice in determining the discharge of municipal duties.[48]

His successor in St Michael's ward recognized the cross pressures that could sometimes result from acting as broker between a strongly marked minority and the wider civic arena. Early in his career (in 1899), Daniel McCabe, second-generation Irish, owner of a family drapery business, who eventually became the acknowledged leader of the Manchester Irish and in 1913 the city's first Catholic lord mayor, warned that

45 Anon., 'The late Mr Charles O'Neill', *The Harvest*, 8:8 (1894), 403. **46** *Manchester Guardian*, 13 Sept. 1884. **47** *Catholic Herald*, 22 Mar. 1889. **48** *Manchester City News*, 17 Nov. 1894.

'while I personally … ardently desire a settlement of the Irish question … I do think it time we should pay more attention to our social advancement in this land in which our lot is cast'.[49]

Dr Cornelius O'Doherty was to acquire a reputation as a notably caring servant of both the Irish community and the needy of Manchester. Born of farming stock in Miltown Malbay, Co. Clare, in 1863, he was schooled by the Christian brothers in Kilrush. The diocesan seminary at Ennis prepared him for university entrance and he went on to study medicine at the Queen's Colleges in Belfast and Cork, where he proved to be an outstanding student, winning the Gold Medal Prize and qualifying as doctor of medicine, master of surgery and master of obstetrics by the age of 21. Leaving Ireland, he found Britain offered him plentiful opportunity for his considerable talents and qualifications. He initially settled in Sheffield and then moved to Manchester and set up his surgery in the working-class Rusholme area on the south side of the city, where he gained a reputation as a particularly conscientious and energetic doctor. But his concerns went beyond the immediately professional. He served the Salford Diocese Catholic Protection and Rescue Society as the medical attendant of its Working Boys' Home and at one of its shelters and was active in the Catholic Literary and Debating Society. For ten years, he served as a Guardian on Chorlton Poor Law Union, which covered the area of his medical practice, and was vice-chair for two years. For eight years he served as a Liberal on Manchester City Council, proving so popular that on two occasions he was returned unopposed. When, early in 1903, the post of city coroner fell vacant, he resigned from the council and applied. Since he had also studied law, he was generally regarded as a strong candidate, but very late in the process technical objections were raised and he was disqualified. There were suspicions that his religion and nationality were the real objections.

In politics, he had a keen interest in Irish affairs, was an active supporter of Home Rule and frequently took a leading part in St Patrick's Day celebrations. In March 1891, he seconded the resolution supporting the majority of the Irish party, their adherence to the Liberal alliance and their stance on Parnell's leadership, describing the former leader as someone who 'would … have crushed their hopes to gratify his own ambition'.[50] In January 1898, he was present at the public meeting in support of a Catholic university for Ireland.[51] In March 1900, with Queen Victoria due to visit Ireland the following month, he performed a delicate balancing act, calling for her to be treated with the courtesy due to her eighty years, while simultaneously hoping the occasion would improve relations between Ireland and Britain.[52] Two months later, at a gathering to celebrate the re-unification of the Irish Parliamentary Party, he moved a resolution warmly welcoming the development and arguing that while the alliance with the Liberals was highly valued, Home Rule was the top

49 Daniel McCabe, 'The social position of Catholics: part two', *The Harvest*, 12:142 (1899), 167. **50** *Catholic Herald*, 20 Mar. 1891. **51** *Manchester Guardian*, 24 Jan. 1898. **52** Ibid., 20 Mar. 1900.

priority. The resolution also called for teaching through the medium of Irish in Irish-speaking districts and the teaching of the language in elementary schools. This provoked appeals from the floor for him to address the meeting in Irish, which he did to great applause.[53] In 1903, he responded to the chairman's toast by asserting that the Irish people had proved their ability to hold their own with any people in both politics and war.[54] True to form, he was actively engaged in caring for his patients a week before succumbing to influenza in March 1905.[55] O'Doherty was a notably well-qualified middle-class professional whose work was very much oriented towards serving his Irish Catholic brethren, a tendency that, it has been argued, explained why they were largely invisible to outsiders.[56]

The great majority of upwardly mobile Irish lived their lives in quiet respectability, far removed from the public eye. The final narrative concerns one such individual, never prominent in public life, but nevertheless clearly regarded by local Catholic leaders as a role-model worthy of emulation. *The Harvest* was the journal of the Salford Diocese Catholic Protection and Rescue Society, founded by Bishop Vaughan in 1886 to 'rescue' Catholic children in municipal care and in danger of being fostered or adopted by Protestant families. The journal has a significant trajectory during this period. In its earliest issues, it is defensive and anxious in tone, preoccupied with what are perceived as spiritual and moral threats to Catholic children, leading to 'leakage' from the faith. By the early twentieth century, however, the tone is increasingly confident, if still somewhat wary. In a series of personality sketches and in its obituaries, it held up selected individuals as respectable, exemplary middle-class Catholics.

One such was Thomas Kennedy Magrath. He was born to Irish parents in 1849 in Demerara (now Guyana) in South America, where his father was serving as an officer in the British Army. Within six months, his father had died and the family returned to Clonmel, where he was educated by the Christian Brothers. Later they moved to Lytham on the Lancashire coast, where he completed his education at another Catholic school. He was employed by the Manchester and Liverpool District Banking Company in their Blackburn and Accrington branches and the Manchester head office. He was then appointed head of their new branch in Salford. On his death in 1913, *The Harvest* wrote glowingly of his personal qualities, proudly noting

> neither his religion nor his nationality, which he never denied or concealed or betrayed, stood in the way of the steady advancement to which his business talents entitled him ... [he] earned for himself a solid reputation as a steady citizen, a practical Catholic and a loyal patriot ... As a Catholic it is

53 Ibid., 14 May 1900. **54** Ibid., 18 Mar. 1903. **55** Ibid., 6 Mar. 1905; Anon., 'Dr Cornelius O'Doherty', *The Harvest*, 18:211 (1905), 82–3. **56** Melanie Tebbutt, 'The evolution of ethnic stereotypes: an examination of ethnic stereotyping with particular reference to the Irish (and to a lesser extent the Scots) in Manchester during the late nineteenth and early twentieth centuries' (MPhil,, University of Manchester, 1982), p. 205.

impossible to do adequate justice to the invaluable and continuous services that he was ever willing to render to Catholic societies and individuals.[57]

The journal went on to list these organizations, including the Society of St Vincent de Paul, the Catholic Truth Society, the Protection and Rescue Society and the Catholic Federation. Noting his happy family life, it also declared: 'With an Irishman's love of good literature, he was well read and an excellent conversationalist ... with a humour truly Hibernian.' Yet, in a remarkable passage clearly intended to subvert a deeply entrenched stereotype, it stressed

> though an Irishman to his fingertips, he had few of the external characteris-
> tics of the Irishman of fiction. He belonged to that larger class of Irishman
> (larger indeed than the enemies of Ireland care to admit), which is quiet and
> cautious in expression and judgment, practical and patient in business, and
> calm and strong in controlling all unnecessary emotions.[58]

It concluded 'he had lived a pious, sincere and loyal Catholic [life]', clearly seeing him as a splendid role model, demonstrating to the world and his fellow migrant Catholic Irish what they could do and should be.[59]

CONCLUSION

In discussion of the nineteenth-century Irish in Manchester and other cities, both contemporary observers and some subsequent academic analysts focused almost exclusively on the difficult lives of what was admittedly the largely unskilled working-class majority. But from quite early on, the Manchester example shows that the Irish in Britain were more than simply one part in the reserve army of labour. Other elements were present in the Irish migrant inflow and some were emerging from a background in the city's professional, industrial and commercial life to play a notable part in their own community and the wider civic arena. The mid-century famine influx clearly altered the socio-economic structure of the Irish population, but a new elite quickly emerged, some the product of upward mobility from second and subsequent generations, others migrating directly from Ireland. They played multiple roles, both formal and informal. Some were active on several stages, serving as brokers and intermediaries with the host society, while others were primarily oriented to the Irish population. Many more lived lives out of the public eye, quietly rising through their professions and occupations by personal competence and char-acter and, as such, were applauded as exemplars of Irish Catholic respectability and enduring faithfulness to creed and country in the challenging circumstances of urban Protestant Britain.

---

57 Anon., 'Thomas Kennedy Magrath', *The Harvest*, 26:308 (1913), 109. **58** Ibid. **59** Ibid., 110.

Men who did not exist? Irish tourists and the definition of a national elite

RAPHAËL INGELBIEN

The gradual democratization of travel in the nineteenth century initiated major shifts in a practice that, originating in the aristocratic tradition of the Grand Tour, had helped define social and cultural elites in the early modern period. The changes were most noticeable in Britain, where the expansion of the middle classes and the improvement of travel infrastructure multiplied the forms that tourism could take and made them accessible to ever greater numbers. Increasingly, complaints were made that the rising numbers of Britons travelling for leisure compromised the distinctive nature of the experience. A difference emerged in English writing between travel and tourism: while tourism was a 'mass' phenomenon, heavily commodified and branded with the stigma of inauthenticity, travel was an individual pursuit through which the better kind of tourists (for such they essentially remained) displayed their refined taste and social superiority. Sociologists write of how 'status distinctions then came to be drawn between different classes of traveller, but less between those who could and those who could not travel'.[1] At the same time, since travel was promoted as a means to social and cultural advancement, such distinctions constantly had to be readjusted: the 'authentic', superior experiences of 'travellers' were quickly imitated by 'tourists' who sought the badge of authenticity and thus compromised the elitist nature of 'travel'. The result is that 'tourism has become an exemplary cultural practice in modern liberal democracies, for it has evolved an appearance of being both popularly accessible and exclusive at once'.[2]

While analyses of nineteenth-century tourism have often drawn on British examples, they have remained silent about Irish tourists – significantly, the now substantial body of work on 'Irish tourism' and 'Irish travel writing' refers to foreign visitors to Ireland, not to Irish subjects who travel for leisure.[3] The emergence of the

---

1 Quoted in James Buzard, *The beaten track: European tourism, literature and the ways to culture, 1800–1918* (Oxford, 1993), p. 81. **2** Buzard, *The beaten track*, p. 6. **3** See, among others, Melissa Fegan, 'The traveller's experience of Famine Ireland', *Irish Studies Review*, 9:3 (2001), 361–72; Glenn Hooper, *Travel writing and Ireland, 1760–1860: culture, history, politics* (London, 2005); Eric Zuelow, *Making Ireland Irish: tourism and national identity since the Irish Civil War* (Syracuse, 2009); Irene Furlong, *Irish tourism, 1880–1980* (Dublin, 2009); William H. Williams, *Tourism, landscape and the Irish character: British travel writers in pre-Famine Ireland* (Madison, WI, 2008); *Creating Irish tourism: the first century, 1750–1850* (London, 2010). While some of those studies pay attention to Irish tourists' experiences of Ireland, Irish tourists travelling abroad have so far remained under the scholarly radar.

'Ryanair generation' signalled contemporary Ireland's membership of the 'modern liberal democracies', where tourism is a common and defining experience, but the consensus in Irish tourism studies is that tourism remained marginal among the Irish population throughout the nineteenth and early twentieth centuries. Little has changed since one historian of tourism wrote that

> in Ireland ... holidaymaking was confined to a relatively small minority of the population until the middle of this [viz. the twentieth] century. Irish coastal resorts were to be the preserve of the Anglo-Irish rural and urban elite up to the First World War ... For the ordinary people, a 'holiday' was an outing to a fair, a 'patron', perhaps a race meeting and a football or hurling match.[4]

This is taken to confirm the widespread view that Ireland 'was not a "modern" society on this count': 'the vast majority of people did not take holidays'.[5] The present essay will not deny that, in numerical terms, tourism remained a minority pursuit among the wider population of nineteenth-century Ireland. It will, however, suggest that the phenomenon was more widespread and more varied than is usually recognized, and that we need to query any elision between tourists and Anglo-Irish elites. The evidence considered here is quantitatively limited and exclusively textual in nature, but it will hopefully draw attention both to other historical evidence that awaits analysis and to a broader corpus of hitherto neglected Irish writing.

The travel books, novels, newspaper articles, reviews and advertisements that will be discussed below all suggest that, in the decades that followed Catholic emancipation, tourism started taking hold as a cultural practice beyond the confines of the Anglo-Irish ascendancy, whose notorious absenteeism was itself tied to the importance of foreign travel among the leisured classes of Western Europe. By becoming tourists, Irish Catholics translated their upward social mobility into a geographical mobility that confirmed their attainment to a higher social and cultural status. An analysis of nineteenth-century Irish tourism will thus complement recent studies that have highlighted the importance of Catholic elites in Victorian Ireland and their participation in lifestyles that were at least partly modelled on those of the British (upper) middle classes.[6] As a historiographic enterprise, the recovery of those experiences is fraught with ideological implications, as Senia Pašeta points out in her own discussion of late-Victorian Catholic elites:

4 John Heuston, 'Kilkee: the origins and development of a west-coast resort' in Barbara O'Connor and Michael Cronin (eds), *Tourism in Ireland: a critical analysis* (Cork, 1993), pp 13–28 at pp 13, 16.   **5** Michael Cronin and Barbara O'Connor, 'From gombeen to gubeen: tourism, identity and class in Ireland, 1949–1999' in Ray Ryan (ed.), *Writing in the Irish republic: literature, culture, politics, 1949–99* (New York, 2000). The essay is also available at http://doras.dcu.ie/14969/1/gombeen-to-gubeen.pdf.   **6** See particularly Senia Pašeta, *Before the revolution: nationalism, social change and Ireland's Catholic elite, 1879–1912* (Cork, 1999); Stephanie Rains, *Commodity culture and social class in Dublin, 1850–1916* (Dublin, 2010); and the project on 'Consumer culture, advertising and literature in Ireland, 1848–1921' recently carried out at the universities of Durham and Sunderland.

> The failure of this [Catholic] elite to assume important roles in the adminis-
> tration of twentieth-century Ireland has ensured that their experiences and
> assumptions have all but disappeared, they have become 'lost' through
> momentous political change and through the subsequent construction of
> modern Irish history.[7]

Putting those Catholic elites on the scholarly radar questions accounts of nineteenth-
century Ireland as a pre-modern colony whose Catholic population were excluded
from full participation in the democratic experiences increasingly granted to British
subjects.

If such perceptions need revising, the blame should not exclusively be laid at the
door of post-independence historians and propagandists. Even *before* independence,
some Irish commentators played down the realities of Irish tourism. Recent scholarly views that only Anglo-Irish elites participated in tourism before the First World
War are belied by texts written in the years preceding the conflict, but those very
texts evince the same tendency to represent the democratization of Irish tourism as
a comparatively recent phenomenon. In 1912, a columnist for the *Irish Independent*
commented that

> [t]he Irish people of recent years have entered into the holiday spirit as they
> never did before, and nowadays it is the rule rather than the exception to find
> *Irish tourists – from remote rural districts, too – penetrating into regions home and conti-
> nental that were only a name to a past generation.*[8]

Writing a couple of years earlier about the apparently thriving resort of Youghal,
another commentator mused: 'My acquaintance with Youghal goes back to the
sixties and early seventies, when *English and Continental holidays were undreamt of except
by the landlord class*'.[9] While those early twentieth-century commentators describe
Irish tourism as a common practice, they also imply that, in a recent past, travelling
for leisure, and certainly travelling abroad, were the exclusive pursuit of the
landowning ascendancy.

Such denials or forgettings spring from a mentality that arguably characterized
even late twentieth-century Irish people's attitudes towards tourism. In one experi-
ment, questionnaires about holidays were submitted to Irish citizens. The answers
they produced prompted sociologist Michel Peillon to observe:

> That [Irish] people ... understate their actual participation in holidaymaking
> suggests the weak cultural basis of modernity itself and of the modern life-
> style practised: they have not been able to appropriate fully, in cultural terms,
> their actual patterns of behaviour ... The strong anti-modernist leaning

7 Pašeta, *Before the revolution*, p. 1.   **8** *Irish Independent*, 2 Aug. 1912. My emphasis.   **9** *Irish
Independent*, 17 July 1908. My emphasis.

which pervades Irish culture makes it difficult to acknowledge a practice deeply rooted in the modernity of Ireland. Holidays ... reveal one of the major tensions within Irish society.[10]

The analysis proposed below will contradict both recent and older perceptions about the absence of tourists among the broader Irish population in the nineteenth century. While helping to chart the experience of rising Catholic elites in post-emancipation Ireland, and painting a picture of Victorian Ireland as a 'modern' nation in the making, this essay will also draw attention to anti-modern elements that informed the very consciousness of those elites. Those elements can in turn explain why Irish debates about the nature of tourism were (and perhaps still are) conducted through terms that were markedly different from those that dominated Victorian travel writing in Britain.

Published in 1835 and based on her visit to Belgium, Lady Morgan's *The princess* is not just a novel about Continental liberalism and nationalism as well as a travel book, it is also a reflection on post-emancipation Ireland.[11] While many of Morgan's characters are English tourists (often modelled on real-life aristocrats and socialites), her travelling set also includes the Irish baronet Sir Ignatius Dogherty. A descendant of a Milesian family and, as his name indicates, of good Catholic stock, Sir Ignatius cuts a striking figure among Morgan's Continental tourists. Dressed in his bottle-green jacket,[12] he is a stage-Irish caricature of the post-emancipation social climber, whose very presence on the Continent asserts his new status. As an Irish tourist, Sir Ignatius often registers a sense of incongruity:

> Hôtel de Belview, Brussels.
> MY DEAR CORNEY – You'll wonder greatly to hear from me in this outlandish place; and it is to my own intire amazement surely that I find myself in it ... when I asked for a bottle of Guinness' porter, which you'd think was known all over the wide world, it's a bottle of crusty port they brought me; and to this blessed hour I've not been able to make them understand me ... the Bellview is a fashionable place, and none of the great English will go nowhere else: although at first, sir, we got into a mighty nate little hotel, called the Tirelemont, for half the price. But my lady would go to the Bellview as soon as there was room ... *NB.* There's a power of Irish here, and a fortune might be made by setting up a raal [*sic*] Irish *Hibernian* hotel – and it would be a fine thing to be after making money instead of spinding it ...[13]

As a blundering tourist rather than a cultured traveller, Sir Ignatius is a recognizable type in British travel writing. Yet his nationality arguably outweighs class as a marker

10 Michel Peillon, 'The Irish on holidays: practice and symbolism' in Barbara O'Connor and Michael Cronin (eds), *Tourism in Ireland: a critical analysis* (Cork, 1993), pp 258–71 at pp 266, 270.   11 Lady Morgan, *The princess, or the beguine* (3 vols, London, 1835).   12 Morgan, *The princess*, i, p. 237.   13 Ibid., ii, pp 134–44.

of difference, and his words point forward to specific strands in the Irish imagination of tourism that will recur in this essay. While his wife is keen to imitate the British upper classes, Sir Ignatius retains his Irishness. His request for porter may typify him as a crass, ill-bred tourist who is unable to leave home behind while abroad (a standard theme in British critiques of tourism),[14] but his disappointment at being served port – a very English drink – gives a subtle Irish nationalist twist to what would otherwise amount to class satire. His irrepressible practical sense betrays the utilitarian concerns of the *nouveau riche*. But Morgan's satire of this new tourist type also turns the tables on the fashionable English travellers as it exposes their essential snobbishness and their ultimately conventional upper-class tastes.[15] The author's own sympathies appear divided between her own determination to shine among fashionable English sets and her keen sense of Irish difference, which made her wear the kind of green garments that Sir Ignatius also sports.[16]

Morgan's travelling stage-Irish baronet was probably more an exercise in speculation than the reflection of an actual trend. His excitement at finding out that there is 'a power of Irish here' is later qualified when he observes of the 'first Irish families on the road': 'maybe there wasn't oceans of them'.[17] Morgan remains sceptical about the development of a travelling culture among the newly emancipated classes, but her novel raises an issue that is also taken up by two texts produced in the following decade. In 1837, Matthew O'Conor, a descendant of the kings of Connaught, published his *Picturesque and historical recollections during a tour through Belgium, Germany, France and Switzerland*, and opened his preface as follows:

> In the hope of inducing the richer classes of his countrymen to mix with the enlightened and polished nations of Europe, to see their manners and adopt their institutions, the writer has endeavoured to develope in the following pages the pleasures of a Continental tour, the facility and cheapness of travelling, and the amusements of some of the watering places in the south of Germany.[18]

O'Conor's 'richer classes' were a plural constituency that was no longer exclusively Anglo-Irish, Protestant and aristocratic. Ascendancy tourists had long mixed with foreign elites on the Continent and did not need O'Conor's advice: his book rather seems to target a new audience for whom the experience of foreign travel would be a novelty, and who were denominationally and politically diverse. Although he sometimes criticizes ecclesiastics, O'Conor frequently defends the Catholic religion

---

14 Buzard, *The beaten track*, p. 8.   **15** This conventionality is attested by their adherence to the itineraries laid out by travel books.   **16** On Morgan's notorious use of fashion to make political statements, see Julie Donovan, *Sydney Owenson, Lady Morgan and the politics of style* (Palo Alto, CA, 2009).   **17** Morgan, *The princess*, iii, p. 359.   **18** Matthew O'Conor, *Picturesque and historical recollections during a tour through Belgium, Germany, France and Switzerland in the summer of 1835* (London, 1837), p. i. O'Conor is mostly remembered for his *History of the Irish Catholics from the settlement in 1691* (Dublin, 1813).

against anti-popish slurs, and he makes several sympathetic references to the plight of Irish peasants, not least in his opening description of his journey from Dublin to Liverpool – recalling that 'the fore-deck of the vessel … presented a scene of great misery – an image of our native country. Pigs, sheep, horned cattle, horses, women, children half naked, spalpeens (Irish labourers) in their thread-bare frieze garments, were so packed together that to move was utterly impossible.'[19]

The readership addressed by Thomas Davis in an 1844 essay on 'Foreign travel' in the *Nation* was probably similar to the one envisaged by O'Conor. 'We lately strove to induce our wealthier countrymen to explore Ireland before they left her shores in search of the beautiful and curious', Davis wrote, 'there are some who had not waited for our call, but had dutifully grown up amid the sights and sounds of Ireland … and there are others not yet sufficiently educated to prize home excellence. To such, then, and to all our brethern and sisters going abroad, we have to say a friendly word'.[20] Given the readership of the *Nation* and the cross-denominational nature of Davis' political agenda, the 'wealthier countrymen' he addressed were certainly not an all-ascendancy elite of Protestant landowners. In the immediate post-emancipation period, the Irish tourists envisaged by Morgan, O'Conor and Davis were all part of an elite whose identity was undergoing considerable transformation, but that remained implicitly defined as affluent and therefore exclusive. More importantly, it was explicitly defined as Irish. While wealthy Irish tourists had access to the many British travel books that were advertised in the Irish press,[21] efforts were made in some quarters to make sure that Irish tourism would remain nationally distinctive. Irish elites had to be taught to behave differently from their British counterparts, even though the form of leisure they adopted made them join British tourists abroad.

The second half of the nineteenth century would see a steady rise in the number of Irish people participating in tourism. An exact quantification of the phenomenon falls outside the scope of this essay, but a study of Irish newspapers that were widely read among the rising Catholic middle classes suggests that the number of tourists in their midst had reached enough of a critical mass to make commercial sense. By the mid-1870s, the pages of the *Freeman's Journal* in the run-up to the summer season included quasi weekly advertisements for various guidebooks and for Thomas Cook's tickets, available from the firm's Dublin offices on Dame Street. Cook was both commercially shrewd and ideologically unblinkered enough to adapt to Irish tastes by proposing Continental tours that left from Dublin and included Lourdes.[22] Such tours remained relatively expensive: letters to newspapers proposed that the Catholic Church should organize a cheaper version for '[p]ersons unable to meet singly the expense of Cooke [*sic*]'.[23]

---

19 O'Conor, *Picturesque and historical recollections*, p. 1.   **20** *Nation*, 17 Aug. 1844. **21** For some early examples of such advertisements for itineraries 'for Continental travellers' and other 'travellers' guides', available from C. Cumming and Co. in Dublin, see the *Freeman's Journal*, 6 May 1819 and 12 Aug. 1828.   **22** See, for instance, the *Freeman's Journal*, 25 Aug. 1875.   **23** *Evening Telegraph*, 1 June 1885.

Irish tourists also flocked in their thousands to more secular destinations. Firms like Thomas Cook offered cheap tickets for international exhibitions.[24] At the time of the 1862 London exhibition, a Dublin publisher ran advertisements for 'THE IRISH TOURIST'S GUIDE TO THE SIGHTS OF LONDON – A glance at EVERY OBJECT OF INTEREST … and specially adapted to the GREAT INTERNATIONAL EXHIBITION', priced at 3*d*. (by post 4*d*.).[25] When the exhibition was held in Paris in 1867, a Dublin correspondent of the *Anglo-Celt* sent the following report, where utilitarian considerations about the effects of Irish travel recur as ironic afterthought:

> A sudden Parisian mania has set in among the citizens this week, and has already carried off thousands from the metropolis to the French capital. Judging from the *enormous efflux of tourists* that have left and are still leaving by every mail from Kingston to Holyhead, en route to Paris, *we are at least minus 2,000 people this week*; and looking at this in a monetary point of view, each individual represents a loss to the city in cash expenditure of £3 on the visit.[26]

By 1884, crossing over to Holyhead seems to have been common enough to justify the publication of a Welsh guidebook for Irish travellers. James Roderick O'Flanagan, a well-to-do retired Catholic barrister, undertook the task after a trip to north Wales, where he had been disappointed to find that 'no guidebook described the principality from the Irish side of the country, all gave the routes the other way'. O'Flanagan wrote his travelogue 'to supply this deficiency', but geographical orientation was not the only issue. O'Flanagan also argued that since '*many tourists, especially from Ireland, are Roman Catholics*, it is requisite they should know where to find Catholic Churches'.[27] The *Freeman's Journal*'s review of *Through north Wales with my wife* hailed O'Flanagan as 'the first Catholic who has written for Irish tourists'.[28] The claim is inaccurate, as O'Conor's 1837 *Recollections* make clear, but it emphasizes that the well-off, cultured O'Flanagan was perceived as being a spokesman for his Irish co-religionists.

The defence of an explicitly Catholic Irish identity became a growing theme with the development of tourism among the middle classes in late nineteenth-century Ireland. O'Flanagan's preface states that 'the guidebooks published have all been written by those who are unacquainted with the Catholic religion, and either omit this information, or, in some cases, mention the Catholic Church in offensive

---

24 Buzard, *The beaten track*, p. 63. International exhibitions were a particularly democratic new form of tourism, since they brought the world within reach of fee-paying visitors. See Angela Schwarz, '"Come to the fair": transgressing boundaries in World's Fairs tourism' in Eric Zuelow (ed.), *Touring beyond the nation: a transnational approach to European tourism history* (Farnham, 2011), pp 79–100. **25** *Freeman's Journal*, 9 Aug. 1862. My emphasis. **26** *Anglo-Celt*, 10 Aug. 1867. My emphases. **27** James Roderick O'Flanagan, *Through north Wales with my wife: an Arcadian tour* (London, 1884), p. vii. My emphasis. **28** *Freeman's Journal*, 17 Oct. 1884.

terms'[29] – another flaw of British travel books that he proposes to remedy.[30] A corre-spondent for the *Freeman's Journal* ended his account of Lourdes by countering insinuations about Bernadette de Soubirou found in British guidebooks:

> I cannot close this little sketch [of Lourdes] without calling attention to a passage in 'Murray's Guide'. It says: – 'The girl subsequently became insane, and is or was taken care of by the Ursuline nuns at Nevers'. To use the words of a well-informed gentleman here – 'It is a calumny – it is a lie'... However, I suppose it is one of the marks of the Catholic Church to have everything connected with it calumniated.[31]

Irish Catholic tourists abroad were regularly called upon to defend their faith; they were also expected to bear their national identity in mind. Anglocentric analyses of travel writing stress how 'superior' travellers could only claim to rise above mere touristic attitudes by shedding their national identities and immersing themselves in foreign environments.[32] Irish travellers, on the other hand, were encouraged to think of home when abroad. O'Conor's *Picturesque and historical recollections* already included many anecdotes about exiled Irish soldiers, priests and monks: 'The historical remi-niscences as connected with [the author's] native country will be uninteresting to many, but to such as feel a sympathy for the misfortunes of a generous nation they will not be felt tiresome or obtrusive'.[33] More assertively, Thomas Davis had sent out Irish travellers abroad with the advice to seek out places of Irish interest, highlighting that some readers

> may delight in following the tracks of the Irish saints, from Iona of the Culdees to Luxieu and Boia (founded by Columbanus), and St Gall, founded by an Irishman of that name ... Our military history could also receive much illustration from Irish travellers going with some previous knowledge and studying the traditions and ground, and using the libraries in the neighbour-hood of those places where Irishmen fought.[34]

The exhortation to Irish tourists to consider themselves as nationalist pilgrims is most clearly present in Eugene Davis' *Souvenirs of Irish footprints over Europe* (1888), which defies any distinction between travel writing and popular history.[35] The Continent's chief interest, for Eugene Davis, lies in its Irish associations: 'I do not envy the Irishmen [*sic*] who can step for the first time on French soil without feeling his

---

29 O'Flanagan, *Through north Wales with my wife*, p. vii.   **30** On Protestant hostility towards Catholicism in nineteenth-century British travel accounts, see Marjorie Morgan, *National identities and travel in Victorian Britain* (Basingstoke, 2001), especially pp 93–100.   **31** *Freeman's Journal*, 15 July 1875.   **32** Buzard, *The beaten track*, p. 8.   **33** O'Conor, *Recollections*, p. i.   **34** *Nation*, 17 Aug. 1844.   **35** On Davis' *Souvenirs* as a 'nationalist' travel guide, see Raphaël Ingelbien, 'Defining the Irish tourist abroad: *Souvenirs of Irish footprints over Europe* (1888)', *New Hibernia Review*, 14.2 (2010), 102–17.

heart throb faster, or without finding himself carried back in fancy to a past that speaks so eloquently on his countrymen's military prowess under the Bourbon flag'.[36] When press commentators described the sights of Italy, they sometimes readily assumed that Irish tourists would be guided by a love of Old Erin: 'Irish visitors to Genoa invariably look for the house in which the great man [O'Connell] died ... Irish travellers [to Lucca] will look for the church of St Frediano, a prince of their country, who became bishop of Lucca.'[37]

Thomas Davis had not only set out a cultural nationalist programme for Irish tourists: in his brand of nationalism, Irish cultural specificity was not an end in itself, but rather a means of cementing national cohesiveness for a further goal, viz. the modernization of Ireland. After listing the antiquarian pursuits in which Irish travellers could indulge, he explained that he 'would not limit men to the study of the past':

> Our agriculture is defective, and our tenures are abominable. It were well worth the attention of the travelling members of the Irish Agricultural Society to bring home accurate written accounts of the tenures of land, the breeds of cattle, draining, rotation, crops, manures and farm-houses, from Belgium or Norway, Tuscany or Prussia. Our mineral resources and water-power are unused. A collection of models or drawings, or descriptions of the mining, quarrying and hydraulic works of Germany, England or France might be found most useful for the Irish capitalist who made it, and for his country which so needs instruction.[38]

Davis' utilitarian message is echoed in O'Flanagan's 1884 Welsh guidebook, where the author pauses in his admiration for local tourist facilities to bemoan the lack of equivalents in Ireland, and to suggest their introduction: 'I have often regretted the absence from our Irish watering-places of these attractions to visitors which enliven English and Continental watering-places ... This would pay in the end, and induce fewer Irishmen to seek strange fields and Welsh bathing'.[39] This would become a prominent theme in attempts to develop an Irish tourist industry, first led by Cook's Dublin agent Frederick W. Crossley and the Irish Tourist Association.[40]

In the context of the present discussion, it is especially telling that O'Flanagan's economic espionage focuses on tourism itself, rather than other types of activities. While Thomas Davis' cultural nationalist message to Irish tourists started a lasting tradition in Irish travel writing, his ambition to modernize Ireland by developing its agriculture and industry fade as a motif as the century unfolds. This does not only reflect gradual improvements (in Ireland's agriculture in particular) which made such

36 Eugene Davis, *Souvenirs of Irish footprints over Europe*, ed. Owen McGee (Dublin, 2006), p. 77. The text originally appeared in the *Evening Telegraph* in 1888.   **37** *Irish Monthly*, Mar. 1899.   **38** *Nation*, 17 Aug. 1844.   **39** O'Flanagan, *Through north Wales with my wife*, pp 100–1.   **40** See Irene Furlong, 'Frederick W. Crossley: Irish turn-of-the-century tourism pioneer', *Irish History: a Research Yearbook*, 2 (2003), 162–76.

calls for modernization less urgent. It also testifies to a growing anti-modernism within Irish nationalist ranks, where some had little time for Thomas Davis' utopian vision of an Ireland where 'our bogs must have become turf-factories … our coal must move a thousand engines, our rivers ten thousand wheels'.[41] Such visions accord little with O'Flanagan's Arcadian pastoral, or with the spiritual idealism of the Irish exiles described in Eugene Davis' *Souvenirs*: 'these Irishmen of past generations had such a large amount of what may be called spirituality in their systems that they very often sacrificed the material or practical to the ideal'.[42] As the nineteenth century drew to a close, Irish elites mostly pursued advancement through liberal professions and education rather than business careers.[43] The main trends in their travel writing partly reflect that development, but they also signal that discourses on Irish nationality were increasingly dominated by a critique of English materialism and utilitarianism.[44] A rejection of utilitarian considerations was of course also a defining feature of Anglo-American travel writing in the period, where the scenes that were depicted had 'no connection with the prosaic modern concerns of useful-ness and rational organization that structure life in the home society'.[45] In the case of Irish travel writers, however, what was rejected was not the routine of economic life at home, but a modern utilitarianism that was identified with England.

The writings considered above give a normative definition of Irish Catholic elites' participation in tourism. The fact that such guidelines were issued from within Ireland does not mean that they were always adhered to – in fact, those texts occa-sionally betray an anxiety that Irish tourists might not be different from their English counterparts. Eugene Davis thus blasted the cruder kind of Continental tourist as follows: 'Every man of *the English, American and, I fear I must add, Irish, tourist type* is not satisfied with himself while in Rome until he has profanely carved the outlines of his obscure name on the broken pillars of the Forum or on the walls of the Colosseum'.[46] Irish tourists did not only read Irish travel advice, they could also read the guidebooks issued by English publishers, which immersed tourists and readers in an upmarket commodity culture. The more mainstream and inclusive Catholic newspapers did not necessarily frown on such publications. After extolling the merits of a new book on Switzerland published by a Leicester firm, the reviewer for the *Freeman's Journal* recommended it to seasoned Irish tourists:

> Those of our readers who are acquainted with the Messrs Bickers' 'Rome', 'Rhine' and 'Italy' will regard this as a strong form of praise in regard of the

---

41 *Nation*, 17 Aug. 1844.   **42** Eugene Davis, *Souvenirs of Irish footprints over Europe*, p. 179. **43** See Pašeta, *Before the revolution*, esp. pp 31, 96.   **44** For an analysis of Thomas Davis' economic thought as part of a 'discourse of improvement' that was rejected by later cultural nationalists, see Helen O'Connell, *Ireland and the fiction of improvement* (Oxford, 2006). For an analysis of the continuities between Eugene Davis and late nineteenth-century anti-utilitarian critiques of earlier nationalist thought, see Ingelbien, 'Defining the Irish tourist abroad', 114–15.   **45** Buzard, *The beaten track*, p. 181.   **46** Eugene Davis, *Souvenirs of Irish footprints over Europe*, p. 34. My emphasis.

'Switzerland'. We mean it as such, and we have no doubt that to the numerous Irish tourists to whom the Alpine scenery is familiar, our estimate will be justified by a moderately careful perusal of the book … It will, no doubt, be a favourite amongst the presentation volumes of the approaching Christmas season, and a handsomer Christmas book no one desires.[47]

For more radical nationalists, however, fears that Irish tourists might give in to an English bourgeois commodity culture reflected a broader anxiety that newly affluent Catholic elites might 'become entwined in a British middle-class culture which stressed the virtues of respectability, professional advancement and social refinement'.[48]

Another way of safeguarding the identity of the Irish tourist was to keep him at home. The promotion of internal tourism at the expense of foreign travel was another staple theme of Victorian Irish travel writing – and its very recurrence suggests that the message was not always heeded.[49] In 1849, the *Nenagh Guardian* observed: 'It has been truly said that the Irish tourist too often prefers exploring the beauties of other lands to those of his own … beauty lies at his feet, but he would rather go a distance to behold it'.[50] In 1855, the *Nation* promoted internal tourism through the figure of Jack Beausir:

> Jack is a fierce nationalist … Jack says: 'Killarney whips Como or Constance hollow – hollow by Jove … no Mont Blanc for me. Why Chamouni is an outlet of London. Every detestable dialect in England is there. Here a Yorkshire squire roars at his groom; there a cockney slangs a chamber maid, occasionally lit up by a mellifluous Galway brogue. It's cursedly common that gadding abroad … Why are we blind to the beauties within a few perches of us? By Jove, sir, there are a thousand beauties within a few miles of Dublin – aye, in the very city itself – that we pass unconsciously'.[51]

From a nationalist point of view, Irish internal tourism combined the utilitarian advantage of keeping Irish wealth in Ireland with the cultural added value of making Irish people discover their own country. While probably best known through Miss Ivors' rebuke to Gabriel Conroy in Joyce's 'The Dead', the reproach to the Catholic Irish tourist abroad actually has a much longer history than is often assumed.[52] Miss

---

47 *Freeman's Journal*, 27 Nov. 1878.   **48** Pašeta, *Before the revolution*, p. 3.   **49** Heuston's generalizations about nineteenth-century Irish tourists are not just based on an exclusive focus on Kilkee and its Anglo-Irish patrons, they may also be skewed by his neglect of Irish tourism abroad. New Catholic elites may well have preferred foreign tourism, for reasons ranging from emulation of British models to a wish to visit places like Lourdes or Rome. **50** *Nenagh Guardian*, 10 Oct. 1849.   **51** *Nation*, 17 Nov. 1855.   **52** Spurgeon Thompson has suggested that 'Joyce's likely model for Miss Ivors is, in fact, Hanna Sheehy-Skeffington, the radical women's suffragist and republican. Sheehy-Skeffington joined the board of the ITA [Irish Tourist Association] in 1927 … Her influence on the board almost certainly

Ivors, we should remember, does not criticize Gabriel for his snobbishness, palpable though it is. Instead, her criticism of Gabriel's Continental trips springs from her view that they are an English pastime – a form of leisure that typifies a 'West Briton'.[53]

For the *Nation's* Jack, what was 'cursedly common' about foreign travel was not the fact that the lower orders were impinging on the pursuits of the upper classes, but the fact that it was English – and that it tempted Irishmen, apparently as far away as Galway, to ape English ways. The *Nation's* denunciations of the 'staring, bawling Britons' who toured Europe with Thomas Cook[54] were not so different from the scorn poured on Cook's 'low-bred, vulgar and ridiculous' excursionists by a Unionist class warrior like Charles Lever, the one Victorian Irish travel writer who most easily fits into Anglocentric analyses of travel writing:

> some enterprising and unscrupulous man has devised the project of conducting some forty or fifty persons, irrespective of age or sex, from London to Naples and back for a fixed sum … all the details of the road or the inn, the playhouse, the gallery or the museum will be carefully attended by this providential personage, whose name assuredly ought to be Barnum![55]

But whereas Lever's critiques of modern tourism, published in exclusive organs like *Blackwood's* and the *Dublin University Magazine*, were informed by a snobbish disdain for the aspiring British middle classes, the *Nation's* strictures reflected its anti-English nationalism. The Yorkshire squire and the London Cockney were equally despicable; if he wanted to avoid being confused with them, the Irish tourist's easiest option was to stay in Ireland. His own class identity was barely an issue; his national credentials, on the other hand, were the main object of contention.

★ ★ ★

This survey of nineteenth-century Irish attitudes to the emergence of Irish tourism yields several hypotheses. One is that the Irish Catholic middle classes engaged in touristic activities in ever greater numbers: despite its greater geographical distance from the centres of Continental tourism, its poorer infrastructure and the different make-up and condition of its rising middle classes, Ireland clearly joined Britain in sending more and more tourists on the paths of home and Continental travel. Any

helped to pressure the publication to step up the internal tourism campaign': see '"Not only beef, but beauty …": tourism, dependency and the postcolonial Irish state, 1925–30' in Michael Cronin and Barbara O'Connor (eds), *Irish tourism: image, culture and identity* (Bristol, 2003), p. 275. The nationalist encouragement to stay at home is much older than what Thompson envisages, leaving Miss Ivors a potentially more over-determined figure. **53** *The essential James Joyce*, ed. Harry Levin (London, 1977), p. 149. **54** *Nation*, 4 May 1872. **55** Quoted in Buzard, *The beaten track*, pp 60–1.

quantification of the participation rate in tourism will require further work, but even a limited study of Irish travel writing already puts paid to the idea that tourism remained an ascendancy pastime in Victorian Ireland: rising Catholic elites were clearly an important new contingent. The ideological significance of this neglected phenomenon is also worth stressing: while Irish tourists had the opportunity to model their behaviour on British practices, they were often invited to shun British attitudes and to adopt distinctively Irish ways of travelling. Comparative investigations can perhaps determine if the idiosyncrasies of Irish travel writing have equivalents in the travel literature produced by other peripheral nations whose modernity was likewise problematic.[56] In any case, the Irish distinctiveness charted in this essay was promoted with such insistence that it cut across or supplanted the class-based distinctions that informed nineteenth-century British travel writing. To the extent that it applies at all, the distinction between (refined) travellers and (crass) tourists that is a staple of Anglocentric travel writing is largely replaced by a distinction between nationally aware Irish tourists and degenerate (West) Britons. Not only did an essentially 'national' understanding of tourism obscure the still inevitably class-bound nature of travel, it also allowed anti-modern strains to colour what was an essentially modern experience. The new elites of nineteenth-century Ireland were afforded ways to think of themselves as first and foremost *Irish* elites who were synecdochically synonymous with the rest of (Catholic) Ireland, and whose experiences were not compromised by the taint of (British) modernity. If later generations managed to forget about nineteenth-century Irish tourists, they were partly helped to do so by the reluctance of Victorian Ireland's new elites to fully take part in what is commonly defined as the modern touristic experience.

---

56 See, for instance, Gayle R. Nunley, *Scripted geographies: travel writings by nineteenth-century Spanish authors* (Cranbury, 2007). Nunley suggests that Spain's economic backwardness and its uncertain place between the West and the Orient produced 'dilemmas of modernity' for Spanish travel writers (p. 19): these could be compared to Ireland's.

A new role for Irish Anglicans in the later nineteenth century: the HCMS and imperial opportunity

TIMOTHY G. McMAHON[1]

I would like to open a line of inquiry that is part of a wider series of questions designed to assess the impact that the British Empire had on Irish identities during the late Victorian and Edwardian eras. Between the 1870s and the 1910s, an under-appreciated conjuncture shaped the future of the United Kingdom and Irish states. I am speaking about the connection between what is often referred to as the age of new imperialism – that period when Europeans scrambled for Africa and Asia, extending their grasp for control in the wider world, and the age of Home Rule – when Irish nationalists of various stripes cooperated uneasily to press for a reworking or revocation of the Act of Union. Often this latter issue is still treated as an Irish or, at best, a United Kingdom domestic concern, though one need only pay attention to the rhetoric of British Tories and Irish unionists to recognize that the spectre of 'the breakup of the empire' loomed large in their imaginations as they opposed Home Rule.

And yet, the imperial enterprise *is* a burgeoning topic of research in Irish studies. It has become rather modish, for instance, to speak of the people of Ireland as impe-rial hybrids – simultaneously colonized and colonizing.[2] In particular, a great deal of basic research has laid out the prominent part that Irish men and women played in the armies, administrations and missionary enterprises of the British Empire. The involvement of colonized peoples alongside colonizers in the imperial enterprise was,

1 The author wishes to thank the members of the Society for the Study of Nineteenth-Century Ireland who offered suggestions to him after hearing an earlier draft of this essay. I wish also to recognize the Graduate School at Marquette University and Boston College-Ireland for support that made it possible for me to conduct some of the research for this essay. **2** Joseph Lennon, *Irish orientalism: a literary and intellectual history* (Syracuse, 2004), pp 149–50. See also Alvin Jackson's comments about the empire acting as both 'a lock and a key' for the Irish in the nineteenth century. Alvin Jackson, 'Ireland, the union and the empire, 1800–1960' in Kevin Kenny (ed.), *Ireland and the British Empire* (Oxford, 2004), p. 136. Several essay collections have appeared in the last fifteen years that provide useful introductions to Ireland and its place in the empire. For example, see Kevin Kenny (ed.), *Ireland and the British Empire* (Oxford, 2004); Keith Jeffrey (ed.), *An Irish empire? aspects of Ireland and the British Empire* (Manchester, 1996); Michael Holmes and Denis Holmes, *Ireland and India: connections, comparisons, contrasts* (Dublin, 1997); and Stephen Howe, *Ireland and empire: colonial legacies in Irish history and culture* (Oxford, 2000).

of course, not a uniquely Irish phenomenon. One can point to numerous examples
of indigenous peoples who played key roles in educating their children according to
imperial norms, in aiding in the administrations of the colonies, and in policing their
home territories or, in the case of the Gurkhas, other regions as needed. But the Irish
are a singular case, I contend, for three reasons: first, during the nineteenth and early
twentieth centuries, they were home subjects, that is, they were subjects within the
United Kingdom state whether they wanted to be or not; second, they were
Europeans, which meant that they carried much of the same racial and cultural
baggage into the wider world that other Europeans did; and third – stemming from
the first two points – they debated the imperial enterprise among themselves and
with the wider Union audience.[3] Further, those debates were informed, as Barry
Crosbie has persuasively argued in his path-breaking book, by networks established
as part of the imperial enterprise, which served 'as mechanisms for the exchange of
whole sets of ideas, practices and goods'.[4] Understanding the place of Ireland within
the imperial enterprise is, therefore, critical to appreciating the development both of
the empire and of competing identities within Ireland. Just as the settler-Irish of
Manchester turned inwards for social mobility in England and gentrified travellers
viewed the Continent through their own cultural lens, so too did the imperial Irish
carry both literal and cultural baggage with them when they left home.

Part of that understanding, however, involves appreciating that there were already
multiple identity groupings in Ireland by the age of new imperialism. Thus, while it
is legitimate from the standpoint of understanding nationalist politics to speak of a
national identity that was largely Catholic and increasingly Gaelicized by the early
1900s,[5] it is equally important not to omit non-Catholic Irish men and women from
the discussion of identity, particularly when they labelled themselves as Irish while
abroad and when they were labelled as such by people from outside Ireland. Their
understandings must be accounted for when studying Irishness, especially within a
United Kingdom context and particularly in the period when Catholic-nationalist
Irish people seemed to be in the ascendant.

3 I recognize that the Irish were not the only imperial subjects resident in the United
Kingdom, and numerous scholars have explored the impact of subjects resident in Britain
recently. For example, see Antoinette M. Burton, *At the heart of the empire: Indians and the
colonial encounter in late-Victorian Britain* (Berkeley, CA, 1998); Shompa Lahiri*, Indians in
Britain: Anglo-Indian encounters, race and identity, 1880–1930* (London, 2000); A. Martin
Wainwright, *'The better class' of Indians: social rank, imperial identity and south Asians in Britain,
1858–1914* (Manchester, 2008). For the Irish case, see Jennifer Regan-Lefebvre, *Cosmopolitan
nationalism in the Victorian empire: Ireland, India and the politics of Alfred Webb* (Basingstoke,
2009).   **4** Barry Crosbie, *Irish imperial networks: migration, social communication and exchange in
nineteenth-century India* (Cambridge, 2011), p. 23. Interestingly, Crosbie has little to say about
the CMS in India, save that the East India Company in the early nineteenth century was
wary about proselytizing by CMS missionaries in the 1820s. See Crosbie, *Irish imperial
networks*, pp 137–8. I am grateful to Ciaran O'Neill for bringing Crosbie's work to my
attention.   **5** See Timothy G. McMahon, *Grand opportunity: the Gaelic revival and Irish society,
1893–1910* (Syracuse, 2008).

I want to explore this last point – that is, competing identities within Ireland – by looking at the work of a missionary organization, the Hibernian Church Missionary Society (hereafter the HCMS) and how its growing dynamism in the late nineteenth century reflected multiple redefinitions of elite status for the Anglican community, both within its ranks and in relation to the wider Irish and United Kingdom communities. It would, of course, be ahistorical to speak of Irish Anglicans as if they were a singular entity: members of the Church of Ireland came from different social classes and status groupings. One need only consider that Protestant tenant farmers, led by T.W. Russell, were among the most vocal advocates for reform of land ownership at the end of the century – a prospect that was inimical to land-lords, many of whom were themselves Anglicans – to recognize their varied economic interests.[6] Irish Anglicans also debated – sometimes hotly – theological questions throughout the period under review. One such division was between those espousing a more High Church theological approach and those espousing an evan-gelical approach.[7] That division constrained the HCMS in its earliest days, but as we will see, the emergence of evangelical Anglicans as prominent church leaders after 1850 lent a prominence to the society that it had lacked initially. More important, the society achieved wider public recognition toward the end of the century because it mollified Anglican fears of social and political decline in the decades after disestab-lishment. Utilizing the emerging techniques of marketing, particularly through exhibitions designed to broaden interest in the wider world, the HCMS provided a vision of outsiders and their relationship to the people of Ireland that gave Irish Anglicans a special sense of purpose in the empire.

Established in 1814, the HCMS was an auxiliary body to the better known and much larger Church Missionary Society (CMS), which had been founded in 1799 by British Evangelicals hoping to spread the Christian gospel message to 'Africa and the East'.[8] Although these organizations came out of a period when evangelicalism encouraged ecumenical activity, the CMS and the HCMS were exclusively Anglican bodies.

Still, the state church initially looked askance at them. In fact, when the HCMS held its inaugural meeting, laymen outnumbered clergy, and those clergy in atten-dance were not senior clerics; thus, from its foundation, lay participation was an essential component to the organization's existence.[9] Clerical reluctance, it seems,

---

6 On Russell's career and its impact on nationalist politics, see Patrick Maume, *The long gestation: Irish nationalist life, 1891–1918* (New York, 1999), pp 40–2.   7 On the interrela-tionship of these groupings, see Alan Acheson, *A history of the Church of Ireland, 1691–1996* (Dublin, 1997), pp 124–37, 148–64. For an account of the so-called Second Reformation, see Irene Whelan, *The Bible war in Ireland: the 'Second Reformation' and the polarization of Protestant–Catholic relations, 1800–1840* (Madison, WI, 2005).   8 The formal name for the organization was the Church Missionary Society for Africa and the East.   9 On the CMS in general, see Kevin Ward and Brian Stanley (eds), *The Church Mission Society and world Christianity, 1799–1999* (Cambridge, 2000). On the importance of lay participation in the HCMS, see Acheson, *History of the Church of Ireland*, p. 125.

had to do with the theological tensions within the Anglican Communion in the 1810s (alluded to earlier), especially in the wake of the still-recent breakaway of the Wesleyans. Indeed, when the Revd Josiah Pratt led a three-man delegation from London to launch the Hibernian auxiliary in 1814, the archbishop of Dublin, Euseby Cleaver, discouraged his clergy from participating, as the society was 'accused of being enthusiastic in the sense of leaning towards Methodism'.[10] Lest Pratt lose heart, however, he received substantial support from Lady Lifford, wife of the dean of Armagh, who established a Ladies Association to support the mission work prior to the founding of the HCMS. She then pressed her husband to encourage clergy in his archdiocese to take a more favourable attitude toward the London society, enabling the Hibernian auxiliary to launch successfully.[11]

Indeed, these lay people were not just any members of the Church of Ireland. They had always included members of elite Anglican families. In the early days, for instance, they included a number of aristocrats and prominent gentry, such as the earl of Enniskillen; the brewing magnate Arthur Guinness; Lady Florence Balfour, mother of Francis Townley Balfour, who would become the first bishop consecrated in what is today Lesotho; and Lady Charlotte O'Brien of Dromoland Castle, a leading sponsor of evangelical causes and the mother of the future Young Irelander William Smith O'Brien.[12] Individuals – male and female – from these strata continued to be the financial backbone of the organization into the early twentieth century, as recorded in the address book of the society's Life Governors and Life Members. These 275 men and women gave literally tens of thousands of pounds to the HCMS.[13]

I must at least acknowledge that the organization raised funds through individual memberships and parish collections from all ranks of Irish Anglicans. In 1878, such collections and individual donations totalled more than £6,540.[14] While income would fluctuate – with the Land War period being particularly lean – recorded donations were impressive. The general trend was for annual donations to increase. In the decennial period from 1889 to 1899, the society collected no less than £130,000 – an average of £13,000 per annum, while in fiscal year 1913, donations totalled more than £23,000. Altogether, between 1870 and 1930, the total income of the HCMS 'was in excess of £1 million'.[15]

10 Jack Hodgins, *Sister island: a history of the CMS in Ireland, 1814–1994* (Dunmurry, 1994), p. 4.   **11** Ibid., pp 4–5.   **12** Patrick Comerford, 'An innovative people: the Church of Ireland laity, 1780–1830' in Raymond Gillespie and W.G. Neely (eds), *The laity and the Church of Ireland, 1000–2000: all sorts and conditions* (Dublin, 2002), p. 192; Acheson, *History of the Church of Ireland*, p. 134.   **13** RCBL MS. 313/5/4, *Address book of life governors and life members*, n.d. **14** *Sixty-fifth report of the Hibernian District of the Church Missionary Society for Africa and the East, for the year 1878, adopted at the annual meeting of the society, held in the antient concert rooms, Dublin, Friday 25 April 1879, with a statement of income and expenditures* (Dublin, 1879), p. 1. Page number indicates beginning of the statement of income and expenditures, which actually appears at the end of the annual report.   **15** Hibernian Church Missionary Society, *CMS centenary and anniversary of the Hibernian CMS, programme of meetings* (Belfast, 1899), p.

Two things are especially important to note here. First, just as women had played a critical role in launching the HCMS, they remained key players throughout the organization's history, in terms both of organizing local committees and of raising money. If we go into the receipts of the HCMS, for example, we find that fully 45.1 per cent of the Life Governors and Life Members were women.[16] At a more prosaic level, women's contributions were essential to perpetuating the society's efforts. For example, according to the printed annual report of the HCMS for 1878, nearly £500 of income came from the annual subscriptions and donations provided by 197 individuals, nearly 43 per cent of whom were women.[17]

Second, the HCMS certainly was not the only organization encouraging missions of various types among Irish Anglicans. Indeed, the Society for the Propagation of the Gospel (SPG) had fully a century more experience than had the HCMS in supporting overseas missions. Typically, the SPG focused on ministries to Anglicans who had moved into the empire, while the CMS and its Irish auxiliary supported efforts to convert or minister to non-Christians. True to its roots among Evangelicals, the CMS sought to bring people unfamiliar with the gospel message into the Christian fold. They did so in part because they viewed it as an imperative at all times to convert individuals to accept that salvation came alone through faith in Jesus, and in part because 'there were strong feelings of millenarian expectancy', with many sensing that missionary work would 'usher in the 1,000-year period of bliss on earth, as foretold in the Apocalypse of St John'.[18]

Still, it would be incorrect to suggest that there was a clear distinction that separated CMS and SPG activities in the field. Thus, in 1900 the Revd H.M.M. Hackett – a long-time activist with the HCMS – became for a time principal of the Montreal Theological Seminar, which educated clergy for the diocese of Montreal (and, according to the *Church of Ireland Gazette*, 'for the wider field of the whole Dominion and in some degree also for the boundless field beyond – the harvest field of the world').[19] Later that same year, in an address at Armagh, the Anglican primate praised both organizations equally before an audience, saying that

2; *Ninety-ninth report of the Hibernian District of the Church Missionary Society for Africa and the East, for the years 1912–13, adopted at the annual meeting of the society, held in the antient concert rooms, Dublin, Friday April 18th 1913, with a statement of income and expenditures* (Dublin, 1913), xvi. See also John Crawford, *The Church of Ireland in Victorian Dublin* (Dublin, 2005), pp 119–20.   **16** RCBL MS 315/5/4, life governors and life members, n.d. Calculation is based on 124 of the 275 governors and members listed.   **17** *Sixty-fifth report of the Hibernian District of the Church Missionary Society for Africa and the East, for the year 1878, adopted at the annual meeting of the society, held in the antient concert rooms, Dublin, on Friday 25 April 1879, with a statement of income and expenditure etc. etc.* (Dublin, 1879), pp 2–3 of the statement of income and expenditure. The exact total was £498 16s. 6d. The average gift was approximately £2 10s. 8d. The overall total from women donors was £216 13s. The women's average gift was approximately £2 11s. 7d.   **18** Nigel Scotland, *Evangelical Anglicans in a revolutionary age, 1789–1901* (Carlisle, Cumbria, 2004), ch. 12, quotation at p. 288. See also Lawrence Nemer, *Anglican and Roman Catholic attitudes on missions: an historical study of two English missionary societies in the late nineteenth century, 1865–1885* (St Augustin, Germany, 1981); and S.J. Brown, *Providence and empire, 1815–1914* (Harlow, 2008).   **19** 'Colonial and American church news',

the spread of the missionary spirit is one of the healthiest signs in the life of the Church, and it is gratifying to notice that the more the difficulties and dangers of missionary work are realized the more eager are the best men in the Church to devote themselves to this field.[20]

Along with domestic missions (such as the Church Mission to the Jews), such efforts received considerable interest from Irish Church members. Of these many organizations, however, the HCMS was the largest, in part, because of the efficiency of its organization. Hence, as Acheson has pointed out, 'in 1873, [the] HCMS was supported by 555 parishes, SPG by 318, and both societies by 123 parishes; by 1897 the parishes which gave no such support had fallen from 461 to 156'.[21]

As these gross numbers suggest, the impact of the HCMS was felt more broadly throughout the island in the latter years of the nineteenth century. In fact, in the years after 1890, the HCMS embarked on an ambitious promotional campaign known as the Three Years' Enterprise (or TYE) that catalyzed these trends. A special subcommittee of the HCMS central committee led the effort, coordinating communications with outside bodies such as the YWCA, as well as with existing HCMS entities, such as the Gleaners' Union and county associations.[22] Most importantly, it sponsored what were known as 'missionary missions', or week-long series of events featuring sermons, lectures and exhibitions designed to raise awareness of the need for foreign missions. In essence, they hoped that their own zealousness would prove contagious.

Shortly after its formation, the TYE subcommittee circularized the Dublin clergy to encourage them to hold a preliminary mission week after the celebration of the epiphany in January 1897. In its letter, the subcommittee stated its goal as 'bringing before the members of our Church the claims of Christ for the Evangelization of the World'.[23] In words that would have heartened those zealous founders of the Irish auxiliary, the committee proclaimed that 'the chief object of this effort is not to raise money, but to give information, to awaken a *heartfelt* interest in the heathen, and first, above all, to bring followers of our Lord and Saviour face to face with his command, and to impress upon them their *personal* responsibility in obeying that command'.[24] Thus, the campaign had a dual nature, entirely in keeping with the earliest soteriological vision of the HCMS – awakening the unenlightened abroad to the Christian message *and* awakening the home audience to the essential part they played in making the missions possible. In spite of the late date – the circular was sent out near the end of November – some thirty-four parishes in the diocese participated.

One essential reason for this quick response was that the society had been

Church of Ireland Gazette, 29 June 1900. In this context, it is important to note that the *Church of Ireland Gazette* reported Hackett's position as colonial church news (meaning efforts to create and staff Anglican dioceses whose primary constituents were United Kingdom settlers or their descendants). **20** 'The primate of missionary enterprise', *Church of Ireland Gazette*, 26 Oct. 1900. **21** Acheson, *History of the Church of Ireland*, p. 221. **22** RCBL MS 315/1/7, TYE missionary campaign sub-committee minute book, entry for 19 Nov. 1896. **23** Ibid. **24** Ibid. Italics in original.

embraced by mainstream church authorities. In part, this was due to the wider acceptance of evangelicals among leading Irish churchmen. Acheson has contended that the fifty years on either side of disestablishment (1845–95) marked the high water mark of evangelicals in the Church of Ireland, as families associated with the evangelical vanguard achieved eminence within the Church.[25] Among the most important for our purposes was William Conyngham, Baron Plunket, who served as archbishop of Dublin from 1884 until 1897. In the 1850s, while working in the west of Ireland, where his uncle Thomas was the bishop of Tuam, Killala and Achonry, Plunket had befriended the missionary Alexander Dallas and became a convinced evangelical.[26] During the early 1890s, he was one of the most zealous proponents of the HCMS, though he died on the eve of the TYE campaign.[27]

In spite of his loss, the campaign still received active participation from leading clerics, including the bishop of Ossory and future archbishop of Armagh John Baptist Crozier and Plunket's successor as archbishop of Dublin, Joseph F. Peacocke – himself an evangelical who had spent four years (1861–5) as secretary of the HCMS.[28] With their encouragement, the subcommittee planned another 'missionary mission' for late October through early November 1897 to expand upon the January success. The CMS in London provided further aid, including seven clergy and a set of magic lantern slides of mission sites around the world. Among the fixtures were special services in St Patrick's Cathedral and Christ Church Cathedral on 31 October and 8 November and a mass meeting for children on 6 November in Dublin's Metropolitan Hall, at which the slides were presented.[29] To promote these activities, the committee distributed some 6,000 pamphlets and 15,000 handbills and organized weekly planning meetings to train parish volunteers.[30] So successful was this 1897 effort that the Hibernian society continued to hold periodic missionary missions, even after the Three Years' Enterprise had run its course.

The most impressive series of mission meetings in the 1890s – and the culmination of the TYE – was the centenary celebration between 9 and 18 April. Indeed, the sequence of meetings held that week serves as a measure of how successful the HCMS had been at insinuating itself into the fabric of the Church of Ireland. Among the featured events of the nine days were the centenary meeting itself, held on Wednesday 12 April and addressed by the primate of Ireland the archbishop of Armagh, the bishop of Meath, the secretary of the Church Missionary Society from London, and the Revd E. Guilford, formerly a resident missionary in the Punjab, and

---

25 Acheson, *History of the Church of Ireland*, p. 182. **26** Georgina Clinton and Sinéad Sturgeon, 'Plunket, William Conyngham' in *Dictionary of Irish biography from the earliest times to the year 2002: vol. 8*, ed. James McGuire and James Quinn (Cambridge, 2009), pp 169–70. **27** Plunket's comments on the importance of mission work at the valedictory meeting, at which HCMS missionaries were feted prior to their leaving Ireland, are instructive: see *Irish Times*, 17 Sept. 1896. **28** RCBL MS 315/1/7, TYE missionary campaign sub-committee minute book, entries for 19 Nov. 1896, 7 July 1897, 23 July 1897, 15 Mar. 1898. On Peacocke, see Georgina Clinton and Bridget Hourican, 'Peacocke, Joseph Ferguson' in *DIB*. **29** Ibid., 10 Mar. 1897. **30** Ibid., 23 July 1897, 16 Sept. 1897.

a public prayer meeting led by the Archdeacon of Glendalough and addressed by the rector of Holyrood parish in Co. Down. Two days later, the HCMS held its annual meeting and a special meeting for ladies interested in missionary work, the latter of which was addressed by a woman named McClellan, who had been stationed as a missionary in Fuh-Kien, China. (The Fuh-Kien mission, which would prefigure the Far East mission usually associated with Trinity College, was in fact an offshoot of the CMS enterprise.) Secondary events included a children's meeting on the evening of 16 April and a social for members of the Gleaners Union two days later. Central to the celebration were special sermons delivered at thirty-five parishes around the Dublin archdiocese on 9 and 16 April, including sermons delivered by the bishops of Ossory, Meath, Cork and Down, and the archbishop of Dublin, as well as by former mission workers from the Punjab and the North Pacific.[31]

Such activity paid dividends not only in terms of burgeoning donations, but in terms of what these monies allowed the HCMS to undertake. For instance, not only did the Irish body continue to make payments to its London-based parent, but it also sponsored exhibitions to promote greater knowledge of the outside world in Ireland. These events ranged from simple lantern lectures and kinematograph presentations by returned missionaries to weeklong bazaars. For instance, in October 1904, the Revd A.B. Fisher, one of the first Christian missionaries into Uganda in 1882, delivered a lecture in the Metropolitan Hall at which Lord Longford presided. Fisher displayed photographs he had taken himself and described how, under his watch, the Anglican community in Uganda had grown from one church with some 300 converts to more than 400 churches with more than 50,000.[32]

Most important, the HCMS began to underwrite the incomes and expenses of missionaries sent out from Ireland to Africa and Asia. Over time, nearly 400 lay and clerical missionaries went out under the sponsorship of the HCMS.[33] Their efforts were directly connected to the church at home rhetorically and practically. Rhetorically, senior clergy spoke at annual valedictory meetings designed to encourage outgoing missionaries and to link their work to the support of ordinary Anglicans in Ireland. Thus, in the same month that Fisher had described his days in Uganda, the Revd Hackett, having returned from Montreal, told those in attendance at one such valedictory meeting not only that their focus should be on those abroad, but that 'it should not be forgotten there was a duty to be done at home, which was just as important. Every assistance possible should be given to those who devoted their lives to the carrying of the Gospel to the heathen.'[34] In the context of the present discussion, it should be noted that, while Hackett was the dean of Waterford in 1904, he had been general secretary of the HCMS in the 1890s and one of the leaders of the Three Years' Enterprise.[35]

31 HCMS, *CMS centenary and anniversary of the Hibernian CMS* (Belfast, 1899), pp 4–15. Pamphlet attached to RCBL MS 315/1/7, TYE missionary campaign sub-committee minute book.   32 *Irish Times*, 4 Oct. 1904.   33 Kenneth Milne, *A short history of the Church of Ireland* (Blackrock, Co. Dublin, 2003 ed.), p. 62.   34 *Irish Times*, 21 Oct. 1904.   35 For example, Hackett had authored and co-signed the original circulars for the TYE campaign.

The assistance to which he alluded was made all the more relevant through clever marketing via a programme known as 'Our Own Missionary', through which parishes 'adopted' a single missionary.[36] As Martin Maguire described it, 'letters and visits from these missionaries provided news from exotic corners of the British Empire and constant reassurance of the good that was being done by their missionary efforts in combating witch-doctors in Africa or heathens in India'.[37] But the connection between missionary and sponsor-parish was not a one-way link. Home parishes held annual 'sales' and bazaars to raise much-needed funds that went directly to benefit 'their' missionary.[38]

Such activities were not, of course, unique to Irish Anglicans, as Presbyterians, Methodists, and, yes, Catholics – were engaged in financing and sending out missionary workers. Nor, as noted above, were the efforts of the HCMS the only ones engaged in by members of the Church of Ireland. And yet the HCMS was not only the largest of the Anglican bodies at the turn of the twentieth century, but its efforts were becoming more activist and had greater success from the time of the Three Years' Enterprise forward. The question remains, why?

While one should not overlook the part played by the TYE and associated campaigns in energizing support, I believe that there are at least three other factors inspiring this dynamism.

The first relates specifically to the psychological perils involved in the imperial enterprise. It goes without saying that Europeans generally and Irish and British people specifically were in more frequent, direct, and occasionally ominous contact with Africans and Asians. In the parlance of the time, it was a clash of races, implying both cultural and biological struggles, and missionaries periodically paid the ultimate price for carrying their notions of civilization abroad. Accounts of attacks on missionaries were frequent in the Irish newspapers, as witnessed by the extensive coverage given to such events as the Boxer Rebellion in China.[39] To counter such violence – which even the nationalist newspaper the *Freeman's Journal* called 'the greatest blow Western Civilization has sustained in modern times' – required the kind of zeal reflected in the HCMS' activities.[40]

Second, within the Irish Anglican community, a particular constituency found mission work particularly attractive and useful in the wake of Disestablishment. These were Anglican women. Within the Church of Ireland, they were not only not allowed to be members of the clergy, but since the General Convention of 1870 – which set up policy within the disestablished Church – they were officially excluded

See RCBL MS 315/1/7, TYE missionary campaign sub-committee minute book, entry for 19 Nov. 1896. **36** Martin Maguire, '"Our people": the Church of Ireland and the culture of community in Dublin since disestablishment' in Gillespie and Neely, *The laity and the Church of Ireland*, p. 286. **37** Ibid. **38** For examples of such events in Rathfarnham and Harold's Cross, see respectively *Irish Times*, 8 Oct. 1904 and 29 Oct. 1908. **39** See Timothy G. McMahon, 'Dash and daring: imperial violence and Irish ambiguity' in Sean Farrell and Danine Farquaharson, *Shadow of the gunman: violence and culture in modern Ireland* (Cork, 2008), pp 79–89 at pp 86–8. **40** *Freeman's Journal*, 17 July 1900.

from participation in the convention or even in general vestries, a status they had held prior to Disestablishment. As we have already seen, women were integral to the formation and financial maintenance of the HCMS. Like their English counterparts in religiously motivated voluntarist causes, these women built on the evangelical assumption that the '"women's mission" was to export the moral education she [*sic*] provided in the home but not beyond the point at which she herself started to become contaminated by the activity.'[41] Having played essentially secondary parts in the early decades of the century, women late in the century assumed a more public and acceptable role in the Church, through philanthropic work, such as planning the events and bazaars that paid for the 'Our Own Missionary' appeals. These events involved weeks of organizing and put an activist spin to the traditional concept of an all-parish festival, and even though the speakers at such events tended to be church MEN, it was church WOMEN who brought them off.[42] Such activity clearly paralleled, and potentially augmented, the social activism documented by Luddy and Walsh, among others.[43] Equally important, women increasingly took on the most prominent role in the HCMS, as missionaries in the widening vistas of the empire. Looking at the published report of missionaries sent out only by the society prior to 1901, thirty-seven of them were women, and they went to every part of the world where the parent organization had set up outposts, including nine going to parts of Africa, five to Japan, eleven to China (including seven to regions outside of Fukien), five to Ceylon, and two to Persia.[44] That total of thirty-seven represents 42 per cent of the missionaries sent out by the HCMS in this period.

Finally, a majority of people in Ireland were expressing their desire to break free from the union, if not from the empire, in a channelled fashion. Of course, that majority was generally not representative of the Church of Ireland community, whose primary allegiance was to the state and the culture of the United Kingdom. Even so, as an entity, the Church was still recovering its bearings from the shock of church Disestablishment in 1869 and the realization that significant numbers of

---

41 M.J.D. Roberts, *Making English morals: voluntary association and moral reform in England, 1787–1886* (Cambridge, 2004), p. 129.   **42** For examples of such events in Rathfarnham and Harold's Cross, see respectively *Irish Times*, 8 Oct. 1904 and 29 Oct. 1908.   **43** Maria Luddy, *Women and philanthropy in nineteenth-century Ireland* (Cambridge, 1995), especially ch. 2, which highlights the role of religious motivations behind much philanthropic work; idem, 'Religion, philanthropy and the state in late eighteenth- and early nineteenth-century Ireland' in Hugh Cunningham and Joanna Innes (eds), *Charity, philanthropy and reform from the 1690s to 1850* (New York, 1998); idem, 'Women and philanthropy in nineteenth-century Ireland' in Kathleen D. McCarthy (ed.), *Women, philanthropy and civil society* (Bloomington, IN, 2001); Oonagh Walsh, *Anglican women in Dublin: philanthropy, politics and education in the early twentieth century* (Dublin, 2005). Cf. Roberts, *Making English morals*, p. 130.   **44** *Eighty-seventh annual report of the Hibernian Church Missionary Society for Africa and the East, for the year 1900, adopted at the annual meeting of the society, held in the Metropolitan Hall, Dublin on Friday, April 19th, 1901 with a statement of income and expenditure, &c. &c.* (Dublin, 1901), 'List of Irish Missionaries at present working in connection with the Church Missionary Society', pp 140–1. See also Oonagh Walsh, *Anglican women in Dublin*, ch. 4.

people in the Church of England 'did not care much about the Irish Church'.[45] At the same time, many of its prominent members were facing declining rent rolls and the political onslaught of land legislation.[46] Taken together, these factors challenged fundamentally the perception that Irish Anglicans had as political and social elites not only on their island but within the wider state. Mission work, whether in the field or vicariously through supporting the work of those abroad, helped them to find a place again. While missionaries throughout the empire could speak about Britain's 'divine mission' as an imperial power,[47] Irish churchmen at valedictory meetings frequently argued that their church had a special place within the wider Anglican Communion because they could draw on Irish Christianity's distinctive missionary heritage.[48] That heritage, which was highlighted by an Irish speaker at a CMS convention as early as 1829, came in direct succession from St Patrick himself.[49] With such a legacy, they could play a unique part in creating a new calling for the United Kingdom. To quote the dean of St Patrick's Cathedral from a mission bazaar in 1908,

> As the growth of the imperial idea of statesmanship began with the first efforts of the state at colonization, so too the efforts of churchmen to carry the Gospel to lands beyond the sea were leading the way to a larger and more imperial − a more catholic, and therefore more evangelical − conception of the Church ... Our colonies have saved the United Kingdom from much of the narrowness and self-sufficiency and intolerance of other races, to which communities insulated by their geographical position, and in some measure shut off from the life of the European Continent, were peculiarly susceptible. The colonies had inspired them with a larger idea of freedom and a more generous idea of human society.[50]

That idea could only be fully realized in a United Kingdom context. Thus, in placing before their audiences this noble vision of the empire as a missionary beacon of freedom, the HCMS sought not only to undercut the value of Irish nationalist arguments on behalf of Home Rule, but also to assert anew the place of Irish Anglicans as elites with a critical niche in that imperial enterprise.

45 G.A. Denison quoted in Brown, *Providence and empire*, p. 257.   **46** Maguire, '"Our people"', pp 277–8.   **47** Brown, *Providence and empire*, p. 435.   **48** *Irish Times*, 18 Oct. 1901.   **49** Acheson, *History of the Church of Ireland*, p. 135.   **50** *Irish Times*, 29 Oct. 1908.

Visual parody and political commentary: John Doyle and Daniel O'Connell

FINTAN CULLEN

In London in August 1833, the poet Tom Moore breakfasted with 'the famous and anonymous caricaturist H.B. …. (who is an Irish artist) a very sensible and gentle-manlike person'. Moore informed H.B., whose real name was John Doyle (1797–1868), that he and some friends had 'agreed that there was a quiet power about his caricatures, producing as they did their effect without either extravagance or ill-nature, which set them, in a very important respect, far above Gillray's'.[1]

This essay will discuss Doyle's political caricatures of the 1830s and 1840s produced in London, and, in particular, will examine a small selection of prints that deal with the satirical representation of Daniel O'Connell, Ireland's most illustrious political success story of the first half of the nineteenth century. As James McCord indicated some twenty years ago in the most sustained examination of Doyle's print satires of O'Connell, the politician featured in about a quarter of all of HB's prints, that is about 225 out of the 900 prints published between 1829 and 1851.[2] In attempting to go beyond McCord's seminal article, the focus here is on Doyle's use of parody (usually of contemporaneous art and literary references) to expose O'Connell's political strategies.

The parodying of works of art, which means, to paraphrase Margaret Rose, the comic reworking of literary or artistic material, had been a common feature of polit-ical satire in London from at least the 1780s and was facilitated by the 'growing visual literacy of the audience' as well as by the rise in public art exhibitions and the greater availability of engraved reproductions of works of art.[3] John Doyle's political satires made full use of these developments and in his depiction of O'Connell he turned to recent oil paintings that had been exhibited in London by a range of emerging and established artists, including the animal painter Edwin Landseer (1802–73). Doyle's use of parody also included references to fairy tales such as 'Little Red-Riding Hood'

---

1 Lord John Russell (ed.), *Memoirs, journal and correspondence of Thomas Moore* (8 vols, London, 1853–6), vi, pp 334–5. For a reference to this diary entry by Moore and a discussion of Doyle in London, see Celina Fox, *Graphic journalism in England during the 1830s and 1840s* (London, 1988), pp 86–90. Doyle's monogram 'HB' was created by placing two 'JD's one above the other, 'J' being a conventional initial for John.   2 James N. McCord, 'The image in England: the cartoons of HB' in Maurice O'Connell (ed.), *Daniel O'Connell, political pioneer* (Dublin, 1991), pp 57–71.   3 Diana Donald, *The age of caricature: satirical prints in the reign of George III* (London, 1996), p. 67; for Margaret Rose, see *Pictorial irony, parody and pastiche: comic interpictoriality in the arts of the 19th and 20th centuries* (Bielefeld, 2011), p. 5.

and to contemporary novels such as *Barnaby Rudge* by Charles Dickens. As these sources suggest, HB's use of parody was up to date in its allusions and popular insofar as it was appreciated by a literate and educated audience.

As well as parodying star attractions at London exhibitions and new publications from Dickens, in his prints of O'Connell Doyle also utilized the well-established tradition of the animalization of politicians. In London such a tradition, like artistic parody, also stretched back into the eighteenth century, where such figures as Charles James Fox could appear in a 1782 print by Gillray (1756–1815), not surprisingly as a fox, while prime minister William Pitt could be cast by Isaac Cruikshank as a locust (1795) or a later prime minister, the duke of Wellington in 1829 at the beginning of Doyle's productive years, was represented by William Heath as a lobster.[4]

The visualization of the Irish political elite as animals in London-based satires, while not as extensive as their English colleagues, was equally varied in its range. During the Regency Crisis of 1789, the Irish political delegation, which had attempted to offer the prince of Wales the regency of Ireland, had appeared in prints as asses (some one-headed, others six-headed) and on a number of occasions as bulls, while a little over a decade later such a prominent Irish hate-figure as John FitzGibbon, the earl of Clare, was represented in at least one print as a 'great mangy, mongrel dog' chased by a group of English Whigs.[5] Given such a visual precedent, it is useful to examine the decision by Doyle to characterize O'Connell, a member of the new Irish elite at Westminster in the 1830s, as, among other creatures, a supine dog or a sly wolf and see why the artist used such a well-worn tradition for a fellow-Irishman.

Doyle's lithographic caricatures were not cheap and were purchased and collected by the English political classes who could afford to buy them.[6] In the mid-1830s, a single print, often hand-coloured, cost two shillings, which was about three times the price of a newspaper.[7] As Doyle's prints tended to appear in pairs or in sets of three or four, sales must have been limited to a few. Unlike previous visual satires, back in the days of Gillray, for example, Doyle prints, as far as is known, were not accessible in other ways.

Given O'Connell's undoubted prominence at Westminster in the 1830s, there is a long list throughout the decade of formal oil and engraved portraits of him, while after his death in 1847 innumerable sculptured memorials were erected throughout Ireland.[8] Political satires of the 'Liberator' are even more numerous and range from

4 For Fox, see Donald, *The age of caricature*, pp 60–1; for Pitt and Wellington, see Richard Godfrey, *English caricature, 1620 to the present: caricaturists and satirists, their art, their purpose and influence* (London, 1984), pp 94, 104. 5 Nicholas Robinson, 'Caricature and the Regency Crisis: an Irish perspective', *Eighteenth-Century Ireland*, 1 (1986), pls 5, 8; Nicholas Robinson, 'Marriage against inclination: the union and caricature' in Dáire Keogh and Kevin Whelan (eds), *Acts of union, the causes, contexts and consequences of the Act of Union* (Dublin, 2001), pl. 27. 6 Fox, *Graphic journalism*, p. 87. 7 McCord, 'The image in England', p. 67. 8 For sculpture, see in particular Paula Murphy, *Nineteenth-century Irish sculpture: native genius reaffirmed* (New Haven and London, 2010), ch. 8; for further discussion of O'Connell

the genially humorous to the aggressive and this is where Doyle plays his part. O'Connell is depicted by Doyle as a large, usually jovial, round-faced man whose political activity is driven by a formidable energy and cunning. Doyle's own politics tended more to the conservative side of the lobby than the Whigs and indeed in 1842 he wrote to Robert Peel when the latter was in No. 10, informing him that the artist's 'political opinions ... may in a great degree be traced in the sketches themselves'.[9] Despite 'being an Irishman and a Roman Catholic' as he informed Peel, Doyle's attitude to O'Connell 'underwent change' and it is necessary to see the satirist's prints of O'Connell in terms of such a growing disillusionment.[10]

Doyle's art has received a mixed press. In his day, he could be lauded, as we have seen with Tom Moore's comments, while *The Times*, as Dorothy George informs us, saw each publication of his prints as an event and praised him highly.[11] By the 1850s, he was largely forgotten. In 1840, William Makepeace Thackeray, in an article on the satirical art of the much more hard-hitting George Cruikshank, was of the opinion that:

> You never hear any laughing at HB; his pictures are a great deal too genteel for that – polite points of wit, which strike one as exceedingly clever and pretty, and cause one to smile in a quiet, gentlemanly-like kind of way.[12]

To the detriment of Doyle, Thackeray compared HB with contemporary French lithographers such as Honoré Daumier, and found the Irish-born artist wanting:

> In looking, for instance, at HB's slim vapour figures, they have struck one as excellent likenesses of men and women, but no more: the bodies want spirit, action and individuality.[13]

imagery, see: M.L. Chappell and J.N. McCord Jr, 'John Doyle, Daniel O'Connell "The Great Liberator" and Rubens: the appropriate and appropriation in political caricature', *South Eastern College Art Conference Review*, 11 (1987), 127–34; Fergus O'Ferrall, 'Daniel O'Connell, the "Liberator", 1775–1847: changing images' in Raymond Gillespie and B.P. Kennedy (eds), *Ireland: art into history* (Dublin, 1994), pp 91–102; Fintan Cullen, *Visual politics: the representation of Ireland, 1750–1930* (Cork, 1997), pp 90–101; Leslie Williams, '"Rint" and "Repale": *Punch* and the image of Daniel O'Connell, 1842–1847', *New Hibernia Review*, 1 (1997), 74–93; Gary Owens, 'Visualizing the Liberator: self-fashioning, dramaturgy and the construction of Daniel O'Connell', *Éire/Ireland*, 33–34 (1998), 103–30; Fintan Cullen, *The Irish face: redefining the Irish portrait* (London, 2004), pp 185–9; Peter Gray, '"Hints and hits": Irish caricature and the trial of Daniel O'Connell, 1843–4', *History Ireland*, 12 (2004), 45–51; Fintan Cullen and R.F. Foster, *'Conquering England': Ireland in Victorian London* (London, 2005), pp 40–1; Ruan O'Donnell, 'The Liberator: images of Daniel O'Connell', *Irish Arts Review*, 23 (2006), 92–7.   **9** BL, Peel Papers, Add. MS 40497, Doyle to Peel, 22 Jan. 1842, fo. 315v.   **10** Ibid.   **11** George, p. xlvi. For Doyle's career, see Rodney Engen, *Richard Doyle* (Stroud, 1983), pp 11–15. For the decline of interest in Doyle, see Graham Everitt, *English caricaturists and graphic humourists of the nineteenth century* (London, 1893), pp 275–6.   **12** W.M. Thackeray, *The Westminster Review*, 34 (1840), 7.   **13** W.M. Thackeray, 'Caricatures

Thackeray's criticisms focused on the fact that Doyle's lithographs 'are admired merely because they are caricatures of well-known political characters', but the problem is that they are not 'witty'.[14] Here, I would like to take Thackeray to task on this latter criticism. While much comment on Doyle has focused on his capacity to accurately capture 'well-known political characters', HB also perfected the use of parody in his compositional and thematic borrowings from topical paintings or well-known stories, either by contemporary writers or ones that had entered into popular lore. These parodies are decidedly witty and potentially acerbic. They are not as 'mundane' as Thackeray would have us believe.[15]

In using contemporary well-known visual references so as to entertain his viewers and to strengthen the point of his satire, Doyle was not attempting plagia-rism, for he always acknowledged his sources and made it very clear where he had found them. Knowledge of Doyle's use of well-known paintings by such artists as Landseer that had recently been on display at the Royal Academy of Arts' annual summer exhibitions held at Somerset House on the Strand in central London was greatly helped by the fact that the *Political sketches* were regularly discussed in *The Times*. The newspaper offered descriptions of the individual sheets and commented on the artist who was described as 'unrivalled' of his 'richness of whim' and his 'display of imagination'. According to *The Times*, HB or Doyle could convey a meaning that was 'serious' and that makes one 'smile freely' but also 'reflect'.[16]

An excellent example of Doyle's use of high art parody is the 1835 lithograph, *Jack in office* (fig. 15.1), 'in which', as Doyle writes on the sheet itself, 'Mr Edwin Landseer's admirable picture is made very free with'. The painting in question is *A Jack in office*, now in the Victoria and Albert Museum in London (fig. 15.2), which had been exhibited two years earlier at the Royal Academy in 1833.[17] In the original painting, a group of dogs gather around a Jack Russell terrier who sits on top of a wheel-barrow. The expression 'a jack in office' refers to a pompous official and is thus a play on both the breed of dog and the psychological role being played by the terrier, which clearly controls whatever morsels of meat the other rather pathetic looking dogs will receive. Doyle's lithograph substitutes five human heads for the group of dogs with Lord John (or 'Jack') Russell wittily replacing the features of the dog sitting on top of the barrow. In the spring of 1835 (HB's print is dated 25 April 1835), after the short-lived government led by Robert Peel, Russell was appointed leader of the House of Commons in London and is seen here seated atop a barrel marked with a 'T' for Treasury, while below he is surrounded by fellow Whigs and radicals who

and Lithography in Paris' in *The Paris sketch book by Mr M.A. Titmarsh* in *The works of W.M. Thackeray*, introduction by Lady Richie (25 vols, London, 1911), xxii, p. 198. **14** Ibid., p. 178. See also Richard Gaunt, 'Wellington in petticoats: the duke as caricature' in C.M. Woolgar (ed.), *Wellington Studies*, 4 (Southampton, 2008), 140–72. **15** W.M. Thackeray, *The works of W.M. Thackeray*, vol. 22, p. 178. **16** *Times*, 27 Jan. 1835; 21 Mar. 1835; 16 May 1835. **17** Ronald Parkinson, *Victoria and Albert Museum: catalogue of British oil paintings, 1820–1860* (London, 1990), pp 144–5; Richard Ormond, *Landseer* (London, 1981), pp 104–6.

15.1 John Doyle, *Jack in office*, lithograph, 1835 (courtesy of the
University of Nottingham, Manuscripts and Special Collections).

aspired to new political appointments.[18] On the far left, the radical MP Joseph Hume
sits quietly observing the scene; in the foreground the former lord chancellor, Lord
Brougham, is caricatured as an 'emaciated pointer'[19] with its tail between its legs,
whose hopes for reappointment are indicated by the plate of liver that he studies with
care, resembling as it does the form of the lord chancellor's ceremonial wig. John
Lambton, first earl of Durham and soon to become ambassador to St Petersburg, is
the sharp-eared terrier in the background, while Daniel O'Connell is the poodle on
the right who, according to a key to HB's *Political sketches* published a few years later,
'puts up his supplicating paws like one long-accustomed to beg'.[20] The resemblances
to the Landseer original are clear: five dogs, one in charge; one sniffing meat in the
foreground. The top dog is overweight and smug in his position of power, a characteristic commented on by many contemporary newspapers and journals when
reviewing the original Landseer painting. The *Examiner* referred to the 'vigilant
watch-dog', while the *Gentleman's Magazine* enjoyed the 'surly looking bull-dog ...
guarding the meat' and the *Athenaeum* spoke of the 'well-fed and much caressed dog,
who, like his friend of the manger, keeps others from tasting the food of which he
has too much'.[21]

18 Thomas McLean, *An illustrative key to the political sketches of HB* (London, 1841), p. 258.
19 Ormond, *Landseer*, p. 105. **20** McLean, *An illustrative key* (1841), p. 258. **21** *Examiner*,

15.2 Edwin Landseer, *A Jack in office*, oil on panel, 50.2x66.1cm, 1833
(courtesy of the Victoria & Albert Museum, London).

Diana Donald has carefully examined Landseer's innumerable animal paintings
and has suggested how, from the late 1820s onwards, in his many narratives of dogs,
he invented a new kind of 'anthropomorphism, where animals were associated with
particular kinds of humans'.[22] To Donald, Landseer's dog pictures are 'complex and
imaginative – sites of hidden conflict'.[23] By transferring Landseer's collection of variously smug, hungry and impoverished dogs as seen in *A Jack in office* (fig. 15.2) into
a contemporary Westminster political clique (fig. 15.1), Doyle offers a critique of the
self-serving role of politicians. Donald goes on to say that Landseer's dogs also suggest
'some insight into the anxieties of the age'.[24] By including O'Connell in this whig-
gish club, Doyle is perhaps saying that a member of the Irish elite has been totally
subsumed into a political grouping where he must beg and fawn to achieve his
goals.[25]

By 1835, when Doyle's *Jack in office* appeared, the fame or renown of paintings
such as the oil now in the V&A would have been such that members of the political elite, either Tory or Whig, would have got the joke. Indeed, Thomas McLean,
who published a *Key to the political sketches of HB*, said as much in 1841:

1320 (19 May, 1833), 309; *Gentleman's Magazine*, 103:1 (1833), 541; *Athenaeum*, 289 (11 May
1833), 298. **22** Diana Donald, *Picturing animals in Britain, 1750–1850* (London, 2007), p. 128.
23 Ibid., p. 127. **24** Ibid. **25** For another Doyle based on one of Landseer's dog
paintings that also relates to O'Connell and Russell and also dates from 1835, see Godfrey,
English caricature, p. 109.

[*Jack in office*] is a parody of the admirable picture, under the same title, by Mr Edwin Landseer, and those only who are acquainted with the original can fully appreciate the merit of the parody.[26]

The need for Doyle's parody to make sense of itself was important, as it greatly increased the humour as well as the visual power of the satire. It is thus important to know that Landseer's *A Jack in office* had been engraved within a year of being exhibited at the RA, while, as has been noted, the leading periodicals of the day carried reviews and discussion of the painting.[27] As a very versatile and speedy technique for print production, by the mid-1830s, lithography had become a popular medium.[28] It allowed for a linear clarity that perfectly reproduced Doyle's dexterity with the pencil.[29] Indeed, at the time of his death in 1868, the *Art Journal* claimed that the artist had 'haunted parliament in search of copy, a quiet, silent unsuspected frequenter of the lobby and gallery'.[30]

An ink drawing of Robert Peel in the British Museum (BM) taken from the life while observing the politician in Westminster, exemplifies Doyle's speedy technique (fig. 15.3).[31] The thinly drawn lines were easily transferred to the lithographic stone and prints could be made in large numbers. As Doyle's political satires were produced in groups of between two and five and later sold in volumes, they can be seen as comparable to a periodical of visual images.[32] McLean carefully marketed HB's *Political sketches* and each print is authenticated by a subscriber's stamp. In the key that accompanies each volume of the *Political sketches*, the publisher warned against 'spurious copies, and imitations of style and signature, much inferior to the celebrated originals'.[33] Although black and white versions of *Jack in office* and other Doyle lithographs dominate in terms of availability, hand-coloured versions do exist and when bound in a tooled-leather volume make for a very attractive collection.[34]

---

26 McLean, *An illustrative key* (1841), p. 258.   **27** Engraving by B.P. Gibbons, 1834: see Ormond, *Landseer*, p. 105.   **28** For the popularity of lithography in the period, see Beatrice Farwell, *The cult of images (Le culte des images): Baudelaire and the 19th-century media explosion* (Santa Barbara, 1977), p. 9. Dave Cole, 'Grant's printmaking technique' in Richard Pound (ed.), *C.J. Grant's political drama: a radical satirist rediscovered* (London, 1998), pp 19–21. My thanks to Brian Maidment for his comments after an earlier version of this paper was given at the Research Society for Victorian Periodicals' annual conference, Yale University, Sept. 2010.   **29** As far as is known, Doyle did not actually make the lithographs himself. During the 1830s and 1840s, the lithographs were printed by a series of London businesses: Motte's 23 Leicester Square and Docôte & Stephen's, 70 St Martin's Lane, which later became known as the General Lithography Establishment; for these companies, see Michael Twyman, *Lithography, 1800–1850* (London, 1970), passim.   **30** *Art Journal* (1868), p. 47.   **31** BM, Department of Prints and Drawings, 1882, 1209.688.   **32** The frequent mention of HB's prints in *The Times* (see n. 16) throughout the 1830s and early 1840s, along with the fact that each print is clearly dated, helps us to follow the publication of the groups of political sketches.   **33** Printed warning with each volume of *Political sketches of HB* (8 vols, London, 1829–43).   **34** There are hand-coloured prints in the British Library's bound volumes of *Political sketches of HB*.

15.3 John Doyle, *Robert Peel*, brown ink over graphite, early 1840s (© Trustees of the British Museum, London).

A BM drawing of O'Connell that possibly dates from the early 1830s would in time be used as the basis for a number of prints, most especially another one of 1835, which shows O'Connell now in the guise of a wolf with Lord John Russell as Little Red-Riding Hood.[35] *Little Red-Riding Hood's meeting with the wolf* (fig. 15.4) appeared on 3 April 1835 and thus pre-dates *Jack in office* by a few weeks. While the latter is based on a recently exhibited painting, the parody of the former is of course derived from the well-known fairy or folk tale. As we have seen, in *Jack in office*, O'Connell is a poodle, while in *Little Red-Riding Hood's meeting with the wolf*, the choice of animal suggests that the Irish politician is perhaps more cunning than merely acquiescent. Published at a time when the Whigs were negotiating a possible deal with O'Connell and his parliamentary followers, known as the Litchfield Compact, O'Connell's wry smile suggests that he has gained complete control of the diminutive Lord John Russell.[36]

35 This BM drawing (1882, 1209.687) was more immediately used as the basis for *View of an interior*, 1832 (no. 225 in Thomas McLean, *An illustrative key to the political sketches of HB from no. 601 to 800* (London, 1844)), a print showing O'Connell at Derrynane, his home in Co. Kerry. See also no. 248 (*A Pealer and a Repealer*, 1833), no. 253 (*Changed at nurse*, 1833), no. 386 (*Robin Hood and Little John fleecing the Church*, 1835). **36** Oliver MacDonagh, *O'Connell: the life of Daniel O'Connell, 1775–1847* (London, 1991), pp 402–3 and Patrick M. Geoghegan, *Liberator: the life and death of Daniel O'Connell, 1830–1847* (Dublin, 2010),

15.4 John Doyle, *Little Red-Riding Hood's meeting with the wolf*, lithograph, 1835 (courtesy of University of Nottingham, Manuscripts and Special Collections).

pp 67–9. The 'Litchfield Compact' was called after the house where the meeting took place, Lord Litchfield's London home in St James' Square: see A.H. Graham, 'The Litchfield Compact, 1835', *IHS*, 12:47 (Mar. 1961), 209–25 at 217; my thanks to Richard Gaunt for this reference.

15.5 John Doyle, *Barnaby Rudge and his raven*, lithograph, 1841 (courtesy of University of Nottingham, Manuscripts and Special Collections).

A few years later in the early 1840s, with the battle for repeal of the union having turned sour as it was prolonged, the image of O'Connell becomes much more negative. Looking older, fatter and more aggressive, Doyle's O'Connell is a parody of a character from Dickens' latest novel, the eponymous *Barnaby Rudge*, which was being serialized in *Master Humphrey's clock* during 1841, with HB's print appearing on 30

August (fig. 15.5). As with the character in Dickens' novel, O'Connell carries a loquacious raven in his bag, which here has the head of Lord John Russell, while the Liberator's satchel carries the legend 'RINT'. Rendered here as if with an Irish accent, the word 'rint' or 'rent' relates to O'Connell's fundraising efforts, which involved a penny-a-month minimum donation initially to the Catholic Association to aid the Emancipation movement in the 1820s and later to aid the Repeal Movement.[37]

Doyle's representation of O'Connell echoes the depiction of Barnaby Rudge himself in Hablôt Knight Browne or Phiz's original woodcut illustration that appeared in volume 3 of *Master Humphrey's clock* in April 1841, some four months earlier (fig. 15.6). In Phiz's illustration, in which Barnaby greets his mother, Rudge is dressed in a ragged coat with torn stockings and he carries a floral-decorated staff with a plethora of wild grasses and flowers in his hat. Doyle repeats these sartorial details in his caricature of the bloated O'Connell. Famously simple, in time, Barnaby blindly gets involved in riotous acts of religious intolerance.[38] Given Doyle's own disillusionment with O'Connell as expressed in his letter to Robert Peel of 1842, by characterizing the Irish politician in the guise of a fanatic, Doyle suggests a comparable lack of judgment on O'Connell's part.

Two years later, in 1843, Doyle continued his less sympathetic representation of O'Connell not by comparing him to an animal or a contemporaneous literary creation, but by returning to another 'admired picture' by Edwin Landseer, this time *A naughty child* of 1834 (figs 15.7, 15.8). Doyle's lithograph, which dates from November 1843, changes the indefinite article of Landseer's title to a definite *The naughty boy*, thus stressing the emphasis on who is depicted. The print appeared at the end of six months of extraordinarily popular monster repeal meetings throughout Ireland, which, according to Oliver MacDonagh, averaged 'nearly two a week'.[39] Closely echoing Landseer's painting of a decade earlier, in which a young girl sulks in the corner of a school-room, Doyle wittily substitutes the now sixty-eight-year-old O'Connell, while the neglected book on the bench is inscribed 'The Laws' and the broken slate on the floor contains the word 'REPEAL'.[40] The implication of both these parodies of the early 1840s, one referring to a Dickens novel, the other to a Landseer painting, is that O'Connell's battle for repeal had got out of hand and that the great Liberator of Catholic Emancipation was using the struggle for his own ends. McLean, in his 1844 edition of his *Illustrative key*, offered an interpretation:

> [O'Connell] has been amusing himself with writing 'Repeal' upon his slate, no bad allusion to ciphering, to which purpose a slate is usually applied, for

37 MacDonagh, *O'Connell*, passim.   **38** For interpretations of Dickens' novel, see Dennis Walder, *Dickens and religion* (London, 1981), pp 92–112; Patrick Brantlinger, 'Did Dickens have a philosophy of history? The case of *Barnaby Rudge*', *Dickens Studies Annual*, 30 (2001), 59–74.   **39** MacDonagh, *O'Connell*, p. 509.   **40** The print dates from 2 Nov. 1843 and is no. 787 in McLean, *An illustrative key* (1844). There is a black chalk drawing by Doyle relating to this print in the BM, Department of Prints and Drawings, 1882, 1209.565.

15.6 Phiz (Hablôt Knight Browne) © the British Library Board.
Charles Dickens, *Master Humphrey's clock*, 3 (1841), p. 28/C194.b.III.

Repeal has been to Mr O'Connell a grand sum in addition. But HB is prophetic – he has sketched the slate, in fragments on the floor; an intimation that when Repeal has done its duty for him who lives and thrives by the word, it will be thrown down like a broken toy and be no more thought of.[41]

An unattractive intransigence permeates the *Barnaby Rudge* print in that the raven (or Lord John Russell) has been taught, as in Dickens' novel, to endlessly call out 'Never say die, Never say die, Hurrah!' Similarly, a self-centred, child-like stubbornness pervades Doyle's representation of O'Connell. Despite O'Connell's original advocacy of non-violence, Britain feared that the year of repeal would end in bloodshed, as if the Irish leader was resolutely ignoring the rule of law. An additional explanation of O'Connell's sulky expression in the print and the broken slate marked 'REPEAL' that lies on the floor may be the fact that after that great summer of huge public assemblies, the last gathering to be held at Clontarf on the outskirts of Dublin on 8 October was banned at the eleventh hour by Dublin Castle.[42]

The aggressive tone that enters Doyle's prints with these later O'Connell satires of the 1840s is one that is ambivalent in its relationship with its target. In his letter to Robert Peel written in 1842, Doyle claimed that his prints were 'an agent of some little influence …', although he had 'scrupulously avoid[ed] all indelicacy, private

41 McLean, *An illustrative key* (1844), p. 189.   **42** MacDonagh, *O'Connell*, pp 522–4.

15.7 John Doyle, *The naughty boy*, lithograph, 1843 (the Tabley Collection and the British Cartoon Library, University of Kent).

scandal and party bitterness'. The work 'should ... amuse [and] be directed to the furtherance of some intelligible public object, and that by such means as would by fair analogy be considered legitimate in political warfare'. In this letter to Peel, Doyle went on to discuss the 'mis-guidance of O'Connell', saying that once the Catholic relief bill had been passed, 'Catholics were bound in honour, if not in conscience, to abstain from all attacks upon the temporalities' of the Anglican Church in Ireland.[43]

Doyle saw his prints, as he said in his letter to Peel, as potential political weapons. And yet it was an art-form that had clear elitist connotations. Doyle's audience was expected to instantly grasp the artistic or literary allusions and such an expectation instantly limited its appeal to a well-educated clientele.[44] Given the renown of his

---

43 BL, Peel Papers, Add. MS 40497, Doyle to Peel, 22 Jan. 1842, fos 314, 316; also McCord, p. 69. For an account of an Irish Tory viewpoint at this time, see Joseph Spence, 'Isaac Butt, Irish nationality and the conditional defence of the Union, 1833–70' in George Boyce and Alan O'Day (eds), *Defenders of the union: a survey of British and Irish Unionism since 1801* (London, 2001), pp 65–89. **44** Fox, *Graphic journalism*, pp 94–5. For more on the elite audience for political prints, see Eirwen E.C. Nicholson, 'English political prints *ca.*1640–

15.8 Edwin Landseer, *A naughty child*, oil on millboard, 38.1x27.9cm, 1834 (courtesy of the Victoria & Albert Museum, London).

visual and literary sources and the celebrity of his political actors and the frequency with which publications like *The Times* praised Doyle's productions, these prints offer a triangular connection between, firstly, the public art exhibition or the popular tale or novel, secondly, the commercially orientated print-market for political satire and, finally, the printed word in newspapers. The public impact of Doyle's 'parodistic appropriations', as Benjamin Buchloh has called such artistic mechanisms,[45] involved the use of acclaimed paintings on show at recent Royal Academy exhibitions (Landseer's *A Jack in office* (1833) and *A naughty child* (1834)), the on-going popularity of such tales as 'Little Red-Riding Hood' and the publication of Dickens' *Barnaby*

Rudge (1841) combined with constant comment on these adaptations and others in *The Times*.

Like Doyle's prints of the 1830s and 1840s, visual political satire in our own day can also be seen as part of a connection between the world of fine art and the greater possibilities of contemporary media. Over the years, the satirist Steve Bell has produced a host of political parodies in the *Guardian* newspaper that echo famous paintings. For example, Michelangelo's fresco of the creation of Adam in the Sistine Chapel, as in *… and Bush created democracy* (2005), or some years earlier Jacques Louis David's famous painting of Napoleon, as in *Blair crossing the Alps* (2000).

What this essay has tried to do is track how Doyle used visual parodies of contemporary art, literature and fairy tales to comment upon the figure of O'Connell in the 1830s and early 1840s. As the dominant Irish political figure in both Ireland and Britain during these years, his appearance in visual satires by such a major London-based caricaturist as John Doyle gives us access to metropolitan attitudes surrounding such an important Irish figure. Parody helped HB to convey a move from toleration to dissatisfaction within the Westminster elite towards their Irish co-parliamentarian, and it helps us to gauge how the visualization of pre-existing narratives (be they from the world of art or from the world of story) can reflect political opinion.

'A *rara avis*': Jeremiah Jordan, Methodist and Nationalist MP

NICOLA K. MORRIS

Elites in nineteenth-century Ireland took many forms: this essay focuses on the polit-ical and religious through the career of Jeremiah Jordan, MP and Methodist. Jordan was elected as Nationalist MP for the constituencies of West Clare, South Meath and South Fermanagh successively, making him one of the most prominent Methodists in the public sphere between his first election in 1885 and his death in 1911. This is all the more remarkable because in 1885 there were less than 25,000 active Methodists in Ireland,[1] and only three other Irish Methodists were elected to the House of Commons in this period, all of whom served less than a decade. Jordan was also an accredited Methodist local preacher, a position recognized by the national church as entitling him to lead public worship, attend circuit leaders' meetings and discipline the faithful.

A merchant of Enniskillen, Jordan rose to prominence in Fermanagh local poli-tics in the early 1880s during the Land War and entered the national political arena in 1885 as one of the new cohort of eighty-six Nationalist MPs returned at the general election of that year.[2] He captured the seat of West Clare with the substan-tial margin of 6,763 votes to 289, despite being both staunchly Protestant and a native of Co. Fermanagh.[3] A faithful Methodist, a Temperance campaigner, Sunday school teacher and local preacher, throughout his career, Jordan maintained a public commitment to the application of his religious principles to his political life. His loyalty to his church was, however, contested by his fellow Irish Methodists, with suggestions that he was a 'Protestant renegade'.[4] This resulted in an uneasy and often acrimonious relationship between Jordan and the national Irish Methodist elite regarding the extent to which he represented the Methodists of Ireland, given that he was the sole member of their church to be elected to national political office. The notoriety associated with public office meant that (as with O'Connell in the previous

---

1 *Wesleyan Methodist conference minutes of Ireland, 1885.* This figure included only those with full membership, not the total that attended Methodist worship. 2 Frank Thompson, 'The Land War in County Fermanagh' in E.M. Murphy and W.J. Roulston (eds), *Fermanagh: history and society* (Dublin, 2004), p. 224; B.M. Walker, *Parliamentary election results in Ireland, 1801–1922* (Dublin, 1978). For further details regarding Jordan's contribution to Fermanagh politics, see Richard McMinn, Éamon Phoenix and Joanne Beggs, 'Jeremiah Jordan MP (1830–1911): Protestant home ruler or "Protestant renegade"?', *Irish Historical Studies*, 36 (2009), 349–67. 3 Kieran Sheedy, *The Clare elections* (Dublin, 1993), p. 275. 4 See McMinn, Phoenix and Beggs, 'Jeremiah Jordan MP'.

essay) an added significance was placed upon Jordan's public persona and reputation by fellow members of his minority sect. This essay will explore how this relationship developed over the course of Jordan's parliamentary career, from his first election in 1885, through to his death in 1911, and will consider whether Jordan did indeed apply Methodist principles, acceptable to the wider church, to the political issues of his parliamentary career.

The 1885 general election is one of particular note, being the first to be fought after the franchise reforms of 1884–5, which tripled the Irish electorate.[5] The priority of the Irish Methodist leadership became to educate new electors among their congregations as to the exercise of conscientious citizenship, particularly with regard to morality in public life. Methodist electors were advised to eschew simple party loyalty and rather assess a candidate's 'attitude to moral questions' before casting their vote and return a 'God-fearing, pure-living Christian man' to represent them.[6] The Belfast-published, quasi-official, Methodist journal, the *Christian Advocate*, highlighted a number of 'moral' issues that were expected to come before the next parliament; principally, education, control of the liquor traffic and repeal of the Contagious Diseases Acts.[7] The *Advocate* was, however, unhappy that Methodism was politically undistinguished, verging on being completely anonymous during the election campaign. In fact, the *Advocate* was able to identify only one Methodist candidate, Thomas Shillington, the Liberal party nominee for North Armagh. Shillington espoused a radical political programme, supporting land reform and broad democratic changes, including female suffrage. Nevertheless, the *Advocate* considered Shillington to be a 'safe pair of hands' on the key 'moral' questions, and the newspaper was thus happy to give his (unsuccessful) campaign prominent coverage and support. By contrast, the *Advocate* made no mention of Jordan's campaign in West Clare, nor indeed his Methodist affiliation, until after the result had been declared.

Jordan's selection for the safe Nationalist seat of West Clare, with the support of the local Catholic clergy, meant that despite his northern Protestant credentials, his election was secured easily with a majority of over 6,000, with only a minimal campaign.[8] The negligible canvass may explain why his candidature was overlooked by the *Christian Advocate*, although it seems improbable that they were completely unaware of his nomination. Jordan was a prominent political figure in Fermanagh, where he had been a leading proponent of the Land War, and was widely credited with securing the support of many Protestant tenant farmers for the Land League prior to the Land Act of 1881.[9] In 1885, Jordan's first preference was to continue his political association with Fermanagh, and unsuccessfully attempted secure nomination for one of the county's two parliamentary seats.[10] Instead, Jordan accepted the

5 The total Irish electorate rose to 728,000: K.T. Hoppen, *Elections, politics and society in Ireland, 1832–1885* (Oxford, 1984), pp 87–8; Jonathan Bardon, *A history of Ulster* (rev. ed., Belfast, 2001), p. 374. **6** William Arthur to John Wallen Jr, 21 Nov. 1885 (Methodist Church Archives, John Rylands Library, Manchester, PLP.P. 2.61·4) and *Christian Advocate*, 27 Nov. 1885. **7** *Christian Advocate*, 27 Nov. 1885. **8** Sheedy, *The Clare elections*, pp 274–5. **9** Thompson, 'The Land War in Country Fermanagh', pp 294–5, 299. **10** *Freeman's*

nomination for West Clare, where his acceptance was lauded by Timothy Healy as a symbol that a candidate's Nationalism was the only credential that mattered, 'not creed nor class'.[11]

As a nominee, Jordan fulfilled many of the criteria laid down by the *Christian Advocate* for political candidates: he was a committed life-long Methodist; an ardent Temperance campaigner in favour of stricter control of the drink trade; favoured high standards of probity in public life; and was interested in both education and broad, democratic reforms. The issue-driven, non-party political approach supposedly followed by the *Advocate*, however, was apparently only applied to 'respectable' political parties and their candidates, not associates of the National League or their political representatives in the Irish Parliamentary Party. Thus, their first substantive comment on Jeremiah Jordan's political campaign came after his successful election on 18 December, when he was denounced for associating 'with a band of men who ignore the moral law and trample underfoot the laws of the land'. One correspondent of the journal also suggested that because of his politics he had forfeited the right to call himself a Methodist, despite previously having held office within the Methodist Church.[12]

This attack on Jordan provoked a flurry of correspondence in the denominational press early in 1886. The London-published voice of English Methodism, the *Methodist Times*, immediately leapt to his aid, permitting Jordan to publish a lengthy defence of his political opinions under the title 'An Irish Methodist's reasons for supporting Home Rule', a move that was decried as 'wanton meddling' by the *Advocate*.[13] In his article, Jordan was anxious to accentuate his Methodist credentials, emphasizing that he was an 'Irish Wesleyan Methodist of the third generation … trained in the principles of Protestant Nonconformity'. Directly appealing to the British Methodist audience, he accentuated his opposition to the monopolies of the aristocracy and his long-standing support for Gladstonian Liberalism, and highlighted the campaigns supported by British Nonconformists as a significant stage in his development as a Nationalist.[14] Jordan also stressed the intolerance of the local Protestant population of Fermanagh, stating that, because of his political opinions, his 'life and property were endangered, and … [his] business boycotted … almost to ruin'. Moreover, he claimed that within Methodism 'to support a Liberal candidate and policy was disqualification for Church office', as it was taken as an indication that the individual was on an inevitable slide towards Catholicism. Given the *Advocate's* support for the radical Liberal Methodist candidate, Shillington, in the election,

---

Journal, 21 Oct. 1885. **11** Ibid., 10 Nov. 1885. **12** *Christian Advocate*, 18 Dec. 1885.
13 *Methodist Times*, 14 Jan. 1886. **14** Ibid. Most notably, British nonconformists had been appalled by atrocities being committed by Turkish authorities against Bulgarian Orthodox Christians. Disraeli's government leant towards supporting Turkey against Russian ambitions, whereas Gladstone reacted by speaking out against Turkish power in Bulgaria, framing the arguments in clear moral terms, and rapidly becoming the champion of the nonconformists: see R.T. Shannon, *Gladstone and the Bulgarian agitation, 1876* (London, 1963), p. 159.

Jordan's claims appear somewhat overstated, conflating his support for Gladstonian policies with his Nationalism. However, the case of Jordan's property being vandalized had previously been raised in parliament by Timothy Healy in 1884. He had questioned the lack of action taken by local Church of Ireland magistrates when a Nationalist was targeted, while they were keen to respond when a Nationalist was the perpetrator.[15]

The burgeoning conflict between Jordan and the Irish Methodist elite was also taken up by the *Freeman's Journal*, who cited the support of the *Methodist Times* for Jordan as evidence that the true views of Methodists were being under-represented by a bigoted Irish denominational press. This was angrily refuted by correspondence to the *Freeman* by a fourth-generation Irish Methodist, Matthew Tobias, who decried the *Methodist Times* and Jordan as both radical and unrepresentative of Methodism.[16] This viewpoint was supported by the news that anti-Home Rule resolutions had been passed by the Committee of Privileges, the governing body of Methodism, confirming the commitment of the denomination to the Union.[17] This move proved controversial with the denomination, as it was seen to be breaking the Wesleyan convention that official organs of the Church should not comment publicly on political issues.[18] During the election campaign, for example, the *Christian Advocate* had been clear to distinguish between 'moral' issues that it was appropriate to comment on, and 'political', especially party political issues, on which it remained neutral. Opinion divided sharply as to which of these categories Home Rule belonged to. Many opponents of Home Rule claimed that it was inherently a moral issue, because a Catholic-dominated legislature would have a significant impact on education and religious tolerance, while others maintained that as a proposed constitutional change, Home Rule was fundamentally a political issue on which Methodism should be officially neutral.

The unprecedented public statement opposing Home Rule by the Committee of Privileges was taken by Methodists with nationalist sympathies as an indication that dissenting opinions were being actively suppressed within the denomination. Consequently, Jordan became the focus for Methodists across Ireland who harboured nationalist sympathies.[19] In their letters to Jordan, they criticized the *Christian Advocate* for rejecting for publication pro-Home Rule correspondence, while

15 *Hansard 3*, cclxxxiv, 1492 (20 Feb. 1884). **16** *Freeman's Journal*, 16 Jan. 1886. **17** *Methodist Times*, 21 Jan. 1886 and *Christian Advocate*, 22 Jan. 1886. **18** For a more detailed discussion of this point, see N.K. Morris, 'Methodist politics in Ireland, 1861–1914' (PhD, University of Liverpool, 2007). **19** It is difficult to accurately assess the number of Methodists that supported Home Rule in 1886. At the annual conference, 137 out of 159 delegates (86%) supported resolutions opposing Home Rule. Of the 22 who voted against the resolutions, only around 10 can be assumed to have supported Home Rule, the others believed that the Methodist Church should not comment officially on political matters. While the conference only included the ministers and a limited number of lay delegates, it appears likely that the small proportion supporting Home Rule reflected Methodist political opinion around the country. *Wesleyan Methodist conference minutes of Ireland, 1886.*

commending Jordan for his stand.[20] Praise was particularly forthcoming for Jordan's maiden speech in the House of Commons during the debate of the Home Rule Bill, commending him for answering the 'rabid Orange members' and confronting 'northern prejudices'.[21] Jordan was careful to acknowledge the reciprocal relationship he had with these correspondents, testifying in parliament that he held 'letters in my pocket from Methodist people in different parts of Ireland' who favoured Home Rule.[22] This gave apparent potency to his argument that he was a true representative of Irish Methodism, despite the boycotting campaign against him by northern Protestants. Jordan was also keen to emphasize the support for Home Rule by English Methodists, particularly the newspaper the *Methodist Times* and its editor, the Revd Hugh Price Hughes, implying that the statements of the Methodist elite in Ireland were not representative of Methodism as a whole.[23]

Jordan's membership of the Irish Parliamentary Party and his overt support for the principle of Home Rule alienated the vast majority of Irish Methodists. They strongly objected to him framing his politics as an outworking of his religious convictions, rooted in his upbringing in Fermanagh. Antipathy to the Irish Parliamentary Party appears to have blinded the Irish Methodist elite to the other aspects of Jordan's politics that were more in line with their own thinking. He was assiduous in attending to constituency affairs in parliament, as well as applying his knowledge of Co. Fermanagh to good effect. In his first year, he raised many questions regarding improvement works for Cos Clare and Fermanagh, particularly harbours and waterways.[24] He also demonstrated concern for the rule of law in the country and fair treatment for farmers and tenants by officers of the law and local boards of guardians.[25] Jordan's moderate stance on these issues was entirely in keeping with both his previous political aims and the political objectives outlined by the *Advocate* for the good governance of the country.

In addition, Jordan actively pursued the 'moral' issues highlighted by the *Christian Advocate* during the election campaign. He was a strong advocate of more stringent controls on drink traffic, consistently supporting legislation to control the sale of intoxicating liquor in Ireland. Moreover, he regularly brought forward bills to that effect jointly with both Nationalist and Unionist MPs – including the only other Irish Methodist MP elected in 1885, the Independent Orangeman, E.S.W. de Cobain.[26] Jordan was uncompromising in his support for Temperance and

---

20 A. Duncan to Jordan, 16 Dec. 1885. **21** G. McNeal to Jordan, 11 June 1886; S.C. McElroy to Jordan, 5 May 1886, PRONI D2073/2/1. **22** *Hansard 3*, cccv, 660 (10 May 1886). **23** Ibid. **24** See, for example, *Hansard 3*, ccciii, 443 (11 Mar. 1886); *Hansard 3*, cccviii, 784 (30 Aug. 1886); *Hansard 3*, cccviii, 1477 (7 Sept. 1886); *Hansard 3*, cccix, 22–3 (10 Sept. 1886). **25** See, for example, *Hansard 3*, ccciii, 447–8 (11 Mar. 1886); *Hansard 3*, cccviii, 1076 (2 Sept. 1886); *Hansard 3*, cccviii, 1728–9 (9 Sept. 1886); *Hansard 3*, cccix, 680–4 (16 Sept. 1886); *Hansard 3*, cccix, 1091–2 (21 Sept. 1886). **26** See, for example, *Sale of liquors on Sunday (Ireland) Act (1878)*, *1878*, H.C. 1888 (86) vi, 531; *Liquor traffic local veto (Ireland)*, 1888 (25) III, 715; *Intoxicating liquors (Ireland)*, 1889 (18) iii, 327; *Sale of intoxicating liquors (Ireland)*, 1894 (83) viii, 179 and *Intoxicating liquors local veto (Ireland)*, 1900 (55) ii, 519. Temperance was one issue where Irish politicians of all parties were prepared to cooperate.

throughout his career persisted in promoting increased control of the drink trade, through restricting liquor licences, local veto and a ban on Sunday sales. Moreover, Jordan persevered with this advocacy into the twentieth century, when Temperance had ceased to be politically expedient for the wider party.[27]

Jordan was also a keen advocate of education, another key issue highlighted by the *Advocate* and one with the capacity to bring him into conflict with both the Methodist and nationalist elites. Jordan was a keen advocate of the national schools, a system that was waning in popularity among his Catholic colleagues. He sponsored parliamentary bills to aid the acquisition of land for building national schools and residential properties for school teachers, as well as regularly raising questions regarding children apparently refused entry to national schools, the closure of schools, and the condition of teachers.[28] He did not publicly advocate Methodist education policy in parliament, however, as it favoured non-denominational schooling, a position that would run contrary to the official Irish Parliamentary Party line of support for denominational education. Nevertheless, he clearly believed that all should have the opportunity to receive an education in an establishment that would not offend their religious sensibilities, and campaigned on that basis.

This issue again came to the fore over the question of university provision for Ireland, where Jordan found himself at odds with both the Methodist elite and his parliamentary colleagues. In contrast to Methodists in both Ireland and Britain who opposed the creation of a Catholic university in Ireland, Jordan supported Catholics in 'their earnest efforts to obtain university education through a medium they can approve of'.[29] In pursuance of this, Jordan advocated negotiating with the sitting Conservative government to formulate a satisfactory solution. He believed this course of action would have the dual benefits of providing higher education acceptable to the majority, and using the Tory-led imperial parliament to negotiate an inflammatory issue helping to avert accusations of endowing Catholicism from Ulster Conservatives and Orangemen and incline them more towards Home Rule.[30] This stance conflicted with the views of many within the Irish Parliamentary Party who believed that the single plank of their platform should be Home Rule, with all other issues relegated and non-negotiable until the national question had been settled.[31] This provoked a public disagreement with Michael Davitt in the pages of the *Freeman's Journal*, in which Davitt accused Jordan of pandering to a 'querulous

There is otherwise little evidence that Jordan and Cobain had much interaction, and Jordan made no public comment when Cobain was expelled from parliament in 1892 for 'acts of gross indecency' (*Report of warrant for the arrest of E.S.W. De Cobain MP for East Belfast*, H.C. 1890–1 (253)). **27** See Elizabeth Malcolm, 'Temperance and Irish Nationalism' in F.S.L. Lyons and R.A.J. Hawkins (eds), *Ireland under the Union: varieties of tension: essays in honour of T.W. Moody* (Oxford, 1980), p. 109. **28** *Freeman's Journal*, 23 Jan. 1886; *Hansard 3*, cccix, 964 (20 Sept. 1886); *Hansard 3*, cccxlv, 344–5 (9 June 1890); *Hansard 4*, xcix, 64–5 (8 Aug. 1904) and *Hansard 4*, cxcvii, 1050 (30 Dec. 1908). **29** *Wesleyan Methodist conference minutes of Ireland, 1898, 1899* and *Hansard 4*, lxxiii, 524 (23 June 1899). **30** *Freeman's Journal*, 12 Sept. 1899. **31** *Hansard 4*, lxxiii, 458–66 (23 June 1899).

and unreasonable Protestantism' and undermining the authority of a future Dublin parliament by removing from its remit any issue that might prove contentious.[32] Jordan objected to these accusations, however, arguing that any measure that promoted fair access to education and avoided sectarian conflict should be pursued – demonstrating that he was at heart interested in providing practical ameliorative solutions to Ireland's problems, whatever form they might take.

Despite clearly promoting Methodist political principles, Jordan's position of these issues did not gain him any credit with his Irish co-religionists. The *Advocate* ignored his progress, except to occasionally denounce his politics and cast doubt on his commitment to Methodism.[33] British Methodists were more sympathetic to the claims of Ireland to Home Rule, positively associating it with broader democratic trends, and they were thus were more welcoming of his politics. A significant number of British Methodists sitting in the House of Commons favoured Home Rule, as did the influential journal the *Methodist Times*.[34] Consequently, throughout his parliamentary career, Jordan was able to build and maintain strong relationships with influential British Methodists, notably the Revd Hugh Price Hughes, editor of the *Methodist Times*. Also among Jordan's friends were the McArthur family, Methodists originally from west Ulster, three members of which represented English constituencies in the Liberal interest between 1868 and 1908.

Arguably the defining moment of Jordan's political career, when both his religious and his political loyalties were severely tested, came in November 1890 with the revelations concerning Parnell publicized by the O'Shea divorce case. Jordan's British Methodist friends had for a number of years been running a campaign through the *Methodist Times* for high moral standards in public life, while simultaneously supporting Home Rule.[35] Parnell's behaviour placed this support in jeopardy, as they were not prepared to support the policies or party of a man that had demonstrated such serious moral failings. The reaction of the *Methodist Times* to the court hearing of 15–17 November 1890 was immediate and damning of the Irish leader. On 20 November, the journal declared that '[o]f course Mr Parnell must go', before apologizing to its readers that circumstances required it to make such an obvious statement.[36] The newspaper maintained that its previous espousal of Home Rule and support for Parnell over the Pigott forgeries vindicated its 'right to speak as friends

32 *Freeman's Journal*, 13 Sept. 1899.   **33** See for example, *Christian Advocate*, 19 Aug. 1892.
34 Following the second reading of the Government of Ireland Bill, in addition to Jeremiah Jordan, the *Christian Advocate* identified 10 English Wesleyan Methodists, 5 (English) Primitive Methodists, and 1 member of the Methodist Free Church who had voted in favour of Home Rule. Only 4 Wesleyan Methodists voted against Home Rule, while Cozen-Hardy from the Methodist Free Church abstained: *Christian Advocate*, 11 June 1886.
35 Hughes was a senior member of the Methodist Conference's Committee for Social Purity and had supported the *Pall Mall Gazette* in forcing Sir Charles Dilke from office over his involvement in the Crawford divorce case in 1885: *Methodist Times*, 18 Feb. 1886; 17 June 1886; Christopher Oldstone-Moore, *Hugh Price Hughes: founder of a new Methodism, conscience of a new nonconformity* (Cardiff, 1999), pp 152–4.   **36** *Methodist Times*, 20 Nov. 1890.

of the Irish people' and that its criticisms of Parnell were in no way born of anti-Irish feeling.[37] It was inconceivable to Hughes that a man who was immoral in his personal life was fit to lead a party or a nation, declaring that 'what is morally wrong can never be politically right'.[38] Hughes further insisted that

> if the Irish race deliberately select as their representative an adulterer of Mr Parnell's type, they are as incapable of self-government as their bitterest enemies have asserted. So obscene a race as in those circumstances they would prove themselves to be would obviously be unfit for anything except a military despotism.[39]

This vicious admonition set the tone of the coverage that journal gave to the crisis. While the Methodist press in Belfast quoted Hughes' statements with glee, they caused much anger in Nationalist circles, where they were perceived as demonstrating anti-Irish sentiment.[40] The stinging riposte of the *Freeman's Journal* read 'if the Irish people abandoned Mr Parnell to follow the Reverend Hugh Price Hughes, a military despotism would be 10,000 times too good for them'.[41] Hughes' represented his statements as an ultimatum to the 'Irish race': demanding that they choose between the continued leadership of Parnell and the support of British nonconformists for the Nationalist cause. While the statements of a Methodist minister in London may have had little direct impact on the views of the Irish people, many were nevertheless aware of the need for the support of British nonconformity for Home Rule if the Gladstonian plan was to successfully pass through the Houses of Parliament.

The beginning of the new parliamentary session hastened the political climax of the crisis, pushing MPs, including Jordan, to take a public stand on the issue of Parnell's continuing leadership. Aware of the increasing opposition among nonconformists, Gladstone met with Justin McCarthy on 24 November to indicate that while he still supported Home Rule, should Parnell remain as leader, the electoral success of the Liberal Party would be put in jeopardy, and furthermore his retention of the Liberal leadership would be rendered 'almost a nullity'.[42] McCarthy was thus charged with representing the views of Gladstone to his own party leader, and appears to have indicated to Parnell that the Liberal leader would 'still fight our cause'.[43] Nevertheless, when the Irish Parliamentary Party met in Committee Room 15 on 25 November to elect their sessional chairman, Parnell received significant support from his colleagues. The sense that British Methodism was dictating the terms of the political debate was unacceptable, and Dr J.E. Kenny explained to Archbishop Walsh that the party would unanimously re-elect Parnell, leaving the

---

37 Ibid., 27 Nov. 1890. **38** Ibid. **39** Ibid., 20 Nov. 1890. **40** *Christian Advocate*, 28 Nov. 1890; *Freeman's Journal*, 24 Nov. 1890. **41** *Freeman's Journal*, 21 Nov. 1890. **42** *Times*, 26 Nov. 1890. **43** Eugene Doyle, *Justin McCarthy* (Dublin, 1996), p. 37 and Christopher Oldstone-Moore, 'The fall of Parnell: Hugh Price Hughes and the nonconformist conscience', *Eire-Ireland*, 30:4 (1996), 94–110 at 102.

decision entirely in his hands.[44] This was both a demonstration of the personal loyalty Parnell commanded and an indication that the party was determined not to be dictated to by outside forces, whether they be the Catholic hierarchy, British Methodism or the Liberal Party. Despite Davitt having published an article critical of Parnell on 20 November, accounts of the meeting note Jordan as the only dissenting voice, describing him as an 'obscure and habitually unassertive member of the party'.[45] Jordan was clearly sensitive to the increasingly vociferous opposition to Parnell among British Methodists, and chose to convey the advantages of Parnell standing down, in order that pressure for Home Rule could be maintained with the support of British nonconformity within the Liberal party. Donal Sullivan, writing to his nephew Tim Healy, recalled that Jordan 'did his work creditably and *most feelingly*' in calling for Parnell to retire, if only temporarily, but that the suggestion was 'received in silence'.[46] Jordan was thus the first to break ranks within the party, acting according to his principles and the desire to see Home Rule succeed.

This private advocacy of retirement for Parnell contrasted markedly with Jordan's public support for his leader. Writing in the *Methodist Times* on 27 November in the wake of Parnell's re-election as leader of the Irish Parliamentary Party, Jordan suggested that the journal had been 'unduly severe' in its criticism of the party and had failed to comprehend the extent of the 'natural homage' that was felt towards Parnell.[47] Hughes, however, dismissed these criticisms, maintaining that he had alluded to a hypothetical situation and referred to the 'proverbial chastity of the Irish people', believing that they would not accept a notorious adulterer as leader. Nevertheless, the *Methodist Times* declared that by re-electing Parnell as leader of the party, the Irish MPs had 'placed Parnellism outside the pale of Christian civilisation' and expressed the hope that Jordan and all the 'respectable members' of the party would rally around Michael Davitt: the only prominent nationalist to have publicly called for Parnell's resignation.[48]

As the political tide began to turn against Parnell, Jordan became more determined that the chairman should resign, a position contrary to that of a majority of his Nationalist constituents.[49] However, Jordan gained no credit for this position among Methodists in Ireland. The Belfast *Christian Advocate* considered the revelations about Parnell vindication for their existing opposition to Nationalism. The *Advocate* maintained that the Irish people had for many years 'blindly' followed nationalist leaders without regard for their personal integrity, resulting in clearly immoral policies and tactics. One correspondent of the journal, Thomas Moran of Enniskillen, suggested that it was inconsistent of Jordan and British Methodists to condemn Parnell for breaking the seventh commandment regarding adultery, when

44 Emmet Larkin, 'The Roman Catholic hierarchy and the fall of Parnell', *Victorian Studies*, 4:4 (1961), 315–36 at 322.   **45** *Labour World*, 19 Nov. 1885; Frank Callanan, *The Parnell split, 1890–1* (Cork, 1992), p. 14; F.S.L. Lyons, *Charles Stewart Parnell* (London, 1977), p. 497. **46** T.M. Healy, *Letters and leaders of my day* (London, 1928), i, pp 322–3.   **47** *Methodist Times*, 27 Nov. 1890.   **48** Ibid.; *Freeman's Journal*, 21 Nov. 1890; Callanan, *The Parnell split*, p. 12. **49** *Freeman's Journal*, 4 and 5 Dec. 1890; Sheedy, *The Clare elections*, pp 286–9.

it was common knowledge across Ireland that the Irish leader had frequently incited and applauded the breaking of commandments six and eight (those forbidding murder and theft).[50] Irish Methodists thus perceived that their Nationalist brethren at home and in England were both selective in their use of scripture and purposely ill-informed regarding the tactics of the Nationalist movement in Ireland. Moreover, at the general election of 1892, the *Christian Advocate* was still openly doubting Jordan's Methodist affiliation, claiming that 'if he be a Methodist, we find it difficult, indeed impossible, to understand how for seven years he has managed to associate, and apparently feel at home with that dreadful "Irish Party"'.[51]

Jordan's stance during the divorce crisis was indicative of his whole political career. His principled stand, stemming from his religious convictions, gained him no credit with the Methodist elite of Ireland, who continued to believe that he applied his ethics only selectively. While his calls for Parnell to resign lost him the support of his Clare constituents, who perceived him as siding with perfidious English noncon-formists against their great Irish leader. Jordan, however, refused to bow to pressure, and, as with his parliamentary contributions, pursued a consistent and principled line. Knowing that he had lost the confidence of a majority of the Clare electors, at the 1892 general election he withdrew from Clare and opted instead to contest the seat for North Fermanagh, a constituency with a small Unionist majority. Jordan's local profile ensured that the contest in Fermanagh was close, although much of his appeal to the Protestant tenantry was nullified by the opposition candidate, R.M. Dane, who stressed to Methodist voters the need for Protestant unity and espoused both Temperance and compulsory purchase.[52] Jordan consequently lost the Fermanagh contest, but was returned the following year for South Meath. At the next general election in 1895, Jordan finally achieved his long-term ambition to represent his home county, being returned for the southern division, where he was able to success-fully appeal to both Catholic and Protestant voters.[53] Jordan represented this constituency until his retirement in 1911, standing unopposed in 1906.

Despite sitting for parliament nearly continuously between 1885 and 1910 (with a brief gap 1892–3), Jordan never sought nor achieved status as a populist politician. His strength of mind nevertheless earned him a measure of esteem within the party, and ensured his nomination at parliamentary elections until his retirement a year before his death in December 1911. Jordan played a prominent role in the unity debates held within the Irish Party in 1899–1900, when he was nominated to repre-sent 'the common sense of the party' in the negotiations with the Parnellites.[54] Throughout his career, Jordan demonstrated that he was never prepared to sacrifice his principles on the altar of political expediency; and eventually this stubborn refusal to bow to pressure gained him the respect of his fellow Methodists. Jordan finally

50 *Christian Advocate*, 28 Nov. 1890. **51** Ibid., 19 Aug. 1892. **52** B.E. Barton, 'The origins and development of Unionism in Fermanagh' in Murphy and Roulston (eds), *Fermanagh, history and society*, p. 313. **53** Ibid., p. 314. **54** *Freeman's Journal*, 5 Apr. 1899; F.S.L. Lyons, *The Irish parliamentary party* (London, 1951), pp 83–5.

retired from parliament at the December election of 1910, citing ill health, and died in December the following year. Despite the country preparing for battle over the Third Home Rule Bill, the announcement of his death in the *Christian Advocate* was glowing in its testimony, describing the regular visits he received from the Methodist ministers of Enniskillen in his last illness and recalling his career as 'an ardent temperance reformer, and a loyal Methodist. He was also a kind friend, and those who knew him best believed most thoroughly in his sincerity and faithfulness'.[55] While the obituary glossed over his political career, its recognition of Jordan's strong religious principles was a far cry from their previous disavowal his Methodist loyalties. The journal also carried a lengthy account of Jordan's funeral and the address delivered by the local Methodist minister. At his death, Jordan was recognized as a '[s]traightforward to the last degree … a man of strict integrity'.[56] The eulogy was clear in recognizing the difficult path that Jordan had chosen to walk, stating that:

> It is well known that in public questions his judgement often differed widely from that of the majority of his co-religionists. His religious convictions, on the other hand, differed from those with whom he associated in politics. Those who knew him best, however, can testify that he never compromised the church to which he belonged on the one hand, or his political party on the other.

This demonstrated that by 1912 the Methodist elite of Ireland recognized Jordan as one of their own, who had faithfully implemented his faith throughout his political career. While they could not entirely approve of his activities as part of the constitutional Nationalist elite of Ireland, they had at least partially reconciled themselves to political diversity within the Church, recognizing that Jordan was indeed 'a *rara avis*, but of course perfectly entitled to his opinion'.[57]

---

55 *Christian Advocate*, 5 Jan. 1912.   56 Ibid., 12 Jan. 1912.   57 Ibid., 22 Jan. 1886.

The Irish revival, elite competition and the First World War

JOHN HUTCHINSON

The study of nationalist movements has been largely the analysis of elites and counter-elites and their ideological struggles to win a popular following. This is but a partial perspective and one now rightly under challenge.[1] But it shaped the framework of my book on Irish nationalism, *The dynamics of cultural nationalism: the Gaelic Revival and the creation of the Irish nation-state*, now twenty-five years old.[2] The editor of this collection has asked to me review its claims in the light of recent scholarship on Irish history and also to discuss how elites are being analysed in the broader scholarship on nationalism. I will first explain the aims and arguments of my study, situating it within the nationalism scholarship of the time. I will then examine more recent Irish historical studies, notably those of Senia Pašeta[3] and Fergus Campbell.[4] Finally, in the light of my current research, I will briefly argue for the neglected centrality of war for understanding crucial developments in Irish nationalist politics.

AIMS OF *THE DYNAMICS OF CULTURAL NATIONALISM*

My book is a work of historical sociology. After finishing an undergraduate degree in history, I had become interested in the origins and social significance of Irish cultural revival of the late nineteenth century, but felt I lacked the conceptual tools with which to tackle the topic. When reading in the then undeveloped field of nationalism research, I came across *Theories of nationalism* by the sociologist Anthony D. Smith.[5] I was impressed by his final chapter, where Smith put forward a set of hypotheses about the origins of nationalist movements which I thought offered a promising avenue for historical research. I applied to do a PhD under his supervision in the sociology department at the London School of Economics, and out of this came my book.

Although my specific topic was the role of cultural nationalist movements in modern Ireland, I was also attempting to make a general contribution to the schol-

---

1 Maarten Van Ginderachter and Marnix Beyen (eds), *Nationhood from below: Europe in the long nineteenth century* (Basingstoke, 2012). **2** John Hutchinson, *The dynamics of cultural nationalism: the Gaelic revival and the creation of the Irish nation-state* (London, 1987). **3** Senia Pašeta, *Before the revolution; nationalism, social change and Ireland's Catholic elite, 1879–1922* (Cork, 1999). **4** Fergus Campbell, *The Irish establishment, 1879–1914* (Oxford, 2009) **5** A.D. Smith, *Theories of nationalism* (London, 1971).

arship on nationalism, in which nationalism is usually conceived of as a state-oriented political project. There was and still is much less scholarly focus on nationalists whose primary aim is the formation of national *communities*. In my book, I argued that we need to give more attention to cultural nationalist movements that precede or accompany state-oriented nationalisms. These movements might arise from small circles of intellectuals, but they could develop (as in early twentieth-century Ireland) into large-scale ethno-cultural projects promoting new historical mythologies, a redefinition of homeland (including in the Irish case a revalorizing of the west), a language and cultural revival, and an idea of nation as a network of activated self-help communities. Such activities had generally been dismissed, by scholars of nationalism, as a surrogate politics, as backward-looking and reactionary, and as transient phenomena that would fade as societies modernized. I argued that their goal was not so much political as the formation of a moral solidarity created through education into national values and promoted through the idiom of regeneration. Moreover, these movements were socially innovative, could become a platform for revolutionary action, and recurred periodically even after independence had been achieved, seeking to redefine the identity of political communities. My two central questions were:

1. How do we explain the origins of such movements?
2. What are circumstances under which they become politically salient?

In addressing the first question, I drew on Anthony Smith's dual legitimation thesis (first developed in *Theories of nationalism*), in which he argues that nationalism arises from the impact of secular modernizing states on societies regulated by religious norms and institutions.[6] Such states, promising by the application of scientific principles and modes of organization to emancipate human beings from nature, threaten the authority of religious organizations that claim to offer transcendental solutions to the problem of evil and suffering in the world. This creates what Smith calls 'a crisis of dual authority' in which first intellectuals and then, as modernization intensifies, more extensive educated strata are forced to choose between science and the idea of progress and the sense of meaning and enchantment offered by traditional religion. There are three logical solutions to this dilemma: modernist, reformist/ revivalist and neo-traditionalist – each of which tends to generate nationalism.

Modernists reject religion outright and aspire to a cosmopolitan polity, but become disillusioned when they discover that their universalist dreams are culture-bound and can be achieved only within a limited territorial state. Neo-traditionalists reject outright the secular state but learn that they can combat it only by adopting modern techniques of political mobilization, and in doing so they have to appeal to mass ethnic sentiments. Reformists see no clash between science and revelation, but in order to undermine, traditionalists have to find a concrete example in the past

6 Ibid., ch. 10.

where secular progress and the spiritual flowering of the people have been combined. This golden past gradually becomes the touchstone by which contemporary religion is judged and the project of the reformist becomes one of historical revival as a means to remake a 'fallen' present. My focus was on the third group, which included modern romantic intellectuals as well as reform-minded clergy and heterodox mystics (for example, theosophists), who created new historical and cultural visions of the nation, and to a lesser extent the disillusioned modernists who transformed these visions into socio-political programmes. Needless to say, these characterizations were ideal types. Real human beings would switch between the three positions or even combine them pragmatically in their response to problems.

For the second question, explaining why and when such visions became politically resonant, I turned to what might be dubbed the 'blocked mobility' hypothesis.[7] This proposes that innovative ideas have the potential to be politically salient when an emerging educated stratum, imbued with expectations of advancement found itself arbitrarily (in its own estimation) excluded by existing power-holders. They then may take up these ideas to find a vocation as leaders of a counter-system movement. The task was to identify whether such an aggrieved stratum existed in Ireland and if so, explain why the revivalist vision resonated with this group.

INTELLECTUAL ORIGINS OF THE IRISH REVIVAL

The central themes of my study were then questions of identity change, elite competition and problems of legitimacy. What was their application to modern Ireland? In Smith's initial model, the revivalist intellectuals had a key role, but only at the beginning when they joined with the modernists, who used their vision of a golden age to organize and inspire political campaigns with the aim of achieving an independent state. In later writings, he argued that each of the three routes could independently produce nationalism, but at first he assumed that that the revivalists would fade in significance once a political nationalism got going.

I found this had to be modified. First, in the Irish case, there were three, not one, significant cultural nationalist revivals – the late eighteenth-century antiquarian revival of Charles O'Conor and Sylvester O'Halloran that founded the Royal Irish Academy; the early to mid-nineteenth-century archaeological and philological revival associated with figures such as George Petrie, John O'Donovan and Eugene O'Curry; and the late nineteenth- and early twentieth-century Anglo-Irish literary revival of W.B. Yeats and the Gaelic Revival of Douglas Hyde and Eoin MacNeill. Each gathered adherents across the sectarian divide and had a following among reform-minded clergy, the third, in particular, among Catholic lower clergy.

---

7 This takes various forms, having its origins in Max Weber's work, but for the purposes of nationalist movements, the best formulation is in A.D. Smith, *The ethnic revival* (Cambridge, 1981), pp 116–20.

Second, there appeared to be a *recurring* and contrapuntal relationship between the cultural nationalists with their communitarian conception of the nation and the political nationalisms whose primary focus was political independence or autonomy for the nation. Indeed, cultural nationalist emerged alongside political nationalist movements, sometimes as allies, sometimes as rivals, and were transformed from coteries of intellectuals into a broader socio-political projects at points of crisis for the larger political movements. In short, I found that that there was a long-running concern with national identity and cultural regeneration that surfaced *episodically* in the three national revivals, each of which emerged at a time of growing political nationalism in the form of state-seeking movements and shared the latter's hostility to the intervention of a centralizing state in Irish life. Each revival had three phases. There was *gestation* led by historicist intellectuals, scholars and artists, often allied with religious reform movements. In phase two, these coteries *crystallized* into cultural institutions at times of internal conflict, arising from the failures of political nation-alism, to propound a new historico-cultural conception of the nation (against what was seen as a divisive, exclusive and political conception) based on a mythical golden age of harmony and progress. Finally, *socio-political articulation* occurred when more modernizing intellectuals (often journalists) translated into concrete socio-political programmes (some of) the communitarian themes of the revival, appealing to a disaf-fected rising educated generation that felt excluded from power. In this third phase, revivalism could develop a broader-based movement, offering an alternative grass-roots politics to that of established statist organizations. By the late nineteenth century, a neo-traditionalist vision was gaining resonance, represented by sections of the Catholic clergy that promoted a rural patriarchal vision of Ireland.

The picture of cultural nationalism is of a different kind of nationalist project, forming individuals disaffected with existing leaders and institutions into a counter-elite and appealing to a range of disaffected groups outside established organizations. Each of the Irish revivals ended in revolt, but in the case of the third revival (the Easter rebellion) with long-term success.

In short then, cultural nationalism is a complex and dynamic phenomenon that has the following characteristics. First, it has a distinct conception of the nation, which is located in its history, culture and people, above all in its golden age, and it pursues grass-roots communitarian strategies rather than the mass organizational modes of political nationalism. In Ernest Renan's terms, the nation is a daily plebiscite defined not in constitutions or state orders but in the formation and refor-mation of a distinctive way of life. Cultural nationalism originated in each case from individuals who are plunged into an identity crisis, often drawn to a pantheism and then to the living community of the nation, exemplified in its folklore, language and literature. They saw themselves as outsiders (even if in the case of Hyde and to a lesser extent Davis and Petrie, they could be classed as part of the dominant commu-nity) who wished to be a new cultural elite. The goal of their historical, philological and artistic endeavours was to create a vision of integration founded on an alleged golden past in which the energies of traditionalists and modernists then in conflict could be redirected, so that they would then cooperate on a grass-roots reformation of a broken society.

Second, it crystallized as a serious cultural project at times of perceived crises when it offered new maps of identity and meaning. For this reason, I describe cultural nationalists as *moral innovators*.[8] Through a vision of the golden age (the early medieval age of 'saints and scholars') traditionalists were to be persuaded that the past legitimized secular achievement and lay initiatives not resistance to change. Modernists, on the other hand, were to be persuaded that it was a mistake to look to British models of progress and to decry Irish culture, because Ireland had once been in the vanguard of European civilization when Britain was in darkness. The task was to build a modern Ireland on Irish lines, and to select those foreign models that could be adapted to Irish circumstances. In the cultural sphere, Yeats looked to the Norwegian drama and to Wagner's Bayreuth Theatre, while D.P. Moran extolled Catholic Belgium's successful industrialization and Arthur Griffith Hungarian examples of political self-help.

Third, although cultural nationalists proposed models of integration, the project itself was unstable, since the intellectual groupings had themselves different goals. The revivalist intellectuals' primary concern was with cultural achievement and identity, but by drawing modernists and also traditionalists into their movement they imported conflicting objectives that threatened to marginalize them. Over the modern period then, the picture was of competing conceptions of the nation interacting in complex ways with each other, and gaining or losing popularity at points of crisis that gave space for the rise of new sets of meanings.

In exploring these developments, I focused on the third and formative revival of modern Ireland, which, to add to the complexity, broke into rival wings – the more Protestant Anglo-Irish literary wing and the much more significant Catholic-dominated Gaelic Revival. Yeats' hope was to create (through the medium of English) an Irish literature and culture of European significance that would transform the moral consciousness of the Irish people, just as Hyde and MacNeill defined their primary goal as the revival of an Irish language civilization. Both saw the newly rediscovered Irish-speaking peasantry of the west as a yet unpolluted reservoir of national myths, legends and social practices that could be used to redeem the fallen urban anglicized Ireland. In contrast, the more political journalists such as Arthur Griffith and D.P. Moran viewed culture in more instrumental terms as a means by which to mobilize the Irish to civil disobedience or individual and collective self-help. Over time, the original cultural mission became appropriated for the political campaigns of the latter, which attracted educated middle and lower middle classes aggrieved at their exclusion from status, occupational advancement and political power. Neo-traditionalists, such as Fathers O'Leary and Dinneen on the other hand, conceived the Irish language as a means to protect religion from the onslaught of

---

8 The term is used by Quentin Skinner, 'Some problems in the analysis of political thought and action', *Political Theory*, 2:3 (1974), 277–303.

British secular ideas and values, and rejected ideas of subordinating the Church to lay nationalist activism, notably in the field of university education. They gained force from 1907 onwards as fears mounted that traditional Ireland was disintegrating, indicated by a rapid exodus from the land and by labour militancy in Dublin, which seemed to suggest that the threat to the Church from British atheistic socialist ideas was now at an acute stage. This is very much in accordance with Tom Garvin's depiction of the Gaelic Revival shortly before the First World War, in which he argued an ethnocentric mood in the countryside and small towns of the west and centre had infected the Gaelic Revival.[9]

SOCIO-POLITICAL RESONANCE: TESTING THE 'BLOCKED MOBILITY THESIS'

Taking the third revival as my main subject, my second task was to examine how far one could explain the take-off of Irish Ireland as a significant social movement by reference to a problem of 'blocked social mobility' among young Catholics.

In my book I was able to marshal evidence of a considerable expansion between 1861 and 1911 in the number of primary, secondary and tertiary educational institutions catering to the Catholic middle and upper middle classes, as well as to an emerging lower middle class. Although there were also occupational advances, particularly in the lower ranks of the civil service, there was also evidence of a relative shortage of positions in the higher professions and upper echelons of the civil service to qualified Catholics. There was ample evidence of 'over-competition' of young Catholics for even more junior positions.[10] However, the 'blocked mobility thesis' was never simply about an oversupply of the qualified relative to suitable positions. It was as much about expectations and a sense of entitlement (occupational and vocational) that was generated by the educational process itself, including ideas of a career open to the talents, of equality and democracy, and the bitterness that arose as a result of the frustration of these expectations. Among these grievances was the reservation of first-class positions in the public administration to Protestants, with the result that Catholics were forced into subordinate positions. There was resentment at policies of ethnic discrimination in the form of the manipulation of examination content with the aim of disadvantaging Catholics. A third grievance was at measures that restricted Catholics playing a decision-making role in public affairs (for example, the bar on political involvement placed on civil servants).[11]

As I argued, this did not explain why aggrieved young Catholics were attracted to the Irish revival rather than the Irish Parliamentary Party (IPP) in the early years of the twentieth century. There was the overhang of disillusionment with nationalist politics after the internecine conflicts between Parnellites, clerical supporters and

---

9 Tom Garvin, *Nationalist revolutionaries, 1858–1928* (Oxford, 1987). **10** Hutchinson, *The dynamics*, p. 273. **11** Ibid., pp 272–6.

proponents of the Liberal alliance after the fall of Parnell. But the key factors were the poor prospects of Home Rule following the Conservative victory in the general election of 1900, the combination of factionalism and oligarchic tendencies in the party, which created entry problems for new aspirants, the perceptions that the leadership of the party was anglicized, and evidence of corruption as Home Rule politicians took power in local government.[12] By contrast, the Irish Ireland ideals of the Gaelic Revival offered a positive vision of a regenerated Ireland based on a rediscovery of a western Irish-speaking and spiritual heartland and outlets for the vocational and leadership generation of a younger generation, better educated than their fathers and frustrated at the *cul-de-sac* of Irish parliamentary nationalism. Hence the born-again quality of many Irish Ireland supporters who spoke of being rescued from a despondency, personal and collective, by their membership of the revival and their discovery of a mission to convert their society from its thrall to English materialism. Moreover, the message of building an Ireland from within appealed to those who could see that even if Home Rule was soon achieved, the main sectors of Irish society – its public administration, major professions and business, dominated by a Protestant elite governed by British norms – still had to be reclaimed for the Irish nation (in practice identified with Catholics).

At the same time, I stressed that supporters of Irish Ireland were not attracted to the radical nationalism of Sinn Féin. Most combined a commitment to the Irish revival and to Home Rule. Indeed, as the strategies of the Gaelic League and its affiliated groups to recreate a viable Irish-speaking Ireland were seen to founder from 1907 onwards and as prospects for Home Rule revived from 1910 onwards, even D.P. Moran embraced the IPP, arguing that, without an independent Irish parliament, the revival itself would falter.

I argued that the real *political* significance of the Irish revival was the creation of a cohesive counter-cultural community, whose values and concept of legitimacy were radically distinct from those of the state and dominant institutions of Ireland, including the IPP, which remained committed to British constitutional norms. The primary allegiance of the leadership and cadres of the Irish revival was to a culturally distinctive and autonomous Irish nation. Support for the IPP and constitutional modes of politics was pragmatic rather than ideological. For this reason, I argued that they were able to give legitimacy to independent and, if necessary, revolutionary action at times of crisis for the nation, when constitutional nationalism was perceived to fail. This occurred at several junctures – the establishment of the Irish Volunteers in 1913–14 and the Easter Rising of 1916.

12 Ibid., pp 280–5.

ELITES AND FOLLOWERS

The framework of the book was Weberian in arguing that new concepts of national identity arise when existing meaning systems are under threat, and ideological innovators are often social outsiders who may view themselves in messianic terms. Without a social constituency, these elite messages are empty, but, should there be such a constituency, the new ideas can act as 'switchmen' of interests, for example by orienting an emerging Catholic middle class to a communitarian rather than a state-oriented politics.

My focus was on elites, or more accurately counter-elites, but, as I have mentioned, these were of different kinds – revivalist intellectuals and more political thinkers and campaigners. When writing my study, there was a variety of interpretations of the relationships between nationalist elites and ordinary people. At one extreme, some like Ernest Gellner viewed nationalist intellectuals as symptoms rather than creators of social change (that is, national formation).[13] But what was notable was that revivalist intellectual circles *preceded* the social movements: indeed, I argued that the new ideas of the nation, when given political translation by figures like Moran, formed individuals who might feel isolated and alienated into a cohesive and militant community. Hans Kohn and, in a very different way, Miroslav Hroch considered the historical and artistic revivalists as crucial only in the earliest phases of nationalism, having their role as identity formers, after which they retire as significant agents to be replaced by political actors and class interests.[14] As I already observed, however, this is too static a picture, for there were three Irish revivals in which intellectuals played a leading role. Defining the nation is a recurring process as a result of internal changes of the given populations, shifting relations of a given population with its neighbours (as Britain transformed in the nineteenth century into the world's industrial power), and new political contexts.

An alternative perspective was Eric Hobsbawm's characterization of nationalists as 'inventors of tradition', which considered nationalist ideas, rituals and symbols as novel means by which emerging groups sought to displace established interests in the struggle for power in the modern world.[15] Paul Brass had a more refined formulation that recognizes the role of external differentiation, arguing that 'the study of nationality was in large part the process by which elites and counter-elites select aspects of a group's culture and attach new values and meanings to them and use them as symbols to mobilize the group, defend its interests and compete with other groups'.[16] The problem with both formulations was an instrumentalist conception of

13 Ernest Gellner, *Nations and nationalism* (Cambridge, 1983), pp 57–61. 14 Hans Kohn, *The idea of nationalism* (New York, 1946), pp 329–41, 429–30; Miroslav Hroch, *Social preconditions of national revival in Europe* (Cambridge, 1985), ch. 6. 15 E.J. Hobsbawm, 'Mass producing traditions: Europe 1870–1914' in E.J. Hobsbawm and T. Ranger (eds), *The invention of tradition* (Cambridge, 1983). 16 Paul Brass, 'Elite groups, symbol manipulation and ethnic identity among the Muslims of south Asia' in D. Taylor and M. Yapp (eds), *Political identity in south Asia* (London, 1979), pp 40–1.

elite actions that failed to account for the popular resonance of nationalist ideas. The term 'invention' underestimated the difficulty of changing the existing meanings of the past in a country in which, to quote William Faulkner, 'the past isn't dead and buried. In fact, it isn't even past'. It viewed nationalist leaders as 'above' or even 'outside' their society, manipulating it in terms of pure power interests, whereas they were very much social products like their followers. Later, Hobsbawm admitted that, though created from above, nations cannot be understood unless analysed from below, in terms of the assumptions of ordinary people, but he did not explore this.[17]

For this reason, I described the revivalist intellectuals not as inventors but as 'moral innovators' who employed ideas of a golden age and comparisons with other countries to show how a reverence for the past could inspire a modernization of Irish society. In doing so, they sought to unite the urban middle classes with the clergy and their supporters under the revivalist umbrella. But I argued that there were real difficulties in doing this, especially when powerful institutions and social groups validated themselves by reference to the past. It was successful only up to a point, and the result was that original conceptions of the early revivalists were transformed as social groups read their own meanings into the ideas, myths and symbols articulated by the intellectuals.

We see the limitations of elite aspirations in the establishing of the Gaelic League, when both Douglas Hyde and Eoin MacNeill invoked the model of the Land League, as a populist project that led to the transformation of rural Ireland. Their aspirations were for a cultivated Irish-speaking, rural, democratic and non-sectarian nation, that, inspired by its eighth-century glories, would be a spiritual beacon in a materialized world. The restoration of a Gaelic social order, however, meant something quite different to the descendants of Land League veterans – to the educated peasantry and lower middle classes of the small towns of Munster. To these individuals, imbued with a xenophobic hatred of an English culture that was steadily penetrating into the rural interior, an Irish Ireland entailed an overturning of the Protestant ascendancy that still dominated Irish social and economic life. The profound dislocations and crises of the First World War, the Easter Rising and the War of Independence brought representatives of these social strata to leadership positions in post-independence Ireland. The Irish Ireland they brought into being was far removed in its puritanism, insularity and anti-intellectualism from the vision of the early revivalists.

These remarks indicate some of the limitations of my study. I had attempted to avoid a static perspective from above by exploring the competition between elite projects (Home Rule political nationalisms v. cultural nationalisms), and the shifting struggles for dominance within revivalist nationalism. The individuals I studied were often from humble backgrounds with aspirations to speak for emerging groups and to become a counter-elite. I also mentioned that cultural revivalists adopted often 'grass-roots' or populist strategies, and suggested that their constituencies translated

---

17 E.J. Hobsbawm, *Nations and nationalism since 1870* (Oxford, 1990), p. 10.

their programmes in ways the founders had not anticipated. Nevertheless, my study was by no means a study of nationalism from below. A full study of the different strata involved in Irish nationalist movements and how they relate to each other is still to be written. Also lacking is an analysis of banal nationalism[18] in Ireland: how national sentiments connect with the concerns and practices of everyday life, and how this banal nationalism articulates with the 'hot' nationalism of ideological movements.

ALTERNATIVE INTERPRETATIONS

One study that went some of the way towards a more extensive analysis of the social bases of radical Gaelic nationalism was Tom Garvin's *Nationalist revolutionaries, 1858–1928*, published in the same year as my monograph. He viewed the Gaelic Revival as a vehicle for the ambitions of a newly educated cohort of Catholics entering an urban world in Ireland or Britain but of farming and peasant origins, 'deeply sensitive to its political subordination, to the inadequacies of its own culture and education, and to the aloofness of the ascendancy'.[19] The roots of this cohort, disproportionately centred in Munster, were traced back to the Fenian traditions that had passed into the Land League, and their frustrations exploded under the pressures of European war into revolution. Garvin's was a penetrating study of the mindset of Irish revolutionary elites and their legacy in post-independence Ireland. His study was sensitive to synchronic developments in Europe in his references to European radical leaderships of the twentieth century.

My study was diachronic in exploring the long-range patterns of Irish revivalism, which, like cultural nationalist movements elsewhere, could take different forms – liberal, populist, socialist or traditionalist – depending on social and political contexts. In other words, the fact that early twentieth-century revivalism took anti-modernist forms was historically contingent. There was nothing intrinsically traditionalist about Irish cultural nationalism as the earlier revivals had shown. Given the disparity in resources and cultural self-assurance between Britain, then the great imperial power possessing a global vernacular culture and an advanced industrial base, and the smaller, more rural Ireland, poorly educated, and religious with a small secular laity, it is not surprising that a cultural nationalism ultimately took such defensive neo-traditionalist forms. In spite of this, the new governing class that arose out the Gaelic Revival, although facing the huge challenges of the years after independence, including a civil war and economic depression, remained committed to an Irish democracy.

In contrast to Garvin, Senia Pašeta has argued that to privilege growing ethnocentric and separatist currents before the First World War is to adopt a winner's historical perspective. Irish Irelanders, she claims, were an unrepresentative minority who glorified an exalted past out of 'a fear of embracing modernity'.[20] Edwardian

---

18 Michael Billig, *Banal nationalism* (London, 1995).   **19** Garvin, *Nationalist revolutionaries*, p. 43.   **20** Pašeta, *Before the revolution*, p. 151.

Ireland was rather a period of Catholic middle-class advance, notable for the rise of women's movements, an expansion of professional opportunities and a commitment to Home Rule politics. If there was evidence of a crisis of vocation among sections of a new educated Catholic stratum, this was due more to perception of Protestant dominance than a dearth of employment opportunities. The Easter Rising was an 'aberrant' event and it was only 'the intervention' of the First World War that disrupted Ireland's steady progress within the British Empire and that cast a young generation of constitutionalist nationalists into oblivion.[21]

There is much of value in Pašeta's analysis. There were potent anglicizing or assimilating trends within Irish society – as I acknowledged in my study. However, this picture rather detracts from what was central to my framework, namely the dynamic interplay between the different options presented to the Irish people that continued throughout this period.[22] Indeed, without the sense of 'anglicization', it would be impossible to explain the fervour and, as time went on, the desperation of Irish-Ireland advocates, such as Pearse, who knew all too well that they were a declining minority. I will take up Pašeta's challenge and make three further observations.

First, there was indeed an apocalyptic tone to some of the pronouncements of revivalists in the early twentieth century, but this was not unique to Irish nationalists. The accelerating arms race between the great powers, explosive urbanization and rural decline, intense class conflict and (in Britain) constitutional crisis induced expressions of panic across the political spectrum in many European countries. All of these could be regarded as aspects of modernity, which one could appreciate Irish revivalists being reluctant to 'embrace'. But, of course, there is no such thing as 'modernity' as such: there are multiple modernities that are always culturally framed. Irish cultural nationalists like Griffith and Moran did not reject modernity as such: they rejected a modernity equated with British secular industrial models. Understandably, they feared that a small Irish rural society in demographic decline and with many of its ablest young looking to emigrate might well be swallowed by the industrial Goliath to which it was yoked. They wished a modernity based on Irish values, promoting Irish industries, supported educational advance and the development of a lay Catholic culture. Many young women graduates were prominent revivalists and active in women's suffrage organizations. Some revivalists (George Russell and later Patrick Pearse and Thomas MacDonagh) could see in Denmark an alternative model of successful modernity – of a small progressive and prosperous

---

21 Ibid., 'Epilogue'. **22** In my understanding of the crosscurrents in late nineteenth and early twentieth century Irish nationalism, I was influenced by several important studies: Alan O'Day, *The English face of Irish nationalism* (Dublin, 1977), which demonstrated the strong assimilation of the Irish political elite at Westminster into British radicalism, even as Patrick O'Farrell, *Ireland's English question* (London, 1971) was sketching the rising Catholic neo-traditionalist revulsion in the countryside and small towns against English currents in the same period. Another significant influence was Tom Garvin, *The evolution of Irish nationalist politics* (Dublin, 1981).

peasant democracy. Certainly, one can find in their writings and those of their contemporaries a horror at aspects of popular culture and exaggerated notions of traditional virtues, but in that they were in no way different to their English or European equivalents.

Second, Pašeta's depiction of limited professional advances for Catholics does not affect my argument about 'blocked mobility'. I expressly noted such advances as well as the growing sway of English values and fashions in the early twentieth century.[23] Moreover, 'blocked mobility' referred not just to career openings but also to a sense of being deprived of playing a significant role in the public life of their country. I cited the frustration of a tertiary educated Catholics, like Arthur Clery, one of the Clongowes cohort, European in their horizons, who wrote for Moran's *Leader*. Clery, among many others, complained of Catholics who should expect to take prestigious positions at the bar or to become cabinet ministers in a future Home Rule parliament, but were compelled to take 'menial' positions in the civil service and teaching.[24] Moreover, such 'menial' positions debarred them from taking an overt part in politics. This frustration was directed also against the corruption and toadying to English ways of members of the older nationalist political elite who were assuming power in local government.

Third, there is ample evidence of the reality of exclusion operating at the higher levels of almost all spheres of Irish society. In my book, I referred to census data which showed the proportions of Catholics in the major professions almost static, while the numbers of those qualified had substantially increased, and I cited figures of 'over-competition' of lower-middle-class Catholics seeking junior civil servant positions, which forced them into employment as postal clerks in the cities of Britain, from where they attempted to return to Ireland.[25] Exposure to an alien secular urban world either in Britain or in Dublin, dominated by English Protestant values, intensified the appeal of a radical Gaelic populism to socially insecure young Catholics.

Support for my analysis has recently come from Fergus Campbell's *The Irish establishment*, which can be seen as an extension as well as a critique of Lawrence McBride's *The greening of Dublin Castle* (1991). Although one might cavil at the idea of a single establishment operating in Ireland, he provides comprehensive data demonstrating that while Catholics were advancing in the lower and middle sections of the civil service, local government, the less prestigious professions and small business, Protestants retained their grip in higher levels of the Irish administration, business, the major professions and the army and police. He argues there was an increasing contrast between the political emancipation of Catholics and their persisting social subordination and the perception of them as second-class citizens. This socio-economic division was sustained by powerful Protestant loyalist upper-class networks centred on the vice-regal lodge and associations such as the Kildare Street Club that bound together a declining landlord class with a rising Protestant business elite. These networks were strengthening during the early twentieth century

---

23 Hutchinson, *The dynamics*, pp 259–65.   **24** Ibid., p. 271.   **25** Ibid., p. 300n44.

in response to the Protestant perceptions of a tilt of the British state to the Irish nationalist interests.[26] The Catholics who greened Dublin Castle were incorporated into the Protestant establishment. It is this contrast between political emancipation and social inferiority, underpinned by ascendancy cultural connections, that I argue gave momentum to the projects of cultural rather than political nationalism. For the focus of the former was making Irish values hegemonic and on nationalizing the dominant institutions of Irish society rather than achieving a Home Rule parliament.

Campbell rejects Pašeta's fortuitous interpretation of the political success of the Irish revival. In doing so, he states that my analysis suggests a logical line between frustrated career and vocational aspirations and attraction to cultural nationalism and finally to a Sinn Féin revolution.[27] In fact, I don't make such a direct connection. As I have already stated, whatever their leaders might say, most Irish Irelanders saw no contradiction between a support for the revival and for the Home Rule movement. I argued rather that once the revival became institutionalized, it could become a platform for revolutionary action at times of a crisis of the state (for example in war) when the official organizations Irish nationalism (the IPP) had also begun to lose legitimacy. He can be forgiven for reading that into my interpretation, however, since I spend so little time discussing how it was that the revival became radicalized in this manner. Central to this was, of course, the outbreak of the First World War, and this raises the question of whether we, like Pašeta, view the war as an intervention that changed the direction of Irish political development.

WARFARE AND IRISH NATIONALISM: ANOMALY OR CONSTITUTING FRAMEWORK

There are two reasons for disputing the view of the First World War as an anomaly. First, to consider war as an intervention is to normalize peace and economic and social developments as the forces that shape national trajectories. If one takes the perspective of Charles Tilly seriously ('war makes the state and the state makes war'), the reverse is true.[28] Without swallowing the full Tilly line, one could make a case that (in the jargon of social science) wars can act as 'critical junctures' that frame new paths of social and political development. Irish–British history has been profoundly shaped by a series of European-wide conflicts that resulted in ethno-political structures that patterned later inter-national relations. Out of the religio-dynastic wars of the sixteenth and seventeenth centuries came the conquest, the land settlements and the establishment of the Ulster plantation. From the wars of the French revolutionary and Napoleonic era crystallized modern Irish Catholic nationalist identities, arising from the 1798 Rising, the Act of Union and the broken promise of Catholic

26 Campbell, *The Irish establishment*, pp 309–12. **27** Ibid., pp 314–16. **28** Charles Tilly, 'Reflections on the history of European state-making' in Charles Tilly (ed.), *The formation of national states in western Europe* (Princeton, NJ, 1975), p. 42.

Emancipation and, in their wake, the rise of O'Connellite mass popular politics. This last phenomenon, formally constitutionalist but yoked to rural millenarian senti-ments, created the template for later parliamentary agitations.

Tilly acknowledges that whereas general European warfare was an almost contin-uous feature of the seventeenth and eighteenth centuries, in the modern period it has been less frequent (if more destructive). Even so, the First World War that resulted in the destruction of the great empires in Europe was not a bolt from the blue. It was the outcome of an accelerating contest for geo-political European and global supremacy between the great powers, which was entangled with ruling-class fears either of imperial disintegration from insurgent nationalisms or of class revolution. In this context, the revolutionary establishment of an Irish nation-state, weakened by civil war and unresolved irredentist claims is very much part of the mainstream of European history.

There is a second reason for bringing war *inside* our analysis. My focus has been on the different conceptions of legitimacy struggling for primacy in early twentieth-century Ireland, and the rise of a conception of Ireland, given body in a sacrificial community of believers, that viewed the nation as radically distinct from that of Britain. Many have claimed that war can be seen as the ultimate test of legitimacy of a state, particularly total war that requires the mobilization for sacrifice of whole peoples. The stresses of the First World War not only occasioned the collapse of autocratic empires; it opened intense cleavages even in democratic ethnically diverse states – in Canada, where the threats to forcibly enlist French-speakers in Quebec threatened its cohesion and in Australia, where efforts to introduce conscription were defeated by opposition from Irish-Australians.

The war was, however, more of a catalyst than the cause of imperial collapse. Just as the advance of Hungarian nationalism before 1914 had all but eroded Habsburg authority, so the radicalization of Irish nationalist and Ulster unionist movements had severely undermined the legitimacy of the British state in Ireland before the war. A key criterion of authority is the ability of the state to monopolize the legitimate use of violence. By this standard, an allegiance to British constitutionalist norms was already withering, as indicated by the recourse to arms of the Ulster and Irish Volunteers (initiated by Eoin MacNeill) and by the British Army mutiny at Curragh. As in much of Europe, the outbreak of war inspired a rallying to the state, although Irish leaders such as John Redmond assumed this would provide strong support for Home Rule after the war. But, as in Europe under the adversities and sufferings of war, the solidarity of the subordinate nationalities with their imperial states snapped. The events following the Easter Rising and the inevitable British response, including attempts to impose conscription on Ireland, showed how fragile support for Britain was.

In short, the Irish revolution needs to be understood as part of a larger European and indeed global context. The First World War and its successor were crucial moments in the transformation of the world from one dominated by world empires into one of nation states. The experience of twentieth-century Ireland – its civil war, irredention, utopianism and insecurity – has parallels with that of other newly independent European post-colonial states.[29] It might be asked if an independent Ireland would have occurred in the absence of the Irish Ireland movement. Counter-factuals are of themselves unanswerable. What one can do is point to the crucial role of the Irish revivalists not just in the struggle for independence but more importantly in the definition of the new Irish nation state. We can answer in similar terms a second question, whether but for the war the Irish Ireland movement would have triumphed. What is important is that an alternative conception of the Irish nation had become institutionalized and hence available as a resource for rethinking possible political futures, should the established nostrums be found wanting. The outbreak of war had only suspended the crisis in Ireland over Home Rule, with the opposing parties seemingly irreconcilable. The strains of war were to bring the crisis to a head, but it is unclear even in the absence of war whether a resolution satisfactory to nationalist Ireland could have been achieved. As the hopes of the Irish Parliamentary Party for a future Ireland participating amicably within a British empire receded, the rival vision of Irish Ireland culturally as well as political autonomous became increasingly credible as a blueprint for the future. The outbreak and fortunes of wars have often resulted in the fall of regimes and the unexpected catapulting of previously marginalized actors into office. The Easter Rising and the War of Independence propelled into power not just a saviour figure but an entire generational cohort, which dominated the first fifty years of the new state, and configured its institutions and ethos. It is this legacy that makes the study of Irish cultural nationalism and the figures that formed it so significant.

29 Some examples: Finland in 1918 combined a liberation war against Russia with a civil war between 'Whites' and 'Reds'. The post-war period was dominated by irredentist dreams of regaining 'lost' Karelian lands. The post-World War settlements generated intense irredentist tensions in Central and Eastern Europe as well as political instabilities, leading to the rise of authoritarian regimes. The independent Hungarian state, after a socialist putsch and brief civil war, lost substantial territory and population to Czechoslovakia, Romania and what later became Yugoslavia and turned to an authoritarian right wing politics geared towards a 'restoration' of greater Hungary. The resurrected Polish nation-state subject to intense political fissures, defined itself in religious terms against the atheistic USSR while in dispute with Lithuania over the status of Vilnius.

Index